THE 1984 OLYMPIC GAMES

SARAJEVO/LOS ANGELES

W9-ATL-705

USA

THE 1984 OLYMPIC GAMES

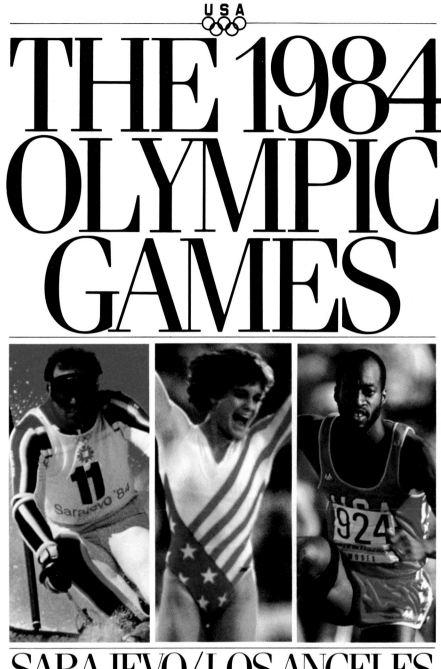

SARAJEVO/LOS ANGELES

BY DICK SCHAAP

WITH AN INTRODUCTION BY JAMES A. MICHENER

RANDOM HOUSE / NEW YORK

ABC PUBLISHING/ABC SPORTS

ACKNOWLEDGMENTS

The author wishes to thank all of the thousands of athletes and journalists who participated in and recorded the events of the 1984 Olympics, especially the dozens of athletes who shared their time and thoughts in interviews and the dozens of journalists whose accounts provided special and intimate views, most notably the men and women of the *New York Times,* the *Los Angeles Times,* the *Los Angeles Herald-Examiner,* the *Boston Globe,* the *Washington Post, Sports Illustrated* and *The Sporting News.* Which is not to say that the men and women of other newspapers and magazines didn't offer equally skillful reportage and commentary. But there is a limit to research, even with the diligent and expert help of Larry Klein, who carried the burden with me. I am indebted, too, to the encyclopedic minds of the ABC Sports research staff, Peter Diamond and Tim Rockwood and Maarten Kooij and Michael Bass and their cohorts, and to the editorial guidance of Ash Green and Tony Schulte of Random House, both of whom offered more than professional enthusiasm and energy. Don Miller and Bob Paul of the U.S. Olympic Committee provided help, insight and information, as usual, and Trish McLeod, my wife, provided infinite patience, as usual. I am also grateful to the producers, cameramen, technicians, electronic editors, assignment editors and correspondents of ABC News, with whom I worked and played in Sarajevo and Los Angeles.

—Dick Schaap

GRAPHIC CREDITS

Project Direction: Anthony Schulte

Editor: Ashbel Green

Art Direction: R.D. Scudellari

Production Director: Karen Tonningsen

Design: Robert Anthony/Robert Anthony, Inc.

Design Associate: Susan Parsons/Robert Anthony, Inc.

Photo Editor: Kaye Neil Noble

Special Assistance: Margarita Pile, Anne Cady

U.S.O.C. Factual Research: C. Robert Paul, Jr.

ABC Factual Research: Michael Bass, Peter Diamond,
    Maarten Kooij, Tim Rockwood

Separations: W.A. Krueger Co., Brookfield, Wisconsin

Printing: W.A. Krueger Co., New Berlin, Wisconsin

Binding: W. A. Krueger Co., New Berlin, Wisconsin

Typographer: Typographic Images, Inc.

LIBRARY OF CONGRESS CATALOGING IN PUBLICATION DATA

Schaap, Dick, 1934–
The 1984 Olympic Games.

1. Olympic Games (23rd : 1984 : Los Angeles, Calif.) 2. Winter Olympic Games
(14th : 1984 : Sarajevo, Bosnia and Hercegovina) 3. Olympic games—Records. I. Title.
GV722 1984.S33   1984   796.4′ 8   84-42909
ISBN 0-394-53678-9
ISBN 0-394-72162-4 (pbk.)

Manufactured in the United States of America

98765432

First Edition

FOREWORD

The Olympic Games are about the spirit of excellence and achievement that the athletes carry with them both on and off the fields of competition. This is the story of one generation of athletes that exemplified this spirit perhaps better than any in Olympic history. I don't think that the U.S., for example, which has fielded more than 1,000 gold medalists and over 12,000 competitors during its history of participation in the Games, has ever been represented by a finer group of men and women than it was in 1984. The Olympic motto of *Citius, Altius, Fortius* has never been more masterfully met nor more universally upheld.

The book Dick Schaap has written succeeds in capturing the excitement and diversity of the extraordinary competitions and the flavor of the broader experiences of the athletes. The staff photographers of the American Broadcasting Company and others have managed to freeze some very precious and memorable moments on film. I congratulate them for combining their efforts to preserve forever in so eloquent a fashion the legacy of what our athletes have accomplished over the last four years.

Although this is the story of our U.S. athletes, this book is dedicated to the almost 13,000 athletes from 150 nations who participated in the 1983 Pan Am Games, the Olympic Winter Games and the Summer Olympics in Los Angeles. It is the story not just of the medalists who received their rewards in the record books and on the podiums, but of every man or woman who had, through sacrifice and discipline, earned the right to say simply that he or she was an Olympian. That alone is a victory worth saluting. As Baron de Coubertin so eloquently stated in the Olympic creed, "The most important thing in the Olympic Games is not to win but to take part, just as the most important thing in life is not the triumph, but the struggle." This is what makes a champion. And champions are what make the Olympics.

—WILLIAM E. SIMON
President,
United States Olympic Committee

The Games of the XXIII Olympiad in Los Angeles climaxed the most successful four-year period in the history of the United States Olympic Committee. More than 1,400 athletes represented the United States in the Pan American Games and the Olympic Games.

No other athletes faced a greater challenge than ours during the last four years. No one had blotted out the unpleasant memory of not participating in Moscow. Perhaps as many as thirty percent of our athletes selected for the Olympic Games in Los Angeles had been members of the 1980 Olympic team. These gallant men and women achieved their personal goal of basking in the Olympic sun.

The 1983 Pan American Games in Venezuela provided us with an excellent measuring stick for 1984 in Los Angeles. Our athletes proved their mettle in head-to-head competition with the best athletes in the Western Hemisphere.

At Sarajevo, our skiers and figure skaters proved themselves best in the world in two of the most competitive sports in the Olympic Games.

And then in Los Angeles our athletes achieved new and personal success and accepted the glory and adulation of a nation understanding and appreciating the pressures they had been under for four years.

Through the generosity of the American public and 37 national corporations, the United States Olympic Committee had a record income, $90,000,000. It was these dollars, spread over the four-year period, that helped repair our dedicated and talented athletes.

On behalf of the United States Olympic Committee I gratefully acknowledge the generous support from the people of the United States, corporate America and the thousands of volunteer workers whose unstinting efforts helped make this the most glorious quadrennial period in the history of the USOC.

—F. DON MILLER
Executive Director,
United States Olympic Committee

CONTENTS

SARAJEVO

LOS ANGELES

INTRODUCTION

Where great national spectacles are concerned, I side with dour John Adams, second President of the United States. On the night of July 3, 1776, following the signing of the Declaration of Independence, he wrote to his wife Abigail:

The Second Day of July 1776 will be the most memorable Epocha, in the History of America…It ought to be commemorated, as the Day of Deliverance by solemn Acts of Devotion to God Almighty. It ought to be solemnized with Pomp and Parade, with Shews, Games, Sports, Guns, Bells, Bonfires and Illuminations from one End of this Continent to the other from this Time forward forever more.

The world needs festivals, so I was philosophically prepared to welcome the Games of the XXIII Olympiad in Los Angeles, but I was not prepared for that majestic show which unfolded the first Saturday in the Olympic stadium. It was big. It was garish. And it was positively breathtaking. I reveled in every minute of it, and when that marvelous display of flashcards covered the surface of the stadium with the flags of the 140 competing nations I shouted to my wife: "We've already won the Olympics!" John Adams would have cheered, too, for it was exactly this kind of emotional release he had in mind.

I would suppose that many who saw the competition on television shared my experience on the first day. I had never seen a bicycle race, had no interest in seeing one, and knew nothing about either the women or the men competing. But I felt honor-bound to see how the Games started, and within a few minutes I was completely hooked. The finish of that women's race, with Connie Carpenter-Phinney of Boulder and Rebecca Twigg of Seattle battling to the last inch, the last gasp, was a magnificent sports spectacle. To think that two young women could race for more than two hours and finish less than a hand's breadth apart was astonishing. A friend who watched with me said: "A finish like that cleans out the sinuses."

The television team from the American Broadcasting Company deserves kudos for the expert manner in which they reported the games. Camera work was exceptional, as when the lens went underwater to record the slap-slap finish of that incredible men's 800-meter relay when Bruce Hayes, trailing the great Michael Gross of West Germany, turned on his afterburner and touched the finish wall first by an inch. He and his team had set a world record.

Throughout the Games I was mindful of my assignment to write the foreword to this volume, so I remained severely neutral, cheering whatever was good and stifling my inclination toward chauvinism. I was not unhappy to see a Korean boxer take a gold from an American, and I applauded the New Zealand and Romanian rowers who swept to multiple victories on Lake Casitas. But as an old-time setter in volleyball, I allowed myself a muted hurrah when our American men's volleyball team made their stunning comeback. In a qualifying game, Brazil had crushed the United States but with the championship on the line, the United States put together a noble effort to win three straight. For me that was one of the golden moments.

But one watchful viewer shared with me her putdown of chauvinism: "Of any fifty American athletes photographed during the playing of the 'Star-Spangled Banner,' only three knew the words."

The desirability of keeping the Olympics as international as possible was proved by the embarrassing superiority in medal count of the host countries in the last two restricted Games. In 1980 the Soviet Union won 80 gold, 69 silver, 46 bronze. In 1984 the United States

tally was 83–61–30. Nevertheless Los Angeles did have a strong international flavor, because forty-six different visiting nations carried home medals.

Many splendid incidents proved that the Games really were international. I, along with millions of other Americans, took pride when delightful Mary Lou Retton won the gold for her all-around performance in gymnastics, but I was equally pleased when that remarkable parade of beautiful Romanian elves led by Ecaterina Szabo won individual honors and the team victory.

I felt the same way when the Chinese women's volleyball team, having been defeated once by the bigger and stronger Americans, performed so flawlessly in the return match and copped the gold. I cheered Pierre Quinon of France when he won the pole vault, and I was awed by the superiority of Britain's Daley Thompson in winning the decathlon for the second time.

Even more touching was the Ivory Coast's Gabriel Tiacoh's earning the silver in the men's 400 meters, first medal ever for that small country, and the public celebration that Morocco put on when one of its women won the gold in the 400-meter hurdles and when one of its men did the same in the 5,000 meters.

But what was especially significant, I thought, was that many medals won by non-Americans were garnered by young people from smaller nations who had attended college in the United States, been trained by American coaches, and been allowed to hone their skills in our track meets. In such victories two nations triumphed, the country of birth and the country that provided an opportunity.

Olympics are sometimes more noted for their scandals than for their attainments. This time several judging problems perplexed me. How could the diving judges report their complicated calculations—total point score multiplied by the difficulty index of the dive—within fifteen seconds while the gymnastics judges could not seem to agree upon or report their major scores within fifteen minutes? The Games had not been underway long when it became obvious that the officiating in boxing must sooner or later produce an uproar. Hesitant decisions, ones that were patently dubious, others that were reversed against all evidence, left an ugly scar on a sport that so often produces controversy.

Incomprehensible was the reluctance of officials to insist that the Swiss marathoner Gabriela Andersen-Schiess leave the track when she was obviously in distress while trying to finish the two-and-a-half-hour run in the heat. Thirty-nine years old, exhausted, and near sunstroke from lack of water, she was allowed to stagger and stumble around the last quarter of a mile in view of thousands who wondered whether she might at any moment faint or die. This was a shocking exhibition, one which would have been halted instantly by the medics had she been a boxer, and it detracted from the splendid running of America's Joan Benoit and Norway's Grete Waitz, both of whom covered the long distance in great time and without incident. Let's hope the quarter-mile horror does not encourage critics who claim that women are not capable of running the longer distances. The officials were to blame, not Andersen-Schiess.

On the other hand, the refereeing of volleyball, a game that produces some very close, judgmental calls, and basketball seemed conspicuously fair. The officiating in water polo was also of high caliber, as was the equestrian judging. Taking all events into consideration, these Olympics had fewer sustainable protests than one might have expected.

There was, inevitably, one mishap which will be debated for decades as The Foul-Up of 1984. If a computer had chosen the two athletes in the Olympiad whose imbroglio would cause the greatest international clamor it would surely have nominated Mary Decker, the fragile, accident-prone darling of American racing, and Zola Budd, the winsome barefoot lass whose contested nationality had already caused a furor: was she South African and barred from the Olympics, or British and eligible? For months, media throughout the world had hyped their confrontation as the race of the century, a hoopla exacerbated by the London newspaper that had engineered Budd's entry into England and was orchestrating the publicity.

More than a medal was involved in this contest. Budd had to be warned by the British Olympic Committee that she would be sent home if she continued to earn money by writing a daily column for her paper, and the *New York Times* revealed that Decker was already earning about $500,000 a year from endorsements. Whichever young woman won stood to earn a bundle.

As the games unfolded I became increasingly aware of adverse criticism, and it hurt. The opening extravaganza was more Hollywood than sport. ABC was overly nationalistic at times. The accomplishments of other nations, especially in sports we do not feature like soccer, which had 1,421,264 total admissions, were frequently ignored, and when an American won, the silver and bronze winners were often overlooked. Newspapers also concentrated so heavily on the American accumulation of medals that perceptive critics became bored, as three Texas headlines on successive days proved:

American Gold Rush Begins
More Embarrassing Gold for USA
U.S. Gold Shines Through the Boos

The boos were for Carl Lewis, who performed so grudgingly in the broad jump, and for Rick Carey, who won a gold in the men's 200-meter backstroke but who sulked because he did not break the world's record. Many sensible observers, men and women who love sports, told me during the progress of the Games: "We've gone over completely to the Vince Lombardi ethic. Only winning counts."

Many observers wondered if these might be the last Games ever to be held in a major nation. Some argued: "They obviously can't go back to either Russia or the United States. Perhaps they'll have to be taken to Greece or Switzerland at some permanent venue." There was widespread speculation that the 1988 Games in Korea could be a disaster because of Russian-Chinese-American animosities.

There were some who questioned the value of continuing the Games at all. Lord Porritt of New Zealand was one bronze winner who was remembered. As Arthur Porritt, a young New Zealand Rhodes Scholar at Oxford in 1924, he finished third in the famous *Chariots of Fire* 100 meters behind Harold Abrahams and Jackson Scholz. Capitalizing on his athletic fame, he later became governor-general of New Zealand and its permanent representative to the International Olympic Committee, which runs the Games. In an interview given at Los Angeles he was pessimistic:

The Olympic Games suffer from gigantism, commercialism, nationalism, racism and drugs. Politics has ruined the organization, and television has ruined the competition. It's sad. I still believe in the Games but I doubt they can be resuscitated. They're trying to do an impossible thing—to keep the Olympic ideal in a modern world.

I interpreted this as the regretful longing of an old warrior recalling battles in a more relaxed age: " I hardly trained at all. I tottered down to the track at Oxford two or three times a week." Such lack of dedication would not get an athlete into the Olympics these days. And as for nationalism as a curse, if it is one, it seems to be ineradicable in the human heart. I'll wager that in the early, pristine Olympics there was ample rivalry between Sparta and Athens.

Still, I did have the mournful feeling in watching these wonderful Games that I might be seeing the last of the breed; powerful forces work against their continuation. But for the time being I could take delight in the fact that the 1984 Games were not merely a success; they were a smasheroo, better by far than cynics had anticipated. Even the Russian absence did not prevent attendance from being far above estimate, and on the second Friday ABC could report that on this night alone more than 350,000 people were paying their way into some game or other. Soccer, from which the American team had long since been eliminated, drew 100,374 to the Rose Bowl for the consolation game between Italy and Yugoslavia. For the France-Brazil final, 101,799.

If the Games do go forward, and six cities are already bidding for 1992, I believe that nonsports like synchronized swimming and rhythmic gymnastics should be dropped. It would be quite wrong to add bowling to the roster, and I even have doubts about baseball. Some complain about equestrian, but this is one of two Olympic sports in which women have won medals competing against men.

I have evaded the crucial question: was the value of these Games lessened because the Soviet Union refused to participate? Let me try to give bedrock answers. First, Russia and her satellites were justified in their boycott, since we had tried to wreck their Games in 1980. Second, the failure of Russia and East Germany to show left a gap that obviously could not be filled. Without question the world was deprived of some great contests. Third, the high scoring of the two Communist nations who did compete, Romania and China, indicates how close the standings might have been had all the Communist nations attended. Fourth, despite their absence the outstanding performances testify to the high caliber of the 1984 Games, and no apologies are required. Fifth, it was Russia, not the United States, who lost in this boycott. These Games were magnificent, and to have missed them was to have missed one of the fine experiences of this decade. I am truly sorry that Russia was not here, and I would have made immense concessions to persuade her to come. But I am not sorry for the United States, who lost so much; I am sorry for Russia and East Germany, who lost so much more. Sixth, and I would like this to stand as my final judgment on the XXIII Olympiad, these Games were a soaring triumph, and they would have been had only eight nations participated. We were ready for an emotional catharsis. We needed to see bright young people competing regardless of national affiliation. We found joy in watching youth stand victorious regardless of point score. Just watching that hyper-excited wrestler Robert Weaver, not much bigger than a bantam rooster, give his victory dance with his infant son in arms was worth a whole Olympiad.

I like national celebrations, especially when 139 guest nations join the party.

—JAMES A. MICHENER
Austin, Texas

SARAJEVO

Neither the ancient Greeks nor Baron Pierre de Coubertin, whose zeal created the modern Olympic Games in 1896, recognized any need for Winter Games. But in 1924 a separate winter program was introduced in Chamonix, France. The Winter Olympics quickly caught on, and in time spotlighted such great athletes as Sonja Henie of Norway, Jean-Claude Killy of France and Eric Heiden of the United States.

For the 1984 Games, the International Olympic Committee selected the first East European site in Winter Olympic history: Sarajevo, Yugoslavia, a city that hoped to become known as a winter resort. Seventy years had passed since the event that gave Sarajevo its enduring identity. In 1914 a 19-year-old patriot, Gavrilo Princip, killed Archduke Franz Ferdinand, heir to the Austro-Hungarian throne, and set off World War I. Now Sarajevo, an industrial city of more than 450,000 people, was staging the XIVth Olympic Winter Games.

The citizens of Sarajevo wanted a new identity, wanted the world to recognize their independence, friendliness, enthusiasm and pride. To help finance the Winter Olympics, they had voted to give up for four years a small percentage of their not-so-substantial earnings. The Sarajevo Organizing Committee had performed a small financial miracle, budgeting $160 million and spending perhaps $20 million less to blend the city and the surrounding mountains and old and new athletic facilities into a suitable Olympic site. Now it was time for the Games to begin, time to put into practice the motto Sarajevo offered the Olympians: "He who wins should be glad, and he who loses should not be sad, for we are here to make friends."

See page 286 for captions identifying opening spread photographs.

The official mascot of the Sarajevo Olympics was Vučko, an amiable Bosnian timber wolf, selected because Yugoslavs consider the wolf, representing strength and courage, the symbol of winter. Perched on a hundred souvenirs, Vučko looked like something out of Disney. But the wolf who was spotted on the back side of Mount Bjelašnica, away from the downhill course, was not a friendly wolf, and the rest of the pack who chased the policeman who shot the wolf did not seem to possess the true Olympic spirit, either.

HOCKEY

Yugoslav soldiers, many armed with Kalashnikov sub-machine guns and some flanked by guard dogs, patrolled the perimeter of Mojmilo, the main Olympic Village, the temporary home for most of the 1,591 athletes representing 49 nations in the 1984 Winter Games.

Memories of 1972, when Palestinian terrorists infiltrated the athletes' quarters in Munich and murdered 11 Israelis, made security a major Olympic concern in Sarajevo. Electronic detectors monitored every item brought into the Village, and electrified fences, seven feet high, discouraged intruders.

A few days earlier, when a pair of American speed skaters tried to steal an Olympic flag flying in front of the Village, Yugoslav militiamen, unamused, caught them in the act, one skater on the other's shoulders, arrested them and detained them for four hours.

Few athletes complained about the security, or about the facilities in Mojmilo—spacious and functional rooms—markedly improved over the cramped Lake Placid quarters that were converted, after the 1980 Games, into a minimum-security prison. Mojmilo would become a housing development. The cultural center, stripped of movies, pinball machines, television sets and disco lights, all the accoutrements of athletic culture, would become a kindergarten, and the sprawling dining room would turn into a department store.

"This is by far the best Olympic Village we've had the pleasure of being in," said Don Miller, the executive director of the U.S. Olympic Committee.

They ate their breakfasts in the dining hall in the Olympic Village and then the U.S. hockey players headed toward their apartments. Their 38-year-old coach, Lou Vairo, who grew up playing roller hockey on the streets of Brooklyn, who never skated on ice till he was in his twenties, paused in the lobby. He was still in shock. "The kids were definitely uptight," Vairo said.

The day before, the U.S. hockey team, successor to the miracle team that beat the Soviet Union and won the gold medal at Lake Placid in 1980, had faced Canada in the opening round of the Olympic hockey tournament, which, because of an expanded schedule, had to begin play before the formal opening of the Games.

Twelve times in the previous year the U.S. and Canada had met, in Olympic tune-ups, and the U.S. had won five games, Canada four, and three had ended in ties. In the final meeting of the two teams, the U.S. had scored a resounding 8–2 victory. Canada had lost five straight games going into the Olympics. The U.S. clearly was favored.

To make its position more precarious, Canada had just lost two players, Mark Morrison and Don Dietrich, both barred from the Games by a bizarre ruling of the International Olympic Committee. After weeks of charges and countercharges, which almost prompted Canada to withdraw from the Games, then confronted by a Finnish protest that at least ten players from a variety of countries were really professionals, not amateurs, the IOC had decreed that any man who had signed a contract with a team in the National Hockey League *and* had played for that team in an NHL game was a professional. Anyone else, no matter how many contracts he may have signed, no matter how much money he may have been paid, was not a professional. Purists were horrified; the IOC had taken a giant step toward "open" competition in the Olympics. But that was small consolation to the two Canadians, two Italians and one Austrian who were ruled ineligible for the 1984 Games.

When the ruling came down, only the day before competition began, the wording was fuzzy, and at first the Canadian goalie, Mario Gosselin, who had signed with the Quebec Nordiques of the NHL but had not played for them, was informed by his coach, Dave King, that he was not eligible for the Olympics. An hour later, King told Gosselin he might be eligible. Gosselin, a 20-year-old French Canadian, spent the evening wandering around the Olympic Village, wondering whether he had wasted a year of his life preparing for the Games. Then shortly before midnight he got a phone call from a talk-show host in Quebec who told him that because he had never played in the NHL, he was eligible to face the United States the following day.

The game was played in Zetra Arena, a $20 million rink with a roof shaped like the official symbol of the Games, an impressionistic snowflake, and even before the opening whistle, Lou Vairo turned to an assistant, Tim Taylor, the Yale coach, and said, "I feel uneasy, Timmy, and I can't pinpoint it."

American hockey coach Lou Vairo.

Soon, Vairo felt even more uneasy. Only 27 seconds into the first period, Canada's Pat Flatley, an All-American at the University of Wisconsin, tipped in a shot for a 1–0 lead. At the end of the first period, despite the cheers of a predominantly American crowd, waving flags and remembering Lake Placid, the U.S. trailed, 2–1. Vairo thought of screaming at his players to shake them up.

"Then I thought about how young our team was," Vairo said. "I didn't want to panic them. We were only down by a goal, so I didn't rip them."

The Canadians ripped them, 4–2, with a teenager, David A. Jensen, getting both U.S. goals. Carey Wilson, who went to Dartmouth, scored the last three Canadian goals, and Goose Gosselin, playing brilliantly, made 37 saves. "I blew it," Vairo said. "I should have yelled."

Canadian goalie Mario Gosselin stops a point-blank shot by American Pat LaFontaine.

On Mount Bjelašnica, outside Sarajevo, the downhill skiers practiced, and a brash young American preached. "All I have to do is come down, be decent, be aggressive and I'll win," said Bill Johnson on the eve of his perilous race.

Johnson had reason to anoint himself king of the downhill. He had the second fastest time of the morning, and in his last three practice runs, he had placed first, second and second, an awesome feat.

Still, his confidence was stunning. After all, no American male had ever won an Olympic gold medal in any event on skis, and no American male had won even a silver or a bronze in the downhill.

Americans simply were not supposed to be downhill racers, especially not Americans who were blond, slender, 23 years old and lived in Van Nuys, in California's San Fernando Valley, an area better suited to surfers than skiers.

Bill Johnson was practically unknown until, a few weeks earlier, in Wengen, Switzerland, he became the first American man to win a World Cup downhill. His shocking victory prompted Austria's Franz Klammer, whose spectacular downhill lit the 1976 Olympics, to refer to Johnson as "a nosepicker," a term common among Europeans, meaning merely one of the racers who stood and waited while the top skiers, the seeded skiers, took their turns.

American reporters, less familiar with the phrase, took it as a personal insult and used it to goad Johnson into outrageous statements. It didn't take much goading. "This is going to be a race for second place," he said. "I don't care who gets that. They'll all be behind me."

ABC Sports had paid $91.5 million for the television rights, a sizable slice of the budget of the Sarajevo Organizing Committee—which had received 2/3 of that amount—and had brought more than 900 employees to Sarajevo. Sixty-eight cameras were ready to deliver 63.5 hours of programming through a Star Wars studio equipped even with an electronic palette enabling artists to paint pictures on the screen, a studio that had been assembled and tested in the United States, taken apart, shipped by sea to Rotterdam, then transported to Sarajevo in 22 40-foot trailers.

Bill Johnson on a downhill practice run.

Nineteen-year-old figure skater Sandra Dubravcic lights the Olympic torch.

In the morning, snow fell on the streets of Sarajevo for the first time in more than a week, but only briefly, barely an inch, and what glistened now inside Kosevo Stadium was imported, trucked in by Yugoslav troops to provide the proper backdrop for the opening ceremonies of the Winter Games. The temperature rose just slightly above freezing, and the sun sliced through the clouds and the thick Sarajevo air for only a few minutes at a time, but the sellout crowd of 50,000—each ticket cost $55, or two weeks' salary for the average Yugoslav—was warmed enough by the occasion, by the dazzling spectacle.

Eight hundred gymnasts, 1,200 folk dancers, 400 cadets and 180 members of the Yugoslav army band lit up the field as the parade of the athletes began, some 1,500 Winter Olympians, all except the ones saving their strength for their events the next day. More than 300 of the athletes were women, who had clearly come a long way since the games of the ancient Greeks; in those days, any woman found at the Games, even as a spectator, was supposed to be thrown off a cliff.

The athletes marched into the stadium behind Yugoslav women carrying signs identifying each country, and behind their national flags. The Greeks, as always, led the Olympic parade, followed by 47 nations in Serbo-Croatian alphabetical order and then, according to tradition, by the host team, in this case 75 Yugoslavs whose appearance, in gray coats, beige pants and blue hats, set off the loudest cheers of the day.

The athletes could not have been a more varied group. The oldest, a Swedish bobsled driver, Carl-Erik Erikkson, was 53. The youngest, an Argentine Alpine skier, Geraldina Bobbio, was 15. The men carrying the Austrian, British and Soviet flags were three of the world's most celebrated athletes: Franz Klammer, the downhill skier; Christopher Dean, the ice dancing

Yugoslav dancers marching in the opening ceremonies.

Frank Masley of the luge team carrying the American flag.

king; and Vladislav Tretiak, the hockey goalie. The men holding the Puerto Rican, Egyptian and the British Virgin Island flags were three of the world's most obscure athletes: George Tucker, a luger; Jamil El Reedy, an Alpine skier; and Errol Fraser, a speed skater, each of whom was born, but none of whom lived, in the land he represented. All three grew up, in fact, in New York State; each was a one-man team for his place of birth.

Tucker almost missed the opening parade. He showed up only 20 minutes before the start, his hands sticky with Fiberglas. With the help of an American luger named Ray Bateman, he had just finished repairing his sled. The day before, on a practice run, Tucker, a 36-year-old candidate for a doctorate in physics at Wesleyan University, had crashed, maintaining his perfect record. He had, after a year of occasional attempts, never yet made it all the way down a luge run without crashing. Even driving to New York's John F. Kennedy Airport to catch a plane to Sarajevo, Tucker had crashed, wrecking his girlfriend's car. "I break cars, sleds, everything," said Tucker, who was born in Puerto Rico when his father was distributing films to South America.

Carrying the flag for the United States team, 124 strong, behind a sign marked SAD, for *Sjedinjene Americke Drzave,* was Frank Masley, a 23-year-old computer expert from Newark, Delaware, who had placed tenth in the world luge championships. Masley's parading teammates included the 1980 flagbearer, figure skater Scott Hamilton, and the 1976 flag-bearer, skier Cindy Nelson. One American athlete, luger Ron Rossi, could catch a glimpse of his wife, Susan Veltman-Rossi, another luger, march-ing for Canada.

American figure skaters on parade.

The Americans wore tan sheepskin jackets, five-pocket blue jeans with red fleece lining and off-white cowboy hats, a small part of the 32-piece wardrobe presented to each U.S. athlete by Levi Strauss, the clothing company which had budgeted $50 million for its Olympic program from 1981 through 1984, only $30 million less than the budget of the entire United States Olympic Committee.

Each country's dress was distinctive, the Moroccans exotic in red shirts and long black robes, the French dapper in tan overcoats with maroon scarves and burgundy pants, the British Virgin Islands singular, in the person of Errol Fraser, in an olive cap, black turtleneck and brown leather pants. Four skiers from Lebanon wore black coats with red-and-white scarves. While they marched, heavy shelling rocked Beirut, the government and its supporters stunned even more by President Reagan's announcement that the U.S. Marines would begin withdrawing. Three of the Lebanese skiers had flown out of Beirut as bombs shook the runway; one of them, Toni Sukkar, had a bullet scar on his left arm, a mark of his country's turmoil. "We are here to be represented," Serge Axiotiades said, "to have our flag flying among all the others, to show that we're still living, we're not only dying."

An occasional hitch spiced the ceremonies—the band played "The Yellow Rose of Texas" when the Italian team marched in—but for the most part the people of Yugoslavia put on a magnificent display of drills and dances, prompting the president of the International Olympic Committee, Juan Antonio Samaranch, to offer his thanks in Serbo-Croatian: "*Hvala,* Yugoslavia, *hvala,* Yugoslavia."

DAY 2
THURSDAY, FEBRUARY 9th

Contrary to popular opinion, the 1980 United States Olympic hockey team did not perform a miracle at Lake Placid. The team performed several miracles. The Americans trailed in six of their seven Olympic games, and yet they did not lose a single game. The Americans were figured not to have a chance against the Soviet Union, and yet they beat the Soviets. The Americans were not ranked among the top four teams in the 1980 Olympics, and yet they won the gold medal.

No one seriously expected the 1984 team to duplicate all those miracles. In fact, the dozens and dozens of magazine articles, newspaper stories and television features devoted to the team emphasized that it was unfair and unrealistic to expect the new team to come even close to the magic of its predecessor. But the cumulative impact of the coverage was precisely the opposite: The new team was so well reported—and, incidentally, so well financed, its budget for the Olympic year a luxurious $1.5 million—that readers and viewers, and writers and broadcasters, began to believe that 1984 could be 1980 revisited.

The pressure on the young American team, its average age barely 21 and its brightest star, Pat LaFontaine, only 18, was enormous, and when the youngsters, during their pre-Olympic tour, held their own against National Hockey League teams and won a six-game series from a visiting Soviet team (of the second rank), the pressure multiplied, and the expectations rose.

Most Americans ignored the reasoned words of Ken Dryden, the articulate goalie-lawyer-author-broadcaster. "If the U.S. team wins the bronze," Dryden said, "that would be considered a major achievement." But even the American players themselves dreamed of gold.

THE GOLD MEDALISTS
SPEED SKATING
WOMEN'S 1,500 METERS
KARIN ENKE, EAST GERMANY
NORDIC SKIING
WOMEN'S 10 KILOMETERS
MARJA-LIISA HAEMAELAEINEN, FINLAND

NORDIC SKIING

The first gold medal of the XIVth Winter Olympics, in the women's 10-kilometer cross-country ski race, went to Marja-Liisa Haemaelaeinen, whose last name is almost as common in Finland as Smith is in the United States.

Haemaelaeinen, the 1983 World Cup champion, led the race at every checkpoint, and when the Finn crossed the finish line, 19 seconds in front of the Soviet runner-up, she collapsed, half in fatigue, half in ecstasy. "I've never been so happy," said the 28-year-old physiotherapist.

King Olaf V of Norway was happy, too. The 80-year-old monarch, who had himself won a gold medal for yachting in the 1928 Olympics, watched one of his subjects, Brit Pettersen, take the bronze.

SPEED SKATING

The first world record of the XIVth Winter Olympics, in the women's 1,500-meter speed skating race, went to East Germany's Karin Enke, a former figure skater who switched to speed because "I didn't like the ballyhoo, the acting, the playing to the audience, the starring role."

By 1984, at the age of 22, Enke has taken over the starring role in speed skating, heiress to Eric Heiden's throne, contender for as many as four gold medals in Sarajevo. "Skating is not hard," said Enke, dark-haired and attractive, a sturdy 5-foot-9 and 158 pounds. "But people look to me, always look to me, and that's hard."

Before she started in the 1,500 meters, skating in the fifth pair, Enke felt uneasy. "For the first time in years," she said later, "I was nervous, very nervous." But she mastered her nerves and beat the time of teammate Andrea Schoene, who had raced earlier.

Marja-Liisa Haemaelaeinen (left), winning the first of her three gold medals, in the 10-kilometer ski race, Russian powerhouse Raisa Smetanina (middle) on her way to winning the silver medal in the women's 10-kilometer cross-country event and East Germany's Karin Enke (right), winning the gold in the 1,500-meter speed skating event.

Halfway up the chair lift, as he approached the 80-mile-an-hour winds that whipped through the fog crowning Mount Bjelašnica, Bill Johnson realized that his bid to win the downhill gold would be postponed. Two hours before the scheduled noon start, the race was officially pushed back a day.

Seven inches of new snow fell on the course, diminishing Johnson's chances—the faster the course, the better for him—but not his confidence. "There's going to be a helluva battle," he predicted. "For second. They might as well give me the gold medal now."

Then Johnson grandly posed for photos with Jean-Claude Killy, the Frenchman who won the downhill, the slalom and the giant slalom at Grenoble in 1968. Killy was working in Sarajevo for French television, one of many former champions turned commentators.

The great Soviet goalie Vladislav Tretiak, in his fourth Olympiad.

HOCKEY

Vladislav Tretiak, the best goalie in the world, was getting ready to play hockey, to face Italy. He was not concerned with the report circulating in Sarajevo that he had been offered a contract by the Montreal Canadiens of the National Hockey League. Tretiak, a 31-year-old army major, had always turned aside such reports with a simple statement: "I am a patriot." He turned aside slap shots even more convincingly.

A big man, 6-foot-1 and 208 pounds, and a superb skater, Tretiak was playing in his fourth Olympics, seeking his third gold medal. The Italians knew they had little chance against Tretiak and his gifted teammates. Three of the Italian players were American born and bred, and as they warmed up for the game, one of them, Dave Tomassoni, whose wife was home in Minnesota, expecting a baby, turned to teammate Mike Mastrullo, another American, and said, "I just felt something. I think my baby is being born."

More than an hour later, in the second period, with the Soviets leading, 4–0, Tomassoni scored the only goal the Italians managed against Tretiak. The final score, 5–1, was close enough, however, to be considered a moral victory for Italy. "The Russians were a little tired," Mastrullo said.

"How could you tell?" he was asked.

"They let us touch the puck once in a while," Mastrullo said.

After the game, Tomassoni called his wife in Minnesota and found out that his first son had been born three hours earlier—as he was warming up for the Russians.

With two-thirds of a hat trick—a son and a score—the new father explained how he happened to be playing for Italy. "Under Italian law," Tomassoni said, "I qualified because my father was born before my grandfather became a naturalized American, and that made my father an Italian, and that made me an Italian."

Not quite so simple as "I am a patriot."

LUGE

Snow sprinkled Mount Trebevic, slowing down the luge track, which was bad news for almost all the lugers, except the star and sole member of the Puerto Rican team, George Tucker. Of all the lugers, Tucker seemed to understand best that lying on his back on a four-and-a-half-foot sled, hurtling down an icy chute, feet first, at speeds approaching 70 miles an hour, turning almost upside down through breathtaking curves, could be dangerous. Tucker was in favor of a slow track. The slower, the better.

During his abbreviated practice runs, Tucker had been getting pushes from the sports editor of *Time* magazine, Tom Callahan. "Each time I pushed him," Callahan reported, "he'd lean back and, in his heartrending voice, say, 'Goodbye.'"

Now, facing the first of his official Olympic runs, one a day for four straight days, Tucker had not only the slick track to fear but also the snow. Still, miraculously, Tucker negotiated the first eight curves without mishap. Only five to go.

"On curve nine," Tucker said later, "my mask was just covered with snow, and I went into the section called The Labyrinth completely blind, and I was waiting for the voice of *Star Wars* to say, 'Let the Force be with you, George, and don't worry about steering.'" The Force must have been with him. Tucker sped safely through The Labyrinth.

"When I got into the final curve," he said, "I knew I had it." Tucker did it, completed a luge run without crashing for the first time in his life. A small but enthusiastic crowd cheered. "All the Yugoslavian people have been tremendously encouraging," Tucker said, "and I really wanted to do it for them and for the people of Puerto Rico."

Tucker's delight at finishing was tempered by his regret that the only luger to finish behind him was a Yugoslav, Suad Karajica, who had been training with him and had become his friend. Tucker would have been happy to place 32nd instead of 31st. But Karajica, in front of the home crowd, crashed before the finish. "I felt terrible for him," Tucker said.

East Germans ran one-two-three among the women, and Italians one-three among the men. But the two best American lugers, neither of whom had any illusions about winning a medal, performed creditably, Bonny Warner eighth among the women, Frank Masley fifteenth among the men.

Bonny Warner of the American luge team.

Warner, a 21-year-old Stanford student, had never *seen* a luge run till three days after the 1980 Olympics. She was in Lake Placid in 1980 only because she had won a contest to be a member of the torch relay. After the Games, after she tried the luge and loved it, she won a "Be All You Can Be" essay contest, sponsored by Levis, and used the $5,000 prize to go to West Germany to learn proper technique on the luge. By 1983, she had learned enough to finish seventh in the world championships. A field hockey goalie gifted enough to have dreams of making the 1988 Summer Games, Bonny was a very bold luger.

"Everyone who watches the sport—unless they're lugers themselves—thinks we're crazy," Warner said. "But you have to be a very sane person, very much in control. The daredevils crash. A schizo wouldn't make it down the hill. Everybody thinks I'm crazy. But I know I'm not."

Frank Masley, who carried the flag in the opening parade, shared Bonny's calm view of the luge sled. "If I couldn't steer it," said Masley, "I wouldn't be on it."

Although he brought no medal home from Sarajevo, David Gilman added to the effort of the young U.S. luge team.

The four Lebanese skiers in Sarajevo, their downhill race postponed, gathered in the Olympic Village, and after an hour-and-a-half wait for an open telephone line, one of them, Michael Samen, managed to get a call through to Beirut. Samen listened, then reported, "There was really heavy shelling for about six to eight hours yesterday. My mother says the Americans moved out of their headquarters. Everybody in my family is okay. They stayed between the walls of the buildings. They always do that."

As the Lebanese ate in the Olympic dining hall, smiling and laughing athletes surrounded them. "All the people here are happy," Toni Sukkar said, "and we—we try to be happy, too. We try to laugh and smile, but inside, we are not happy."

After the Olympics, Samen would be returning to school, at the University of California at Davis. "Sometimes you feel guilty," he said, "because all your friends are home in Beirut suffering. They have no electricity, no water."

HOCKEY

The United States hockey team took the ice against Czechoslovakia knowing it was in a precarious position. Another defeat would make it very difficult, almost impossible, to reach the medal round. But to beat the Czechs, generally considered the second-best team in the world, behind the Soviet Union, was a very difficult, almost impossible, task.

The Americans played with a fury and a dedication they had not shown in the opening game against Canada, and late in the first period the score was tied 1–1, each team having scored a shorthanded goal. An upset seemed possible. But then a power shortage darkened the lights in the arena for 15 minutes, and when the lights brightened again, the Czechs dimmed U.S. hopes by scoring a pair of power-play goals. The Czechs went on to win decisively, 4–1.

Pat LaFontaine shooting at the Czech net.

LaFontaine. A few weeks later he would be playing professionally for the New York Islanders.

In other games, Finland beat Norway, 16–2, and Canada beat Austria, 8–1, keeping both those teams, like the Czechs, undefeated.

"At least we played as hard as we can play," coach Vairo said. "This time we didn't lose. We were beaten." Then, in defense of his young players, Vairo added, "If our country was at war and the enemy was coming, I'd take these twenty and fight with them because the enemy wouldn't get through without killing every one of us."

Mike Eruzione, the captain of the 1980 team, working in Sarajevo as an ABC commentator, offered a less passionate assessment. "It was unfair from the beginning," Eruzione said. "We expected too much."

"You know," said Eddie Olczyk, a 17-year-old American star, "I was coming off the ice and I just blinked my eyes, and the whole year had gone—right before my eyes."

O f all the events in the Winter Olympics program, none is so beautiful nor so controversial as figure skating. Nine judges assess every individual competitor or pair, and each judge assigns point values to both technical and artistic skills, a task that murders objectivity. To compound the problem, politics, past performances and personal prejudices occasionally intrude and make the judging even more—to use the kindest word—subjective.

The result is a catch-22 situation in which every skater knows the judging is unfair, but also knows that if he or she complains, then the judging will, to his or her detriment, become even more unfair. Since the most prominent skaters are generally favored by the judges, the most prominent skaters rarely complain and the less prominent rarely find an audience for their complaints. The strangest thing is that the best skaters still usually win. Usually.

The two things about figure skating that are not debatable are, first, that it is beautiful, a marvelous blend of grace and strength and spectacle, and second, that it is, for the winners, very profitable, a tradition dating back to Sonja Henie. The Norwegian beauty, who made her Olympic debut at 11 and won three gold medals by the time she was 23, was earning a million dollars a year by the time she was 26.

Today every Olympic skating champion anticipates a rich professional contract, which explains why not since Henie, among the women, won her third title in 1936, and not since Dick Button, among the men, won his second in 1952, has any individual Olympic figure skating champion successfully defended his or her title. The temptation is simply too great to turn professional, to be measured from then on by applause and by income, and no longer by sometimes capricious judges.

THE GOLD MEDALISTS

SPEED SKATING

MEN'S 500 METERS
  SERGEI FOKICHEV, SOVIET UNION

WOMEN'S 500 METERS
  CHRISTA ROTHENBURGER, EAST GERMANY

NORDIC SKIING

MEN'S 30 KILOMETERS
  NIKOLAI ZIMYATOV, SOVIET UNION

Snow had come back to Sarajevo, 12 inches in 24 hours, spreading a white coat over the valley city, hiding the mud, brightening the Olympic Village. Winds gusting up to 120 miles an hour stormed through the mountains shielding Sarajevo, forcing the postponement once again of the men's downhill. The postponement, until Sunday, was announced so early Bill Johnson didn't even have to go to the mountain to deliver his sermon of confidence once more.

NORDIC SKIING

Neither the wind nor the snow stopped Nikolai Zimyatov, who won three gold medals at Lake Placid in 1980, from retaining his championship in the first Nordic skiing event for men in Sarajevo, the 30-kilometer cross-country race. The 28-year-old Soviet Army officer, wearing a red wool cap to match his red racing outfit, defeated a countryman, Aleksandr Zavialov, on a track softened by fresh snow. "Zimyatov floats like a deer on a soft track," said Bill Koch, who had in 1976 become the first American to win a Nordic skiing medal, a silver.

In Sarajevo, Koch again finished first among the Americans, but only 21st in the race. "A soft track is not my kind of track," he said. "I know a lot of people will be disappointed. But I hope they will appreciate my effort. It was the best I skied all year."

Don Nielsen, a member of the American biathlon team, offered his own tribute to Zimyatov. Nielsen, a classics major at Dartmouth, was contributing columns to the *Denver Post*. "Days like today you want to tie your horse to a good tree so it won't blow away," Nielsen wrote. "You must wake up in a special mood to race well in a winter hurricane. Zimyatov was rumored to have kicked the cleaning lady's cat before leaving the hotel to race. This can't be: Zimmy has a cat of his own back in Russia.

"When the weather is mean, the best approach is a perverse pleasure in battling it, skiing till your eyes cross, with a leer on your face. Zimyatov faced the gale with the right combativeness and skied like a man walking on feathers. Elbows splayed to the side and with a head-on profile as thin as an Irish setter's, he foiled the wind and let the pressure of this 18-mile sprint slide over his hunched back.

The food in the Olympic Village was created more for gourmands than gourmets: mountains of stewed lamb and bony fish, washed down by cases and cases of Coke, the only item more ubiquitous in Sarajevo than photographs of Tito. Rosalynn Sumners, the women's world figure skating champion, called home to the U.S. for canned tuna, canned chicken and sugarless gum, but most athletes settled for the Village fare. Most settled for the Village air, too, except Scott Hamilton, the men's world figure skating champion, who, to combat the soot and sulfur of Sarajevo, put a purifier in his Mojmilo room. "I hold my breath all day," Hamilton said, "and then I go back to my room to breathe."

America's Bill Koch working through soft snow to a 21st-place finish in the men's 30-kilometer cross-country.

Nikolai Zimyatov, Russia's triple gold winner at Lake Placid, repeats his winning performance in the 30-kilometer.

"He is his gentle, quiet self again tonight, but we'll see the same look on his face before the 50-kilometer, and the house cat had better stay in bed that morning. . . .

"Reactions after a race are as mixed as the moods before. Thomas Wassberg of Sweden is downstairs sawing his skis in half, teaching them a lesson."

Rumors swirled through Sarajevo early in the morning, triggered by reports that somber music had replaced regular programming on Soviet radio stations, an indication, historically, that a significant Soviet official had died. The rumors focused upon the Soviet president, 69-year-old Yuri Andropov, who had not been seen in public for several months, who had, according to unconfirmed reports, recently undergone a kidney transplant. Russian athletes, striding through the Olympic Village, were asked if they had heard of Andropov's death. They knew nothing, they said, and hurried off to their competitions, their practices.

LUGE

Midway through the luge competition, after the second run, East Germans still held the first three places among the women, and had moved into first and third places among the men. Steffi Martin, 21, the world champion, led the women, and Bonny Warner of the United States remained in eighth place, gaining confidence and, with two days and two runs to go, dreaming of moving up.

For the second day in a row, for the second time in his life, George Tucker completed the luge run without crashing. He was, cheerfully, the slowest finisher, directly behind his Yugoslav friend, Suad Karajica.

SPEED SKATING

The snow delayed the start of two speed skating finals, the 500-meter races for men and women, and when the track finally was ready, a young American, 20-year-old Nick Thometz, was paired with a Soviet star, Sergei Fokichev, in the first heat. Thometz, caught leaning, was charged with a false start; then, fearful of being disqualified, he got off to a costly legal but slow start.

Over the final 400 meters, Thometz outskated Fokichev, but he had spotted the Russian too much of a lead. Fokichev won the gold medal, and Thometz wound up fifth, .37 seconds behind the champion. "If Nick hadn't jumped," said his coach, Bob Corby, "I think he would have walked out of here with the gold or silver."

Yoshihiro Kitazawa, in second place, became the first Japanese to earn an Olympic speed skating medal. Canada's Gaetan Boucher came in third and Dan Jansen of the United States placed fourth.

Among the women, Karin Enke—"Monster Woman," as coach Corby called her, with awe—also got off to a relatively slow start, which cost her a chance for her second gold medal of the Games. Enke, the 500-meter champion at Lake Placid, finished second to an East German teammate, Christa Rothenburger, a 24-year-old physical education student.

Karin Enke (top left) and Christa Rothenburger (right)—East Germany's silver and gold medalists in the women's 500; and Yoshihiro Kitazawa (bottom left)—Japan's first-ever speed skating medalist.

Not long after noon, the rumors turned to reality: The Soviet Union confirmed that President Yuri Andropov, leader of the Communist Party and the communist world, was dead. "Well, what to say?" said Nikolai Zimyatov, the cross-country gold medalist. "It was quite unexpected for all of us. But we will continue to struggle for high performances."

The International Olympic Committee, with expressions of sympathy, announced that the Games would go on, and the Soviet Olympic delegation said that its team would not withdraw. The Russians quickly organized a memorial service for the Olympic Village and arranged for their flag, among the 49 flying in the Village, to be lowered to half-mast. Yugoslavia and the Eastern bloc countries lowered their flags, too, a mark of respect for the Soviet leader.

No one suspected at that moment that the death of Yuri Andropov might have a critical impact upon the Summer Games in Los Angeles.

ICE DANCING

Bestemianova and Bukin—second only to the incomparable Torvill and Dean.

"Their Greatnesses," the British press hailed them in headlines that abandoned all pretense of restraint. "The best thing to come out of Nottingham since D. H. Lawrence and Raleigh bicycles," suggested the *London Daily Mail.* They had been on the Queen's honors list. They had been received at Buckingham Palace and at 10 Downing Street. They were an ex-insurance clerk and an ex-policeman, Jayne Torvill and Christopher Dean, a pair of impeccable blonds in their mid-twenties, and they had become, beyond question, the best ice dancing team in the world.

Torvill and Dean, T&D, a tandem as recognizable to most Englishmen as Charles and Diana, launched their bid for their first Olympic title, after winning three straight world championships, by performing the three compulsory dances, in this competition the paso doble, rumba and Westminster waltz. They performed the first two exquisitely, the last, in the opinions of three judges, perfectly. They got three 6.0 scores, the first perfect scores for a compulsory dance in the history of Olympic ice dancing, a history that dated back only to 1976. But brief history or not, the achievement was stunning. In fact, of the 27 scores they received for their three compulsory dances, T&D had thirteen 5.9s and only one so low as 5.7.

A Soviet pair, Natalia Bestemianova and Andrei Bukin, placed second in the compulsory dances, and an American duo, Judy Blumberg and Michael Seibert, third. For their first dance, the U.S. team had received a 5.7 from the one American judge, a 5.3 from the one Soviet judge. "You expect that," Blumberg said. "It's the same old story," said Seibert.

Even though the compulsory dances counted for only 30 percent of the final score in ice dancing, the odds were infinite that neither the Soviets nor the Americans would seriously challenge Their Greatnesses. "The gold medal we concede to Jayne and Chris," Seibert had said even before the competition began, "but we won't concede the silver."

Small wonder T&D had earned the Order of the British Empire, plus the freedom of the city of Nottingham, an honor that permitted them, historically, to drive their sheep across the city square without penalty. When Dean was a rookie policeman, before he turned full time to skating, he worked on occasion in the city square. His Greatness once arrested a citizen for publicly disrobing.

The Soviet "hammerhead shark."

BOBSLED

The two-man bobsleds braved the snow and the wind and 13 curves along the 1,300-meter Mount Trebevic course, and in the first two runs, half of the two-day competition, Wolfgang Hoppe, a 25-year-old East German soldier, piloted his team into first place, followed by another East German team and by Soviets in third and fifth.

The Russians employed a revolutionary new sled, copied from Formula 1 racing cars of the 1960s and 1970s, a sleek machine variously described as "bullet-like" and "cigar-shaped" and "a hammerhead shark" and "the one with the fins on the outside and Russians on the inside." German and Swiss competitors rejected similar designs because the sleds seemed too risky, too liable to overturn, the driver and the brakeman squeezed dangerously close together.

The emergence of Bill Johnson seemed to signal the end of an era in men's Alpine skiing in the United States, the era of the Mahre twins, Phil and Steve, a pair of 5-foot-9, 170-pound, 26-year-old, married, astigmatic, prematurely balding all-around athletes from the state of Washington. And at a news conference in the Olympic Village, the Mahres, the dominant Americans in their sport for almost a decade, offered their own signals that their careers would soon end.

"I'm not as hungry as I used to be," said Phil, by four minutes the older of the twins. "If I don't win any medals, I won't have any problem." Steve seemed equally at ease. "I have no qualms about leaving the sport," Steve said. "I'm ready to go on."

Their careers had been remarkable. Phil Mahre smashed his left ankle so badly in 1979 that Dr. Richard Steadman had to use seven screws and a metal plate to reconstruct it. Yet in 1980, Phil won the silver medal in the Olympic slalom, and for the next three years, from 1981 through 1983, he won the World Cup overall championship, a title no American had previously earned. Steve Mahre won the giant slalom at the World Alpine Championships in 1982.

Both Mahres had always been candid about the state of amateurism in their sport. "It just doesn't exist at the top levels," said Phil, who admitted that, to earn his endorsement checks, "I'll always put the skis between me and the commentator because if you don't, they cut them out."

Torvill and Dean's paso doble.

FIGURE SKATING

It was no surprise that Elena Valova and Oleg Vasiliev, the reigning world champions, dominated the short program of the figure skating pairs competition. None of the nine judges gave the pair from Leningrad a 6.0 either in required elements or in presentation, but the Soviets earned enough 5.8s and 5.9s to build a commanding lead.

But it was surprising that an American pair, Kitty and Peter Carruthers, tied for second place in the short program, which counted 29 percent toward the final standings. The U.S. youngsters, who were adopted separately from the Home of the Little Wanderers in Boston and raised in Massachusetts, had finished only fourth in the 1983 world championships, and Kitty, at 22, two years younger than Peter, had been suffering from tendinitis in her right ankle during the week leading up to the competition. She had to skate with foam rubber wrapped around the ankle.

The Carrutherses opened to the sounds of Earth, Wind and Fire, then skated to the theme music from *Hawaii Five-O* and, performing seven elements in two minutes, collected enough 5.5s and 5.6s to tie Larisa Selezneva and Oleg Makarov, a little-known Soviet couple. Among the 4,500 spectators who cheered Kitty and Peter at Zetra Arena, the site of the two American hockey defeats, was Lou Vairo, the U.S. hockey coach. "Peter is staying in the same building with our players," Vairo said. "He comes to the hockey games to cheer us on. I came here to cheer him on."

The parents of the American pair also cheered. "When we adopted Peter," Charles Carruthers said, "we were asked what kind of child we wanted. They meant a boy or a girl, but I said, 'We want an active child.' We like to go camping and canoeing. When we adopted Kitty, we asked for another active child."

Kitty and Peter were such active children their father built a makeshift rink for them on their Massachusetts farm. He and his wife, Maureen, also built their lives to a great extent around the children's skating, a commitment that cost close to $200,000. "We both held teaching jobs," Charles Carruthers said, "spent sparingly, drove the same car for eleven years and 200,000 miles and ate a lot of spaghetti and meatballs."

Valova and Vasiliev, world champions and gold medalists.

Kitty and Peter Carruthers.

Once a childhood playmate taunted Peter, "Your parents *bought* you," but Peter responded, "My parents *picked* me out. But your mother and father *had* you, and boy, did they get stuck!"

As Kitty and Peter's skating blossomed, they moved to Wilmington, Delaware, to train under Ron Ludington, who helped them develop, in practice, a maneuver called the Big Quad, a quadruple throw Salchow in which Kitty would do four full airborne left turns, then land on the back outside edge of her right foot. No one had ever executed a Big Quad in world or Olympic competition, but Kitty and Peter, who sometimes pulled it off in practice and sometimes didn't, were prepared to use it in their freeskating program if the situation demanded a dramatic, but dangerous, moment.

The freeskating would be held two days after the short program. Coach Ludington said that Kitty and Peter would not attempt the Big Quad. "To risk a Quad," Ludington said, "I would be very derelict in my duties."

Kitty and Peter Carruthers already had a silver or a bronze medal within reach, and no American figure skating pair had won any kind of Olympic medal in twenty years.

DAY 4
SATURDAY, FEBRUARY 11th

The biathlon is a sport few Americans understand, and only a couple of hundred perform, which may explain why, since the event was added to the Olympics in 1960, no American has placed among the top ten in any individual race. But if the Americans drawn to the biathlon are few, they are a precious few, uncommonly articulate, uncommonly versatile.

Of the six American biathletes competing in Sarajevo, three went to Dartmouth, and one of them, 32-year-old Don Nielsen, graduated magna cum laude in classics. In 1980, Nielsen says, he mortgaged his family's farm to finance his biathlon training, a story that doesn't have the standard happy ending: the bank foreclosed. Teammate Lyle Nelson, 35, who captained his high school football, track and ski teams in Idaho, set a record for the obstacle course at West Point, served as a captain in the Army, then earned a master's degree in business at the University of Southern California.

"We sit down at the dinner table," Nielsen says, "and talk about everything from Buddhism to calculus to Andropov. We don't talk about things like ski wax that the regular cross-country skiers talk about. Our world is not defined by ski wax."

Obviously, uncommon men for an uncommon sport, a blend of cross-country skiing and rifle marksmanship, two contradictory disciplines. "Try sprinting full out around the neighborhood," suggests Marie Alkire, the U.S. team's rifle coach, "then stopping to thread a needle."

"Skiing and shooting is a marriage made in hell," Don Nielsen says. "Biathlon is turning from a rabbit to a rock and then back again."

THE GOLD MEDALISTS
BIATHLON
20 KILOMETERS
  PETER ANGERER, WEST GERMANY
BOBSLED
TWO-MAN
  WOLFGANG HOPPE
  DIETMAR SCHAUERHAMMER, EAST GERMANY

Kitty and Peter Carruthers awoke at 4:45 A.M. and were on the ice practicing at 6:00 A.M. Coach Ron Ludington, who shared a bronze medal in the pairs in 1960, wanted them to polish their four-and-a-half-minute freeskating program, which would count 71 percent toward their final score.

LUGE

Bonny Warner, after the crash.

Bonny Warner decided to gamble, decided to try for an extraordinary luge run that might lift her from eighth place, after two runs, to fifth or sixth. The gamble failed. After a brilliant start, Warner crashed into the wall entering the final stretch, fell off her sled, cut her arm, but still clung to the sled and crossed the finish line legally. She had, however, lost so much time she tumbled to 16th place among the women, still the best of the Americans, but far behind the world champion, Steffi Martin, leading a one-two-three East German parade.

"When you take a few chances," Warner said, "sometimes they don't pay off."

Among the men, with one run to go, Paul Hildgartner of Italy, the silver medalist at Lake Placid, moved into first place. Puerto Rico's George Tucker made it three straight runs without crashing and tightened his grip on last place.

BIATHLON

Once again, in the 20-kilometer biathlon race, the Nordic athletes found nature their fiercest foe. Early in the race, the deep soft snow on Mount Igman tripped up Odd Lirhus of Norway, the leader in the World Cup standings, and Lirhus stumbled and fell. He arose so shaken that at the first of the four shooting stations—the first standing, the second prone, then standing, then prone, all with a .22-caliber rifle on a 50-meter range—Lirhus missed all five of his shots. With a one-minute penalty for each miss, Lirhus shot himself out of contention.

The leader going into the final fourth of the race was a Czech, Jan Matousch, but on the last shoot, he had to blow snow out of the sights of his rifle and missed four of five. Peter Angerer of West Germany, a 24-year-old soldier, a member of the mountain patrol, clicked off his last five shots perfectly, charged past Matousch and won the gold medal. "I concentrated on the target until I could not see the snow," Angerer said.

Biathlon gold medalist Peter Angerer of West Germany.

Sweden's Tom Sandberg soaring into first place in Nordic Combined.

NORDIC SKIING

In the first sixty years of Olympic competition in the Nordic combined, an event combining jumping and cross-country skiing, no American had ever won even a bronze medal. But the favorites in Sarajevo included a 26-year-old Coloradan named Kerry Lynch, one of the few Americans who could say, honestly, that he was capable of playing drums, riding bulls, racing on skis and jumping on skis. Lynch's forte was the cross-country phase of the Nordic combined, and the jumping came on the first day of the two-day event. Surprisingly, on the 70-meter jump, another Coloradan, 23-year-old Pat Ahern, stole the spotlight from Lynch—and almost earned a medal.

On his first jump—the best two out of three count in the scoring for the Nordic combined—Ahern soared 292 feet, the longest jump until the 19th of 28 skiers, Rauno Miettinen of Finland, traveled 295. The judges then interrupted the competition and decided that the skiers were landing too far down the course, too close to the area where the hill flattened out, threatening serious injury. The first round was ordered restarted, from a safer point. His first jump wiped out, Ahern then sailed 274 feet, a very respectable distance.

On the second round, Ahern jumped 282 feet and moved into first place. But when Hubert Schwartz of West Germany floated 302 feet, the judges again stopped the competition, again huddled and again ordered a new start—even though only four skiers still had to jump, and only one of those four was in contention. Ahern then jumped 257 feet, not a very respectable distance.

On the third round, Ahern leaped 265 feet. He had lost his two longest jumps, which, judged on form and distance, might well have put him in the lead, and his two best surviving jumps, 274 feet and 265, placed him no better than 16th. Ahern said he could understand stopping the first round, but not the second.

Kirk Douglas, the actor, played a central role in a small drama in Sarajevo. He and a few friends dined in a local restaurant and, instead of being charged 5,400 dinars, roughly $44, the proper modest amount, they were charged 54,000 dinars, or an immodest $440. When Yugoslav authorities confirmed the incident, they shut down the restaurant. Sarajevo was proud of the fact that its merchants, for the most part, were not gouging Olympic visitors.

Biathlon winner Angerer alone on his way to the gold.

Colorado's Pat Ahern outjumped the mountain, lost his two best jumps and a possible medal.

"The guys here are all good skiers," Ahern said. "We should be jumping down to the bottom. Someone jumped there, and the jury freaked out. Stopping the second round was outrageous. This is the Olympic Games. They should expect long jumps."

Jim Page, the director of the U.S. Nordic program, called the restarts "basically a political move, but not anti-American." The judges were a West German, an East German, a Norwegian and two Yugoslavs. "I think that in their esteemed judgment, they ordered restarts because most of the West German and Norwegian jumpers were having a bad round. For someone like Pat, wiping out a good jump just kills your spirit. He had a chance for the gold, and they took it away."

Going into the cross-country phase, Tom Sandberg of Norway, the world champion, was in first place, and Sergei Tchervyakov of the Soviet Union was second. Kerry Lynch stood 22nd, his dream of an Olympic medal shattered.

On the eve of the rescheduled men's downhill, the seeded racers, the top fifteen, drew once again for starting places, and Bill Johnson caught the least favorable first position. He would have to ski down the hill before the course had been packed. "It makes no difference," said Johnson after his practice runs on Mount Bjelašnica. "It's the same course, and it still belongs to me."

HOCKEY

For the first time, 29 handicapped skiers were an unofficial part of the Olympics, living and training among the other athletes. In the giant slalom, they raced in four divisions— skiers with one arm, with no arms, with one leg and with one leg amputated above the knee—and the winners represented four different nations: Paul Neukomm of Switzerland, Lars Lundstrom of Sweden, Markus Ramsaur of Austria and Alexander Spitz of West Germany. In the evening the handicapped champions stood atop the victory stands outside Skenderija Arena, the scene each night of the Olympic medal ceremonies, and accepted gold medals.

The United States hockey team hit bottom. A Norwegian team that had lost its first game to Czechoslovakia by six goals and its second to Finland by 12 rose up and tied the U.S., 3–3, a result that both embarrassed the Americans and eliminated them, erasing even the most remote mathematical possibility of reaching the medal round. "Before the Olympics," a reporter asked coach Lou Vairo, "could you have envisioned being tied by Norway?"

"No way," said Vairo. "No way, no way, no way, no way."

The key to Norway's victory was its goalie, 30-year-old Jorn Goldstein, born in Norway after his father was liberated from a concentration camp at the end of World War II. Goldstein stopped 34 shots, the last a spectacular glove save on David A. Jensen's 18-foot slap shot in the closing minutes. "Our honor is back," said Hans Ivar Westberg, the Swedish coach of Norway.

Yugoslavia salvaged a small measure of honor against the Soviet Union, holding the Russians even, 1–1, during the second period. The Soviets won the other two periods, 8–0. Ivan Scap, who scored Yugoslavia's only goal, on a 15-foot wrist shot over the glove of Vladislav Tretiak, retrieved the puck and kept it as a souvenir. The Yugoslavs in the crowd cheered. Like their American visitors, they had not yet had a medal winner to cheer in the Sarajevo Games.

Canada and Czechoslovakia each won its third game in a row, matching the Soviet Union for the best record in the hockey competition. The Czechs beat Austria, 13–0, and the Canadians beat previously undefeated Finland, 4–2, a victory that, for this tournament at least, established Canada as America's Team.

BOBSLED

Dietmar Schauerhammer and Wolfgang Hoppe steered their way down the treacherous course to win gold in the two-man bobsledding event.

A pair of sergeants in the East German Army, both former track and field athletes, teamed up to win the two-man bobsled championship. Wolfgang Hoppe, a decathlete turned driver, and Dietmar Schauerhammer, a sprinter turned brakeman, broke the course record on both their final runs and still ended up, after four runs, less than half a second in front of their countrymen, Bernhard Lehmann and Bogdan Musiol. Revolutionary cigar-shaped sleds from the Soviet Union settled for third and fourth places.

Hoppe and Schauerhammer hurtling to their gold in the two-man bobsled.

DAY 5
SUNDAY, FEBRUARY 12th

Three days of competition had passed, 21 medals had been awarded, and yet the United States still had not won a single medal, gold, silver or bronze. The U.S. had never been shut out of medals since the Winter Olympics began, but, at this point, only true alarmists were truly alarmed. As a matter of cold fact, the United States was not running far behind its traditional winter pace.

In Winter Games, the U.S. had won roughly one of every ten medals awarded, including one of every ten gold medals. That average had dipped slightly since 1956, when the Soviet Union first participated, and slightly more since 1968, when East Germany began competing as a separate and athletically powerful nation. Statistically the U.S. was running barely two medals behind its normal pace, and not even one behind its normal gold pace.

Coming into Sarajevo, the United States had won 36 gold medals, 42 silver and 31 bronze, a total of 109 Winter awards. Only the Soviet Union, with 62, and Norway, with 51, had more gold medals, and only the same two nations had earned more total medals, Norway 154 and the USSR 141. Incidentally, even though Norway and the Soviet Union clearly dominated winter sports, the United States could argue that its athletes dominated winter sports <u>on skates</u>. American skaters, including hockey players, had won 75 medals, more than any other nation. But Americans had won only 17 medals on skis, and 17 more on sleds.

The U.S. had never gone through a Winter Olympics without winning a gold medal, but four times had managed only one, most recently in 1968, when Peggy Fleming, on figure skates, saved her country from a shutout.

THE GOLD MEDALISTS

FIGURE SKATING

PAIRS
ELENA VALOVA AND
OLEG VASILIEV, SOVIET UNION

LUGE

MEN'S SINGLES
PAUL HILDGARTNER, ITALY

WOMEN'S SINGLES
STEFFI MARTIN, EAST GERMANY

SPEED SKATING

MEN'S 5,000 METERS
TOMAS GUSTAFSON, SWEDEN

NORDIC SKIING

NORDIC COMBINED
TOM SANDBERG, NORWAY

WOMEN'S 5 KILOMETERS
MARJA-LIISA HAEMAELAEINEN, FINLAND

70-METER SKI JUMP
JENS WEISSFLOG, EAST GERMANY

Marja-Liisa Haemaelaeinen, Finland's indomitable "snow queen," racing her way to a second cross-country gold.

NORDIC SKIING

In the women's 5-kilometer cross-country ski race, an event she did not expect to win, Finland's Marja-Liisa Haemaelaeinen became the first athlete to collect two gold medals in the XIVth Winter Olympics. Haemaelaeinen had feared the distance was too short for her. "I was most afraid of Aunli," she said, "whom I consider the world's best at this discipline."

But Berit Aunli of Norway, the 1982 world champion at 5 and 10 kilometers, who had skipped the 1983 season to have a baby, lost a contact lens at the start—"I had to run the whole race practically one-eyed," she said—and had to struggle to earn the silver medal behind Haemaelaeinen.

Haemaelaeinen, who was engaged to a member of the Finnish men's team, had been racing internationally for more than a decade, but had enjoyed little success till 1983. The Finnish press had often criticized her for her failures. "A hundred times they're written that I would never become anybody," Haemaelaeinen told Leena Jokinen of Helsinki's *Ilta-Sanomat,* "and I want to show people that I am somebody."

"She is the snow queen," said Immo Kuutsa, the coach of the Finnish cross-country team.

SPEED SKATING

Tomas Gustafson of Sweden, who traveled to the United States in 1979 to train at the side of Eric Heiden, was in the first pair of speed skaters, and when he completed the 5,000-meter race almost ten seconds slower than Heiden's Olympic record, he figured he had little chance for a bronze medal, no chance for a gold. "Let's go inside and watch some figure skating," Gustafson suggested to his parents. "Let's get away from all this."

But the pockmarked ice was slow, and got slower, and when Gustafson returned to the outdoor rink, he found out that he had won by the slimmest margin in the Olympic history of the event, defeating Igor Malkov of the Soviet Union, 7:12.28 to 7:12.30, the difference precisely two-hundredths of a second or 27 centimeters or half the length of a skate blade.

Sweden's Tomas Gustafson (right) beat Soviet Igor Malkov (left) by the thinnest of margins in the 5000-meter speed skating event.

NORDIC SKIING

After their disappointing restarts in the jumping phase of the Nordic combined, neither Pat Ahern nor Kerry Lynch had any chance of becoming the event's first American medalist. Ahern's desire, he admitted, had been drained. "You have a lot of energy going into the Olympics," he said, "and most of mine was taken away yesterday." Ahern placed 17th in the 15-kilometer cross-country race, 17th overall.

But Lynch, who had been so successful on the World Cup circuit, had something to prove. "Oh, yes, I was motivated," he said. "I just wanted to blow their doors off, to show them." Lynch finished third in the cross-country race, good enough to lift him to 13th overall.

The gold medal went to Norway's Tom Sandberg, a 28-year-old school-teacher, second in the cross-country after winning the jumping, and the silver and bronze medals went to a pair of Finns.

Second in the 15-kilometer cross-country race, after placing first in the jump, Norwegian Tom Sandberg won the Nordic combined gold.

For the fourth straight day, snow fell steadily on the streets of Sarajevo, and while the city coped efficiently with the storm, keeping traffic flowing, blizzards far more severe struck the nearby mountains and the northern areas of Yugoslavia. The main highway between the major cities of Belgrade and Zagreb was shut down, thousands of passengers had to be rescued from snowbound buses and Army helicopters dropped emergency provisions to motorists stranded in snowdrifts up to seventeen feet high. The men's downhill race was postponed once again, this time for four days, till Thursday, to await the arrival of predicted better weather, and the delay inspired the Austrian downhill skiers to leave Sarajevo, to fly home to practice on more manageable mountains.

NORDIC SKIING

For Yugoslavia, which had never won any medal in any event in any Winter Olympics, and for the United States, which had won only one medal in 60 years of Olympic ski jumping, the results in the 70-meter jump were disappointing. Primoz Ulaga, a handsome 21-year-old Yugoslav who had finished first in six major international meets during the previous three years, started the first of his two runs with the cheers of his countrymen ringing across Igman Plateau.

But when Ulaga, arms and legs flapping awkwardly, produced the shortest jump of the day, the cheers turned first to groans, then to derisive whistles. Ulaga's second jump was respectable, but he still finished 57th, next to last. "They want only medals," Ulaga said of the fickle crowd. "But you are man, you are not machine."

The United States' only Olympic jumping medal, a bronze medal, was earned in 1924 by Norwegian-born Anders Haugen, but Haugen was not conceded his award until 50 years later, in 1974, when a Norwegian researcher discovered that a mathematical error had incorrectly placed Haugen fourth.

The breath-catching view from the top of the 70-meter ski jump.

No athlete received more publicity than the man working the starting gate at the ski jumping competition at Malo Polje on the Igman Plateau. He had appeared on television in the United States hundreds of times, and yet hardly anyone knew his name. His name was Vinko Bogataj, and every time he appeared on television, he suffered a broken ankle, a concussion and an assortment of bruises. He was the man in the opening sequence of ABC's Wide World of Sports, the flailing, falling ski jumper who, following the ecstasy of victory, personified the agony of defeat. Bogataj, a Yugoslav, was only 22 years old when, in 1970, in Oberstdorf, West Germany, he suffered the spill that made him an international celebrity.

Tiny Jens Weissflog of East Germany at the 70-meter launching pad.

Jeff Hastings, who hoped to match Haugen's achievement without waiting so long, had a first jump he called "awful," though it was not nearly so awful as Ulaga's. "It was gag city," Hastings said, describing his own tenseness. "Tight turtleneck. Tight, tight, tight." With a strong second jump, Hastings rose to ninth place, the best 70-meter showing by an American since the event was placed on the Olympic program in 1964.

A wisp of an East German teenager, Jens Weissflog, only 5-foot-6 and 114 pounds, even with snow clinging to him, cut through the air magnificently to win the 70-meter gold medal. The 19-year-old East German outjumped a 20-year-old Finn, Matti Nykaenan, equally famous for his talent and for his temper. "He might blow up any minute," said Nykaenan's coach, Matti Pulli. "He doesn't really talk, he gripes."

Nykaenan's philosophy of jumping was simple. "I have to stay mad," he said. "I must."

LUGE

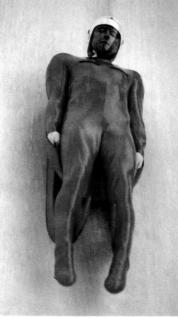

The futuristic luge sled.

When the final luge run was completed, the individual champions were, like the champions in the two-man bobsled, both converted track and field athletes. The men's leader was Paul Hildgartner of Italy, the so-called grandfather of his sport, at 31 the veteran of four Olympic competitions, a former sprinter and an avid hunter, a silver medalist at Lake Placid and a gold medalist in doubles in 1972. The women's was Steffi Martin of East Germany, at 21 competing in her first Olympics, a former shot-putter, discus and javelin thrower who was, at 5-foot-11 and 172 pounds, an inch taller than Hildgartner and three pounds lighter.

Soviets finished second and third among the men, East Germans second and third among the women. The leading Americans moved up on the final run, Frank Masley to 14th place among the men, Bonny Warner to 15th among the women, but neither cracked the top ten, a pre-Olympic goal. Puerto Rico's George Tucker reached his goal—the bottom of the run, in one piece—for the fourth straight day and wound up 30th among the 30 men who completed all four runs.

Over the four runs, the difference between Hildgartner, in first place, and the 29th-place finisher was 15 seconds. The difference between the 29th-place finisher and Tucker, in 30th, was 14 seconds.

The elegant, and unassailable, Torvill and Dean.

ICE DANCING

Their Greatnesses, Jayne Torvill and Christopher Dean, simply waltzed through the paso doble, the rhythm designated for the original set pattern dance, collected four 6.0s and a flock of 5.9s and strengthened their already comfortable lead in the ice dancing competition. The original set pattern dance counted 20 percent toward the final score; the free dance, to be held in two days, would count 50 percent.

Behind Torvill and Dean, the order remained as it was after the compulsory dances—Natalia Bestemianova and Andrei Bukin of the Soviet Union second, Judy Blumberg and Michael Seibert of the U.S. third and Marina Klimova and Sergei Ponomarenko of the Soviet Union fourth—and the judging remained questionable.

The British judge, Courtney Jones, who had designed costumes for Torvill and Dean, gave the contending Soviet pair no better than a 5.4 for both presentation and composition, and scored the other Soviet pair a lowly 5.3 and 5.4. Jones also judged Blumberg and Seibert severely with a 5.5 for composition, but awarded the Americans a lofty 5.9 for presentation. At the other extreme, a Canadian judge gave Blumberg and Seibert only a 5.3 for presentation. "That's a huge range at this level," said Michael Seibert, tempering his displeasure.

The Americans had to cope not only with the vagaries of the judges but also with their position in the program, skating immediately after Torvill and Dean. While Blumberg and Seibert were on the ice, trying to impress the judges, Torvill and Dean were in the stands, accepting congratulations from one of their admirers, a woman who had studied with their coach. The woman was Princess Anne. Photographers were torn between shooting the skating Americans or the three regal spectators.

Soviet notables Bukin and Bestemianova (top), and Klimova and Ponomarenko.

The formidable Russian figure skating competition: Selezneva and Makarov (top and bottom left), and star duo Valova and Vasiliev (right).

FIGURE SKATING

The two leading Soviet figure skating pairs skated before the American challengers, and the team of Elena Valova and Oleg Vasiliev—despite one noticeable flaw in their routine, despite one anxious moment when Valova had to steady herself with her hand—were accorded scores that virtually assured the world champions of Olympic gold: two 5.7s, nine 5.8s and seven 5.9s.

The less celebrated Russian duo of Larisa Selezneva and Oleg Makarov, who started the free skating tied for second place, earned less remarkable scores —five 5.6s, eleven 5.7s and two 5.8s—and so, as Kitty and Peter Carruthers prepared to take the ice, the Americans knew almost exactly what they had to do: They needed a miracle to win the gold medal, a powerful performance to capture the silver and a good performance to take the bronze.

Peter turned to his coach, Ron Ludington, and said, "This is going to be it. This is going to be a great performance." Then he turned to his sister. "Something special happened," Kitty said later. "Peter looked into my eyes, and I knew it was going to be magic."

It *was* magic. They dazzled the audience filling Zetra Arena, 17 separate elements, split triple twists, triple Salchow throws, double Axels, all executed with a grace close to perfection.

When the four-and-a-half-minute free skating came to an end, almost everyone in the crowd of 8,000 was standing, cheering and applauding, and at the center of the ice, Kitty and Peter Carruthers, sister and brother adopted as infants, wrapped their arms around each other and hugged

Peter and Kitty Carruthers gliding toward America's first medal at Sarajevo.

and hugged and hugged. "I told him I loved him," Kitty said. "I told him I was happy we had worked so hard and achieved our goal. I was so proud."

Then the Carrutherses skated over to Ludington, who greeted them, "Fantastic job," confident that his pupils' scores would lift them easily into second place. But the suspense was not over. The judges were not quite so moved. The scores were posted: one 5.5, four 5.6s, eleven 5.7s, one 5.8 and one 5.9, almost identical to the points awarded Selezneva and Makarov. Now the duel for second place came down to a most complicated scoring system: How many judges had ranked the Americans ahead of the Soviets? How many judges put the Soviets ahead of the Americans?

The computer took minutes to come up with the answers: The score was five to four in favor of the Americans. Peter and Kitty Carruthers skated to the victory stand with tears in their eyes. They climbed up and waved to a section of the stands jammed with Americans, including their parents. "When the American flag went up," Peter Carruthers said, "it was a moment I will never forget."

"It looked so good," Kitty said. "You dream about it when you are little, but you never believe it will happen."

The United States had its first medal of the XIVth Winter Olympics, its first silver medal in the figure skating pairs in 32 years.

But the Soviet Union, with its gold and its bronze, plus the speed skating silver won in the morning by Igor Malkov, now had a grand total of 77 medals won on skates, one more than the United States.

DAY 6
MONDAY, FEBRUARY 13th

The United States history in men's figure skating was a strikingly erratic one. In six Olympic competitions before World War II, including a Summer Games figure skating championship in 1908 in London, the U.S. did not win a single medal, not a gold, a silver or a bronze. But immediately after World War II, American men took four straight gold medals, plus a silver and two bronze. Then as suddenly as the American dynasty rose, it fell. In the next five Olympics, from 1964 through 1980, no man from the U.S. won the figure skating title, and only one placed as high as second. Scott Hamilton was expected to end that dry spell.

Hamilton was a remarkable young man, raised in Bowling Green, Ohio, by a pair of university professors. Like Kitty and Peter Carruthers, by stunning coincidence, Hamilton had been adopted in infancy. But while Kitty and Peter had always been active children, Scott Hamilton had suffered in his childhood from a disease once thought to be cystic fibrosis, which in time would have been fatal. Later, the disease was correctly identified as Schwachman's syndrome, which prevented Scott from digesting food and, from age five to age eight, stopped him from growing. The symptoms vanished almost miraculously when Hamilton began ice skating, but the three lost years left him, at age 25, in 1984, 5-foot-3 and 110 pounds.

Scott Hamilton was small, but he was a splendid athlete. Since 1980, when he finished fifth in the Olympics and in the world championships, he had won 15 consecutive competitions, including three world championships in a row. All the experts agreed he was a cinch to be an American gold medalist in Sarajevo.

But he would not be the first.

THE GOLD MEDALISTS

SPEED SKATING

WOMEN'S 1,000 METERS
  KARIN ENKE, EAST GERMANY

ALPINE SKIING

WOMEN'S GIANT SLALOM
  DEBBIE ARMSTRONG, USA

NORDIC SKIING

MEN'S 15 KILOMETERS
  GUNDE SVAN, SWEDEN

FIGURE SKATING

The men's compulsory figures started at 7:00 A.M. in Skenderija Rink, a secondary arena with room for fewer than 2,000 spectators. There was no fear of overcrowding. When the figures began, perhaps 50 people were on hand, the early skaters, the judges, a few friends, a few reporters. The figures are not a spectator sport; except to expert eyes, they are both boring and baffling.

Scott Hamilton was neither baffled nor bored. "It's not boring," he said, "because you're working toward perfection, and you never get it."

In winning three straight world championships, Hamilton had never finished first in the compulsory figures, which counted for 30 percent of the final score. He had been fourth once and second twice, first place going, all three times, to a Frenchman, Jean-Christophe Simond, whose uninspired free skating invariably cost him a medal.

Now, in Sarajevo, Simond, Hamilton and 21 other skaters had to perform the group of three compulsory figures selected by draw the night before, all variations on the figure 8, first the inside rocker, then the forward paragraph double three and finally the backward change loop, pure hieroglyphics to the nonskater, pure inspiration to Scott Hamilton. "The figures force you into discipline," he said.

The competition dragged on for more than six and a half hours, enlivened mostly by a breach of discipline and form on the part of a Canadian skater, Gary Beacom, who, instead of hiding his displeasure at being placed tenth in the second figure, swore at the judges and kicked a hole in the sideboards of the rink.

Hamilton, of course, was impeccable. "When he finished," Frank Litsky, one of the sturdy spectators, reported in the *New York Times*, "the judges, wearing coats and boots because they stand for long periods on the ice, studied the tracings. Were the figures accurate? Was the size proper? Were the tracings clean? The judges squinted, peered and made notes. Then they held up scorecards."

Hamilton received the highest scores for the first figure, the highest for the second and the highest for the third. He was stunned and delighted. "Winning the figures was something I always wanted to do before I retired," he said.

Then, mischievously, he told one reporter, "I've never worked harder, I've never felt physically or emotionally better. No girl problems and the drug rehabilitation really worked." He paused. "Just kidding," he said.

If Hamilton had been an overwhelming favorite before the figures, he appeared unbeatable afterward. His two closest rivals in the world championships, Norbert Schramm of West Germany and Brian Orser of Canada, placed ninth and seventh in the figures. Even Hamilton himself said, "I guess it sets me up pretty good."

He clearly was approaching the end of his amateur career, yet he still seemed ambivalent about turning professional. On the one hand, he said, "There is such a thing as raping the gold, and I don't want to do that," but on the other, he asked, "What am I going to be as soon as I'm off the ice, a neurosurgeon?"

On one point, however, Scott Hamilton had no hesitancy. "What would you like to be?" someone asked.

"Tall," he said. "For 20 minutes."

She was an Olympian herself, an equestrienne who had endured an embarrassing spill in Montreal in 1976, but Princess Anne of Great Britain came to the bobsled run as a fan, to cheer on her bobsledding subjects. One asked her if she would care to sit in the sled before their practice run. "I suppose so," said Princess Anne, "as long as you don't push it down the hill."

She slid into the sled, and the British athletes promptly pretended to start her down the chute. "Don't you dare," said the princess, and her obedient subjects didn't.

NORDIC SKIING

Harri Kirvesniemi of Finland hugs his fiancée Marja-Liisa Haemaelaeinen

Gunde Svan could talk to the gods. But they didn't respond immediately. When he woke up the morning of the first men's cross-country race, the 30-kilometer, Svan yelled out the window, "Stop snowing!" Now, only three days later, the snow stopped, and in the men's 15-kilometer race, Svan, who had come in third at the longer distance, skied his way to a decisive victory. He seemed surprised. "I never really counted on 1984," said the 22-year-old Swede, who started skiing when he was three. "I thought I might win in 1988."

Two Finns trailed Svan, Aki Karvonen, earning the silver medal, and Harri Kirvesniemi, the fiancé of Marja-Liisa Haemaelaeinen, adding a bronze to the family collection.

SPEED SKATING

In the women's 1000-meter speed skating race, precisely as in the women's 1,500-meter speed skating race four days earlier, Karin Enke finished first, her East German countrywoman Andrea Schoene second and Natalia Petruseva of the Soviet Union third. There was only one difference. "This one was comparatively easy," Enke said, after setting an Olympic record.

The East German star now had two gold medals, one silver and one race to go, the 3,000 meters. "Let's just wait with calling me a superstar till we are through with our schedule," Enke said.

Mary Docter of the United States called her pampered. "She has a masseur and a coach and a private doctor who are with her all the time," said Docter, who was considered a threat to win a medal in the 3,000-meter race. "She has her blood tested three times a day. She knows when she's building up, and when she's tearing down."

Docter hoped Enke would not be up for the 3,000 meters.

ALPINE SKIING

The United States women's Alpine skiing team began its Olympic training on the Fourth of July, 1983, in Hawaii, ten days of intensive conditioning, including karate drills. By the time the team reached Sarajevo, its Hawaiian tans had long faded, but its image had brightened: The American women were considered the best Alpine squad in the world. The two most celebrated members were Cindy Nelson, at 28 the sentimental favorite in the Games, and Tamara McKinney, at 21 the logical favorite.

(Left) Christin Cooper rounds a gate. (Right) Perrine Pelen of France, whose third-place finish stopped an American sweep of the women's giant slalom medals.

The powerhouse American women's giant slalom team: from left, Debbie Armstrong (gold), Tamara McKinney, who finished in fourth place, and Christin Cooper (silver).

Nelson, a bronze medalist in the downhill at Innsbruck in 1976, tore ligaments in her right knee barely two months before the Sarajevo Olympics, and only the gifted work of Dr. Richard Steadman, who had performed surgical magic on either the knees or the ankles of every leading member of the U.S. women's team, enabled her to be ready to compete.

In 1983, McKinney became the first American woman to win the overall World Cup championship. Her mother was a ski instructor and a horse trainer, and her father a Hall of Fame steeplechase jockey, which explains why Tamara was born in Lexington, Kentucky, a terrific birthplace for a thoroughbred, but not for a skier. McKinney now lived and skied in Squaw Valley, California. Her older brother was the first person to go 200 kilometers an hour on skis, and her older sister was a promising skier until, in a downhill race, she crashed into a wooden post and suffered head injuries so severe she was unable to walk or speak normally for almost a year.

Besides McKinney and Nelson, the U.S. team included Christin Cooper and Holly Flanders, both of whom were among the handful of Americans to have won World Cup races, Cooper in the slalom and Flanders in the downhill. And then there was Debbie Armstrong, freshly 20 years old, never a winner in a World Cup race, up from the B team, a face for the future.

The future was now.

On the first run of the women's giant slalom, the first Alpine race to outlast the storms of Sarajevo, Debbie Armstrong skied 15th, the final seed. Nelson and McKinney did not have strong first runs; Cooper had a super run. As she faced the slope on Mount Jahorina, Armstrong told herself she was as good as anyone. "Well, I know that," she said to herself, "so why don't I go and do it and show everybody else, too?"

She raced down the mountain into second place, only a tenth of a second behind Cooper. Then the two American women, the leaders, sat down to lunch together. Cooper ate lightly, Armstrong ate nothing. "I was afraid I couldn't keep it down," she said.

But back at the top of the hill, Armstrong showed no signs of nervousness. She was the fourth skier on this run, directly ahead of Cooper. Armstrong turned to her teammate and lunchmate and said, "When you go down, I want you to relax and have fun, because that's what I'm going to do. I'm going to have fun! Have the best run of your life!"

And then Armstrong, a late-blooming skier, once the most valuable soccer player at Garfield High School in Seattle, was off, on the most important run of her life, zigging and zagging down the giant slalom course, gracefully and swiftly.

Cooper skied next and, five gates from the top, she slipped momentarily. "My hip touched the ground," she said later. "I don't know what happened or why." Quickly Cooper regained her balance, but she had lost precious fractions of a second, and when she reached the bottom of the hill, her cumulative time was four-tenths of a second behind Debbie Armstrong's.

Tamara McKinney, with the fastest second run of the day, moved up to fourth place and only France's Perrine Pelen, in third, kept the United States from a clean sweep of the giant slalom, a feat never achieved by any nation.

"How do you feel?" someone asked Armstrong, and an enormous smile danced across her face, and she replied, "Yaaaaaaweeeeeee!" Later, she translated: "Not in my wildest dreams did I think I'd win gold. I just had fun. It was a gas. It was the time of my life. I didn't think today. I just skied."

Her teammates shared Armstrong's delight. Even Cooper did not seem disappointed. "I could have easily fallen and then I wouldn't even have gotten what I did," Cooper said. "I'm happy to get the silver. Look, a year ago today I was lying in a bed in South Lake Tahoe and I wasn't sure I would ski race ever again."

Cindy Nelson, Armstrong's roommate and mentor, beamed. "Debbie's no fluke," Nelson said. "She's gonna be around a long time."

Debbie's father, Hugh Armstrong, a professor of psychology at the University of Washington, put his daughter's achievement in perspective. "It's a real sweet spot in time," he said, "when something like this happens."

Perrine Pelen of France.

HOCKEY

Finally the United States won a hockey game. Finally Pat LaFontaine exploded, the 18-year-old star scoring three goals, a hat trick, blending with his fellow teenagers, Eddie Olczyk, who had four assists, and David A. Jensen, who added two goals, to turn back Austria, 7–3. "It's a big donkey off our back," Olczyk said. "It's a good feeling." The young Americans looked at the bright side: If they won their remaining games, they figured, they could finish fifth in the Olympics.

But the gold medal they had dreamed of would go, almost certainly, to one of the three teams that stretched their winning streaks to four games, most likely the Soviet Union, which beat West Germany, 6–1, or, if the Soviets faltered, Czechoslovakia, which defeated Finland, 7–2, or, the long shot, Canada, which outscored Norway, 8–1.

The unexpected success of the Canadians revived memories of the days when Canada ruled the hockey world, especially the Olympic hockey world. The Canadians won six of the first seven Olympic hockey championships, and the only one they lost was to a British team made up almost entirely of Canadian citizens. In its first sixteen Olympic hockey games, Canada outscored its opponents, 197 goals to 6.

But with the emergence of Soviet hockey in the 1950s, plus the pair of American miracles in 1960 and 1980, Canada came to Sarajevo without an Olympic championship in 32 years, a long and painful drought. "There was the urge in all Canadians," Ken Dryden said, "to scream out, 'Wait a minute, you don't understand. Back home we have these professionals who can beat your teams very easily. We want you to know that. We're *desperate* that you know that."

Canada's best professionals were still back home, and the young players in Sarajevo assessed their chances realistically. "I think the Czechs can be beaten," Mark Morrison said. "The Russians, that's a different story."

"That would be a real miracle," said the Canadian coach, Dave King. "That would be a greater miracle than 1980."

DAY 7
TUESDAY, FEBRUARY 14 th

The people of Yugoslavia deserved a medal. They deserved a medal for the warmth and charm with which they hosted the XIVth Winter Olympics, and for the efficiency and economy with which they staged the Games. They deserved medals, too, for being able to breathe in bars choked with cigarette smoke, for being able to converse in nightclubs throbbing with the sounds of Michael Jackson and for being able to swallow slivovitz in the morning and still survive the day.

The cabdrivers of Sarajevo deserved a special medal for refusing tips they considered excessive, on top of fares that were shockingly low, and for negotiating twisting mountain roads at dizzying speeds without losing a single visitor.

Clearly the Yugoslavs deserved a medal. The question was: Would they get one? No Yugoslav had ever won a medal in the Winter Olympics, not a gold or a silver or a bronze, not on skis or or on skates or on sleds. But no country had ever hosted the Winter Olympics without capturing at least a bronze medal.

In recent years, in fact, athletes from the host nations, cheered on by so many of their countrymen, had performed far beyond expectations. In 1980 in Lake Placid, the United States achieved its hockey miracle; in 1976 in Innsbruck, in the 90-meter jump, Karl Schnabl became the first Austrian to win a Nordic skiing event; in 1972 in Sapporo, in the 70-meter jump, Yukio Kasaya the first and only Japanese to win a Winter gold medal; and in 1968 in Grenoble, Jean-Claude Killy the first and only Frenchman to sweep the Alpine events, to win the downhill, the slalom and the giant slalom.

The Yugoslavs weren't greedy. They would settle for one medal, even a bronze.

THE GOLD MEDALISTS

BIATHLON

10 KILOMETERS

ERIK KVALFOSS, NORWAY

FIGURE SKATING

ICE DANCING

JAYNE TORVILL AND CHRISTOPHER DEAN, BRITAIN

SPEED SKATING

MEN'S 1,000 METERS

GAETAN BOUCHER, CANADA

ALPINE SKIING

MEN'S GIANT SLALOM

MAX JULEN, SWITZERLAND

BIATHLON

Hans Hiltebrand was angry. The Swiss electrician was 39 years old, and although he had once shared the world two-man bobsled championship, he had never won an Olympic medal. But even though he guided his four-man sled, the number three Swiss sled, to the fastest practice run of the day, he was told he would not compete in the official race in three days. So in the middle of the Olympics, Hiltebrand sold his sled to the United States bobsled team for $10,000, the sale financed by Bob Landau, an American businessman.

"We had hoped to buy an East German sled," said Lester Fenner, the American coach, "but they wouldn't sell us one."

Peter Angerer of West Germany glided up to the firing range for his second and final time, needing only to hit five of five targets from the standing position to win the 10-kilometer biathlon, to earn his second gold medal of the Games. Shooting was Angerer's strength; he had fired his five shots from the prone position perfectly.

"I didn't think I had a chance," said Erik Kvalfoss of Norway, a swifter skier who had finished the course and, because he missed two shots, was in second place.

But, under pressure, Angerer missed one of his five standing shots and was forced to ski a 150-meter penalty lap, and when the extra lap cost the German the gold medal by eight seconds, Kvalfoss let out a Bavarian yodel to celebrate his surprising victory. "I am the world champion and I wanted to win real bad," said Kvalfoss, who took the bronze medal when Angerer won the 20-kilometer biathlon three days earlier.

"One gold and one silver—what more could I want?" said Angerer.

Erik Kvalfoss, Norway's surprise gold medalist in the 10-kilometer biathlon.

Nick Thometz , America's disappointed gambler in the 1000-meter speed skating race.

Soviet sprint champion Sergei Khlebnikov.

SPEED SKATING

His false start had cost him a medal at 500 meters, and now, in the 1000-meter speed skating race, Nick Thometz, a 20-year-old Minnesotan, wanted an Olympic medal so badly he decided he would try to push his body to new limits. He was going to go as fast as he could for as long as he could.

Thometz was paired with Kai Arne Engelstad of Norway, and this time Thometz got off to a perfect start, a sizzling start, skating as he had never skated before. He reached 600 meters in 45.18 seconds, four-tenths of a second faster than he had ever raced the distance, almost eight-tenths of a second faster than Engelstad and fully seven-tenths of a second faster than an earlier skater, one of the favorites in the event, the 1982 world sprint champion, Sergei Khlebnikov of the Soviet Union.

Warming up, watching Thometz's time on the scoreboard, Gaetan Boucher of Canada, the runner-up to Eric Heiden at 1,000 meters in Lake Placid, seemed worried, concerned that once again an American might beat him out.

But the torrid pace tired Thometz, and in the final 400 meters he slowed down perceptibly. "I hit the wall," Thometz said metaphorically. "My legs started screaming. I couldn't get 'em under me. I had no power." Engelstad caught him and beat him by one-tenth of a second. Khlebnikov was another tenth of a second faster than Engelstad, and Boucher was still to race. Thometz knew his bid for a medal was doomed.

Boucher, his confidence restored, skated to a decisive victory, his first gold medal, his third Olympic medal, the most medals ever won by a Canadian, a perfect way for him to mark, at the age of 25, his third and final Olympics.

ALPINE SKIING

They came on a perfect day, crisp and bright, to cheer for Bojan Krizaj, thousands and thousands of Yugoslavs, lining the men's giant slalom course on Mount Bjelašnica. They stood behind orange fences and shouted, *"Hop, hop, hop!"*—"Go, go, go!"—and smacked wooden spoons against metal buckets to demonstrate their enthusiasm. They even had a 15-piece orchestra to accompany their cheers for Krizaj, who in 1980 in the giant slalom at Lake Placid came within two-hundredths of a second of winning a bronze medal. Now the 27-year-old Krizaj had another chance to become the first Yugoslav ever to win a Winter Olympic medal.

More than a hundred skiers started in the giant slalom, many of them true amateurs who knew they had no hope for a medal. The sole Egyptian representative, 18-year-old Jamil El Reedy, born in Cairo of an Egyptian father and an American mother, was raised and taught to ski in New York State, not far from Lake Placid. His father decided to prepare him for the Olympics mentally by taking him back to Egypt, to the Sahara, and leaving him in a cave, alone, with only food and water, for 40 days, a coming-of-age ritual that made El Reedy realize, "I was like a snowflake in the universe." Understandably, he was delighted to be out of the Sahara and in Sarajevo, even though his previous skiing experience centered on his high school team. Like El Reedy, the four Lebanese skiers, their training too often disrupted by battle, were no threat to Bojan Krizaj and the rest of the world's best skiers. El Reedy fell on his first run, but so did 22 other skiers, including Pirmin Zurbriggen of Switzerland, one of the favorites.

He couldn't reach them on the mountain immediately after their one-two finish in the giant slalom, but a day later, President Reagan got a phone call through to Debbie Armstrong (left) and Christin Cooper (right). "Is that you, Mr. President?" Armstrong asked. "Did you watch?"

It was, and he had, but he still probably wasn't prepared for Cooper's greeting. "Hi, Ronnie," she said. "It was a neat day for America, for sure."

The President told Cooper he knew about her broken leg in 1983 and he said he thought she was, to borrow the phrase of an earlier President, a profile in courage. "I told him I thought he was, too," said Cooper later.

First-ever Winter Olympics medalist for Yugoslavia, Jure Franko took a silver in the men's giant slalom.

Liechtenstein captured the giant slalom bronze with the performance of Andreas Wenzel.

Switzerland's Max Julen won the gold.

Krizaj did not have a good run, no better than 12th place. But the anguish of the spectators turned quickly to hope when another Yugoslav, skiing behind Krizaj, a 21-year-old from Slovenia near the Italian border, Jure Franko, blazed down the course, two-thirds of a mile long, and through its 56 gates in 1:12.15, the fourth-fastest time of the run. Max Julen of Switzerland had the fastest time, followed by the 1980 silver medalist, Andreas Wenzel of Liechtenstein, and by Franz Gruber of Austria.

The *"Hop, hop, hop"* of the crowd grew to a roar during Franko's second run. "I felt the pressure," he said later. "I felt it in my heart."

Franko responded to the pressure perfectly, attacking the icy slope so fiercely that he recorded the fastest time of the second run, a pace swift enough to lift him past Gruber, past Wenzel and into second place, swift enough to give this son of a ski jumper a silver medal, Yugoslavia's first medal of any Winter Olympics. The crowd exploded.

The gold went to Julen, the 22-year-old son of a downhill racer. "The course was steep and hard, just the way I like it," Julen said.

"Yugoslav skiers are good enough to compete with anybody," Franko said, "and now I have broken the ice for them."

"Yur-ee! Yur-ee! Yur-ee!" the crowd chanted, to the drum beat of spoons banging against buckets. Flags and banners flew, and horns blared, and all the considerable pride of the people of Yugoslavia poured into the achievement of Jure Franko. "There has been no bigger day in the history of sports in our country," said Anton Hocevar of the Yugoslav Olympic Committee.

And the celebrations of a perfect day were just beginning.

FIGURE SKATING

Spectators shouted "Scotty!" and called on him to clinch a gold medal for the United States, and even though he had endured so many finals before, the attention, the pressure of the Olympics got to Scott Hamilton. "I was fine until the middle of the warm-up," he said after completing the short program, worth 20 percent toward his final score, "and then it was dum-dum-DUM-BIG TIME! Here we go! Aargh!"

Nervous, excited, Hamilton didn't skate his best. He was noticeably slow going into the camel spin, one of the required elements, and when the scores were posted, Hamilton's were—in the eyes of six of the nine judges—only second best, to Canadian Brian Orser's, the first time in two years the world champion failed to dominate a short program. Still, because Orser had placed seventh in the compulsory figures, Hamilton remained in a most comfortable position. He could lose the gold medal only if he failed to finish among the top four in the freeskating, and he had finished first in his last 15 freeskating competitions.

"I was hoping to sweep the three days," Hamilton said, "but that's getting greedy at this level."

Orser concluded that overtaking Hamilton would be almost impossible, but he said he was happy with his position, poised to earn the silver medal or the bronze. His Canadian teammate, Gary Beacom, who had sworn at the judges after the compulsory figures, was still fuming. "We're not trained monkeys," said Beacom, who dropped to 11th place after the short program. "We're human beings. We should be able to demand fair play."

The brilliant figure skating short program of Canada's Brian Orser (left) was not enough for him to surmount Scott Hamilton's overall lead.

ICE DANCING

They began on their knees, on the ice, in a simulated embrace, and before they fell to the ice again, four minutes later, to signal the tragic end of their free dance, Jayne Torvill and Christoper Dean moved exquisitely through a slow and sensuous interpretation of Ravel's "Bolero." With tender touches, with tortured looks, with consummate grace and style, they danced the story of two doomed lovers who, unable to live together, elect to die together, to throw themselves into a volcano.

Torvill and Dean danced the story so magnificently that all nine judges gave them perfect 6.0s for artistic impression, three gave them 6.0s for technical merit and six gave them mere 5.9s, a set of scores unprecedented in the history of ice dancing. The audience that filled Zetra Arena, including Britain's Princess Anne, was equally generous with its cheers. "It was the ultimate of our career," said Dean, at 25 a year younger than his partner. "We've reached the pinnacle."

Superlative artists in their event, Jayne Torvill and Christopher Dean electrified the ice dancing judges.

The two Britons played the two lovers so convincingly one reporter asked if they were getting married. "Not this week," said Dean casually. But both he and Torvill had addressed the subject more seriously in their best-selling biography, titled simply *Torvill and Dean*. "We were very close at one time," said Dean in the book. "I think we fell in love and out again."

"I have, of course, a deep affection for him," Torvill said. "Where does deep affection end and love begin? I just do not know."

But while Torvill and Dean shared a magic moment, the American ice dancers, Judy Blumberg and Michael Seibert, shared only pain. Like Torvill and Dean, they, too, had flouted ice-dancing tradition and, instead of using four segments of music, as the rules encouraged, had used only one, Rimsky-Korsakov's "Scheherazade."

"We felt we came in with a silver-medal program," said Seibert, who with his partner started the free dance in third place, within easy striking distance of second. In royal gold and purple costumes, Blumberg and Seibert dazzled the crowd, but, instead of moving up in the standings, moved down. They failed to dazzle the judges, especially an Italian named Cia Bordogna. She gave them only a 5.5 for artistic impression; no other judge gave them less than a 5.7. If she had given them a 5.7, they would have won a medal. "Their music didn't have the proper tempo," Bordogna argued.

Because of Bordogna's low score, Blumberg and Seibert finished in a mathematical tie for third place with a Soviet couple, Marina Klimova and Sergei Ponomarenko, and in ice dancing, ties are broken by the scores in the free dance. Five of the nine judges placed the Soviets ahead of the Americans in the free dance. Their countrymen, Natalia Bestemianova and Andrei Bukin, got the silver. "We're very surprised and disappointed," Seibert said.

"I guess what we did wasn't appreciated by the judges," Blumberg said. Then, asked about the Italian judge, Blumberg said, "She's been a swing judge for us before. She's always swung to the Soviets."

Torvill and Dean left Zetra with stars in their eyes, Blumberg and Seibert with tears.

America's Blumberg and Seibert did not fare as well.

DAY 8
WEDNESDAY, FEBRUARY 15th

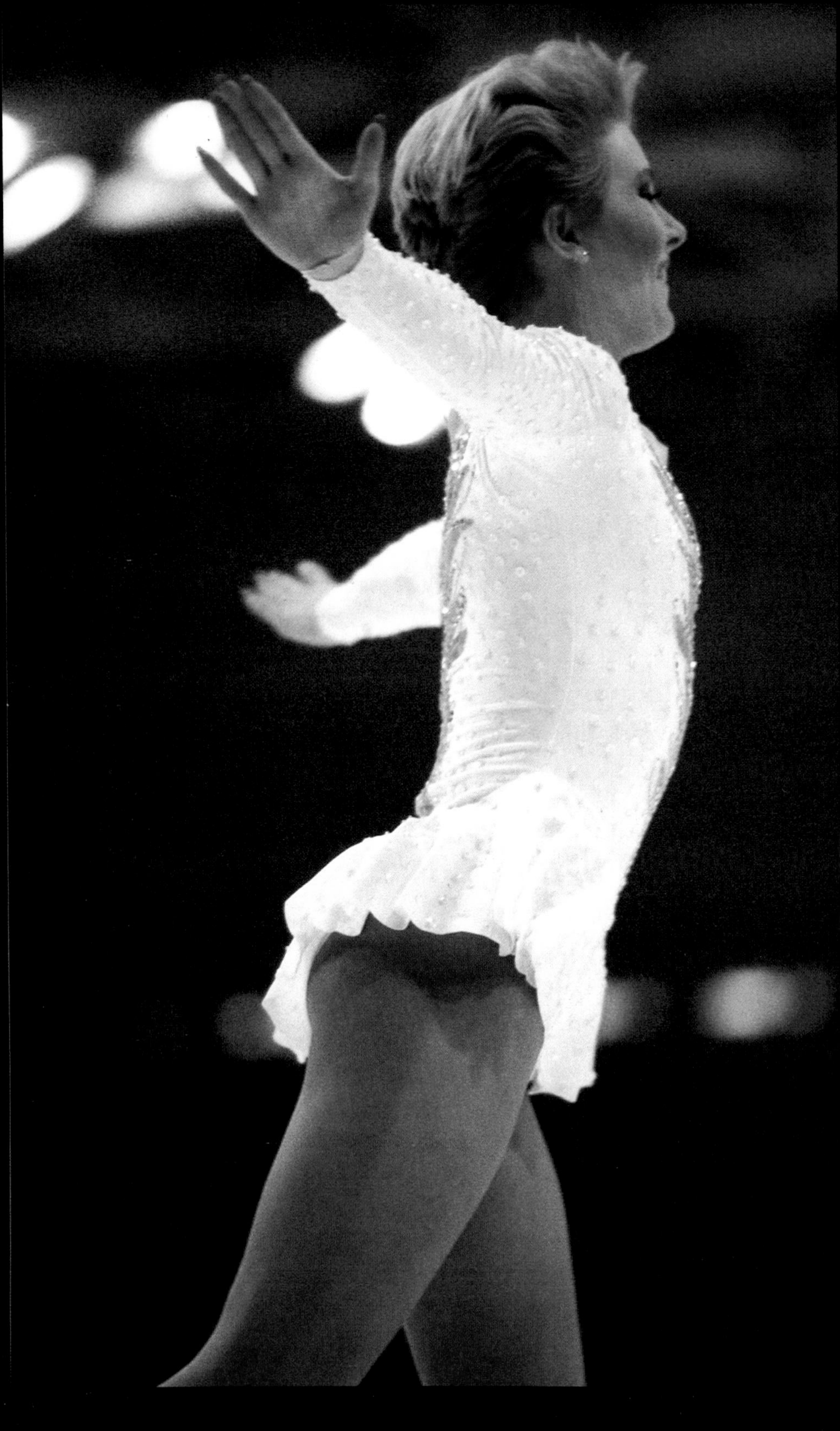

They came from all over the world, from the U.S. to China, more than 3,000 of them, newspapermen and newspaperwomen; some working single-handedly to inform their readers of the events in Sarajevo; some, from larger papers like the Washington Post, New York Times, Izvestia and Figaro, often working in teams of three or more, one dashing off to the mountains, another to the rinks, a third cruising the Olympic Village for interviews.

They grumbled, of course, about the incredible hours ("Eighteen hours a day, finish at four in the morning, go home, put on my red L.L. Bean pajamas, take a sleeping pill and go to bed," said Jane Leavy of the Washington Post), about the freezing snow ("I was jumping up and down to keep my feet warm, and my hands finally just became spasticized from the cold, and I had to call off the interview," said Ed Pope of the Miami Herald) and about the dearth of opportunities to enjoy the hospitality of Sarajevo ("Unlike the magazine people who can go out for dinner every night and have a lot of nice wine and enjoy it, newspaper people come back every day, and it's sort of like ultra-marathoning every day," said Neil Amdur of the New York Times, who took a job with a magazine not long after the Winter Games ended).

But the writers all agreed that with the Olympics going on in Yugoslavia, they didn't want to be anywhere else. "The Winter Olympics is like the Masters, the Super Bowl, the World Series, the Kentucky Derby," Ed Pope said. "If you're a sportswriter, you can't miss it."

"It's one of those classic assignments," Jane Leavy said. "You bitch if you don't get it. You bitch if you do get it. You bitch all the way through it. And then you go home and say, 'It's the greatest thing I ever did.'"

THE GOLD MEDALISTS
LUGE
MEN'S DOUBLES
HANS STANGGASSINGER
FRANZ WEMBACHER, WEST GERMANY
SPEED SKATING
WOMEN'S 3,000 METERS
ANDREA SCHOENE, EAST GERMANY
NORDIC SKIING
WOMEN'S 4 × 5-KILOMETER RELAY
NORWAY

FIGURE SKATING

The excruciatingly precise opening phase of the women's figure skating competition, the compulsory figures, worth 30 percent of the total score, lasted for six and a half hours, and when the ordeal was over, Rosalynn Sumners of the United States, the world champion, had skated herself into first place, by the thinnest of margins, and her fellow American teenagers, Elaine Zayak and Tiffany Chin, had skated themselves out of contention for even a bronze medal.

The daughter of a New Jersey bartender, the survivor of a childhood power-mower accident that cost her part of her left foot, the 1982 world champion at the age of 16 but the victim of a stress fracture of her right ankle at 17, Zayak was clearly frustrated and disappointed. "Elaine seemed nervous," said her coach, Peter Burrows, "and she skated poorly."

Zayak placed 13th, one spot behind the 16-year-old Chin, who remained cheerful. "I'd like to be higher, but the people in front of me are well-established," Chin said. "I'm young. My figures will get better as I go along."

"It was the most relaxed and confident I've ever felt with the compulsory figures," Sumners said. "I had a good pep talk with my mom last night, and I was completely oblivious of the judges."

Sumners' performance, paired with Scott Hamilton's a few days earlier, marked the first time in 28 years Americans had finished first in both the men's and women's compulsory figures. The last duo to trace such impressive figures was Tenley Albright and Hayes Alan Jenkins, both of whom went on, in 1956, to win gold medals.

But Sumners could hardly count on gold. Elena Vodorezova of the Soviet Union had actually scored higher than she on two of the three figures and just slightly lower on the third. Still, Vodorezova, in second place, did not seem too great a threat, because the compulsories were the strongest part of her skating. More menacingly, third place belonged to the European champion, a lovely 18-year-old East German named Katarina Witt, whose compulsories were the weakest part of her skating.

"I'm right where I want to be," said Witt.

NORDIC SKIING

In the seven previous Olympic Winter Games since the women's cross-country relay became an Olympic event, Soviet quartets had won three gold medals, three silver and one bronze, and after the first three legs of the relay in Sarajevo, the Soviet women, in second place behind Norway, seemed likely to keep that medal streak alive.

But on the final leg, as Norway remained in front, both the Czechs and the Finns overtook the Soviets and dropped them into fourth place, out of the relay medals for the first time. The last leg was skied for Finland by Marja-Liisa Haemaelaeinen, who, adding a bronze to the two earlier golds, kept her own medal streak alive.

SPEED SKATING

Mary Docter put pressure on herself. She admitted she desperately wanted to end her speed skating career, at the age of 23, with an Olympic medal. Ironically, her younger sister, Sarah, a more gifted skater, might have been a favorite to win a medal in Sarajevo if she hadn't given up racing, if she hadn't retired because she disliked the pressures of international competition.

Mary Docter didn't expect a gold medal or a silver in the 3,000-meter race—she conceded those to the East Germans—but she would have been delighted with a bronze. For 2,000 meters—"I skated as hard as I could"

Karin Enke (left) and Andrea Schoene (right), both of East Germany, shared the gold and silver medals in the 3,000 meters, as they had in two previous women's speed skating races.

—she was on a medal pace. But in the last 1,000 meters, she tired, tired badly, and faded back to sixth, precisely where she finished at Lake Placid four years earlier.

"I'm going to have to forget about what happened and concentrate on starting to be a good person," Docter said later. "I'm a free girl now. I can go to school. I can knit. I can have a boyfriend."

Karin Enke, who used to have a husband till a divorce in 1983, placed second in the 3,000 meters, winning her fourth medal of the Games, two silver and two gold, a glittering performance that made her more than a heroine but less than a Heiden. Her teammate, Andrea Schoene, second to Enke at 1,000 and 1,500 meters, won the 3,000-meter race. "I wanted to win my third gold medal," Enke said, "but I'm glad I lost it to Andrea."

LUGE

If ever an event belonged to a nation, luge belonged to East Germany. From 1972 through 1980, East German lugers won all three men's singles championships and all three men's doubles championships. But in 1984, only a few days after an Italian won the men's singles, a pair of West Germans, Hans Stanggassinger and Franz Wembacher, with a brilliant second run, overtook a Soviet twosome for the gold medal, and the favored East Germans, the reigning world champions, had to settle for third.

Long considered invulnerable, the East German men's doubles luge team was able to capture only the bronze at Sarajevo.

The new American bobsled seemed well worth its $10,000 price tag. Driving it down the bobsled chute for the first time, Jeff Jost posted the fastest U.S. training time in Sarajevo. "It's like driving a fast sports car after driving a big Mack truck," Jost said.

Prince Alexandre de Merode of Belgium, the president of the medical commission of the International Olympic Committee, announced a significant medical breakthrough, the imposition of a two-beer limit at the doping control stations. The cause: four hockey players who, in order to produce the necessary specimens, had among them devoured 54 bottles of beer. In the future, athletes would get two beers free and have to pay to quench their thirst any further. Let them drink fruit juice, suggested the prince.

For the 1984 Olympics, the Americans purchased and repainted a Swiss bobsled—and were pleased with the results.

The Canadian hockey team emerged scoreless against the tough Czechs.

Fog and snow made the course almost invisible, caused one Canadian to rip up her skis and, after 10 of 32 skiers had made their way, or attempted to make their way, down Mount Jahorina, forced a one-day postponement of the women's downhill. Michela Figini of Switzerland, in first place, was furious. Holly Flanders of the U.S., in second, wasn't too happy either.

The men's downhill skiers were back on Mount Bjelašnica for one final practice run, trying to regain their form. The bold American, Bill Johnson, had never lost his. He was first in the practice run and first in confidence. "I'm gonna smoke those guys," he said. "I don't care who I race against."

HOCKEY

In the final preliminary-round games of the hockey tournament, the United States encountered one more surprise, and Canada encountered reality. With 38 seconds to play, Bob Brooke's shorthanded goal gave the U.S. a 3–2 lead over Finland and a rare chance to celebrate.

But while the Americans were congratulating themselves, the Finns pulled their goalie and, with 21 seconds left, Anssi Melemetsa scored, lifting Finland into a tie and into third place in its division, its record two victories, two defeats and one tie, just ahead of the United States, with its one victory, two defeats and two ties. The Americans were reduced to one last face-saving game against Poland, the fourth-place team in the other division, the winner to be awarded seventh place overall.

Canada finally lost, 4–0, to undefeated Czechoslovakia, with both teams advancing to the medal round, the Czechs to face Sweden, the Canadians to face the Soviet Union, which had won its fifth straight game, handing Sweden its first defeat, 10–1. "We're not going to concede with a white flag," said Dave King, the Canadian coach, "but we're outmanned."

DAY 9
THURSDAY, FEBRUARY 16th

Finally, after a week of delays caused by fog and wind and swirling snow, a week of nature prolonging the drama, it was time for the running of the men's downhill, the heart of Alpine skiing. Sixty-one men were ready to face the mountain, to attack a Mount Bjelasnica course not quite two miles long, with a vertical drop from start to finish of almost half a mile, a fairly straightforward run by downhill standards, demanding more courage than cunning, more speed than style.

The downhill belonged, by tradition and geography and logic, to the countries which shared the jagged peaks of the Alps, to France, Italy, Switzerland and Austria—especially to Austria. The French had their wines, the Italians their opera, the Swiss their clocks. But to the Austrians, the downhill was everything, their trademark, their identity.

In the nine Winter Games since the downhill became an Olympic event, the Austrian men had won four gold medals, three silver and three bronze, almost twice as many medals as any other nation. Franz Klammer of Austria had taken the gold medal on Austrian snow at Innsbruck in 1976; four years later, in Lake Placid, Leonhard Stock and Peter Wirnsberger of Austria had won the gold and silver.

No American man had ever won an Olympic Alpine event. No American man had ever won even a silver medal or a bronze in the downhill. In the World Cup standings for the five years leading up to the Sarajevo Olympics, not once had an American ranked even among the top ten downhill skiers. History, tradition, geography and logic lined up against the U.S.

But Bill Johnson promised he would smoke them all.

THE GOLD MEDALISTS

FIGURE SKATING

MEN'S
  SCOTT HAMILTON, USA

SPEED SKATING

MEN'S 1,500 METERS
  GAETAN BOUCHER, CANADA

ALPINE SKIING

MEN'S DOWNHILL
  BILL JOHNSON, USA

WOMEN'S DOWNHILL
  MICHELA FIGINI, SWITZERLAND

NORDIC SKIING

MEN'S 4 × 10-KILOMETER RELAY
  SWEDEN

NORDIC SKIING

Anatoli Karpov, the king of chess for almost a decade, came to Sarajevo to cheer for Vladislav Tretiak and to help promote the opening of an exhibition highlighting "Winter Sports in the Soviet Union." Karpov also staged his own exhibition, playing 20 chess matches simultaneously, his challengers ranging from a pair of medal-winning Soviet figure skaters to a Yugoslav bobsled pilot to an American tourist.

Boris Radjenovic, the bobsled pilot, claimed he would beat Karpov, but admitted he didn't know how. Twenty kings folded in barely two hours, including Radjenovic's and Dan Peterson's. "It feels great," said Peterson, a Californian who dropped in at the exhibition and was offered a board. "I'm really happy. I mean, this is something I'll remember all my life, being slaughtered by Karpov."

The Swedish strategy in the men's cross-country relay was simple: Have the veteran, Thomas Wassberg, the gold medalist at 15 kilometers in Lake Placid, take the early lead; let the Soviet Union, the defending champion, set the pace in the middle stages; then have the young star, Gunde Svan, the gold medalist at 15 kilometers in Sarajevo, finish up, overtake the Soviets and win the race.

The Soviet strategy was even simpler: Build a big lead before the final leg. "We tried to gain at least 35 seconds over the Swedes because we knew that we had no chance against Svan," said Aleksandr Zavialov, the silver medalist at 30 kilometers in Sarajevo.

Wassberg and Zavialov played their roles perfectly. Wassberg gave Sweden the lead on the first 10-kilometer leg, with the Soviets second and the United States, represented by Dan Simoneau, surprisingly in third place. And on the second leg, as the U.S. began to fade, Zavialov charged into first place and built a 12-second lead over the Swedes.

On the third leg, however, Sweden cut deeply into the Soviet lead, and when the last leg began, Svan, a Swedish soldier, was only half a second behind a Soviet soldier, Nikolai Zimyatov, who had won three gold medals in Lake Placid, in the 30-kilometer race, the 50-kilometer and the relay. He had already won one gold medal in Sarajevo, at 30 kilometers. "I dreamed about racing Zimyatov on the last leg," Svan said later.

For nine kilometers, Svan stayed on Zimyatov's heels. Then the Swede spurted, took the lead and breezed home ten seconds in front of the Soviet star. "I could have overtaken Zimyatov even earlier, but I stuck to our plan," said Svan, who added the relay gold to a gold at 15 kilometers and a bronze at 30. He was off to a strong start toward catching up to the Swedish cross-country skier who had won more medals than any other athlete in the history of the Winter Olympics. Between 1956 and 1964, Sixten Jernberg won four gold medals, three silver and two bronze.

The United States, anchored by Bill Koch, wound up eighth among 17 teams, and Mongolia came in 15th, a fact worth noting only because one of the Mongolians, Purevjal Batsukh, was among the nonmedal winners selected at random to be tested for the use of banned drugs. Batsukh became the first, and only, athlete to be disqualified from the Sarajevo Olympics because of drugs. Traces of anabolic steroids were found in his blood.

But if almost all athletes tested clean, Prince Alexandre de Merode, the head of the IOC medical commission, still was not totally pleased. He said the commission strongly suspected that some athletes were engaged in "blood doping," a procedure not yet detectable in which blood is removed from an athlete, frozen and then, before competition, reinjected, increasing the athlete's oxygen capacity. "Our commission condemns this practice," de Merode said. "It can cause cardiovascular damage, and our tests show the practical results in relation to improving performances are not very high. It is not on our doping list, but it would be if we found a way to detect it."

SPEED SKATING

Gaetan Boucher could pinpoint precisely the difference between Sarajevo in 1984 and Lake Placid in 1980. "Then it was all maybe Heiden has a bad day, maybe he makes a mistake and falls, maybe someone else will win," Boucher said. "It's all different now because he is not here. Everybody has a chance to win."

Boucher made the most of his chances. In the 1,500-meter race, as in the 1,000 two days earlier, Sergei Khlebnikov of the Soviet Union, the favo-

Canadian Gaetan Boucher winning the men's 1,500-meter speed skating race.

rite, skating early, set the mark for the rest of the field to aim at. And once again Boucher took perfect aim.

Halfway through the race, Boucher was a full second ahead of Khlebnikov's pace. On the final lap, Boucher weakened noticeably, but he still managed to come home half a second in front of the Soviet star. "If I had died in the last lap," said the 5-foot-7, 154-pound Canadian, "I still would have had the edge."

His edge made Boucher the first Canadian to win two gold medals in a Winter Olympics, only the second Canadian to win two gold medals in any Olympics. More than half a century earlier, in Amsterdam in 1928, Canada's Percy Williams, a sprinter without skates, had won the 100- and 200-meter dashes.

"Mon bonhomme, tu l'as fait!" Boucher's father told him in a phone call from Canada. "My good man, you've done it!"

Each of the skiers who waited atop Mount Bjelašnica in the restaurant that sheltered the start of the men's downhill had his own dream. Jamil El Reedy of Egypt dreamed of finishing—anywhere. Bill Johnson, of course, dreamed only of victory. He stared out the back window of the restaurant toward distant peaks. "There was nothing but blue sky as far as I could see," he said. "The wind was blowing toward us. That was the first time it really hit me. This was the Olympics! I really started getting nervous. I had to cool down. I put everything out of my mind and started concentrating."

Above, and below left, women's downhill gold medalist Michela Figini.

ALPINE SKIING

Several miles east of Mount Bjelašnica, on Mount Jahorina, the women downhillers faced their own course, almost a mile and quarter long, the vertical drop more than a third of a mile, a course, like the men's, favoring the gliders, the specialists in pure speed. The course was ideal for Michela Figini, the red-haired Swiss teenager who had held first place when the event was postponed the previous day. Two weeks earlier, on a similar course in Megeve, France, Figini had won her first World Cup downhill.

The fifth woman to start, racing in light snow and good visibility, her countrymen chanting, "Figgy, Figgy," Figini flashed down Jahorina at an average speed of 57 miles an hour and crossed the finish line precisely five-hundredths of a second ahead of her Swiss teammate, Maria Walliser, who led the World Cup standings.

Figini, who had won a bronze medal in the world junior giant slalom championships in 1983, became, at the age of 17, the youngest person to win an Alpine gold medal in the Olympics. "I have never been so happy in my life," she said. "I have no words to express it."

Beaming, surrounded by reporters and good wishes, Figini called herself "a child of the sun," and on the far side of the finish area, her countrywoman, the silver medalist, the favorite, Maria Walliser, loser by the slimmest margin in Olympic downhill history, stood alone, watching quietly. "Naturally," Walliser said, "I came here to win."

Holly Flanders, second before the postponement, finished far back, in 16th place. And for the first time in 28 years, for only the second time in Olympic history, not one Austrian woman earned a medal in the downhill.

ALPINE SKIING

He stood at the top of the mountain, surrounded by Austrians and Swiss, men with names like Mueller and Steiner and Klammer and Zurbriggen and Hoeflehner, names that sounded as if they belonged at the tops of mountains, names that conjured up the Alps. *Bill Johnson.* The name didn't quite have the ring of a mountaintop to it.

Johnson, wrapped in peach-and-white *Descente* stripes, was the sixth man to start, and he knew the time he had to beat was 1:46.05, posted by Pirmin Zurbriggen of Switzerland, almost a full second faster than the run of the 1976 champion, Austria's Franz Klammer.

"It takes guts to throw yourself down the mountain," Johnson said later.

He dropped out of the gate and threw himself down the mountain, slipping into his tuck, his skiing stance, and speeding smoothly through the upper part of the course, hitting the first intermediate timing three-hundredths of a second faster than Zurbriggen.

In the middle of the course, through the carousel turns, two icy and treacherous curves that had tested him in practice, Johnson descended safely, but not, by world-class standards, very swiftly. He slipped two-tenths of a second behind Zurbriggen.

But then came Johnson's part of the course, basically flat, with three bumps that would lift the racer into the air for dizzying spells. "I just smoked," Johnson said. "I went down into my tuck, got some good air off the bumps and just smoked." On the first bump, fighting to stay coiled in his egg-shaped tuck, the best aerodynamic stance to combat the air and the clock, Johnson momentarily lost control, straightened up, pumped his arms to regain his balance, then resumed his tuck and rocketed toward the finish.

He hit the line in 1:45.59, almost half a second faster than Zurbriggen, but the race was not yet his. There were still Austrians and Swiss to ski, men with great talent and a lifetime of attacking mountains. Johnson stood by the finish area, glanced at the electronic scoreboard, watched the men challenge the course and his time. He heard the roar of the crowd as Peter Mueller of Switzerland, one of the favorites in the race, reached the two-thirds mark faster than Johnson had. Mueller, like Johnson a gifted glider, certainly had a chance to take the gold. But he failed. He reached the finish line in 1:45.86, more than a quarter of a second behind Johnson.

The men's downhill medalists: Anton Steiner (bronze), Bill Johnson (gold), Peter Mueller (silver).

Switzerland's Peter Mueller (above) racing, and failing, to better the sizzling performance of American Bill Johnson (below, left).

Then an Austrian, Anton Steiner, one of the stars of the World Cup circuit, made his bid, and when he approached the final third of the course, he was fully half a second ahead of Johnson's pace, a sizable margin. But the Austrian couldn't come close to matching the American on the flats, and he came home in 1:45.95, almost a tenth of a second behind Mueller.

Only two seeded skiers followed Steiner, and when neither threatened his time, Johnson knew the gold medal was his, knew that none of the 46 unseeded skiers, the "nose-pickers," as the Austrians called them, would surpass him. Johnson saw the disappointment in the Swiss and the Austrians he had defeated.

"They think they should always win," Johnson said. "I like to stick it to 'em now and then."

Johnson also stuck it to his own coach, Bill Marolt, who once had dropped him from the U.S. team for being out of shape. "He's probably taking all the credit," Johnson said as Marolt was actually giving the skier all the credit. "But I thought it was me up there."

Jamil El Reedy fulfilled his dream and finished, even though he was last, almost a minute and a half behind Johnson, more than a minute behind the next-to-last, the 59th, finisher.

And Bill Johnson fulfilled his dream. "What will it mean?" he was asked. "Millions," he replied. "We're talking about millions here."

FIGURE SKATING

When Rosalynn Sumners arrived at Zetra to perform her short program, the second part of the women's figure skating competition, she flashed her athlete's badge and started to enter the ice arena. Guards stopped her, demanded to see her ticket. Sumners did not have a ticket.

"She doesn't need one," an American called out. "She's the world champion."

The guards were not sufficiently impressed. The world champion had to argue for ten minutes before she was admitted.

And two hours later, the judges were not sufficiently impressed by Sumners' two-minute program, not enough to keep her in first place. She performed an excellent triple toe loop, then tried a double Axel, but instead of landing on one foot, as required, landed on both feet. "I was coming into the double Axel too slow," Sumners said afterward. "I wasn't nervous. Just too slow."

The mistake was costly. The judges gave Sumners mostly 5.3s for technical merit, uncommonly low scores for her, and 5.8s for artistic impression. Her chief rival for the figure skating gold, Katarina Witt of East Germany, earned mostly 5.8s for both technical merit and artistic impression and rose into first place.

The two leaders' scores were so close, however, that whichever one finished higher in the freeskating two days later would be certain to win the championship. "I'm happy with the standings," Sumners said. "This is where I like to be going into the long program."

In the 1983 world championships, Sumners had surpassed Witt in the free skating; in the 1982 world championships, Witt had outskated Sumners.

Elaine Zayak, sixth in the short program, inched up to 11th overall, but the most dramatic advance was achieved by Tiffany Chin, the 4-foot-11 91-pound Californian who, with the second-highest scores in the short program, climbed to sixth overall. "I have mixed feelings about Tiffany's chances for a medal," said her mother, Marjorie Chin. "If she wins a medal, it may be too much too soon. If she comes close, she has a goal for the next Olympics."

East Germany's stunning gold medalist, Katarina Witt.

The two main competitors in the men's figure skating, Canada's Brian Orser (left) and Scott Hamilton (right) of the United States.

FIGURE SKATING

Scott Hamilton followed Brian Orser onto the ice at Zetra. Orser, the young Canadian who was Hamilton's chief rival, had skated magnificently, earning 11 5.9s from the nine judges in the two categories, technical merit and artistic impression. He had earned roses, too, bouquets thrown by cheering spectators. Some of the roses still lay on the ice to greet Scott Hamilton.

Hamilton lifted Orser's roses and dropped them over the rail, off the ice. Thanks to his magnificent compulsory figures, Hamilton still had a comfortable lead. But he was not comfortable. "I felt the pressure," Hamilton said afterward. "I felt like I was carrying twenty-pound weights around with me."

He also carried an infection, in his right ear, and whether it was the infection, or the legal antibiotics he had taken, or, as he suggested, simply the weight of the occasion, he did not skate with his usual fire, his usual flair. Of course there were golden moments. "His camel spin was so correct, so flat that you could have balanced a tray of wine on the small of his back and not spilled a drop," Bob Ottum wrote in *Sports Illustrated.* But the *New York Times* called Hamilton's performance "subdued, tentative and flawed." He failed to execute a planned triple jump, and his triple Salchow turned, timidly, into a double. "I wanted it to be perfect," Hamilton said. "I wanted it to be my greatest moment. But there was no way I could do it."

When he finished his four-and-a-half-minute program, the 25-year-old world champion skated straight up to his coach, Don Laws, and said, "I'm sorry." When his scores were posted—more 5.8s than anything else, with a smattering of 5.6s and 5.7s for technical merit, great scores by normal standards, poor by Hamilton's, scores inflated at least to a small extent by his reputation, his image, rather than his performance—and Hamilton, by a narrow but clear margin, was the Olympic champion, he was still sorry, still frustrated. "I'm happy with the gold," he said. "I worked four years for tonight. But I wish it could have been something special."

When Scott Hamilton followed Bill Johnson to the top of the victory stand on February 16, 1984, it was the first time that two Americans had earned gold medals on a single day in the Winter Olympics in 36 years, and only the third time ever.

On February 5, 1948, in St. Moritz, Switzerland, an 18-year-old schoolboy and a 28-year-old housewife won gold medals for the United States, Dick Button in men's figure skating and Gretchen Fraser in the women's slalom. Fraser was the first American to win an Alpine skiing event—no American man matched her feat till Bill Johnson came along—and Button was the first to win a figure skating event.

On February 4, 1932, in Lake Placid, a pair of American speed skaters won gold medals, John Shea at 500 meters and Irving Jaffee at 5,000. Shea and Jaffee each earned two gold medals in 1932, the only Winter Olympics in which the U.S. won more gold medals than any other country.

Orser, who finished first in both the short program and the long, after placing seventh in the compulsory figures, was a gracious silver medalist. "It's a fair scoring system," the Canadian said. "You've got to do well in all phases of the competition."

Hamilton, Orser and Josef Sabovcik, the Czech who came in third, collected their medals, then took a victory lap around the ice. Hamilton grabbed an American flag from a spectator in a front-row seat and waved the flag as he skated, the gold medal dangling from his neck. "It wasn't pretty, but I did it," Hamilton then told a news conference. "I don't think people understand how difficult it is to be unbeaten for four years." He smiled at the army of reporters in front of him. "Try it, folks," Hamilton said. "It's tough."

Scott Hamilton displays America's banner.

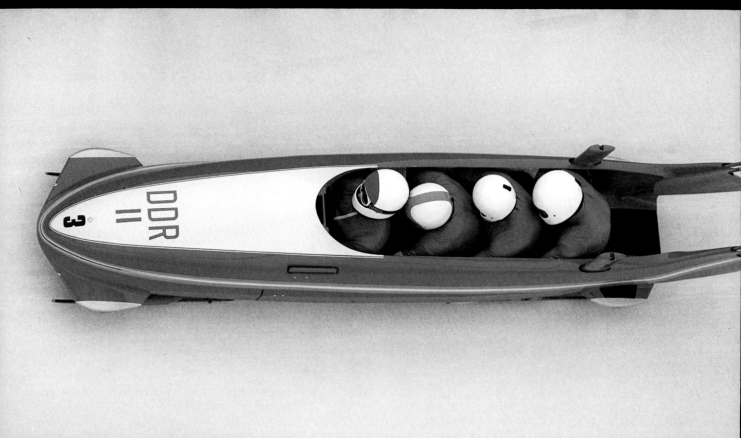

Traditionally, bobsledding in the United States was a party sport, a good excuse for good friends to hurtle down a frozen chute at exhilarating speeds, then repair to a bar to celebrate their feats. The main requirements for the sport were easy access to Lake Placid, site of the only bobsled run in the U.S., plus considerable courage and a matching thirst.

Still, in the early years of international bobsled racing, the high-spirited Americans did quite well, winning the first two Olympic two-man competitions, in 1932 and 1936, and three of the early four-man competitions, in 1928, 1932 and 1948. The 1932 four-man sled carried Eddie Eagan, the 1920 Olympic light-heavyweight boxing champion, the only man or woman to win gold medals in summer and winter Olympics.

But since 1956, the United States had not won any kind of medal for bobsledding, mainly because other countries, notably East Germany, Switzerland and Italy, took the sport much more seriously.

By the 1980s, bobsledders realized that, to succeed, they needed a good driver, who could find and hold the fastest line down the run; a good machine, aerodynamically efficient; and, perhaps most important, good athletes, to push the sled off to a powerful start.

The U.S., later than its more successful rivals, had begun to recruit good athletes for its bobsleds. Willie Davenport, who won the gold medal in the 110-meter hurdles in 1968, was on a four-man U.S. sled at Lake Placid, and in Sarajevo, the crew of the four-man sled piloted by Jeff Jost included Joe Briski, a national-class hammer thrower. The United States was starting to take bobsledding more seriously.

THE GOLD MEDALISTS

BIATHLON

4 × 7.5-METER RELAY
    SOVIET UNION

ALPINE SKIING

WOMEN'S SLALOM
    PAOLETTA MAGONI, ITALY

BIATHLON

Norway had Erik Kvalfoss, who had won one of the individual biathlon championships, and West Germany had Peter Angerer, who had won the other. But even though Kvalfoss turned in the fastest leg of the relay, and Angerer the second fastest, and even though East Germany held the lead after three legs, the Soviet Union, anchored by Sergei Buligin, rallied and won the biathlon relay for the fifth straight Winter Olympics, proving that, on a team basis, no one turned from rabbits into rocks better than Russians.

Christin Cooper of the USA is comforted after she failed to finish in the women's slalom.

Liechtenstein's determined Ursula Konzett won the bronze.

Paoletta Magoni erupted from obscurity to capture the slalom gold for Italy.

ALPINE SKIING

The United States Alpine ski team had elected to enter only two women in the slalom, but since the two were Tamara McKinney, the 1983 World Cup champion, and Christin Cooper, who had already won a silver medal in the giant slalom, the Americans were still brimming with confidence. But the slalom is an unforgiving event, and on the first of two runs down a steep Mount Jahorina course, both McKinney and Cooper straddled gates and failed to finish. "In the slalom," McKinney said, "you just have to whale on it. You have to go all-out. I just took one chance too many."

The winner was a woman who had never in her life won a big race, never finished among the top three in a World Cup event, Paoletta Magoni, one of six children of an Italian bricklayer. She was 19, which meant that Debbie Armstrong, only two months out of her teens, was the oldest of the women's Alpine champions.

Fourth after the first run, Magoni blazed through treacherous fog on her second run and became the first Italian woman to win an Olympic Alpine gold medal. "It was as if they had designed the course for me," Magoni said.

BOBSLED

Jeff Jost, once a state high school wrestling champion, now a state trooper, understood the risks of bobsledding. In the 1981 world championships, at Cortina d'Ampezzo, Jost was riding behind Jim Morgan, one of eleven children of an almost legendary American bobsledder named Forrest "Dew Drop" Morgan. On the final turn, Jim Morgan's sled hit a rut and flipped, and Morgan was thrown headfirst into an ice wall. He died instantly.

"After that, I had a lot of trouble getting back into it the next year," Jost said. "You do a lot of thinking. You've got to drive the fine line, but that year I was driving the middle line instead of the fine line. I was playing it a little safe. Now I'm back driving the fine line again."

On the first two of the four four-man bobsled runs, no one drove the fine line finer than the East Germans, who placed first and second, the leading sled driven by Wolfgang Hoppe, the former decathlete who had won the two-man competition. The 36-year-old Jost, despite a lack of familiarity with his new Swiss-built sled, tied for ninth place.

No one was injured, not even Christopher Dean, the ice dancing champion, who enjoyed a practice run in the British bob.

HOCKEY

President Reagan placed the obligatory phone call to congratulate Scott Hamilton for his gold medal, but the former governor of California did not speak to his former constituent, Bill Johnson. The reason was logistical, not political. The fastest man down the hill was also the fastest man out of town. Johnson had already left Sarajevo and was on his way to the United States, not reachable by telephone.

In the semifinals of the hockey championships, against the brilliant team from the Soviet Union, Canada performed half a miracle. Halfway through the game, halfway through the second period, the score was 0–0. Mario Gosselin, the Canadian goalie, the man who had feared he might be disqualified before the tournament began, turned away 14 Soviet shots in the first period alone. Vladislav Tretiak, the veteran Soviet goalie, did not have to stop a Canadian shot until 15 minutes had gone by. Obviously, the game was being played with the puck in the Canadian end, but as long as the puck wasn't in the Canadian goal, the underdogs had a chance.

Then Canada's Bruce Driver, skating out of the penalty box, got the puck on a breakaway, raced in on Tretiak and fired. Tretiak deflected the shot, and the dream of a miracle was over. A minute later, the Soviets scored their first goal, and they went on to a 4–0 victory, their closest call so far, but still a decisive margin.

In the other semifinal, Czechoslovakia survived its toughest game, a 2–0 victory over Sweden, and advanced to the final everyone had anticipated, against the Soviet Union.

And in a consolation game, the United States beat Poland, 7–4, and the Americans, with a record of two victories, two defeats and two ties, wound up in seventh place, precisely as they had been seeded.

Left: Vladislav Tretiak's skills as goalie for the Soviet hockey team were not sorely tried by the Canadian challengers.

DAY 11
SATURDAY, FEBRUARY 18th

Duringuring the days of the ancient Greeks, women could neither compete in the Olympic Games nor, with the exception of one special priestess, observe. The penalty was so severe, death by being thrown from a cliff, that only one woman was known to have taken the risk. Pherenice of Rhodes, disguised as an athlete, accompanied her son, Pisidores, to the Games, and when he won the boxing championship, she embraced him so eagerly her robe slipped, revealing her sex. Only because her father and brothers had been Olympic champions, and because her husband had died while their son was in training, Pherenice was spared. But from then on, to avoid similar deception, all athletes in all events had to compete naked.

When the modern Games began in 1896, all 285 entrants were clothed and male. In 1900, in Paris, women made their Olympic debut, six of them in golf and tennis, but the first real Olympic star among women was a Winter Olympian, Sonja Henie of Norway, who won three consecutive figure skating gold medals in 1928, 1932 and 1936. She was followed by such outstanding Winter Olympians as Lydia Skoblikova, winner of four speed skating gold medals in 1964; Galina Kulakova, who earned three cross-country skiing gold medals in 1972; and Rosi Mittermaier and Hanni Wenzel, the two women who came closest to sweeping the Alpine skiing events, each with two gold medals and a silver, Mittermaier in 1976 and Wenzel in 1980.

Now, in Sarajevo, the individual stars were two gifted women: Karin Enke, the only winner so far of four medals, two gold and two silver in speed skating, and Marja-Liisa Haemaelaeinen, about to bid for her fourth medal, and her third gold, in cross-country skiing. And either Katarina Witt or Rosalynn Sumners would spring from their free-skating confrontation to stardom.

THE GOLD MEDALISTS

BOBSLED

FOUR-MAN
  EAST GERMANY

FIGURE SKATING

WOMEN'S
  KATARINA WITT, EAST GERMANY

SPEED SKATING

MEN'S 10,000 METERS
  IGOR MALKOV, SOVIET UNION

NORDIC SKIING

WOMEN'S 20 KILOMETERS
  MARJA-LIISA HAEMAELAEINEN, FINLAND

90-METER SKI JUMP
  MATTI NYKAENEN, FINLAND

Two competitors in the exhausting women's 20-kilometer cross-country race; Julia Stepanova of the USSR (left) and Anne Jahren of Norway (right). who took a surprising third place.

NORDIC SKIING

The 20-kilometer cross-country ski race, a new Olympic event, more than 12 miles long, was the easy part for Finland's Marja-Liisa Haemaelaeinen. Dressed in blue and white, her national colors, and wearing a pair of tiny rhinestone earrings, Haemaelaeinen defeated her closest competitor, a Soviet skier, by fully 41 seconds. Then came the hard part. "When I finished and saw the reporters," Haemaelaeinen said, "I almost panicked." But the shy 28-year-old physiotherapist survived the army of interviewers and emerged, with three gold medals and one bronze, the individual star of the Sarajevo Games.

SPEED SKATING

Reversing of the 5,000-meter result, Igor Malkov of the Soviet Union (below, right) narrowly defeated Tomas Gustafson of Norway (above) in the men's 10,000-meter speed skating race.

In the final speed skating race of the XIVth Olympic Winter Games, the 10,000 meters, Igor Malkov of the Soviet Union did to Tomas Gustafson of Sweden what Gustafson had done to him at 5,000 meters. Gustafson won the shorter race by two-hundredths of a second, or one skate blade; Malkov won the longer race by five-hundredths of a second, a difference of less than three skate blades over a race more than six miles long.

Mike Woods, an anesthesiologist from Milwaukee, led the American finishers, but faded to seventh place, which meant that, for the first time since 1956, the U.S. speed skaters, men and women, had been shut out, not a single medal among them. "For the last ten laps," Dr. Woods said, "my legs felt like there were dogs gnawing at them. It's like getting a flat tire on your bicycle. You're pushing, but it's not happening."

If it were any consolation to the American speed skaters, all five of the Olympic records Eric Heiden set in Lake Placid in 1980 still stood, not one of them matched in Sarajevo.

Finland's ski jumping star Matti Nykaenen confirmed his reputation with a gold in the 90-meter event.

NORDIC SKIING

Patriotic Finns show their colors.

The jumpers moved, for their final event, to the 90-meter hill, but the duel was still expected to be the same, Jens Weissflog, the controlled 5-foot-6 East German teenager, the Olympic 70-meter champion, against Matti Nykae nen, the feisty 5-foot-10, 20-year-old Finn, the world 90-meter champion.

The anticipated duel materialized, but not before Jeff Hastings, the veteran American, surprisingly thrust himself into the medal picture with the second of his two jumps, a magnificent leap of 351 feet that lifted him into first place with only four men still to jump.

Three of the four men, including Weissflog and Nykaenen, surpassed Hastings, and he slipped back to fourth place, still the best finish by an American in 60 years, since Anders Haugen earned the bronze medal he was officially awarded half a century later.

Nykaenen took the 90-meter gold, ending a frustrating string of second- place finishes, and earned Hastings' praise. "He's incredible," Hastings said. "He's only 120 pounds and, at five-foot-ten, he's got a lot of flying surface. He's like a feather in the air."

BOBSLED

Wolfgang Hoppe's four-man bobsled, with the best time in each of the four runs, captured the gold medal convincingly, with another East German sled second, and Swiss sleds third and fourth. There was a Swiss sled in fifth place, too, but this one was driven by Jeff Jost, the sled purchased for $10,000 by the U.S. from Hans Hiltebrand, the disillusioned Swiss bobsled- der. Jost's last two runs were swift enough to raise him from a tie for ninth place, to carry him to the brink of a medal. "If I could have had a couple of more training runs," Jost said, "I think we would have won a medal."

Ladislav Lukatch of Czechoslovakia (right) soars above the spectators in the men's 90-meter jump.

In contention for the women's figure skating gold: Rosalynn Summers of the USA (left), and East Germany's Katarina Witt (right).

FIGURE SKATING

At 19, Rosalynn Sumners had been skating competitively for more than half her life, since the age of eight. She won the national novice championship when she was 14, the junior world championship when she was 15, the United States championship when she was 17 and the world championship when she was 18. She trained. She dieted. She sacrificed. And yet, despite all her effort and all her success, she knew that if she did not win the Olympic championship, if she did not capture a gold medal, she would never enjoy the enduring fame of a Peggy Fleming, a Dorothy Hamill.

She would still be a great skater, but hers would not be a name immediately recognizable to people outside figure skating. She would go on to ice shows, to financial rewards, but she would be among the Linda Fratiannes, the Janet Lynns, the ones who almost made it. It wasn't fair, of course, so thin a dividing line between ultimate success and apparent failure, but it was, in Rosalynn Sumners' sport, an inescapable fact. Under this kind of pressure, in front of a capacity crowd at Zetra Arena, wearing a white costume with light blue trim, Rosalynn Sumners took the ice at the end of a long and lovely evening of figure skating.

Katarina Witt of East Germany had skated right before Sumners. Five-foot-five, 112 pounds, dazzlingly beautiful in a raspberry outfit, Witt skated to tunes more familiar to Americans than to the citizens of her hometown, Karl-Marx-Stadt: "I've Got Rhythm," "Mona Lisa" and "Embraceable You." She gracefully blended triple jumps, double Axels, a camel spin and pirouettes, faltering only once, a minor stumble coming out of a double flip.

The audience was visibly impressed, and so were the judges, who rewarded her with two 5.7s, eleven 5.8s and five 5.9s, scores that almost, but not quite, clinched the championship for her. Don Laws, Scott Hamilton's coach, studied the East German's scores, performed a little mental mathematics and concluded, "Five judges have left enough room for Rosalynn to win. But she has to skate a perfect program."

Then Sumners went out and skated a magnificent program and, despite one flaw—a planned combination of a split jump and a triple toe loop turned into a split jump and only a double toe loop—in the opinion of one judge, a perfect program. The Italian judge gave her a 6.0 for artistic impression, the only 6.0 of the Games for either a male or a female individual figure skater. But the other judges were not quite so generous. There were six 5.9s, seven 5.8s, one 5.7 and three 5.6s, including a 5.6 for artistic impression, the range from 5.6 to 6.0 for the same program a very unusual range. The 5.6 came from a Yugoslav judge, who also gave Sumners a 5.6 for technical merit. Asked to explain his low scores, the judge replied, "Job of judge like being leper."

Still, the scores were so close that when Witt looked up and saw Sumners' totals, she was not certain she had won, or lost, the gold medal. She had won—by the most slender of margins. Five judges rated Witt first; four judges rated Sumners first. If either the West German or the Canadian judge had given Sumners a 5.9 instead of a 5.8 for technical merit, she would have won the gold medal. "I think if I had landed that triple," Sumners said, "I would have won the gold." It was that close.

"I think I was getting excited toward the end," Sumners said, explaining the triple that turned into a double. "I think I let up too soon."

The other two American skaters, Tiffany Chin and Elaine Zayak, placed third and fourth in the freeskating, which elevated them to fourth and sixth, respectively, in the final standings, an astonishingly good performance for Chin, a high school sophomore who almost certainly would be among the favorites in 1988, and a satisfying one for Zayak, who, like Sumners, would soon join an ice show, to be introduced night after night as a former world champion, but never as an Olympic winner.

Tiffany Chin placed third in the freeskating—and showed her promise for the 1988 Olympics.

DAY 12
SUNDAY, FEBRUARY 19 th

Rosalynn Sumners was a winner. Tamara McKinney was a winner. Bill Koch was a winner. Each was, at one time, the best in the world at his or her sport, and yet, because each had failed in Sarajevo to live up to the expectations of others, each was called, as the Games drew to a close, a loser. The label was not only unfair. It was inaccurate.

"The important thing in the Olympic Games is not winning, but taking part," said the Baron Pierre de Coubertin, the founder of the modern Games, and while disciples of Vince Lombardi or George S. Patton (who, ironically, took part in the 1912 Olympics, but did not win) might debate de Coubertin's Olympic Creed, the French nobleman was right: The important thing in the Olympic Games is always striving to win, striving to do one's best, yet still appreciating the other rewards of the experience, the opportunity to meet so many people from so many cultures, to share their dreams and their fears, to grow as an athlete and as a human being.

Sumners won, Koch won ("It's the effort that counts, not the outcome"), McKinney won ("I tried my best, and it didn't happen, and I can live with it, it's not the end of my life"), and so did George Tucker of Puerto Rico and Jamil El Reedy of Egypt and the four Lebanese who enjoyed two weeks without bullets or bombs.

"Which prepared you better for the rest of your life?" Phil Verchota, captain of the 1984 U.S. hockey team and member of the 1980 team, was asked. "Winning in 1980? Or losing now?"

"This might be better in the long run," Verchota said.

Phil and Steve Mahre were winners, and now each had one final chance to be an Olympic champion, too.

THE GOLD MEDALISTS

ICE HOCKEY
SOVIET UNION

ALPINE SKIING
MEN'S SLALOM
PHIL MAHRE, USA

NORDIC SKIING
MEN'S 50 KILOMETERS
THOMAS WASSBERG, SWEDEN

NORDIC SKIING

Gunde Svan of Sweden emerged from the grueling 50-kilometer cross-country ski race as the most bemedaled man in the XIVth Winter Games, but he did not get the third gold medal he had sought. He settled for a silver, his fourth medal of the Games, and the gold went to his countryman, Thomas Wassberg, who completed the exhausting run in just under two hours and 16 minutes. Finns came in third and fourth, with Harri Kirvesniemi, Marja-Liisa Haemaelaeinen's fiancé, just missing another medal for the family. "I skied my best," said Bill Koch, typically, after placing 17th.

ALPINE SKIING

Fifty thousand spectators lined the men's slalom course on Mount Bjelašnica, and on the final day of competition, the brightest sunshine of the Olympics lit up the largest crowd. Most of the spectators were Yugoslavs, hoping they might see Jure Franko or Bojan Krizaj win a second medal for their country. An hour before the race began, early in the morning in Scottsdale, Arizona, Holly Mahre, the wife of Phil Mahre, gave birth to the couple's second child, their first son. While she delivered, her husband, unaware, studied the slalom course. Then he delivered.

On the first of two runs, Phil Mahre posted only the fourth-fastest time, seven-tenths of a second behind the surprising leader, his brother Steve. Merely getting through the demanding course was an achievement. Max Julen, Jure Franko and Andreas Wenzel, who had finished one-two-three in the giant slalom, all failed to finish their first runs in the slalom.

On his second run, Phil Mahre concentrated harder, took greater risks and stormed into first place. Then he grabbed a walkie-talkie from an American coach and radioed advice to his brother, who was at the top of the mountain, awaiting his turn to ski. Phil warned Steve, "The bottom is slick."

"He's telling me what I've got to do to beat him," Steve Mahre said later.

Phil's counsel was wise, but Steve's execution was not perfect. By his own

In the men's slalom Phil Mahre captured America's third Alpine skiing gold medal.

count, Steve made three mistakes during his run, and those mistakes dropped him .21 of a second behind Phil, who was four minutes older. At least Steve was cutting down the margin between them.

No one else could challenge the twins. After a trying winter season, after weeks of downplaying the importance of the Olympics, approaching the end of their competitive skiing careers, Phil Mahre won the gold, and Steve Mahre the silver, the finest showings by siblings in a single Olympic race since the Goitschel sisters of France, Marielle and Christine, finished one-two in both the slalom and the giant slalom in 1964.

The Mahres' medals gave the U.S. Alpine team an unprecedented total of five, three gold and two silver, but Phil Mahre still refused to be caught up in the Olympic fervor. "It's just another notch in your skis," he said. "This doesn't compare with World Cup victories. Those were more of a test."

Phil still didn't know that he was a new father.

"If I had to lose," Steve Mahre said, "at least I'm happy that Phil won."

Of all the racers, none was happier than the teenaged Jamil El Reedy. It took him almost twice as long as the Mahres to ski the course, but at least he had beaten somebody. He came in 46th of 47 finishers and, flushed with success, predicted that in 1988, in Calgary, he might be an Olympic champion. His smile was broader than Phil Mahre's.

HOCKEY

Vladimir Caldr knew he was going to score. From only ten feet away, the Czech wing fired at the corner of the Soviet goal, an almost perfect shot. But Vladislav Tretiak, playing in his fourth and probably final Olympics at the age of 31, reached out and blocked the puck with his forearm. Caldr fell to his knees in disbelief, and the Czechs fell to the Soviets, to Tretiak, 2–0 —the winning goal scored by Alexander Kozhevnikov on a slap shot that bounced off the crossbar. For the sixth time in eight Winter Olympics, the Soviet Union won the Olympic hockey championship.

The Russian hockey team celebrates its return to Olympic dominance.

Exultant Soviet goalie Vladislav Tretiak.

When the game ended, the Soviets embraced each other, not quite so ecstatic as the Americans had been in 1980, but still obviously delighted, and relieved, to have regained the title they had so stunningly lost in Lake Placid.

Every member of the Soviet squad received a gold medal, but Tretiak's was special. He played six of the seven games and permitted only four goals. He finished with a pair of shutouts in the two most significant games. On the victory stand, Tretiak held up his third Olympic gold medal and kissed it twice.

The Swedes collected the bronze medals, their reward for beating Canada, 2–0, the third straight shutout for the Canadians after their four opening victories.

"When might Tretiak play his first game for the Montreal Canadiens?" someone asked Viktor Tikhonov, the Soviet coach, at least half in jest.

Tikhonov considered the question. "In two thousand years," he said.

As Phil Mahre strode through the Olympic Village on his way to the medal ceremony at Skenderija Square, Donna de Varona of ABC Sports, a former Olympic champion herself, walked up to him. "Do you know that you're the father of a baby boy?" she said.

Mahre had not heard. Tears came to his eyes, and he could say little, and later, when the gold medal was around his neck, when reporters crowded around him and asked him about his new son, the tears returned, and Mahre managed to say, "It's not worth missing, I'll tell you."

"Which event was more important?" someone asked. "The son? Or the gold?"

"That's a ridiculous question," Mahre replied.

Still, on his way out of a sport that had consumed him for a decade, he offered skiing a final compliment. "I was never in the sport to win one thing," he said. "I was here to compete. I was here to perform to my abilities. I was in the sport because I loved it, and I love it to this day."

"What do you think you'll be doing a year from now?"

Phil Mahre smiled. The tears were gone. "Probably baby-sitting," he said.

Victors in the men's slalom (left to right): Steve Mahre, silver; Phil Mahre, gold; and Didier Bouvet of France, bronze.

The audience at the closing ceremonies was treated to a magnificent figure skating display by Olympic champions Hamilton (left) and Torvill and Dean (right).

The XIVth Olympic Winter Games were over, the medals counted, 25 for the Soviet Union, including six gold, 24 for East Germany, including nine gold, 13 for Finland, nine for Norway and eight apiece for Sweden and the United States. But the numbers meant little. To the Yugoslavs, one medal was as precious as 25 were to the Soviet Union.

Inside Zetra Arena, the Games ended with a dazzling figure skating exhibition, with the champions on display, followed by the briefest closing ceremony in Olympic history, only 33 minutes long, spanning songs and dances and the traditional parade. Each nation was allowed six marchers, plus a flag-bearer, and the U.S. nominated its medal winners, the two Mahres, the two Carrutherses, the two individual figure skaters, Scott Hamilton and Rosalynn Sumners. The other three skiing medalists, Bill Johnson and Debbie Armstrong and Christin Cooper, had already left Sarajevo, but Tamara McKinney marched to represent them. Phil Mahre carried the American flag.

The four Lebanese skiers marched. Two of them had made it down the slalom course, but now they faced a far more dangerous journey that would take three of them from Sarajevo to Belgrade to Athens to Cyprus and then, by boat, to Beirut. "We don't care about dangers," Toni Sukkar said. "We just want to live in our country."

"I'm happy to go back to Beirut," Serge Axiotiades said. "I'm not afraid."

Several Yugoslavs, dressed as Vučko, the mascot of the Games, joined in the festivities. Some of them skated on the Zetra ice, and others danced on the mats that shielded part of the ice, and then the athletes broke ranks, and as the Olympic flag came down, and the Olympic flame flickered out, the athletes were dancing with the wolves in Sarajevo.

DAY 1
SATURDAY, JULY 28th

The last time the Summer Olympic Games were held in the United States, in 1932, in Los Angeles, Babe Didrikson starred in the Coliseum and Katharine Hepburn starred in the movies. Fifty-two years later, when the Games came back to Los Angeles, to the edge of Hollywood and the threat of massive traffic jams and choking smog, Hepburn and the Coliseum endured, a pair of awesome institutions.

The Coliseum, once again the site of the Opening Ceremony and the track and field championships, symbolized perfectly the efforts of the Los Angeles Olympic Organizing Committee to utilize existing facilities, to keep the cost of the Games, financed entirely by private enterprise, under $500 million, a limit that would ensure a profit.

The playing sites for the Games of the XXIII Olympiad sprawled from the edge of Santa Barbara to the edge of San Diego, a span of almost 200 miles. The athletes were scattered, too, in three separate Villages.

The major disappointment of the 1984 Games was the Soviet Union's decision not to participate. The Soviets cited insufficient security and violations of the Olympic spirit among their reasons for staying away. They did not mention revenge, nor the fact that their new premier, Konstantin Chernenko, had been very close to Leonid Brezhnev, the Soviet premier who had been embarrassed, in 1980, by an American-led boycott of the Moscow Games.

Most of the Soviet-bloc countries joined the boycott of Los Angeles, but still the 1984 Games would surely dwarf the 1932 Games, which attracted 37 countries and a total of 1,400 athletes.

Babe Didrikson won two gold medals and a silver for her efforts in 1932. Katharine Hepburn won an Oscar for hers.

Peter Ueberroth, president of the Los Angeles Olympic Organizing Committee.

David Wolper, the man who produced the epic television series *Roots,* put together the Opening Ceremony of the 1984 Olympic Games. The Olympic show made *Roots* look like a news brief. In a three-and-a-half-hour spectacular, Wolper managed to juggle a cast of at least 110,000, including a chorus of 1,000 voices, an all-star college marching band of 750, an orchestra of 100, 84 pianists playing 84 grand pianos that seemed to materialize out of nowhere, countless dancers and flagbearers, plus more than 7,000 marching athletes and officials and 92,655 spectators—some paying as much as $1,000 for a pair of $200 seats—who obediently followed directions in five languages to pull off a dazzling card stunt depicting the flags of all 140 participating nations.

On a smaller scale, Wolper employed one man who was capable of flying, who rocketed into the Coliseum wearing a jetpack on his back, and staged the entire production without using a single eagle. Wolper had planned to feature a bald eagle named Bomber, but a few days before the Opening Ceremony, Bomber died, a victim, at the age of 22, of either—the diagnoses varied—the pressure or the smog. Wolper's set was brightened considerably by banners of magenta, vermilion, lavender and pink, setting off the dyed green of the Coliseum grass, and his musical numbers included works by, in alphabetical order, Beethoven, Ellington, Gershwin, Woody Guthrie and Michael Jackson, one end of the musical scale to the other.

Wolper also worked into the act the president of the Los Angeles Olympic Organizing Committee, the president of the International Olympic Committee and the President of the United States. Nearly a dozen former Olympic champions played parts, too, most of them as walk-ons, one as the star. The result was a musical mystery, a blend of Busby Berkeley and Alfred Hitchcock, the suspense being not who-done-it but who's-going-to-do-it. Who's going to light the Olympic flame?

Peter Ueberroth encouraged the mystery by offering no more than hints to the identity of the person who would ignite the flame. He said it would definitely be a citizen of the United States, killing rumors that it might be Nadia Comaneci, the retired Romanian gymnast who was visiting Los Angeles as a guest of the LAOOC. But Ueberroth started new rumors by saying first that the torch would be lit by someone who was immediately recognizable, and then that it might be more than one person. Guesses ranged from the logical, Muhammad Ali or the 1980 U.S. hockey team, to the absurd, Michael Jackson.

Before the mystery was solved, two billion television viewers and the Coliseum crowd enjoyed singers, dancers, musicians and the traditional parade of the athletes. Greece, of course, marched first, followed by the 139 other teams. Some had names few Americans recognized—Benin, Bhutan, Djibouti and Lesotho, for instance. The flagbearer for the Fiji Islands wore a grass skirt, the athletes from Bahrain wore red and gold gowns and white headdresses, and the Bermudans, naturally, wore shorts. The U.S. team wore the latest version of Levi Strauss red, white and blue.

Ed Burke led the American team, the flag held firmly in one outstretched hand. He was 44, a hammer thrower, a veteran of the 1964 and 1968 Games who had retired in 1969. Burke had retired once before, in 1962, after an errant practice throw sailed through the window of his own car, cracked his wife Shirley in the side of the head and put her in the hospital. "I thought I'd killed her," Burke said. Shirley had to undergo plastic surgery; Burke, in shock, gave up the sport. But when Shirley recovered, she persuaded her husband to resume hammer throwing.

Twenty-five hundred pigeons take flight from the Coliseum.

Greece leads the parade of athletes and officials.

Hammer thrower Ed Burke carries the U.S. flag at the head of his team.

Juan Antonio Samaranch, president of the International Olympic Committee.

On the Coliseum television screen, President Ronald Reagan declares the 1984 Games open.

His second retirement was a lengthier one, lasting ten years, until his two daughters, watching a hammer thrower on television, expressed curiosity about the event. Ed offered to demonstrate—and found that his skills had barely faded. Again, Shirley Burke stepped in, assuring her husband that he could make a comeback in his 40's. At the age of 44, the former world-record holder was throwing farther than he had ever thrown before.

When Burke heard he had been selected to carry the American flag, he was as delighted as if he had won a gold medal. "I've already got what I came for," he said. "Walking into the Olympic Stadium and hearing the crowd roar, that's what does it for me."

The American delegation, more than 600 athletes and officials strong, marched into the Coliseum last, evoking the greatest roar, logically. But three other national teams also received special ovations: The People's Republic of China, for its first full-scale Olympic team, although a Chinese swimmer had competed in Helsinki in 1952; Yugoslavia, for its hospitality during the Winter Games; and Romania, the most enthusiastic reception accorded any visiting team, for its courage in standing up to the Soviet Union and refusing to join the boycott. Three nations—Bangladesh, Burma and Tonga—were each represented by only one athlete, and Denmark's marchers included one of the very few participants to have won gold medals in four separate Olympics, Paul Elvstrom, a yachting champion from 1948 through 1960, now, at the age of 56, sailing again, with his daughter as his deckhand. Elvstrom wasn't the oldest Olympian, however; Switzerland had a 66-year-old alternate yachtsman named Fredric Rochat, and France nominated a 70-year-old shooter named Roger Riard. The youngest entrant was a 12-year-old Belgian, Philip Cuelenaere, a coxswain.

After the parade, Peter V. Ueberroth, the president of the Los Angeles Olympic Organizing Committee, praised the athletes of the world, then introduced Juan Antonio Samaranch, who concluded his remarks, "God Bless America," then introduced Ronald Reagan, who could not resist rearranging his script, the 17 words he was limited to by Olympic mandate—built-in protection against politicians. Instead of saying, "I declare open the Olympic Games of Los Angeles, celebrating the XXIII Olympiad of the modern era," President Reagan said, "Celebrating the XXIII Olympiad of the modern era, I declare open the Olympic Games of Los Angeles." Earlier, meeting with the U.S. athletes at their headquarters in the Olympic Village at the University of Southern California, the President had offered a more familiar speech. "Do it for the Gipper," he said, recalling his movie role as George Gipp, the Notre Dame football star.

Then eleven Americans carried in the Olympic flag, eight of them former gold medalists, sprinter Wyomia Tyus, decathlete Bruce Jenner, swimmer John Naber, divers Sammy Lee and Pat McCormick, runner Billy Mills, shot putter Parry O'Brien and discus thrower Al Oerter, a gifted bunch representing almost every ethnic group from American Indian to Japanese American. They were joined by Mack Robinson, who won a silver medal in 1936 and was the older brother of baseball's Jackie Robinson; Richard Sandoval, a boxer who made the 1980 team that didn't get to compete in Moscow; and Bill Thorpe, Jr., the grandson of Jim Thorpe, the hero of the 1912 Olympics.

Then, after 2,500 pigeons flew off from the Coliseum, attention focused upon the tunnel leading to the track. Everyone wanted to see who would come in carrying the torch, running the anchor leg of a relay that had twisted across the United States for 82 days, the runners ranging from the mayor of Los Angeles to a member of the Hell's Angels, from a child to a 91-year-old former Olympian named Abel Kiviat, from a blind man to a baseball star.

Gina Hemphill, granddaughter of four-time gold medalist Jesse Owens, carries the Olympic torch into the Coliseum.

Soon a figure emerged, clearly a woman, but not immediately recognizable. She was, however, quickly identified as Gina Hemphill, 26 years old, the granddaughter of Jesse Owens, the American star of the 1936 Olympics, the man who had upstaged Hitler by winning four gold medals in track and field in Berlin.

Gina Hemphill had been one of the first two runners in the torch relay after the flame arrived in New York from Mount Olympia, sharing the first lap with Jim Thorpe's grandson Bill. In the Coliseum, Hemphill, often slowed to a walk by the packs of athletes who crowded in on her, managed to complete one lap around the track, then with a dazzling smile handed off the torch to the man who would light the flame, the same man who had handed her the torch for her run 82 days earlier, Rafer Johnson.

The American team, led by hurdler Edwin Moses and gymnastics judge Sharon Weber.

Johnson, the 1960 Olympic decathlon champion, trotted to the peristyle end of the Coliseum, raced up the permanent steps to the rim of the stadium, then continued up temporary steps that ascended almost magically, enabling him to reach a ledge high above the crowd but well below the bowl that would hold the Olympic flame. Johnson lifted the torch high to salute the crowd, then thrust the flame into a duct above his head. The flames licked through the duct, swirled brightly around five symbolic Olympic rings, then darted upward toward the bowl. Within seconds, the flame that would burn for the two weeks of the Games leaped dramatically to life.

The Coliseum roared. Johnson, the essence of athletic dignity, stood proud —and relieved. Only a few days earlier, he had injured his leg, raising the possibility that, on the brink of 50, he might not be able to make the tough climb to the flame. In case Johnson faltered, an understudy was already on the track, Bruce Jenner, the 1976 decathlon champion. But Johnson needed no help. He persevered, just as he had persevered in his exhausting decathlon duel with C.K. Yang in a darkened stadium in Rome in 1960.

Edwin Moses, the greatest 400-meter hurdler in the world, the 1976 Olympic champion, undefeated in his specialty since 1977, then recited the Olympic Oath on behalf of all the participating athletes. Moses stumbled over some of his words, but managed to complete the course.

Finally, as a young woman named Vicki McClure sang "Reach Out," a musical call for understanding and peace, the athletes of the world joined hands and began to sway and sing and dance. Bright smiles lit up some faces; tears of joy rolled down others. In his seat not far from the President of the United States, the Secretary of State, George Shultz, said softly, "Chernenko, eat your heart out."

DAY 2
SUNDAY, JULY 29th

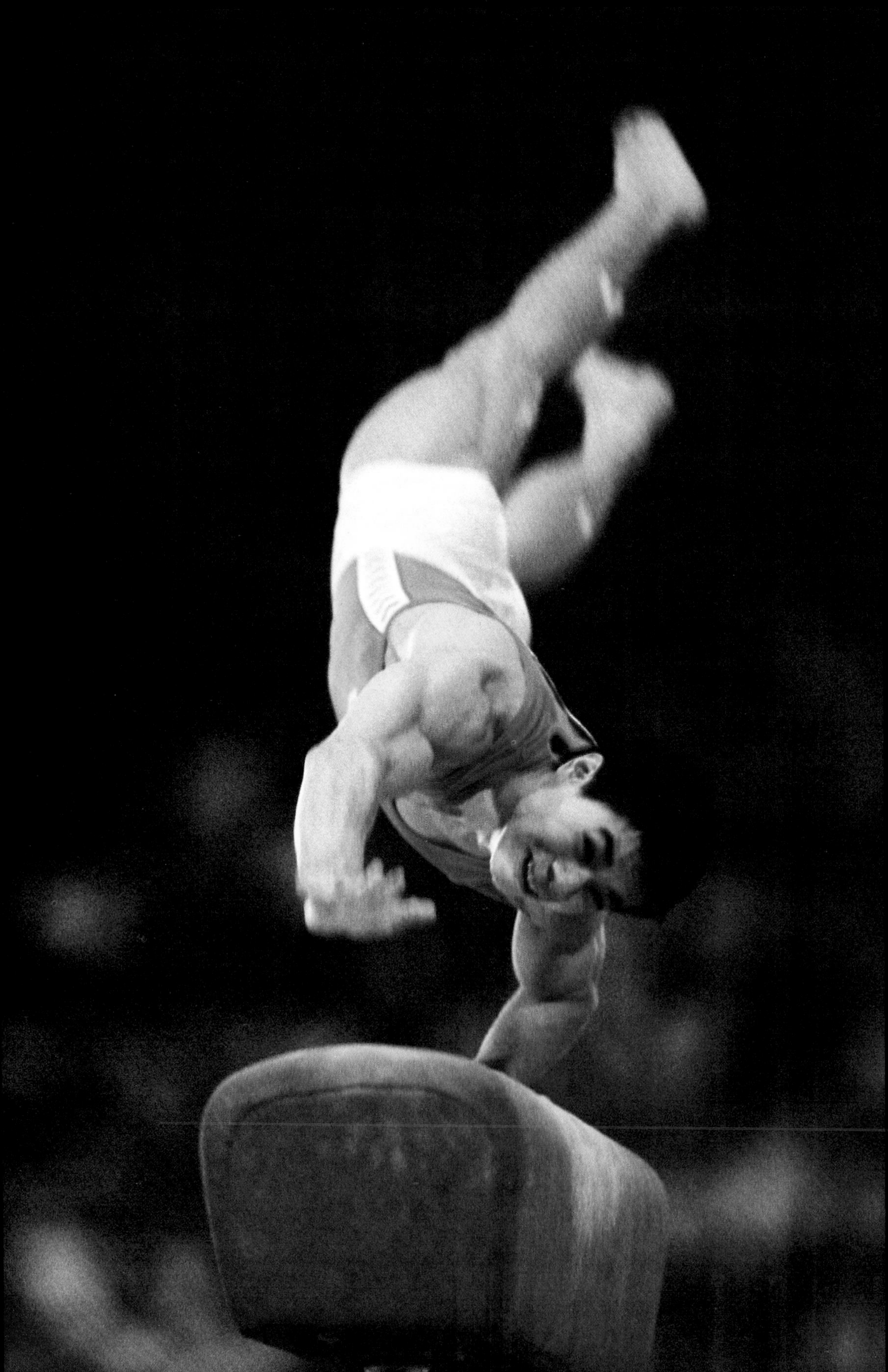

Mainland China—the People's Republic of China—with the largest population of any nation in the world, slightly more than one billion, had never won an Olympic medal, gold or a silver or a bronze, before the Los Angeles Games. In all fairness, the Chinese had not tried terribly hard. They had not competed in the Olympics before 1932, for sociological reasons, or after 1952, for political.

In the 1960s, while the United States and the Soviet Union waged sublimated warfare on the athletic fields, the Chinese Cultural Revolution spawned a revolutionary sports slogan: Friendship First, Competition Second. Late in the 1970s, a Chinese basketball team, touring the United States, saw no reason to play an overtime period after a game ended in a tie. Winning or losing, the Chinese suggested, was immaterial. Vince Lombardi would have been stunned by such dialectical immaterialism.

But by the 1980s, the Chinese had decided to compete athletically against the rest of the world—they sent winter teams to Lake Placid in 1980 and Sarajevo in 1984, mainly for the experience—and by 1984, the Chinese had a world-record holder in track and field, the high jumper Zhu Jianhua, plus the world's best team in men's gymnastics and world-class performers in diving, shooting, weightlifting and women's volleyball.

The Chinese sent 213 athletes to Los Angeles, the ninth-largest team at the Games, and each one knew that if he won a gold medal, he would be well rewarded, reportedly with a $2,000 prize. The Chinese, adjusting to international ways, called the prizes "scholarships." "If we win ten gold medals," said Lu Jingdong, the assistant chief of the Chinese mission, "I'll be a happy man." His team was going to make Lu a very happy man.

THE GOLD MEDALISTS

SWIMMING

MEN'S 200-METER FREESTYLE
  MICHAEL GROSS, WEST GERMANY

MEN'S 100-METER BREASTSTROKE
  STEVE LUNDQUIST, USA

WOMEN'S 100-METER FREESTYLE
  CARRIE STEINSEIFER, USA
  NANCY HOGSHEAD, USA (Dead Heat)

WOMEN'S 400-METER INDIVIDUAL MEDLEY
  TRACY CAULKINS, USA

SHOOTING

MEN'S FREE PISTOL
  XU HAIFENG, CHINA

WOMEN'S SPORT PISTOL
  LINDA THOM, CANADA

CYCLING

MEN'S INDIVIDUAL ROAD RACE
  ALEXI GREWAL, USA

WOMEN'S INDIVIDUAL ROAD RACE
  CONNIE CARPENTER-PHINNEY, USA

WEIGHTLIFTING

52 KILOGRAMS
  ZENG GUOQIANG, CHINA

SHOOTING

The first gold medalist, China's Xu Haifeng (left), winner of the men's free pistol.

Xu Haifeng of the People's Republic of China, who as a youngster sharpened his shooting eye by knocking off birds with a slingshot, became the first gold medalist of the 1984 Summer Games and the first in the history of his country by winning the men's free pistol championship. The tall, slender marksman shared the honor of being the first Chinese medalist with Wang Yifu, the national free pistol champion, who, upset by Xu, settled for an Olympic bronze.

The historic significance of Xu's victory was not lost upon Juan Antonio Samaranch and Peter Ueberroth, both of whom attended the medal ceremony.

CYCLING

Connie Carpenter-Phinney leads in the women's 49-mile cycling road race (top). Gold medalist Carpenter-Phinney (bottom).

A pair of American cyclists, Connie Carpenter-Phinney and her husband, Davis Phinney, had a chance to make history. Three chances, in fact. She was trying to win the first Olympic cycling event for women ever, a 49-mile road race, and he was trying, in the men's 118-mile road race, to become the first American man to win any kind of cycling medal since 1912, the first to win a cycling gold since 1904. Together, the Phinneys were trying to become the first husband-and-wife team to win gold medals in separate Olympic events since Czechoslovakia's Emil Zatopek, in the distance runs, and his wife, Dana, in the javelin, brought home four gold medals between them in 1952. No American couple had ever won separate championships.

The women's race was run first, in the morning, on the streets of Mission Viejo, and six women soon broke away from the rest of the field, the leaders including Connie Carpenter-Phinney, who had represented the U.S. in speed skating in the 1972 Games, and Rebecca Twigg, a 21-year-old former biology major at the University of Washington. Over the last 200 meters, the two Americans shared the lead, sprinting wheel to wheel until, with a closing burst, Carpenter-Phinney hit the finish line half a wheel-length in front, a difference of inches after more than two hours of pedaling.

The two women, supposedly unfriendly rivals, clasped hands, and Carpenter-Phinney said that, at 27, she had completed "the best race of my life, the last race of my life." An Olympic champion at last, she would now be content to concentrate on her husband's cycling career.

Davis Phinney led for a good part of the men's race, but after nearly five hours of facing punishing hills and 92° heat, he faded, eventually to fifth place, and the men's race became a duel between another American, Alexi Grewal, and a Canadian, Steve Bauer. Grewal almost missed the Olympics. Two weeks earlier, he was suspended from cycling for 30 days because he failed a drug test. To combat asthma, unable to get his usual medication, Grewal had taken a Chinese herbal tablet, with its label written in Chinese. The tablet had contained traces of a banned substance. Grewal appealed the suspension, explained the situation and was reinstated only six days before the road race. "I don't think I'll ever take a Chinese herb again," he said.

On the last lap of the demanding men's race, Grewal looked like he needed more than herbs to survive. He was obviously tiring, and the lead he had built up over Bauer was quickly vanishing. But somehow Grewal, a skinny 6-foot-3 23-year-old, summoned fresh strength just before the finish and dashed home ahead of Bauer, not quite so dramatic a victory as Carpenter-Phinney's, but a similarly exciting one. The two tight finishes, perfect for television, lifted American cycling, at least for a day, out of obscurity.

Alexi Grewal of the U.S. victoriously crossing the finish line of the men's 118-mile cycling race.

BOXING

Mark Breland went into the Olympic boxing championships with a brilliant record, 104 victories in 105 fights, and an even better reputation. Experts proclaimed him the best amateur boxer in the world, and Thomas Hearns, one of the best professionals in the world, said Breland was the best welterweight alive, amateur or professional. Breland had already turned down million-dollar offers to turn pro. He wanted gold from the Olympics first.

He was the first American to fight in the 1984 Games, and he ran into a Canadian named Wayne Gordon, who showed little respect for his reputation. Midway through the second round, Gordon landed a right to the jaw that staggered Breland and prompted a standing eight-count. But the 6-foot-3 147-pounder from the Bedford-Stuyvesant section of Brooklyn had built up a big lead in the first round, added to his margin in the third round and escaped with a unanimous decision. Breland said afterward that a former Olympic champion had advised him to build up a comfortable lead in the first round. The advice came from Muhammad Ali.

American Mark Breland, (left), outpointing Wayne Gordon of Canada in a first-round 147-pound bout.

More than 100 miles south of Los Angeles, at their training base on the outskirts of San Diego, two members of the British track and field team, key figures in two of the most glamorous matchups in the Games, held a news conference, an opportunity for one to demonstrate his glibness, the other to demonstrate her shyness.

Daley Thompson, bidding to become the second man in Olympic history to win the decathlon for the second time, spoke of his chief rival, West Germany's Juergen Hingsen. Six-foot-seven and 235 pounds, Hingsen held the world record in the decathlon, but in seven face-to-face confrontations had never defeated Thompson. "I understand Juergen has promised the German people he's bringing home the gold medal," Thompson said, "and I think there's only two ways he's going to do that. He's either going to steal mine—or do another event."

Pressed further about his opponent, Thompson feigned dismay. "All these questions about Juergen," he said, "are giving me a headache." Then he pulled off his hat to reveal a head wrapped in bandages, and when the reporters, appreciating his joke, laughed, Thompson absolutely beamed.

Zola Budd, the other star of the news conference, barely smiled. She was the shy 18-year-old South African whose barefoot middle-distance running had excited the world. To become eligible for the Olympics, she had moved from outcast South Africa to England and, because her grandfather was born in the United Kingdom, had been granted immediate British citizenship. Budd's switch stirred up both controversy and anticipation, anticipation of a 3,000-meter Olympic duel with the world champion, Mary Decker of the United States. The reporters were told that Budd would not speak of political matters or of sociological matters, but she would speak of the Olympic race. "I think of it as a race against people, not just Mary Decker," Budd said softly, almost inaudibly. She also said that Mary Decker was her hero. In South Africa, she kept Mary Decker's picture over her bed.

GYMNASTICS

The Chinese men were strongly favored to win the team championship in gymnastics, and when their star, Li Ning, earned a pair of early 10's in the compulsory exercises, the world champions moved smartly into the lead. But before the first day of the two-day competition ended, Li Ning made a costly slip, and a pair of UCLA gymnasts, competing in their home gym, each turned in a 10—Mitch Gaylord on the parallel bars, the first 10 ever for an American gymnast in the Olympics, and Peter Vidmar on the pommel horse. The U.S., to the amazement and delight of the Pauley Pavilion crowd, had taken over first place. In the individual all-around standings, Vidmar was tied for first with Koji Gushiken, a Japanese. Vidmar and his teammates would now have to wait two days to complete their event, a modest wait considering that the U.S., in 52 years, had won only one medal in gymnastics, a bronze in 1976.

Li Ning on the pommel horse.

Mitch Gaylord of the U.S. on the parallel bars.

BASKETBALL

The Chinese men lived up to expectations in their opening basketball game. They lost, convincingly, to the magnificent U.S. team selected and molded by Bobby Knight, the resident genius at Indiana University, and his gifted staff. The score was 97–49, and in the true spirit of Friendship First, Competition Second, the Chinese did not seem discouraged by their defeat. In fact, the players smiled and laughed throughout the game, every time they heard the public-address announcer mishandle one of their names.

SOCCER

First-round football games—or soccer games, as most Americans called them—were played at four different sites around the country, in Annapolis, Cambridge, Palo Alto and Pasadena. At Stanford Stadium in Palo Alto, 78,265 people turned out to watch two of the weaker Olympic teams, Costa Rica and the United States. The largest crowd ever to see a soccer game in the United States witnessed a rare sight, a U.S. soccer victory, 3–0, its first in the Olympics in 60 years. In 1924, the U.S. beat Estonia, 1–0.

WEIGHTLIFTING

The People's Republic of China started its day with a gold medal—and ended its day with another, this one in weightlifting, in the flyweight division. Zeng Guoqiang earned the gold, and Zhou Peishun took the silver, giving the People's Republic, on the first competitive day of the 1984 Olympics, a better showing than any other country in the world, except the United States.

SWIMMING

Steve Lundquist congratulated by teammate John Moffet (in water) after the 100-meter breaststroke.

America's swimmers were, by the standards of their sport, an elderly lot, some of them actually of voting age, a legacy of the 1980 boycott. Teenagers deprived of a chance to compete for a medal in Moscow stuck to their sport, or returned to it, to compete in Los Angeles. Nancy Hogshead, 22, a Floridian who had given up swimming for sixteen months between Olympics, and her Olympic roommate, Carrie Steinseifer, 16, a Californian, spent the morning of their 100-meter freestyle race watching The Three Stooges on television together, then spent the evening swimming together, precisely together, each touching the wall at the same time, the first dead heat in Olympic swimming history, giving the United States two gold medals in one event. "This whole team is really close," Hogshead said.

In the men's 100-meter breaststroke, the U.S. had another closely matched pair, 23-year-old Steve Lundquist and 20-year-old John Moffet, who had taken turns setting the world record in the event. But in the preliminaries, Moffet tore a thigh muscle and, despite massages, ice packs and a shot of Xylocaine, feared he would be unable to swim his best in the final. "If something goes wrong with my leg," Moffet said to Lundquist before the start, "get the gold for the USA." Lundquist got the gold—and regained the world record in the process. Moffet swam in obvious pain, and only courage lifted him to fifth place. "I kind of feel nine years were put down the drain," said the Stanford star.

After seven years of brilliant swimming, seven years in which she established 66 American or world records and earned 48 national and 12 collegiate titles, Tracy Caulkins, at the age of 21, finally made her Olympic debut, a spectacular debut in the 400-meter individual medley. She turned in the second-fastest time in history, set an American record and finished fully 15 meters ahead of her nearest rival. Caulkins was, once again, the queen of the pool.

Michael Gross of West Germany was the king. A slender 6-foot-7, 20-year-old, nicknamed The Albatross because of his huge 89-inch arm-span, Gross climaxed the first day of swimming by setting a world record in the men's 200-meter freestyle for the fourth time in 14 months, earning a gold medal and the highest of praise from John Naber, the best swimmer in the 1976 Games. "I think Gross is the best swimmer ever," said Naber. "If he were an American, he could win three relays plus four other golds. He's better than Mark Spitz."

Steve Lundquist (top), setting a world record in the 100-meter breaststroke, Tracy Caulkins (middle) on the butterfly leg of her winning 400-meter individual medley and the Albatross, Michael Gross (bottom) of West Germany, swimming away with the 200-meter freestyle.

DAY 3
MONDAY, JULY 30th

During the nine years coach Arie Selinger shaped the United States women's volleyball team, drove it toward the Olympics, changed it from an international also-ran to a world power, his critics called him egotistical, insensitive, arrogant and tyrannical, which meant, on the whole, they didn't like him. His players called him Abba, which meant on the whole they did.

Abba is the Hebrew word for "father," and Selinger, a Polish-born Israeli who took over the U.S. team in 1975, certainly was a stern father. He demanded that his players practice eight hours a day, six days a week, month after month after month. He demanded that they give up school, jobs, social life, even, in one player's case, her engagement. He demanded that they risk shoulders, elbows and knees, diving at the floor, saving shot after shot after shot.

Asked if Selinger, like a National Football League coach, put his players through two-a-day drills, the team's star, Flo Hyman, who had been with Arie from the beginning, even through the boycott, laughed and said, "No. Just one a day. All day." But Hyman thrived on Selinger's demands. "Pushing yourself over the barrier is a habit," she said.

In 1982, Selinger's women finished third in the world championships, but he wasn't satisfied. He added players, shifted players and drove the women harder. Some who left the team told reporters they couldn't stand the regimentation, the discipline. One said playing for Selinger was like being in a concentration camp, an especially cruel image. Selinger spent three years of his childhood in a concentration camp. His father was killed at Auschwitz. He became an Israeli commando. "I am not trying to ruin people," Selinger said. "I am trying to make an Olympic gold medal team."

Cheryl Miller, driving for a lay-up against Yugoslavia.

A funny thing happened on the way to the Forum and the Los Angeles Memorial Sports Arena and Pauley Pavilion: Hardly anyone got into a traffic jam. Even at rush hour on the first weekday of the Games, the tie-ups predicted by pessimists failed to materialize. Why?

1. Fewer tourists than anticipated: The non-Olympic attractions in Southern California, such as Disneyland, suffered particularly.

2. Fewer local people than antici-pated: Many had elected to take their vacations during the Olympics and to flee from the area.

3. Both tourists and local people leaning heavily on public transpor-tation set up for the Olympics.

The result was that even though attendance at the Games was living up to or exceeding expectations, traffic was lighter than usual. As an extra bonus, smog levels had dropped below normal, too.

Miller measuring a foul shot.

BASKETBALL

A lively discussion among American teammates (left to right) Kim Mulkey, Cheryl Miller and Pam McGee.

The game between the U.S. women's basketball team and Yugoslavia started at nine o'clock in the morning, and half an hour later, the Ameri-cans woke up. Cheryl Miller sounded the alarm when her team, an overwhelming favorite, trailed by two points with a little more than four minutes to play in the first half. "I just knew we had to start running," said the 6-foot-1 All-American from the University of Southern California. "I knew I had to go to the boards, get a key steal, do anything to get something started."

Miller did everything: went to the boards, got a key steal, hit a twisting jump shot, passed, ran, defended and cheered. She scored ten points before halftime, and so did her teammates. Yugoslavia managed only four, and the two-point deficit turned into a 14-point U.S. lead. At the intermission, Miller had 17 points, seven rebounds, five assists, three steals and a blocked shot. "She is," said Jasmina Perazic, the star of the Yugoslav team, "how do you say, flashy?"

Wide awake, the Americans doubled their margin to 28 points at the end of their opening game. "I *am* a morning person," said Cheryl Miller.

SHOOTING

Like many teams and several individual athletes, the United States shooting team had its own sports psychologist in Los Angeles. His name was Ed Etzel, a candidate for a Ph.D. in psychology and an instructor in sports psychology at the University of West Virginia, and he understood the pressures shooters faced unusually well. He was a shooter on the Olympic team.

Under pressure, in the U.S. Olympic trials, Etzel had shot a perfect 600 with the small-bore rifle, prone position, 60 straight bull's-eyes, matching the world record.

Etzel responded almost as well to the pressure of the Olympics. "When it would bother me," he said, "I would breathe very slowly. Then I would ask myself, rationally, 'What's the worst that could happen? I shoot a nine?'"

The worst happened—once. Etzel shot one nine and 59 bull's-eyes, which gave him a score of 599, tying the Olympic record, and gave him, at the age of 31, a gold medal.

BOXING

Paul Gonzales came out of the *barrio* of East Los Angeles, a Mexican-American, wiry and tough. When he was 12, a member of a rival gang fired shotgun pellets into Gonzales' head. His cousin plucked them out with a pair of tweezers. A ghetto cop named Al Stankie persuaded Gonzales to use his toughness in the ring, and by the time he was 20, 5-foot-9 and only 106 pounds, he was a light-flyweight—with a punch. He had lost only five times in almost 200 amateur bouts, and he had knocked out 140 opponents, going into the Olympics.

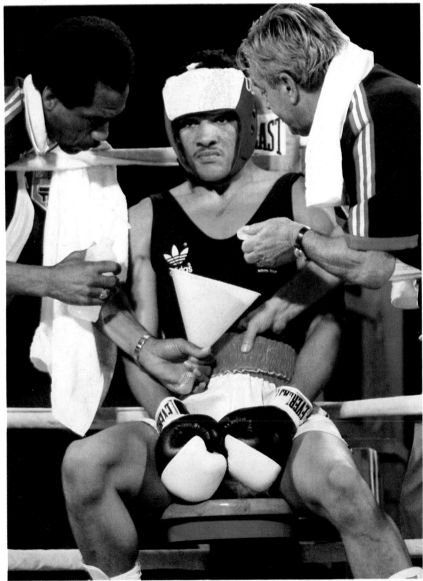

Paul Gonzales getting between-rounds advice from Roosevelt Sanders and Pat Nappi.

In the first round, Gonzales faced, by random draw, probably his sternest opponent, a Korean named Kim Kwang-Sun, who didn't know how to back up and wasn't supposed to lose. But Gonzales knocked Kim down with a right early in the first round, then staggered him with another right for a standing eight-count later in the round. Kim fought back and punished Gonzales in the second round, and only a bizarre move by Gonzales—clinching, he wrestled off Kim's headgear and got a needed rest when the referee stopped the action to replace the protective helmet—saved him from worse punishment. Gonzales, jabbing smartly, clearly won the third round—and a unanimous decision.

The fight was held in the Los Angeles Memorial Sports Arena, a ten-minute drive from the *barrio*. "I want to win the gold not just for myself," Gonzales said, "but for kids like me who are always told, 'You're nothing.'"

SWIMMING

The men on the American swimming team were starting to feel like the shipmates of Coleridge's Ancient Mariner. The sight of the Albatross was downright depressing. Swimming's Albatross, Michael Gross of West Germany, picked up exactly where he had left off the night before, setting a world record and winning a gold medal, his second of the Games, in the 100-meter butterfly, a race too short to be one of his stronger events. Gross came from behind and upset the world-record holder, Pablo Morales of the United States. "I swam my best time," said Morales, who also bettered the record, "and got beat by a great athlete."

The Albatross, Michael Gross, winning the 100-meter butterfly.

Cynthia Woodhead (silver medal) and Mary Wayte (gold) enjoying their success after the 200-meter freestyle.

Gross reacted far more enthusiastically to winning the butterfly than the earlier freestyle. "This is absolutely unbelievable," Gross said, after he leaped out of the pool. "I concentrated on the last ten meters of the race, since I thought Morales would die at that point, which he did."

In the women's 200-meter freestyle, Mary Wayte of the U.S. won the gold medal, and teammate Cynthia Woodhead the silver. Four years earlier, Woodhead had qualified for four individual events and two relays in Moscow, but in 1984 she had earned only one shot at a medal. Still, she showed no trace of bitterness, merely delight with winning the silver. "I'm as happy as if I had won the gold," she said.

In the men's 400-meter individual medley, Canada won its first swimming gold medal in 72 years. Although the champion, Alex Baumann, who broke his own world record, had come to Canada by a most circuitous route—from Czechoslovakia, where he was born, to New Zealand to Ontario—he obviously considered himself a Canadian. He had a maple leaf tattooed on his chest.

In the women's 200-meter breaststroke, Canada took its first swimming gold medal in 23 minutes. Pumped up by the strains of "O Canada!"—played to mark Baumann's triumph—Anne Ottenbrite scored the first victory ever for a Canadian woman swimmer.

Near the finish of the 800-meter freestyle relay, Bruce Hayes, bottom, overtaking Michael Gross for a U.S. gold medal.

The day's final event was the men's 800-meter freestyle relay, an emotional moment for at least one American swimmer, Jeff Float, a University of Southern California graduate who was left almost totally deaf by a child-hood attack of viral meningitis. "I broke down and cried before the race when I saw my friends and family in the stands," Float said.

He recovered in time to swim the third leg for the U.S., and when he finished his 200 meters, he turned over an eight-foot lead to Bruce Hayes, who had to face the Albatross on the anchor leg. One hundred meters later, Gross was even with Hayes, and with 50 meters to go, Gross was in front by a foot and a half, and Hayes' chances seemed as slim as, say, the 6-foot-7 186-pound German. But Hayes refused to give up, caught Gross with his last few strokes and touched the wall, in front by perhaps three inches. If Gross needed any consolation to go with his silver medal, he had swum the final 200 meters in 1:46.89, the fastest leg in history.

The cheers that greeted the American quartet that turned back the Albatross were thunderous, so loud that Jeff Float, who could feel the vibrations and who had a sense of humor, said, "The noise was deafening."

Bruce Hayes is congratulated by his American teammates after he came from behind to defeat Michael Gross in the 800-meter freestyle relay.

Start of the woman's 200-meter freestyle: Cynthia Woodhead, bottom, Mary Wayte, middle.

VOLLEYBALL

Arie Selinger's U.S. women's volleyball team began its quest for a gold medal with a solid, but not spectacular, victory over West Germany, 17–15, 15–8, 15–10. The two teams most likely to challenge the U.S. for the gold medal also had tougher times than expected, China beating Brazil and Japan beating South Korea, a moral victory for the South Koreans, who became the first team—except for the Soviet Union—to win even one game from Japan in Olympic competition. "The pressure's on," Selinger said. "We were all nervous. And the three teams that didn't have much to lose all played very well. Hopefully, the more we play, the more we'll loosen up."

GYMNASTICS

Not everyone raved about the Opening Ceremony. Mark Spitz felt he should have been one of the former gold medalists carrying the Olympic flag. "It's the biggest blow I've ever had in my life," Spitz said. "I'm sad. I'm humiliated, to be honest, not to be considered." In 1972, in Munich, swimmer Spitz, a native Californian, won seven gold medals, a record for one Olympics. In 1984, in Los Angeles, working as an ABC swimming commentator, Spitz watched the Opening Ceremony from the stands.

Mark Spitz.

After the early session of team competition in women's gymnastics—a session featuring the U.S. team—the American head coach, Don Peters, was livid. He called the judging "abominable," filed four fruitless protests and implied that one of the judges, a Romanian named Julia Roterescu, should have been removed from her post.

But after the late session of the compulsory exercises—a session featuring the Romanian team—Peters had mellowed. "The judges did a good job of trying to hold the scores in line," he said. "I'm relieved. I thought we'd lose more ground than we did."

Peters's mood had shifted noticeably because his second-place team, going into the optional exercises two days later, trailed favored Romania by less than half a point, 196.15 to 195.70. "It'll be a dogfight now," Peters said.

In the afternoon, two incidents in particular infuriated the Americans: a less-than-perfect score for Mary Lou Retton for her floor exercise and a less-than-decent score for Tracee Talavera on the balance beam.

When Retton, a sturdy 4-foot-9 16-year-old from West Virginia, completed her floor exercise, the crowd chanted, "Ten, ten, ten," and Retton herself said, "I thought it was the best floor exercise I ever did." But the judges gave her a score of 9.95, brilliant yet disappointing.

"With that fantastic tumbling, and no errors at all, Mary Lou deserved a ten," said her personal coach, Bela Karolyi, the man who had nurtured Nadia Comaneci before leaving his native Romania.

When Talavera completed her performance on the balance beam, every judge awarded her scores ranging from 9.60 to 9.80, except the Romanian judge, Roterescu, who gave her a 9.40. "We got hammered," Peters said.

In the evening, with both Retton and Comaneci watching from the stands, Ecaterina Szabo of Romania received a 10 for her floor exercise, the only perfect score of the day. "In my opinion," said Zhou Jichuan, coach of the Chinese women's team, "the Romanian girl was only one of several gymnasts who did the same routine, all of them perfect. But she was the only one who got a ten."

The battle for the individual all-around championship was even closer than the team competition. Szabo and her teammate, Lavinia Agache, shared the lead, only .05 of a point ahead of Retton, who was seeking to become the first American woman to win an Olympic individual medal of any kind in gymnastics.

Mary Lou Retton (right) performing the vault.

They were going to play baseball in Dodger Stadium and football in the Rose Bowl, and if that didn't make the 1984 Olympics sound like an American festival, nothing did. But the games being played in Dodger Stadium were only Olympic "demonstrations," and the game being played in the Rose Bowl was not American-style football, but rest-of-the-world-style football, the sport Americans historically called "soccer." Still, it seemed a nice touch that America's national pastime and the world's favorite pastime were being offered head-to-head in handsome stadia not many miles apart.

Baseball had been exhibited at the Olympics before—during the first modern Olympics, in fact, in Athens in 1896, a group of American athletes organized a pick-up game, and after the rules were explained, Prince George of Greece pitched for one team and Crown Prince Constantine caught—but never on such a grand scale. Seven countries sent teams to challenge the U.S. in Los Angeles. The field included Chinese Taipei, commonly called Taiwan, which had several players who, in younger years, had starred on championship teams at the Little League World Series in Williamsport, Pa.; Italy, which, even more than the Italian hockey team in Sarajevo, featured players of Italian descent who were born in the U.S.; and Nicaragua, whose Sandinista government considered the baseball diamond a mock battlefield for its grudges against the U.S.

The United States, even though its players were young and, technically, amateur, stood a good chance of winning the non-Olympic gold medal in baseball, a far better chance than it had of succeeding, with a predominantly professional team, in soccer. The last time the U.S. qualified for an Olympic soccer tournament, in Munich in 1972, the Americans played three games, lost three and were outscored, ten goals to none.

THE GOLD MEDALISTS

SWIMMING
MEN'S 100-METER FREESTYLE
  ROWDY GAINES, USA
MEN'S 200-METER BACKSTROKE
  RICK CAREY, USA
WOMEN'S 400-METER FREESTYLE
  TIFFANY COHEN, USA
WOMEN'S 100-METER BACKSTROKE
  THERESA ANDREWS, USA
WOMEN'S 400-METER FREESTYLE RELAY
  USA

SHOOTING
TRAP
  LUCIANO GIOVANNETTI, ITALY
RUNNING GAME TARGET
  LI YUWEI, CHINA
WOMEN'S AIR RIFLE
  PAT SPURGIN, USA

GYMNASTICS
MEN'S TEAM
  USA

WEIGHTLIFTING
60 KILOGRAMS
  CHEN WEQIANG, CHINA

SHOOTING

Three shooting champions were crowned, and while one, Luciano Giovannetti of Italy, in trap shooting, was the first 1980 gold medalist to repeat, the other two were teenagers, 19-year-old Li Yuwei of the People's Republic of China, in the running game target, and 18-year-old Pat Spurgin of Billings, Montana, in a new event, the air rifle for women.

BASKETBALL

Australia might have won in cricket, and Canada in ice hockey, but since the schedule called for basketball, neither the Australian women nor the Canadian men came close to threatening the United States. The American men beat Canada by 21 points, and the American women beat Australia by 34, prompting the coach of the Canadian men, Jack Donahue, to call the U.S. men "the best basketball team I've ever seen," and the coach of the Australian women, Brendan Flynn, to call the U.S. women "the greatest women's team I've ever seen." With the Russians away, neither "the best" nor "the greatest" seemed likely to be challenged in L.A.

BOXING

A pair of American boxers won their opening bouts, Frank Tate by decision and Steve McCrory by default, but the most heated action was in the audience, with Emanuel Steward, who trained both fighters at the Kronk Gym in Detroit, storming out of the arena because he was, at first, denied a ringside seat. Steward eventually came back, but he wasn't happy, not with Pat Nappi, the coach of the U.S. team, nor with Josephine Abercrombie, a Texas boxing promoter whose $150,000 gift to the U.S. Amateur Boxing Foundation may have helped her get her ringside seat.

DECATHLON

For three hours, Juergen Hingsen drove himself through a workout at the University of California at Irvine, exercising, jogging, sprinting, skipping rope, honing his magnificent body for his decathlon showdown with Daley Thompson, only eight days away. Then he relaxed and laughed when he was told what Thompson had said about his chances of winning a gold medal. "Daley is the better talker," Hingsen said. "I am the better athlete."

Juergen Hingsen narrowly leading (and narrowly defeating) Daley Thompson in the 110-meter hurdles in the decathlon at the '83 World Championships.

The army of security personnel assigned to the Olympics, 20,000 men and women, at a cost close to $100 million, represented local police, the FBI, the Department of Defense and volunteers, a total of 50 different jurisdictions. Remarkably, with very little open display of weapons, the system seemed to be working smoothly, except for an occasional case of excessive zealousness. When a coach working with sprinters on the track at the University of Southern California Village took out a starting pistol, a security officer tackled him and wrestled him to the ground. When someone dropped a purse outside the UCLA Village, the area was cleared and the bomb squad summoned—to remove gingerly from the purse a hairbrush, a wallet and an Olympic program. Earlier, officers had lifted a paraplegic archer out of her wheelchair, despite her protestations, and searched the wheelchair. The LAOOC apologized to the archer.

Wayman Tisdale scoring a lay-up against Canada.

SWIMMING

A victory salute by Rowdy Gaines of the U.S. after the 100-meter freestyle.

Michael Gross did not swim, and with that Albatross off their necks, the Americans owned the pool. First, an 18-year-old Californian named Tiffany Cohen won the women's 400-meter freestyle in the second-fastest time in history. Then, in the men's 100-meter freestyle, an old man by swimming standards, Ambrose Gaines IV, known, at the age of 25, as Rowdy, got off to a splendid start, so splendid the Australians officially protested, to no avail, and an American teammate, Mike Heath, unofficially protested, "Several of us got robbed."

But Gaines, who was robbed of a chance to win as many as five gold medals in 1980, got away clean and won his first gold medal of 1984, setting an Olympic record for the event and for exuberance. He fired his fist in the air as soon as he knew he had won. "We all went through hell in eighty," Gaines said, "but this makes it all worth it."

In the only major surprise of the day, Theresa Andrews, a 21-year-old from Maryland, one of twelve children of a retired Navy captain, won the women's 100-meter backstroke, then handed the gold medal to her 20-year-old brother Dan, who had watched the race from poolside, in a wheelchair. A year earlier, riding on his bicycle, Dan Andrews had been struck by a car, and his legs paralyzed.

Against a background of tall blond Californians, Rick Carey, a 5-foot-11 black-haired New Yorker, did not look like a swimmer—until he got in the water. Then, at 21, Carey was the world's best in the backstroke. But when he won the Olympic 200-meter championship, in a time he considered mediocre, more than a second-and a half off his own world record, he hung his head as if he had lost. The second- and third-place finishers were delighted. Carey was depressed. A perfectionist, the John McEnroe of his sport, Carey didn't show even a hint of the joy Rowdy Gaines displayed. "I just feel that it's a pretty slow time," Carey said. "I can do that in a workout. I don't find it the least bit satisfying. It just hurts." Not even the fact that his hometown, Mt. Kisco, New York, had the previous night renamed the street on which he lived "Rick Carey Lane" could lift the swimmer's dark mood.

At the opposite extreme, for the second time in three days, Nancy Hogshead and Carrie Steinseifer were happy to win gold medals in the same event, and this time two other Americans, Jenna Johnson and Dara Torres, the remaining members of the women's 400-meter freestyle relay team, shared the pleasure. "This gold was more fun because I have three people to share it with," said Hogshead. She paused, then added, "Not that I was alone the first time."

Royalty reigned in Los Angeles during the Olympics, and many of the princes and princesses in attendance also enjoyed less regal titles: Princess Anne was president of the British Olympic Association, and her father, Prince Philip, president of the International Equestrian Federation. The exiled King Constantine of Greece was a judge in yachting (and a former gold medalist), and Prince Albert led Monaco's Olympic delegation. Prince Faisal, son of King Fahd, outranked a handful of Saudi Arabian princes at the Games, and when he craved royal company, the King and Queen of Sweden, the Sheik of Kuwait, the Grand Duke of Luxembourg and Princess Nora of Liechtenstein were also around.

Start of the women's 100-meter backstroke (top). Tiffany Cohen (bottom), on the way to a gold medal in the women's 400-meter freestyle.

Rick Carey's start in the 200-meter backstroke.

WRESTLING

When an American, Steve Fraser, upset Frank Andersson of Sweden, the three-time world champion in the 198-pound class, then defeated Greece's George Pozidis, he advanced to the semifinal round of the Greco-Roman wrestling tournament, clinching the first Greco-Roman medal ever for the United States.

GYMNASTICS

It wasn't quite a miracle on mats. It wasn't quite the impossible dream that the ice hockey team achieved in 1980. But it was, once again, a stunning moment, a crowd and a team swept together on waves of patriotism and pride. This time, instead of Eruzione and Craig, it was a bunch of lithe and limber young men, the best gymnasts ever to represent the U.S.

Many of the spectators in Pauley Pavilion actually understood gymnastics and understood the magnitude of the American victory over the world champions from the People's Republic of China. They waved flags and cheered and cried, and the athletes responded in kind. Tears slid down Peter Vidmar's face, and Bart Conner's. Gold medals hung from their necks.

America's team gold medalists in gymnastics: left to right, Tim Daggett, Scott Johnson, Mitch Gaylord, James Hartung, Peter Vidmar, Bart Conner.

The men's team victory, by an Olympic record score of 591.40 to 590.80, was a team effort. Tim Daggett on the horizontal bar, Mitch Gaylord on the rings and Conner, the survivor from 1980, on the parallel bars all earned 10's, matching three 10's for the Chinese, and Vidmar ranked so consistently high he took the lead in the individual all-around standings.

Still, near the end, there was a precarious moment, a critical moment. Mitch Gaylord faced the horizontal bar needing only a 9.80 to ensure an American victory. All he had to do was a safe, smooth routine. But he wanted to go for the spectacular. He wanted to perform the Gaylord II, a maneuver blending a one-and-a-half somersault with a half twist, a maneuver so risky no one else had ever tried it in competition.

Mitch performed the Gaylord II successfully about half the time in practice; in the week leading up to the Olympics, he had improved his success rate to 75 percent. But if he failed, his score would plummet, and his team could lose. He stole a glance at the American coach, Abie Grossfeld. "He was looking at me strangely," Gaylord said. "I think he wanted to come over and tell me not to do it."

"There was no way I should have let him do it," said Grossfeld later.

But Grossfeld did not stop Gaylord. "I guess I just knew how bad he wanted it," the coach said.

Gaylord went for the Gaylord II, and caught it, and when he did, he earned himself a score of 9.95, and the gold medal belonged for certain to the United States. The gymnasts fell upon each other, hugging and smiling. "We made history for the U.S. today," Vidmar said, and Gaylord added, "It's a whole new era for gymnastics in the United States."

The LAOOC confirmed a report that it had paid $60,000, and the IOC another $60,000, toward the $180,000 transportation costs of the Romanian Olympic team. Originally, Romania had planned to share a chartered plane with another Eastern European nation. But when the other country withdrew, the LAOOC and the IOC, eager to have the Romanians attend, agreed to ease their financial burden.

The LAOOC also had agreed to pay $290,000 for a chartered flight that brought 120 athletes and coaches from needy African nations to the Olympics.

Bart Conner (left) on the parallel bars. Victory celebration for the U.S. men's gymnastics team (right).

In the battle between the national pastime and the international pastime, baseball and football both won. Both attracted large crowds and provided close games. In baseball, the United States beat Taipei, 2–1, with 52,319 fans flocking to Dodger Stadium, and in soccer, the United States lost to Italy, 1–0, with 63,627 fans cheering in the Rose Bowl.

Soccer filled more seats—and left more empty. The Rose Bowl holds 99,000, Dodger Stadium 56,000.

DAY 5
WEDNESDAY, AUGUST 1st

Gold medals can be gold mines. Johnny Weissmuller went from Olympic swimming champion to playing Tarzan in the movies. Buster Crabbe went from Olympic swimming champion to playing Flash Gordon in the movies. Bob Mathias went from Olympic decathlon champion to playing Bob Mathias in the movies. And pole vaulter Bob Richards and decathlete Bruce Jenner went from the Olympics to the Wheaties box, living symbols of "The Breakfast of Champions."

But the American Olympic gold medalists who did the best financially—not counting pole vaulter A. C. Gilbert, who invented the Erector set, nor rower Benjamin Spock, who invented the baby, neither of whom had to capitalize on his athletic fame—were probably a pair of boxers, Muhammad Ali and Sugar Ray Leonard, each of whom earned, in his post-Olympic career, between $25 million and infinity.

Who among the 1984 Summer Olympians were most likely to become absurdly wealthy? In track and field, Carl Lewis, bidding to win four gold medals, envisioned a show business career—as broadcaster, actor and singer—that would enable him to indulge all his elegant tastes. Edwin Moses, the unbeatable hurdler, admitted that, under the liberalized rules of enlightened amateurism, he already earned $500,000 a year in endorsements and appearance money. But the best bet for fantastic riches was, once again, a boxer, Mark Breland, the young welterweight, who had already appeared in a film, The Lords of Discipline. Breland's skill and style could fill the charisma gap in pro boxing created by Ray Leonard's retirement. America's basketball players, too, were incipient millionaires, and even the men's gymnastic team could expect to profit from its sudden fame. Perhaps archers, fencers and a handful of others still competed only for glory.

THE GOLD MEDALISTS

CYCLING
4,000-METER INDIVIDUAL PURSUIT
  STEVE HEGG, USA

SHOOTING
MEN'S SMALL-BORE RIFLE, THREE POSITIONS
  MALCOLM COOPER, BRITAIN

GYMNASTICS
WOMEN'S TEAM
  ROMANIA

WEIGHTLIFTING
67.5 KILOGRAMS
  YAO JINGHUAN, CHINA

MODERN PENTATHLON
INDIVIDUAL
  DANIELE MASALA, ITALY
TEAM
  ITALY

GRECO-ROMAN WRESTLING
48 KILOGRAMS
  VINCENZO MAENZA, ITALY
62 KILOGRAMS
  WEON KEE KIM, SOUTH KOREA
90 KILOGRAMS
  STEVEN FRASER, USA

Ecaterina Szabo sails off the uneven bars.

GYMNASTICS

Mary Lou Retton performing the floor exercise.

All through the night, the U.S. men's gymnasts celebrated, wheeling around Los Angeles in a borrowed limousine, using the phone in the limo to call friends around the world. In the morning, the six heroes were back on television, on tape and in person. Obscure only a few days earlier, suddenly they were celebrities, with the media and the public thirsting to know everything about them. Bart Conner's mother, Jackie, revealed that her son used to walk home from school on his hands, that he spent so much time upside down she learned to stand on her head to talk to him. James Hartung, one of the six gymnasts, called Peter Vidmar the team leader. "Peter is the kind of guy you look up to because he just does everything right," Hartung said. "Except for going and getting married. That's the only aspect of Peter we don't look up to." The rest of the gymnasts were bachelors, another fact not lost on approximately 50 percent of the public.

Carl Lewis, the world's fastest and springiest human, showed up for his news conference in the Main Press Center more than half an hour late, a leisurely pace that annoyed many of the 800 reporters who were waiting for him and amused the rest. They were equally amused by the red leather sleeveless shirt Lewis wore with his blue jeans, and by his new flat hair cut, which made him look strikingly like Grace Jones, the singer. Lewis' business manager, Joe Douglas, who joined in the news conference, preferred to compare Lewis to another singer. "We hope he can make as much as Michael Jackson," said Douglas when asked to estimate the mod athlete's commercial worth. Douglas did not smile. Lewis had a straight face, too, when he told the reporters he had been avoiding for a week, "I'd like to be a role model more than a millionaire."

Simona Pauca on the beam.

Steve Hegg pedaling his funny bike.

CYCLING

Cyclist Steve Hegg was born Cregg Hegg, in California, then raced under the name Steve Ingram when he lived and competed in Canada, but at the age of 20, representing the United States in the 4,000-meter pursuit at the Olympic Velodrome in Dominguez Hills, Hegg made a name for himself. He rode one of the U.S's so-called funny bikes—the front wheel on one of these thirteen-pound machines, developed at a cost of $60,000, was three inches smaller than the back wheel, which was a solid disc with no spokes—and he rode so well he beat out West Germany's Rolf Golz for the gold medal, the third gold medal for the American cycling team.

Golz, a German army private, was not a gracious loser. "You wouldn't have beaten me in Germany," Golz said after he crossed the finish line.

"I would have beaten him in Germany," Hegg said. "I would have beaten him anywhere. This was my week." Then Hegg rode a victory lap, carrying in his arms Edward Borysewicz, Jr., the six-year-old son of the U.S. cycling coach.

The night before his cycling race, Hegg had dreamed about skiing. Actually, it wasn't such a strange dream because Hegg had had a chance to make the U.S. Winter Olympic team, too, as a downhill skier, before he decided to concentrate on cycling. "No way you can be a world-class skier and a world-class cyclist at the same time," Hegg said.

But Hegg certainly came close to world class in both sports. Two years before he struck gold in Los Angeles, in fact, Hegg defeated Bill Johnson, the Sarajevo gold medalist, in a downhill race. "When Johnson won his medal, it made me train even harder," Hegg said. "I wanted a gold medal, too."

A victory lap for gold medalist Steve Hegg and his coach's son.

BASKETBALL

Even though the United States men's basketball team defeated Uruguay by 36 points, 104–68, its third victory in a row, Ramon Etchamendi, the coach of Uruguay, thought it was possible for his team to beat the Americans. "Perhaps if we played seven against five," Etchamendi suggested.

MODERN PENTATHLON

The modern pentathlon offered, as always, a stern test of versatility— riding, swimming, fencing, shooting and running, spread over four days— in which military men, and Swedes, historically excelled. But the final day of the 1984 competition was a tough one for the military—the individual championship came down to a race between a medical student and a physical education instructor—and an even tougher one for Swedes.

First, in the morning, in the pistol shooting, the event which in 1912 ruined the medal chances of a young American army lieutenant named George S. Patton, Jr., one of the Swedish contestants, Roderick Martin, was caught cheating, firing two shots at a single target. Pentathletes had three seconds to fire at each target, and when Martin, losing his concentration, failed to fire at one target, he tried to compensate by using that bullet, plus another, on the next. It wasn't a horrendous case of cheating—not close to the classic case of the Soviet Union's Boris Onishchenko, who in 1976 was disqualified for rigging his electronic épée to register imaginary touches—but it was bad enough to destroy Sweden's chances for a very likely silver or bronze medal in the team competition, a development that infuriated the Swedish coach, Bengt Gorgan. "It was a stupid thing to do," said Gorgan. "You might get away with it in some competitions, but not the Olympics."

America's leading pentathlete, Mike Storm.

Scoreboard for the modern pentathlon.

Then in the afternoon, in a stirring finish to the 4,000-meter run, the last leg of the pentathlon, another Swede stumbled. For the first time in Olympic competition, the pentathletes started the run in the order of their standings, the intervals between runners calculated so that the man who crossed the finish line first in the race would win the gold medal. An Italian, Daniele Masala, 29, a physical education teacher in Rome, started first, with a Swedish medical student, Svante Rasmusson, 28, following him, only eight seconds behind.

Fifty meters from the end of the punishing race, Rasmuson had made up the eight seconds and was even with Masala. Then, with a brave effort, the Swede started to pull in front. But as he did, clearly in agony, fighting fatigue, he lost his balance, tripped and almost fell. Masala darted past him to the gold medal. Rasmuson struggled to the finish, won the silver, then collapsed on his face. "Have you ever been so tired that you can't control what you're doing?" Rasmuson said when he revived. "I was almost unconscious."

The United States took the silver medal in the team competition, led by Michael Storm, fifth in the individual standings, a business school graduate from Virginia who at the age of 24 placed first in the shooting part of the pentathlon, the first American ever to win any phase of the event.

WEIGHTLIFTING

For the fourth day in a row, the fourth weight class in a row, the People's Republic of China earned a gold medal in weightlifting. But the streak was likely to end with 148-pound Yao Jingyuan. "We have to stop today," said the Chinese coach, Huang Qianghui. "Tomorrow we have no promising lifters."

GYMNASTICS

The law of lightning held up. The United States women's gymnastic team did not match the men's success, did not upset Romania. The American women had unexpected trouble on the balance beam early in the evening, and from then on, catching up was an almost hopeless cause, despite dazzling 10s for Julianne McNamara, in the uneven bars and the floor exercise, and for Mary Lou Retton, in the vault. The Romanians, who had a pair of 10s themselves, won the team competition by one point, 392.20 to 391.20. Still, the American achievement was remarkable, finishing second to the second-best team in the world, the Romanians having been outscored by the Soviet Union in the last world championship and in the last Olympics.

Romanian Mihaela Stanulet on the balance beam.

Julianne McNamara coming off the vault.

Don Peters, the coach of the American team, had no complaints with the judging during the optional exercises—"I thought the right team won," he said—and Bela Karolyi, the Romanian expatriate, had mixed emotions. Karolyi trained both Retton and McNamara, and before he left Romania, he tutored Ecaterina Szabo, the star of her country's team.

The U.S. women's hopes for Olympic gold were far from dead. Retton led in the individual all-around standings, with Szabo second and McNamara, who fell off the balance beam, tied for third. The final standings would be determined in two days.

WRESTLING

Steven Fraser made the United States' first medal ever in Greco-Roman wrestling a gold one, beating Romania's Ilie Matei for the 198-pound championship. Fraser, a 31-year-old graduate of the University of Michigan, was the 1983 national champion in Greco-Roman wrestling and the 1984 national champion in freestyle. When he wasn't polishing both techniques, he was a deputy sheriff in Ann Arbor, a sturdy symbol of law and order.

Another superb performance, on the beam, by Ecaterina Szabo.

Final in the 90-kilogram Greco-Roman wrestling class, Steven Fraser (right), defeating Ilie Matei (left), for America's first Greco-Roman gold medal.

BOXING

Muhammad Ali sat at ringside and watched Mark Breland, who was half his age, knock out a Puerto Rican named Carlos Reyes in the third round, strengthening his bid for a gold medal. Ali admitted, in a soft voice, he was sorry he didn't have his gold medal anymore, the one he earned in Rome in 1960, the one he threw in the Ohio River a short time later when a restaurant in his hometown of Louisville refused to serve him. Ali told the story of throwing the medal away in his autobiography. In private, he told friends he still had the medal, but he couldn't resist a good story.

Every U.S. team playing a team sport won its match, five for five, including a pair of historic victories: one for the women's handball team, over China, and one for the women's field hockey team, over Canada. American women had never before played an Olympic handball or field hockey game.

The most dramatic victory came in women's volleyball. Arie Selinger's squad lost the first two games to Brazil, then, on the brink of defeat, won the next two, then slid back to the brink again, trailing 12–9 in the decisive fifth game. The Americans scored six straight points to win. "They needed confidence under pressure," Selinger said. "This should make them believe."

Then Selinger warned that the next game, against China in two days, would be the key to the Olympic tournament.

DAY 6
THURSDAY, AUGUST 2 nd

In the half century since Johnny Weissmuller stopped swimming competitively, his best times in his best events—the 100-meter freestyle, the 400-meter freestyle and the 800-meter freestyle relay—had been surpassed not only by mediocre men, but by almost every reasonably swift teenaged girl. Tarzan couldn't have made the finals in the trials for the 1984 U.S. women's swimming team.

In no other sport of measurable skills had world records improved so dramatically. Why? John Naber, a former Olympic champion, pointed to, among other things, the introduction of the Nautilus machine, enabling swimmers for the first time to stretch and strengthen relevant muscles, and to the development of "faster" pools, changes in depths, gutters and lane dividers all reducing turbulence and increasing speed.

All of the world's fastest men, with one notable exception, Vladimir Salnikov, the Soviet master of the longer freestyle races, were competing in Los Angeles, and none of the world's fastest women, with two notable exceptions, Tiffany Cohen, the American mistress of the longer freestyle races, and Mary T. Meagher, the madam of the butterfly events.

One of eleven children in her Louisville, Kentucky family, Meagher set her first world record when she was 14, then at 15 earned a spot on the 1980 Olympic team in three events, both butterfly races and the 200-meter freestyle. But after the opportunity to go to Moscow vanished, Meagher slumped, partly because she let herself gain fifteen pounds as a college freshman. A year before the 1984 Games, however, she resumed training in earnest and now, ready to challenge her own three-year-old records in the butterfly events, she was about to make her delayed Olympic debut, an old-timer at 19.

THE GOLD MEDALISTS

SWIMMING

MEN'S 400-METER FREESTYLE
  GEORGE DICARLO, USA

MEN'S 200-METER BREASTSTROKE
  VICTOR DAVIS, CANADA

MEN'S 400-METER FREESTYLE RELAY
  USA

WOMEN'S 100-METER BUTTERFLY
  MARY T. MEAGHER, USA

WOMEN'S 100-METER BREASTSTROKE
  PETRA VAN STAVEREN, NETHERLANDS

WEIGHTLIFTING

75 KILOGRAMS
  KARL-HEINZ RADSCHINSKY, WEST GERMANY

GRECO-ROMAN WRESTLING

52 KILOGRAMS
  ATSUJI MIYAHARA, JAPAN

74 KILOGRAMS
  JOUKO SALOMAKI, FINLAND

OVER 100 KILOGRAMS
  JEFFREY BLATNICK, USA

SHOOTING

WOMEN'S SMALL-BORE RIFLE, THREE POSITIONS
  WU XIAOXUAN, CHINA

MEN'S RAPID-FIRE PISTOL
  TAKEO KAMACHI, JAPAN

GYMNASTICS

MEN'S INDIVIDUAL ALL-AROUND
  KOJI GUSHIKEN, JAPAN

SHOOTING

In the women's small-bore rifle match, Wu Xiaoxuan became the first Chinese woman to win an Olympic gold medal, the first Chinese athlete, male or female, to win two Olympic medals (she took a bronze in the women's air rifle) and the second Wu to win a gold medal (weightlifter Wu Shude was the first). Wu used positive thinking to maintain her shooting rhythm. "I just concentrated on the music of our national anthem and shot," she said. They played Wu's song afterward.

WATER POLO

They were losing, 3–2, in the third quarter, but then, in two and a half minutes, the United States water polo team scored four goals and coasted to its second straight victory, 10–4, over Brazil, clinching a berth in the medal round. An enthusiastic crowd turned out at Pepperdine University, drawn partly by the skills of the Americans and partly by the builds of the Americans, a perfectly bronzed and bicepped collection of Californians. Spectators seemed to study Terry Schroeder especially, again for two reasons: First, he was voted "World's Best Player," and second, he was the model for the nude headless statue of an athlete that now stood outside the Los Angeles Coliseum, an enormous monument to masculinity. It had not been revealed who was the model for the nude headless female statue, equally impressive, that stood next to Schroeder's likeness.

The U.S. scores in its 10–4 water polo victory over Brazil. Players are Jody Campbell (11), Paulo Abreau (3) and goalie Roberto Borelli.

The Olympic swimming and diving pool on the campus of the University of Southern California.

SWIMMING

George DiCarlo, after his victory in the 400-meter freestyle.

There were five events on the swimming calendar, and in each of the five, the Olympic record fell, and in two of the five, the world record fell—a routine day in world-class swimming, except for one unusual note, a written apology from Rick Carey. Carey admitted he was wrong to sulk after his victory in the 200-meter backstroke two days earlier, but said, "I found it very difficult to smile when my performance didn't live up to my expectations." After he released his statement to the media, Carey added out loud, "I made a mistake. I definitely increased my John McEnroe look."

None of the other swimmers had anything to apologize for, except, perhaps, Thomas Fahrner, who was sorry that he did not swim as well in the morning as he did in the evening in the 400-meter freestyle. Fahrner lived most of his life in France, represented West Germany and intended to enter the University of Southern California. In all three languages, he was swift, but in the morning, Fahrner, with the ninth-fastest time, failed to qualify for the 400-meter final. In the evening, in a consolation race, he broke the Olympic record for the event, set only a few minutes earlier by the winner of the final, the gold medalist, George DiCarlo of the United States.

In the 100-meter butterfly for women, the Mary T. Meagher fan club, some twenty relatives sitting in the stands in "Mary T" T-shirts, cheered Madame Butterfly to an Olympic record in the morning heats, then to a gold medal in the final. It was the eighth straight swimming gold for the U.S., the first for Meagher, who had to overtake 16-year-old Jenna Johnson, her conqueror in the trials. "I'm happy for Mary T," Johnson said. "This is one of her last meets. I'll be here in '88."

The string of American triumphs ended in the next event, the 200-meter breaststroke, with Canada's Victor Davis, still smarting from his defeat at 100 meters, breaking his own world record by more than a second and beating the runner-up by more than two seconds. "I wanted to set a record that would be unreachable for several years," Davis said. Etienne Dagon, in third place, gave Switzerland, better known for peaks than pools, its first Olympic swimming medal.

A more traditional swimming power, the Netherlands, produced the champion in the women's 100-meter breaststroke, Petra Van Staveren, but the United States came back to the winners' stand in the day's last event, the men's 400-meter freestyle relay, a second gold medal for Rowdy Gaines. Swimming the anchor leg, Gaines barely beat out an Australian challenger, then celebrated with a series of wild gyrations in the water.

"I just thank God I don't have to compete against these guys any more," said Gaines, who was retiring, of his U.S. teammates.

"And we're glad you're done," said teammate Mike Heath, who had been favored but had failed to beat Gaines in the 100-meter freestyle.

Mary T. Meagher's family rooting section (top left). The gold medalist in the 100-meter breaststroke, Petra Van Staveren of the Netherlands (bottom left). Rowdy Gaines greeting his teammates in the 400-meter freestyle relay (right).

Canada's Victor Davis (top), gold medalist in the 200-meter breaststroke. Mary T. Meagher (bottom) slashes her way through the water in the 100-meter butterfly.

GYMNASTICS

Peter Vidmar on the rings.

Gymnastics had become, at least temporarily, *the* glamour sport of the 1984 Games, and once again spectators jammed Pauley Pavilion to cheer and tremble, to see if Peter Vidmar could hold first place in the all-around standings, to see if the 23-year-old American could add an individual gold medal to his team gold. Li Ning, the 20-year-old Chinese star, seemed to offer the sternest challenge, but while the spotlight focused on Vidmar and Li, a 27-year-old Japanese named Koji Gushiken began edging toward the top.

After two rotations, after three and after four, Li and Vidmar shared first place, dead even, but on the fifth rotation, the next-to-last apparatus, Li earned only a 9.80 on the parallel bars and Vidmar 9.90 on the vault. With 9.95 on the horizontal bar, Gushiken suddenly moved into the lead.

Each man approached his final apparatus. Li Ning, going to the horizontal bar, was .125 behind Gushiken, and when the Japanese veteran earned 9.90 on his floor exercise, Li was finished, mathematically eliminated from contention for the gold. But Vidmar still had a chance. He needed 9.95 or better on the parallel bars—the brink of perfection—to win the gold. "Let's go, Pete," teammate Tim Daggett shouted from the stands. "Do it."

Vidmar responded bravely to the pressure. He was perfect, or almost perfect, until the dismount. He did not land cleanly. He hopped. Half a hop—just enough so that his score for the apparatus was 9.90, just enough so that he lost to Gushiken by .025, by less than half a hop. When his score flashed on the board, Vidmar did not cry. Gushiken did. After sixteen years as a gymnast, after an injury kept him from the Olympics in Montreal and a boycott kept him from Moscow, Gushiken was the Olympic all-around champion.

Gushiken's scores bordered on the incredible—a 10, two 9.95's and three 9.90's, 59.60 of a possible 60. Vidmar did not complain. He insisted that nothing could have tasted so sweet as the gold medal in the team competition, and that the silver in the all-around, the first all-around Olympic medal ever for an American, exceeded his expectations, exceeded his dreams.

Chinese gymnast Li Ning performing on the parallel bars.

Gushiken on the rings.

WRESTLING

Jeff Blatnick didn't dare dream of Olympic glory, not in 1982, two years before the Games, when doctors looked at a line of lumps on his neck and told him he was suffering from a form of cancer called Hodgkin's disease. "The worst thing was the thought of telling my parents," Blatnick said. "They had lost one son, and now this."

In 1977, Blatnick's older brother, David, died in a motorcycle crash. Late in 1982, Jeff went into a hospital, and surgeons removed his spleen and his appendix. Then he started radiation treatment. Then he started training again. "I never thought of not wrestling again," Blatnick said. "But when I started wrestling again, it was hard. I got tired very easily, and for a wrestler, that isn't good."

Blatnick, who comes from upstate New York, was a very good super-heavyweight Greco-Roman wrestler before the surgery, but afterward he was neither very good nor a super-heavyweight. But he built himself back up to 248 pounds, and he rebuilt his strength and his skills, too, rebuilt them so well that he had made it to the Olympic finals, to a match against Sweden's Thomas Johansson, who outweighed Blatnick by 30 pounds. Blatnick dedicated the match to the memory of his brother David.

Before the match began, Blatnick met with his parents under the stands at the Anaheim Convention Center. "It's so close, Jeff, so close," his father said. "The Swede is big, but you've come too far to let anything stop you now."

"For David, Jeffrey," his mother said. "For David."

"I kept thinking about him," Jeff Blatnick said later. "It helped keep me calm at a time when it would have been easy to get overexcited."

Thomas Johansson of Sweden (blue) wrestling Jeff Blatnick (red) of the U.S. in the final of the Greco-Roman super-heavyweight class. Blatnick won the gold, and Johansson was later disqualified for use of steroids.

Blatnick being interviewed after the final.

He went out to the mat, a big man, 6-foot-4, in a little red singlet, seeking to become the second American to win a Greco-Roman gold medal, and with a minute and four seconds remaining in the six-minute match, neither he nor the Swede had scored a point. Then, in the corner of the mat, Blatnick dropped Johansson, and half a minute later, he scored another take-down, for a 2–0 lead that soon became a 2–0 victory.

As time ran out, Blatnick dropped to the floor, crossed himself and lifted his hands high in prayer. Then he bounded from the mat and into the arms of a friend, a fellow wrestler named Brad Rheingans. Jeff Blatnick spotted his parents and his girlfriend and began to cry. He cried all through the post-match television interview, and the man interviewing him, Russ Hellickson, had to fight back tears, too.

"The last time Jeff cried was when David died," his mother said.

"I'm embarrassed," Jeff Blatnick said later, "but I'm not ashamed. I guess it's like people always say. The big guys are the babies."

BOXING

With a pair of unanimous decisions, featherweight Meldrick Taylor and bantamweight Robert Shannon lifted the American boxing record to ten victories in ten matches. "We're in a groove," said Taylor. "I did not want to be the first to lose," said Shannon.

The United States men's volleyball and baseball teams remained undefeated in the 1984 Olympics, and the men's handball and field hockey teams remained without a victory. The soccer team neither won nor lost, but its 1–1 tie with Egypt eliminated it from the medal round. The soccer team departed with a record of one victory, one defeat and one tie, the best ever for an American Olympic team.

DAY 7
FRIDAY, AUGUST 3rd

Before 1972, the names of the best female gymnasts in the world were hardly household names in the United States. Few households had ever heard of Latynina, Caslavska and Turishcheva. Then, in 1972 in Munich, a teenaged Soviet sprite named Olga Korbut emerged. When Korbut missed a backwards somersault on the balance beam, she cried, her face wrinkled in misery, and half the world adopted her. Korbut was not the best gymnast in Munich—Turishcheva was—but Korbut won the hearts and the headlines and the television time.

Four years later, an eternity in the fickle and fast-moving world of instant celebrity, Korbut was able to walk through the Olympic Village in Montreal almost unnoticed while the cheers rang for a 14-year-old Romanian named Nadia Comaneci. She was so light, so cool, so graceful she leaped onto the cover of national magazines and vaulted into millions of living rooms. At the same time, interestingly, men's gymnastics received relatively little attention. The male star of the '76 Games, Nikolai Andrianov, won seven medals to Nadia's five, four golds to her three, yet he was little noted nor long remembered.

The women were the attraction, and while Americans adored both Nadia and Olga, they obviously thirsted for a heroine of their own. They didn't expect her to have thick muscular legs, to be 4-foot-9 and weigh 94 pounds, to wear size 3 shoes, to be openly infatuated with the young actor Matt Dillon and to have, as her coach, the same Transylvanian who had trained Nadia. But Mary Lou Retton from Fairmont, West Virginia, who as an eight-year-old had watched Nadia on television and had been awed and inspired, was perched to become the new darling of gymnastics. All she had to do was what no American woman had ever done: Win.

THE GOLD MEDALISTS

SWIMMING

MEN'S 200-METER BUTTERFLY
  JON SIEBEN, AUSTRALIA

MEN'S 100-METER BACKSTROKE
  RICK CAREY, USA

WOMEN'S 800-METER FREESTYLE
  TIFFANY COHEN, USA

WOMEN'S 400-METER MEDLEY RELAY
  USA

WOMEN'S 200-METER INDIVIDUAL MEDLEY
  TRACY CAULKINS, USA

GYMNASTICS

WOMEN'S INDIVIDUAL ALL-AROUND
  MARY LOU RETTON, USA

GRECO-ROMAN WRESTLING

57 KILOGRAMS
  PASQUALE PASSARELLI, WEST GERMANY

68 KILOGRAMS
  VLADO LISJAK, YUGOSLAVIA

82 KILOGRAMS
  ION DRAICA, ROMANIA

100 KILOGRAMS
  VASILE ANDREI, ROMANIA

TRACK AND FIELD

WOMEN'S SHOT PUT
  CLAUDIA LOSCH, WEST GERMANY

MEN'S 20-KILOMETER RACE WALK
  ERNESTO CANTO, MEXICO

FENCING

MEN'S INDIVIDUAL FOIL
  MAURO NUMA, ITALY

SHOOTING

MEN'S AIR RIFLE
  PHILIPPE HEBERLE, FRANCE

CYCLING

SPRINT
  MARK GORSKI, USA

MEN'S POINTS RACE
  ROGER ILEGEMS, BELGIUM

Beth Anders of the U.S. swatting a field hockey ball.

FIELD HOCKEY

The American women's field hockey team, in its first Olympics, lost for the first time, but gained stature in defeat, outplaying the world champions from the Netherlands for much of the 2–1 game. Beth Anders scored the American goal, her fourth in two games.

CYCLING

American cyclists Mark Gorski (with son) and Nelson Vails after their one-two finish in the 1,000-meter sprint.

Nelson Vails, a black from Harlem, and Mark Gorski, a Californian from Costa Mesa, had a lot in common. They were both 24 years old, both born in January, both fathers and both in the final of the 1,000-meter sprint, the first all-American final in Olympic cycling history. But they had certainly ridden different routes to the final. Vails, nicknamed Cheetah, didn't start racing seriously till he was 21, then polished his skills while he worked as a messenger, on a bicycle, in New York City. Gorski began racing competitively when he was 14, won the national sprint championship when he was 20, gave up the sport briefly after an accident in 1981, then decided to compete again after backpacking and bicycling through France with his wife. A pack of French racers flew past the picnicking Gorskis one day, reviving Mark's interest.

In the final, Gorski flew away from Vails, winning two straight heats and the gold medal. Vails, who had the New York City skyline painted on his racing helmet, settled for the silver and the spotlight in the post-race interviews. He lit up when someone mentioned the possibility of a movie about him. "A Hollywood movie?" Vails wondered. Then he said, "Nah. Commercials. Like the American Express card. Doublemint gum. We do chicken right. I'm out here to sell your products, folks."

Vails in the velodrome.

Karen Stives, aboard Ben Arthur, jumping a fence in the three-day event.

Karen Stives in another phase of the three-day event.

EQUESTRIAN

Medal winners in the equestrian three-day event: left to right, Karen Stives (silver), Mark Todd (gold), Virginia Holgate (bronze).

Karen Stives had two gold medals within her grasp, two in the three-day equestrian event, the first pair of medals ever for a woman in a competition considered, until 1964, too hazardous for them. The 5-foot-3 33-year-old New Englander knew that she and her mount, Ben Arthur, needed a perfect ride in the show jumping, the final phase of the three-day event, to earn the team championship for the United States and the individual championship for herself.

Stives and Ben Arthur negotiated the first ten obstacles flawlessly, but at 11B, the third-to-last fence, they knocked down a rail, and her chance for the individual gold was gone. But she cleared the final fences and wrapped up the team gold for the United States, captained by Michael Plumb, who at 44 was competing in his sixth Olympics. The medal was also his sixth. Plumb and Stives embraced on the victory stand; they shared a home as well as a medal.

Mark Todd, a farmer from New Zealand, won the individual gold, Stives the silver, and the bronze went to Virginia Holgate of Great Britain, further proof that women could not only survive the event, but flourish.

BASKETBALL

The undefeated American basketball teams won with almost embarrassing ease. The men beat West Germany by 58 points, which pleased coach Bobby Knight but did not satisfy him. His players suggested he would be satisfied only when they held an opponent scoreless. The women beat China by 36 points, completely dominating the rebounds despite Chinese players 6-foot-9 and 6-foot-7. The victories were impressive but not historic, that honor saved for an American referee, Darlene May, who, in a women's game between South Korea and Australia, became the first woman to officiate an Olympic basketball game. "She's the best female official in the world," said Ed Steitz, the president of the Amateur Basketball Association of the U.S. "She's paid her dues." May would not, however, be officiating in any of the men's games, which meant she would not get a chance to please, or displease, the volatile Knight. She hadn't paid that much dues.

They feared Black Friday would bring a monumental traffic jam to Los Angeles, to the vicinity of the Coliseum, the Sports Arena and the Swimming Center, all active simultaneously, the sites of track and field, boxing and swimming, events expected to bring more than 100,000 extra people into the area. But the traffic continued to move well, and Olympic visitors were left to grumble about the heat, which was only seasonally sweltering, and the high cost of parking, ranging up to $50 for choice spots. Southern California businessmen grumbled more, the tourist invasion smaller than anticipated, a surprising number of hotel rooms empty, restaurants uncrowded and rental cars idling.

U.S. coach Pat Head Summitt talking to Pam McGee.

Tracy Caulkins in the breaststroke leg of the 200-meter individual medley.

SWIMMING

Tiffany Cohen after her victory in the 800-meter freestyle.

America's three C's—Carey, Cohen and Caulkins—each won a second gold medal in individual races. Then Caulkins got her third—and so did teammate Hogshead—in the women's 400-meter medley relay. Still, the pride of the pool on the penultimate day of the swimming competition was neither an American nor, equally surprising, an Albatross. An Australian outshone them all, a 17-year-old named Jon Sieben, who, based on past performances, barely belonged in the Olympic pool.

Before this day, Sieben had never swum the 200-meter butterfly faster than 2:01.17, more than four seconds slower than the world record set by the favorite in the event, Michael Gross of West Germany. Gross understandably expected his sternest competition to come from Pablo Morales of the United States and Rafael Vidal of Venezuela, the men with the second- and third-fastest qualifying times. Sieben, although he trailed Morales in his qualifying heat, did break two minutes for the first time in his life—by .37 of a second.

In the final, Gross drew lane four, perfect position, flanked by the two main challengers, Morales in lane three and Vidal in lane five. Sieben drew lane six—and not much attention. He was fifth among eight swimmers after 50 meters, seventh after 100 meters and fourth after 150.

Then, in the last 50 meters, defying all logic, Sieben overtook Morales, overtook Vidal and finally overtook Gross, beating him to the wall, by .36 of a second, in 1:57.04, one-hundredth of a second faster than Gross' world record. Vidal, in third place, and Morales, in fourth, also broke 1:58, and the top four became the four fastest men in the history of the event.

Rick Carey's start in the 100-meter backstroke.

"I wasn't nervous because there was no pressure on me," Sieben said. "I was just going hell for leather for the wall."

Gross, deprived of a third gold medal, said he wasn't really disappointed. Why not? "To be second, in a very good time, the second fastest of my career, wasn't bad," Gross said.

Morales, deprived of a medal, didn't seem disappointed, either. "When a person takes four seconds off his best time to set a world record and win the Olympics, that's a beautiful thing," Morales said.

And the coach of the U.S. team, Don Gambril, who called Sieben's performance "a miracle," surely wasn't disappointed. After the Games, Gambril would go back to his regular job, head coach at the University of Alabama. After the Games, Sieben would enroll, as he had planned, as a freshman at the University of Alabama.

"I knew he was one of the toughest mentally," said Sieben's Australian coach, Laurie Lawrence, who was at the least ecstatic. "I knew he could do it. He was frightened of no one."

Sieben's courage and speed almost obscured the fact that Tracy Caulkins, in her final competitive race, and Nancy Hogshead, who also had a silver, became the first 1984 Olympians to collect three gold medals, that Tiffany Cohen, in the 800-meter freestyle, broke the Olympic record and came within a third of a second of the world record, and that Rick Carey, even though he failed to break his own world record in the 100-meter backstroke, managed to act as if he were happy with his victory.

Mary Lou Retton performing in the all-around. Above right, with coach Bela Karolyi.

GYMNASTICS

In his morning column in the *Los Angeles Times,* Jim Murray, a man with a gift for language and a yen for similes, compared Mary Lou Retton to Shirley Temple and Doris Day, to Jennifer Beals and Peter Pan, to Pete Rose and an earlier baseball player named Burleigh Grimes, and to a Cabbage Patch doll. In the evening, in a battle of gymnastic giants—4-foot-9 giants—Mary Lou lived up to that impossible billing.

Her coach, Bela Karolyi, called her "Little Body." All through the evening, he stood behind a barrier—because he was not an official U.S. coach—and shouted advice and encouragement. Between Retton's routines, Karolyi talked. Three years after his defection from Romania, he told reporters he was a Transylvanian, not really a Romanian, because Transylvania had once been part of Hungary. (An earlier emigré, Bela Lugosi, earned a good living in Los Angeles playing a Transylvanian count with unusual sleeping habits.)

Retton started the showdown for the all-around title .125 points ahead of her Romanian rival, Ecaterina Szabo, the margin Mary Lou had earned during the team competition. But after two rotations, after a 10 and a 9.95 for Szabo, Retton suddenly trailed by .125. "It is killed, it is over," Karolyi groaned to a newspaperman. But to Retton, he barked, "It is all right. You have to work now. You have to work like you have never worked in your life. Okay? Never!"

Ecaterina Szabo in a mid-air split in the floor exercise.

Juan Antonio Samaranch, the president of the IOC, and many visiting athletes and officials complained about the emphasis ABC television was placing on American sports, American athletes and American victories. "Tell me, mate," said Daley Thompson, the British decathlete, "are there any other nations competing?" But ABC explained that its cameras were making almost all events available to other nations as they happened, leaving each nation free to select and show its favored sport, and that for ABC's own programs, geared to an American audience, the inescapable story, emotionally and journalistically, was the success of the American teams and individuals.

On the third rotation, after Szabo scored 9.90 on the vault, Retton hit 10 on her floor exercise and closed to within .05, with only one apparatus to go, the uneven bars for Szabo, the vault for Retton. "Run strong, then bang, hit it!" Karolyi commanded. "Then high, okay? Strong! Bang! High! Okay?"

Szabo went first. Retton watched, a clean performance, a 9.95, possibly a 10, until the dismount. Then Szabo took a step. A 9.90. Now Retton knew she needed 9.95 on the vault to tie, perfection to win. "Now or never," Karolyi said. "Okay?"

"Okay," Retton said.

Then she took off, using all her speed, all her strength, the athletic attributes that separated her from other gymnasts. Strong! Bang! High! A perfect landing. "Yes!" Karolyi yelled.

He knew, and Retton knew, and Szabo knew. Retton's vault was perfect. Her vault was a 10, her second straight 10, a gold-medal 10. Retton spun and raced again, straight for her coach. "We did it!" she shouted, and leaped into his arms, and he shouted back, "We did it," and buried her in an embrace.

"When I come here first," Karolyi told Tony Kornheiser of the *Washington Post,* "I say, 'I am going to make Olympic champion,' and people say, 'You crazy, there is no time.' I have eight years with Nadia and only two with Mary Lou. I am going like a lonely rider through the desert." He paused. "But it is done now," he said. "Yes?"

The United States had its own Nadia, its own Olga, its first Olympic gymnastics champion, part Shirley Temple and part Pete Rose, the hyperactive daughter of a 5-foot-7 former West Virginia basketball player and minor-league baseball player.

Over and over, Karolyi was asked to compare Mary Lou and Nadia. "Both great," he said, but in terms of technical ability, "is like Nadia was performing in last century. Gymnastics progressing so fast, so dramatically, so obviously. What Mary Lou performs today, in 1976 was in order of dreams."

Karolyi's dream had come true, and he was ready to sleep. But because his hotel reservation had run out, because he could not sleep in the Olympic Village with the official coaches, he walked out to the parking lot behind Pauley Pavilion, climbed into the back seat of a Datsun, closed his eyes, tried to stretch out and tried to sleep.

Gold medalist in the 20-kilometer walk, Ernesto Canto of Mexico.

TRACK AND FIELD

On the first day of track and field, Edwin Moses ran 400 meters, winning his heat of the hurdles, his 103rd straight victory, and Carl Lewis ran 200 meters, winning his heat and his quarter-final in the 100-meter dash, the first of his four events. Neither of the American stars had to put in even a full minute's work. Both advanced to the semifinals, to the delight of the crowd.

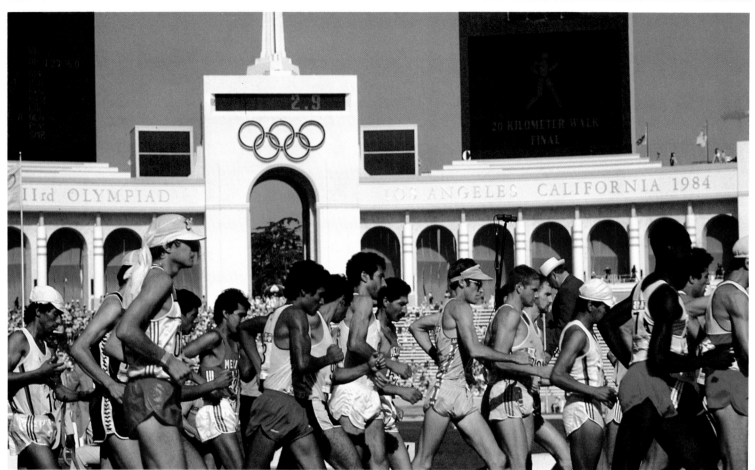

Competitors in the 20-kilometer walk leave the Coliseum.

Only two track and field finals were held, the 20-kilometer walk and the women's shot put. When a Mexican, Ernesto Canto, won the walk, shouts and signs of "Viva Mexico!" greeted him, and someone among the celebrating crowd of Mexicans and Mexican-Americans gave him and the runner-up, another Mexican, Raul Gonzalez, black-and-silver sombreros to wear on their victory lap.

When West Germany's Claudia Losch rallied on her final throw and won the shot put by a quarter of an inch, she got a less pleasant surprise. "Please stand for the anthem of the German Democratic Republic," said the track announcer. He quickly corrected himself, "Federal Republic of Germany." The GDR, East Germany, was boycotting the Games.

VOLLEYBALL

If Arie Selinger was right, if the match between China and the U.S. was the key to the Olympic championship, then the United States women's volleyball team was in very good shape. The Americans, after almost two hours, outlasted China, 15–13, 7–15, 16–14 and 15–12, advancing to a semifinal confrontation with Peru. China, defeated only once, advanced, too, to meet Japan, the team Selinger considered the greatest threat to the U.S. in the tournament.

Selinger had been right about one thing. He had argued, strongly and successfully, for the United States to wear blue uniforms against China. The Chinese, who also preferred blue, wound up in red. Selinger held out because, he said, the U.S. had never lost to China while wearing blue.

BOXING

The United States won three boxing matches, running its record to 13–0, and almost lost one boxing coach. Pat Nappi was so upset by criticism of his coaching and training methods—the criticism coming from Mark Breland, Frank Tate and Steve McCrory, disciples of Emanuel Steward—that he drove to the airport, apparently planning to leave Los Angeles. American Boxing Federation officials intercepted Nappi and persuaded him to return. Breland, Tate and McCrory offered their apologies.

The victory "walk" of Raul Gonzalez (2nd) and Ernesto Canto (1st).

DAY 8
SATURDAY, AUGUST 4 th

*I*f there were an Alvin E. Kraenzlein Fan Club, the members would have approached the 1984 Olympics ambivalently. Their hero's record was safe (that was the good news), but so was his obscurity (that was the bad).

As hardly anyone remembered, Alvin E. Kraenzlein was the only man to win four individual gold medals in track and field in one Olympics. In 1900 in Paris, representing the University of Pennsylvania and the United States, Kraenzlein won the 110-meter hurdles plus one event that has been renamed (the broad jump) and two that have been discarded (the 60-meter dash and the 200-meter hurdles). He then retired. "I am through with athletics," he said, "and shall devote myself to something more serious." He became a coach.

If Carl Lewis had decided he wanted to win four individual gold medals in 1984, Alvin E. Kraenzlein's name surely would have been resurrected, his achievements rescued from obscurity. But Lewis had less lofty goals. He merely wanted to win three individual gold medals and one relay gold to match Jesse Owens' four victories in front of Hitler in Berlin in 1936. Jesse Owens' name did not need to be resurrected. He was already revered.

Owens was voted, in 1950, the outstanding track and field athlete of the first half of the twentieth century, an honor he earned both for his magnificent Olympic performance and for a more impressive performance a year earlier. On May 25, 1935, in the Western Conference championships, Owens—within two hours—won the 100-yard dash, the 220, the 220-yard low hurdles and the broad jump, setting three world records and tying the fourth.

Carl Lewis said Jesse Owens was his inspiration, his role model and his target.

The American women's eight-oared crew celebrates its gold medal.

ROWING

The women of Romania came tantalizingly close to sweeping Lake Casitas, the site of the rowing competition. The Romanians won five of six finals, and in the sixth, the last event, the eight-oared race, they finished barely a second behind the United States. The gold medal was the first for the U.S. in the brief history of women's rowing in the Olympics, and one of the winners, Carrie Graves, 31, who gave up her job coaching the Harvard women's crew to prepare for the Games, said the moment of victory was worth the months of sacrifice. "It was a moment you want to last and last and last," Graves said.

SHOOTING

When he appeared on the TV show *That's Incredible,* Matt Dryke, an army marksman from Fort Benning, Georgia, held his shotgun over his head, between his legs, upside down and while riding a unicycle—and still hit his targets. In the Olympics, while most of the competitors in the three-day skeet shoot stood tall, Sergeant Dryke crouched low and hit 198 of 200 targets, two short of his own world record, but good enough to win the gold medal. Dryke was the first American to win an Olympic medal in skeet shooting.

JUDO

Edward Liddie brought international credentials to the sport of judo. He was born in France, lived in New York and trained in Japan, and his father was a police judo instructor. In Los Angeles, in the extra-lightweight division, Liddie matched the best judo performance ever by an American—a bronze medal—then said, "I feel like I just died and went to heaven." The most recent American bronze medalist, a heavyweight named Allen Coage, competed in 1976, then went not to heaven, but to become a bodyguard to soul singer Aretha Franklin.

SWIMMING

Steve Lundquist displays a towel after the U.S. victory in the 400-meter medley relay.

The swimming segment of the Olympics ended with one more brilliant burst for the United States, three gold medals and two silver, lifting the total to 21 gold and 13 silver, a remarkable showing in 29 events. Michael O'Brien won the 1,500-meter freestyle for his first gold medal, Mary T. Meagher won the 200-meter butterfly for her third and Rowdy Gaines and Rick Carey each collected his third, joining Pablo Morales and Steve Lundquist to set a world record in the 400-meter medley relay. Gaines and Lundquist closed their swimming careers in the relay, and Lundquist—clutching a towel bearing the words AMERICA, THANK YOU FOR A DREAM COME TRUE!—offered one final comment. "They say you're only as good as your last race," he said. "Well, that one was pretty good."

Meagher's was pretty good, too, her third-fastest time ever, the world's third-fastest time ever. Teammate Nancy Hogshead placed fourth, just missing an opportunity, in her final competition, to become only the third female swimmer to earn five medals in one Olympics.

Jolanda De Rover, a 6-foot Dutchwoman, won the 200-meter backstroke, and the outstanding individual performance came from a Canadian, Alex Baumann, who won his second gold and broke the world record in the 200-meter individual medley. "With the Soviet bloc not here," Baumann said, "records were important, too."

The men broke world records in ten events, the women in none.

Mary T. Meagher (top) winning the 200-meter butterfly. Canada's Alex Baumann (bottom), setting a world record in the 200-meter individual medley.

Gold medalist Li Ning on the rings.

GYMNASTICS

Li Ning doing the floor exercise.

China's Li Ning, who went into the 1984 Olympics with the best reputation of any gymnast and came out of the team competition and the individual all-around with only a silver medal and a bronze, revived his reputation with a stirring performance in the individual apparatus finals. In six events, Li won three gold medals and one silver. But he wasn't consoled. "I feel I should have received the gold in the all-around," Li said, "if the judging were fair."

As a final touch to the best performance ever by American men, Peter Vidmar and Bart Conner each took a gold in the apparatus finals, and Mitch Gaylord earned a silver and two bronze.

The biggest loser in gymnastics was the scoring system. Before the 1984 Games, only five men had ever scored 10's in Olympic competition. But on their final night in Pauley Pavilion in 1984, seven different men achieved 10's, and Li Ning got two. "It's getting so that a 9.9 is just like a certificate of participation," said Bart Conner, who earned one of the 10's. "I'd like to see a wonderful routine get a 9.5 and something really special get a 9.8 or 9.9."

The fact that Conner could complain about scores being too *high* showed how far America's gymnasts had come.

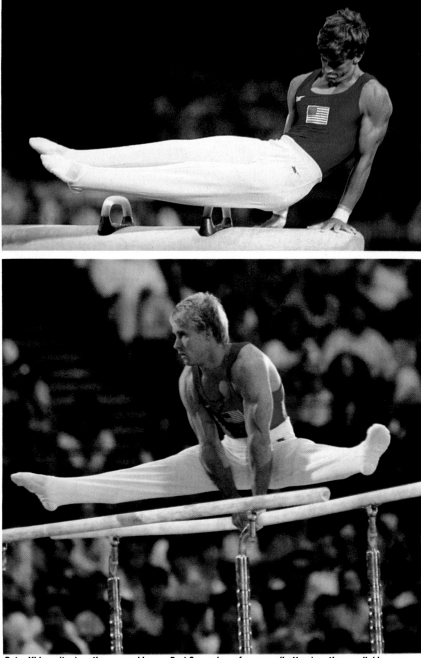

Peter Vidmar (top) on the pommel horse. Bart Conner's performance (bottom) on the parallel bars won him a gold medal.

TRACK AND FIELD

The most elaborate and expensive drug-detection system ever set up for an athletic competition—"So sensitive that it can pick up one part in a billion," said Dr. Anthony F. Daly Jr., the medical director of the LAOOC—caught its first two violators, a pair of weightlifters whose urine tests revealed traces of anabolic steroids, forbidden muscle-building drugs. The punishment was swift and strong. The International Weightlifting Federation announced that Ahmed Tarbi of Algeria and Mahmoud Tarha of Lebanon, neither a medal winner, would be banned for life from international competition.

Carl Lewis began his historic pursuit of Jesse Owens, and after 100 meters, the two men were even, one gold medal apiece. Lewis considered the 100-meter dash the most difficult of the four events he aimed to win, and after his victory, he sent a note to the media—instead of appearing, as all other champions did, in person—which said, "As far as I am concerned, 60 percent of it is over."

Lewis had no difficulty in the 100 meters. He won his semifinal handily, then, in the final, overtook Sam Graddy, who had predicted he would upset Lewis, at 60 meters and hit the tape in 9.99, beating Graddy by two-tenths of a second, approximately seven feet, the widest margin in Olympic history. As Lewis claimed the title, "The World's Fastest Human," he celebrated by lifting both hands over his head. Then, as he jogged around the track, he borrowed an American flag from a spectator and lifted that, too, over his head, leading the crowd in waves of cheers.

He had a legitimate excuse for avoiding the post-race press conference. He would be competing the next day in the qualifying round of the long jump, and the following day in the long jump final and the qualifying round of the 200-meter dash. Lewis was a strong favorite to win both events. "Since I couldn't get him," Graddy said, "I don't see anything stopping him."

Lewis was the first American gold medalist in track and field, but he was joined a few minutes later by the triple jumper Al Joyner, who hopped, stepped and jumped 56 feet 7½ inches on his first effort and could have skipped the next five. Joyner did skip his fourth jump so that he could stand by the edge of the track, cheering for his sister, Jackie, in the 800-meter run, the final event of the heptathlon.

After six of the seven events, Jackie Joyner held first place, 31 points ahead of Glynis Nunn of Australia, 80 points ahead of Sabine Everts of West Germany. If Joyner could finish the 800-meter run within two seconds of Nunn, and within seven seconds of Everts, the American would win the gold medal.

Carl Lewis, raising his arms in triumph after the 100-meter final.

The 100-meter final, left to right, Lewis (1st), Donovan Reid (7th), Sam Graddy (2nd), Ben Johnson (3rd).

Al Joyner on the victory stand for his gold medal in the triple jump.

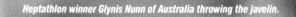
Heptathlon winner Glynis Nunn of Australia throwing the javelin.

Six hundred meters into the race, Everts held a slim lead over Nunn, with Joyner some 20 yards back, on the edge between victory and defeat. On the final turn, entering the straightaway, Al Joyner ran next to his sister, on the infield, urging her to go faster. But Jackie Joyner, a bandage wrapped around an injured hamstring in her left leg, could go no faster. Everts and Nunn accelerated. Joyner faded. Everts finished a second and a half in front of Nunn, who was more than two seconds in front of Joyner.

It took several minutes for the computer to figure out the final standings in the heptathlon, but when the calculating stopped, Nunn was the champion, three points ahead of Joyner. If the American had run the 800 meters six-tenths of a second faster, she would have matched her brother's gold. Still, the Joyners—one of nine sets of siblings representing the United States in the 1984 Olympic Games—were the first brother and sister ever to win track and field medals on the same day. Carl Lewis and his long-jumping sister, Carol, hoped to be the second.

Silver medalist Jackie Joyner competing in the heptathlon events.

Patrick Ewing, USA, struggling with Juan Antonio Corbalan, Spain, for a rebound.

BOXING

Pat Nappi was back working the corner, and the American boxers were back working over their opponents. Steve McCrory, Paul Gonzales and Evander Holyfield ran the U.S. record to sixteen victories, no defeats.

FENCING

The gold medal in the sabre went to a classic fencer with a classic fencing name, Jean-Francois Lamour of France, but the loudest cheers from a crowd of 3,000 went to a 32-year-old New Yorker named Peter Westbrook, who was, like Nelson Vails in cycling, one of relatively few blacks in his sport. Westbrook became the first American in 24 years to win a fencing medal, the first in 80 years to win a sabre medal. He promptly gave credit to his earliest instructor, the sword-swinging, wrong-righting Zorro, the Hollywood hero. "I grew up watching those movies," Westbrook said. "He's an elegant guy."

As a child, Westbrook used to dash around his home, carving the mark of Zorro, a bold Z, wherever he could. He survived his mother's anger when he once sliced a Z into a brand-new table. Later, in 1979, he survived a bizarre injury. His instructor's blade broke, struck Westbrook's throat, pierced his larynx and esophagus and yet missed all the arteries. Hardly bleeding, Westbrook realized he was injured only when he discovered he was breathing through his neck. A week later he placed second in the national sabre championship, a title he captured eight times.

In men's team sports, the United States remained a model of consistency. The baseball and basketball teams continued to be unbeaten, and the field hockey and handball teams continued to be beaten. The one surprise was that the American basketball team led Spain by only three points in the final seconds of the first half. The Americans won by 33.

DAY 9
SUNDAY, AUGUST 5th

Women made their debut in Olympic track and field in 1928, in a total of four events, and when several of the athletes had to drop out, exhausted, before the end of the 800-meter run, Olympic officials decided women were constitutionally unsuited to running such a debilitating distance. Women did not run any farther than 100 meters in the Olympics for the next twenty years.

The women did get a 200-meter run in 1948, an 800-meter run once again in 1960, a 400-meter run in 1964 and a 1,500-meter run in 1972—all events short of a mile. Then, in 1984, after several years of lobbying, women were told they could run 26 miles, 385 yards in the Olympics. They could have their own marathon.

"It's a psychological, cultural and physiological breakthrough," said Holly Turner of the Women's Sports Foundation, one of the advocates of the marathon. The marathon was both a breakthrough and a symbol, a sign of the status women had achieved in the Games. Of 7,575 athletes competing in Los Angeles, 1,718 were women. (Boxing, judo, wrestling, weightlifting, soccer, water polo and the modern pentathlon had not yet opened up to women.)

But if women represented less than 25 percent of the Olympic competitors, they certainly represented more than 25 percent of the excitement. On the ninth day of the 1984 Games, the day of the historic first women's marathon, the spotlight also shone on sprinter Evelyn Ashford, gymnast Ecaterina Szabo and the American women's volleyball and basketball teams. For this one day at least, Edwin Moses and Carl Lewis both were overshadowed.

TRACK AND FIELD

In the first 60 years of the men's Olympic marathon, from 1896 through 1956, out of the hundreds of men who entered the race, only one ran the distance in less than 2 hours and 25 minutes. The only one was Emil Zatopek, who was merely the greatest all-around distance runner in Olympic history.

In the first women's marathon, in 1984, Joan Benoit, from Freeport, Maine, a 5-foot-3, 105-pound 27-year-old, ran the distance in 2 hours 24 minutes 52 seconds. "It was kind of like following the yellow brick road," said Benoit. "I don't know how to say this without sounding cocky, but it was a very easy run for me today."

Fifty women from 28 nations started the historic race, and Benoit ran with the pack only for the first couple of miles. After three miles she was in front by 20 yards, and then she began opening up, stretching out her lead, running smoothly, easily, her left arm swinging slightly higher than her right, turning in her fastest miles before the temperature climbed from the mid-60s to the mid-70s, before the humidity soared from the 70s to the 90s.

Benoit ran alone, along the Pacific, along the freeways, a short, compact woman by marathon standards. She wore a white painter's cap, the peak turned backward at the start, then flipped to shade her forehead from the sun, and she wore the silver uniform, with white lettering and red trim, of the U.S. women's track and field team.

She barely blinked as she pounded out mile after mile, permitting herself a smile only once along the course, at Venice Beach, when the Bowdoin College graduate spotted the black-and-white Bowdoin banner "that seems to follow me wherever I go." She took advantage of many but not all of the drinking stations, splashed water on her head and face occasionally, used yellow sponges to cool her neck.

The anticipated challenge from the gifted Norwegians, Grete Waitz and Ingrid Kristiansen, never materialized. Every rival faded far out of sight. It was difficult to believe that in April, only seventeen days before Benoit won the U.S. Olympic trial, she underwent arthroscopic surgery to ease a locked right knee.

As she approached the Coliseum, and the end of the race, Benoit forced herself to ignore the mural Nike had plastered on the side of a nearby building, a giant rendition of Benoit winning the 1983 Boston Marathon. But when she entered the Coliseum, she could not ignore the honest cheers that greeted her, the chants of "U!S!A!" and the flags waving by the hundreds, the appreciation being shown by women, and men, for what she had done.

Benoit took off her painter's cap, waved it at the crowd, tentatively at first, not quite at home in front of some 200,000 eyes. She preferred the solitude of picking blackberries, making jam, trapping lobsters. She reached the finish line in competitive solitude, almost a minute and a half in front of Waitz. Benoit's condition was as remarkable as her margin. She seemed incredibly fresh.

Benoit had so many people to thank. "If it hadn't been for the work of countless women," she said, "I wouldn't be here today." And the work of at least one man, her fiancé, Scott Samuelson, whose sacrifices and support Benoit had acknowledged before the race.

The race had been essentially a one-woman show, but, suddenly, fifteen minutes after Benoit finished, it was transformed into a drama, with intimations of tragedy. A runner, Gabriela Andersen-Schiess, 39 years old, a Swiss-American representing her native Switzerland, staggered into the Coliseum, her energy spent, her stride more a stumble. Dehydrated, suffering from heat prostration, Andersen-Schiess evoked images of Dorando

The winner of the marathon, Joan Benoit, strides into the Los Angeles Coliseum.

Pietri, the Italian who, in a similar state, leading on the last lap of the 1908 marathon, was carried across the finish line in front of Johnny Hayes of the United States. Pietri, of course, was disqualified for being helped.

Andersen-Schiess wanted no help. Medical officials approached her as she began the final lap, and she veered away from them, something inside her compelling her to finish, and to finish without aid. Arms flailing, legs buckling, she weaved, she lurched, she slowed to a walk, and she went on.

Other images sprang to the minds of observers who knew the history of the marathon. They thought of Jim Peters, a British marathoner who punished his body so severely in the 1954 Empire Games he never raced again, and of Francisco Lazaro of Portugal, who suffered sunstroke during the 1912 Olympic marathon in Stockholm and died of heart failure the following day.

"It is horrible, yet fascinating, this struggle between a set purpose and an utterly exhausted frame," wrote a reporter at the 1908 marathon, the man who created Sherlock Holmes, Sir Arthur Conan Doyle.

Andersen-Schiess pressed on. "Someone should go out and stop her," Marty Liquori, once a brilliant runner himself and now a commentator for ABC, told his television audience. "Someone should stop her and worry about the consequences later."

Many people agreed with Liquori. Some disagreed. Some felt Andersen-Schiess deserved the right, like earlier male marathoners, to push herself beyond reasonable limits. People cried. People shuddered. People cheered her. But no one stopped Andersen-Schiess. Six women failed to finish the marathon, but she was not among them. She took five minutes to negotiate the final 400 meters, five minutes that passed like hours. She placed 37th. Then she collapsed into the arms of waiting officials.

Amazingly, a few hours later, she was feeling almost fine. Her temperature, which had soared above 101, had subsided. She remembered almost nothing of the final mile, but she was able to appear on television, to smile, even to kid about the unexpected attention she received, the controversy she inspired.

"Because of personal attachment, I probably would have tried to take her off the course," said her husband, Dick Andersen. "But that doesn't mean that was right."

Gabriela Andersen-Schiess' painful finish in the marathon.

After the finish of the men's eight-oared race: Canada (gold medal), foreground; United States (silver medal), background (top). The tall Finn, Pertti Karppinen, winning the single sculls (bottom).

ROWING

Unlike the women's rowing finals, which were dominated by Romania, the men's belonged to the world, eight different nations dividing the eight championships. The individual star was a giant Finn, 6-foot-7 Pertti Karppinen, who, at 31, won the single sculls for the third straight Olympics, matching the 1956–60–64 reign of Russia's Vyacheslav Ivanov. The collective stars were the members of the crew that gave Canada, unexpectedly, its first Olympic eight-oared championship. The United States had its own heroes, a fisherman and a financial analyst, Paul Enquist and Brad Allen Lewis, who, reserves at first, came very close to quitting the U.S. rowing team, then joined forces in the double sculls, won the trial and went on to earn the Olympic gold. "As a single," Enquist said, "I couldn't row my way out of a paper bag."

BOXING

Bantamweight Robert Shannon, the only member of the 1980 U.S. boxing team who didn't turn pro, the only one who decided to wait four more years to try for a gold medal, became the first U.S. boxer to lose in Los Angeles. Leading Korea's Sung-Kil Moon after two rounds, Shannon refused to play the third round safe, went for a knockout and, instead, midway through the round, caught a straight right hand on the jaw. Shannon went down, and the referee stopped the fight. Three of Shannon's teammates then ran the American boxing to record 19–1.

TRACK AND FIELD

Carl Lewis made only a cameo appearance in the long jump. He raced down the runway once, leaped a couple of inches beyond 27 feet, far enough to qualify comfortably for the final, then left the Coliseum to rest on, and for, his laurels.

Edwin Moses, a graduate of Morehouse University with a degree in physics, settled for a costarring role in the 400-meter hurdles. He did the physical work. He won the event for the 105th straight time, a flawless victory that was never in doubt; he broke 48 seconds for the 28th time, a feat the rest of the world had accomplished only five times; and he ran only a tenth of a second slower than he ran in 1976 when, at the age of 20, he won the gold medal in Montreal. He joined Paavo Nurmi in history, the only runners to win the same individual Olympic event twice—*eight years apart.* Danny Harris, an American teenager, came in second, and Harald Schmid, a West German veteran, the last man to defeat Moses, in 1977, finished third.

Moses costarred not with his rivals, but with his lovely West German wife, Myrella. She did the emotional work. As the race approached, and the television camera zoomed in on her, she displayed every nuance of feeling from anxiety to anguish. She cried. She trembled. She buried her face in her hands. Myrella knew, and she showed, much more than he did, how much the race meant to her husband.

"This one was for my dad, who passed away in December," Moses said after his victory. Then he and his wife and his mother all shed tears, their arms engulfing each other.

Ed Burke, who carried the American flag in the opening parade, refused to play the tragic role in the hammer throw. His comeback ended when he failed to qualify for the final, but Burke saw the bright side. "I tried," the 44-year-old Olympian said. "I got out there and tried. The only people who have anything to be ashamed of are the people who don't try."

Tom Petranoff tried, too, but the former world-record holder in the javelin also failed to qualify for his final. "I don't have any excuses," the American said. For the first time in twenty years, but the sixth time in Olympic history, a Finn, Arto Haerkoenen, won the event.

Arto Haerkoenen revives Finland's traditional domination of the javelin throw.

The 105th consecutive victory of Edwin Moses in the 400-meter hurdles.

Ashford winning the 200-meter dash: l to r, Merlene Ottey-Page (3rd), Angela Bailey (6th), Ashford, Heather Oakes (7th), Angela Taylor (8th).

Evelyn Ashford's emotional reaction to the gold medal award.

The headliner for the evening show in the Coliseum was clearly the opening act, Evelyn Ashford, ten pounds heavier, two inches taller and one month older than Joan Benoit, who headlined the matinee. Ashford had been one of the world's best sprinters for years—and one of the most injury-prone. In 1980, when she was ranked number one in the world, the boycott kept her out of the Olympics and a pulled muscle kept her out of the trials. In the 1983 World Championships, she was leading halfway through the 100-meter dash when her right leg gave out, and she fell to the track with a pulled hamstring. In the 1984 U.S. trials, she nursed a pulled muscle in her right leg, still won the 100 meters with her leg heavily taped, then pulled up in the 200, afraid she might injure the leg so severely she would miss the Olympics. Guided by her husband, Ray Washington, and her coach, Pat Connolly, Ashford was a dedicated and frustrated athlete who wanted an Olympic victory desperately.

She got it. She won the 100. She set an Olympic record of 10.97 seconds, and she beat the runner-up, Alice Brown, almost as decisively as Carl Lewis beat Sam Graddy. Ashford and Lewis were the first Americans in sixteen years to win Olympic 100-meter races, and on the victory stand, with the gold medal she had sought for so long finally around her neck, Evelyn Ashford cried. She was entitled to.

It was her day, and it was women's day. Not girls. Women. Benoit and Ashford, each 27 years old. Even their first names—Joan and Evelyn—were real women's names, grown-ups' names, not girls'.

Thomas Johansson of Sweden, who lost the gold medal in the Greco-Roman super-heavyweight division to Jeff Blatnick of the U.S., lost the silver medal to drug testing. His urine sample tested positively for steroids, and Johansson became the first 1984 medal winner to be disqualified. He admitted that three months before the Olympics, after losing 20 pounds when he was hospitalized for surgery on a broken nose, he took an injection of Primobolan, an anabolic steroid. Johansson thought all traces would vanish from his system before the Games.

Bronze medalist Mary Lou Retton on the uneven parallel bars.

GYMNASTICS

Mary Lou Retton had a bad day. In the individual apparatus finals—four for the women, against six for the men—she won *only* one silver medal and two bronze, or three medals more than any American woman had won in all previous Olympics. But this was 1984. American gymnasts were getting spoiled. Retton thought she should have won the vault. "Yeah, I was really upset," she said. "I still think I deserved the gold."

Ecaterina Szabo had a great day. She won three gold medals, giving her, with the team gold, four for the Olympics, the most so far for any athlete in Los Angeles, male or female. She wasn't satisfied, either. She still thought she should have won the all-around.

Julianne McNamara of the U.S. won a gold and a silver, but of all the female gymnasts, only Kathy Johnson seemed truly ecstatic. She won one bronze. She was almost 25, the oldest gymnast in the competition, a woman pitted against elves and sprites, Little Bodies or—depending on how you interpreted Bela Karolyi's accent—Little Buddies.

Kathy Johnson treasured the bronze she won in the balance beam, to go with her silver from the team, and she recalled all the dances and dates she had given up to remain a gymnast. "Twenty-five years from now," she said, "I'm going to have this medal, instead of all the dried flowers from all the proms. I've always tried to imagine what this would be like. I imagined what the crowd would be like, and the lights, and the television cameras. But the feeling—I could never imagine the feeling. I had to wait for the feeling."

Winning the gold on the vault, Ecaterina Szabo.

The two gold medalists in the uneven parallel bars, Ma Yanhong (left) and Julianne McNamara (right). Kathy Johnson (right), bronze medalist in the balance beam.

Mary Decker, an athlete almost as elusive as Garbo or Carl Lewis, met the press and announced a miracle, the fact that her inflamed right Achilles tendon seemed to have healed, and an engagement, her own to Richard Slaney, a gentle 6-foot-7 290-pound British discus thrower. Decker seemed happy with both developments, but not so happy when pressed for insights into Zola Budd. "What do you want me to say about her?" Decker said. "She's obviously talented. She's here to do the same thing everyone else is here for. I don't know her personally." They would encounter each other soon.

The U.S. women's volleyball and basketball teams each won easily, over Peru in volleyball and Canada in basketball, and each advanced to its championship game to face, in two days, a rival it had already defeated, China in volleyball and South Korea in basketball.

"Whether we get the gold medal or not, our mission is complete," said Arie Selinger, the coach who turned the American volleyball team into a world power. "I'm fulfilled at this point and very happy with myself and very happy and proud for my players."

The U.S. women's handball team lost, 33–20, to Yugoslavia, whose Jasna Kolar-Merdan, the leading scorer in the world, demonstrated her art with seventeen goals, an Olympic record.

DAY 10
MONDAY, AUGUST 6th

O n October 18, 1968, in the rarefied air of Mexico City, an American long jumper named Bob Beamon thundered down the runway, drove his right foot into the takeoff board and launched himself into space. When he came down two seconds later, Beamon had soared 29 feet 2½ inches, almost two feet beyond the world record, more than two and a half feet beyond the Olympic record.

Arguably, it was the greatest individual athletic achievement in history. Statistically, it was as if the first man to break four minutes in the mile had run that distance in three minutes and forty-five seconds. Metaphorically, it was as if the first astronaut had skipped right past the moon and had landed on Mars.

Now, sixteen years later, Bob Beamon still owned the record and the event. But, finally, the record was under siege, threatened by 23-year-old Carl Lewis, who as a child paced out in his yard 29 feet 2½ inches. "It looked like two Cadillacs," Lewis recalled. "I couldn't believe anyone could jump that far."

Lewis, going into the Olympics, had jumped farther than 28 feet 21 times, his longest 28 feet 10¼ inches. Only three other men in history had jumped beyond 28 feet, and none of the three—including Beamon—had gone so far more than once.

Six-foot-2, 174 pounds, his mother and father both track coaches, his sister and two brothers all superb athletes, Lewis had often indicated that he felt he not only could break Beamon's record but could jump thirty feet.

Beamon had made a beer commercial that was aired during the 1984 Games and alluded to Lewis. "Hope you make it, kid," said Beamon.

THE GOLD MEDALISTS

TRACK AND FIELD
WOMEN'S 400 METERS
  VALERIE BRISCO-HOOKS, USA
WOMEN'S 800 METERS
  DOINA MELINTE, ROMANIA
WOMEN'S JAVELIN
  TESSA SANDERSON, BRITAIN
MEN'S 800 METERS
  JOAQUIM CRUZ, BRAZIL
MEN'S 10,000 METERS
  ALBERTO COVA, ITALY
MEN'S 110-METER HURDLES
  ROGER KINGDOM, USA
MEN'S LONG JUMP
  CARL LEWIS, USA
HAMMER THROW
  JUHA TIAINEN, FINLAND

DIVING
WOMEN'S SPRINGBOARD
  SYLVIE BERNIER, CANADA

WEIGHTLIFTING
100 KILOGRAMS
  ROLF MILSER, WEST GERMANY

JUDO
71 KILOGRAMS
  BYEONG KEUN AHN, SOUTH KOREA

FENCING
MEN'S TEAM FOIL
  ITALY

TRACK AND FIELD

Carl Lewis survived his most grueling day of the Games. He actually had to put in almost a full minute of fierce physical labor. The rest of the day, he didn't have to do a thing except endure constant pressure. He merely had to cope with adulation, envy and unrealistic expectations, all of which he himself had created with his skill and with his personality.

In the morning, he won his first heat in the 200-meter dash, straining every muscle for 21 seconds. At noon, he took half a second less to win his second heat in the 200-meter dash. Then he turned to Thomas Jefferson, a fellow American sprinter, and said that in the evening, if he felt right, he would go for Bob Beamon's record on his first jump.

In the evening, on his first jump, Lewis sprinted down the runway, covering 171 feet in 23 strides and accelerating to a speed of 27 miles an hour, and took off. He landed, for the 22nd time, beyond 28 feet, but only a quarter of an inch beyond, more than a foot short of Beamon's record.

Lewis jumped once more, another seven-second expenditure of energy, and fouled and then, confident that he had clinched his second gold medal, passed his final four jumps. "I got a little sore and I didn't want to risk the chance of injury," he said later. That sounded reasonable. "Even if someone had jumped farther," Lewis added, "I wouldn't have jumped again." That strained belief.

When the spectators realized that Lewis was not going to jump again, many of them—even the same people who had cheered his first gold medal, in the 100-meter dash—booed his second. "I was shocked at first," Lewis said. "But after I thought about it, I realized they were booing because they wanted to see more of Carl Lewis. I guess that's flattering."

Lewis leading Julian Thode, Netherlands Antilles, in a 200-meter heat.

Valerie Brisco-Hooks winning the women's 400 meters.

By the same reasoning, several newspaper columnists filed harsh reports that could not be considered flattering. More than one compared Lewis' abbreviated appearance to a Frank Sinatra concert in which Sinatra sang only one song, probably "My Way," and then took the rest of the night off.

Some people had paid $60 a seat at the Coliseum, or $30 a jump.

The women's 400 and 800-meter finals were scheduled only fourteen minutes apart, which would have been a sturdy test even for Jarmila Kratochvilova, the sturdy Czech who held the world championship and record in both events. Her absence turned both races into contests.

In the 400, Valerie Brisco-Hooks, a 24-year-old American, the wife of an ex-pro football player and the mother of a two-year-old, took an early lead and saved enough strength to hold off a closing challenge from teammate Chandra Cheeseborough. Brisco-Hooks still had the energy, after a prayer of thanks, to leap first into the arms of her husband, Alvin Hooks, who was holding their son, and then into the grasp of her coach, Bob Kersee, who, unencumbered by a child, wrestled Valerie to the ground and joyfully mauled her. She escaped to mount the victory stand and cry through the national anthem.

In the 800, Doina Melinte of Romania moved in front with 200 meters to go and outlasted a young American named Kim Gallagher. Melinte did not have to worry about sharing the moment three ways, with a husband and a coach. Her husband and her coach were the same person.

Melinte was the first Romanian to win the 800, Brisco-Hooks the first American to win the 400 and Tessa Sanderson the first British woman to win the javelin. Sanderson upset the world champion, Tiina Lillak of Finland, who, bothered by an ankle injury, had to settle, unhappily, for a silver medal.

Gabriella Dorio leads in the 800 meters, but it was Doina Melinte, center, and Kim Gallagher, right, who won the gold and silver (top). Brisco-Hooks hugs her husband and son after the 400 meters (left). The women's javelin winner, Tessa Sanderson of Britain (right).

Renaldo Nehemiah, who earned his living playing football, was not allowed to run in the Olympics against Greg Foster, who earned his living running the 110-meter hurdles, because, in the eyes of the International Olympic Committee, Nehemiah was a professional, and Foster was not. So much for Olympic logic. Nehemiah, who held the world record, sat in the ABC television booth and commented on the 110-meter hurdles.

The world-record holders in the 800 and 10,000-meter runs, Sebastian Coe of Great Britain and Fernando Mamede of Portugal, were also in the Coliseum, but even though each was running in the final of his specialty, neither was given much more of a chance to win than Nehemiah.

Coe's problem was physical, the lingering effects of a rare gland infection in 1983 compounded by a muscle pull in his right leg only two months before the Olympics. Coe, the silver medalist at 800 meters in Moscow in 1980, set the world record in 1981, but had not come close to his record time since and had not won a major 800-meter race in almost three years.

Mamede's problem was more psychological, a persistent inability to approximate his world record in major competitions. He was 33 and had never won a significant international event.

The favorites in the flat races were Brazil's Joaquim Cruz at 800 meters and Italy's Alberto Cova at 10,000, and each came through, Cruz the more spectacularly, the 21-year-old University of Oregon junior speeding to

Alberto Covo of Italy wins the 10,000-meter run by more than three seconds over Martti Vainio of Finland.

The men's 800-meter run: left to right, Johnny Gray, Sebastian Coe (silver), Joaquim Cruz (gold) and Edwin Koech.

Roger Kingdom didn't know he'd won the 110-meter hurdles until he saw it on the Coliseum screen.

victory in 1:43 flat, the third-fastest 800 ever run. The man who had run the two fastest, Coe, surprisingly won the silver medal again, in 1:43.64, his swiftest time in years, the first hint that he might successfully defend his Olympic championship at 1,500 meters. Coe's countryman and long-time rival, Steve Ovett, the 1980 champion, came in last, collapsed at the finish line and, dizzy and dehydrated, had to be hospitalized. Ovett still hoped to run in the 1,500 meters, in which he held the world record.

Cruz, the first Brazilian to win an Olympic running event, knew his victory would be hailed in Oregon, but doubted he would become a national hero in his homeland. "The first sport in Brazil is soccer," Cruz said, "the second is volleyball, and track and field would be last."

In the 10,000, the world champion, Cova, known for his kick, needed it to overtake Martti Vainio of Finland, whose pace turned the event into, essentially, a two-man race. Mamede failed to finish.

Foster had made a career of chasing Nehemiah in the hurdles, but this time, with his rival perched 79 rows up in the Coliseum, Foster expected to win. Despite a moment's hesitation after he thought he'd false-started, Foster moved in front and led most of the way. But after clearing the final hurdle, he stole a glance at the field, and when he did, he was overtaken by Roger Kingdom, a former football player who had dropped out of the University of Pittsburgh. Kingdom had never beaten Foster before—and had never run 13.20 before, an Olympic record—and didn't know he'd won, by .03 of a second, till he watched the replay on the scoreboard. "Foster made a crucial mistake," commentator Nehemiah commented. "He looked across to see where the others were."

The favorite did win in the hammer throw, Juha Tiainen of Finland, but he wasn't particularly thrilled by his victory. "I came to the Olympics knowing I should get the gold." Tiainen said. "It's not the same without the Eastern bloc countries here." In the previous six Olympics, Soviets, Hungarians, an East German and a Pole had won eighteen of eighteen medals in the hammer throw.

Juha Tiainen of Finland won the hammer throw by four inches.

Attendance soared beyond the hopes of the LAOOC—average crowds of 46,000 for baseball, 34,000 for soccer, 9,000 for field hockey, even 5,000 for team handball—and on this, the first day of synchronized swimming competition in Olympic history, 12,000 spectators flocked to the Olympic Swimming Stadium. They watched young women, their hair lacquered in place by a firm blend of unflavored gelatin powder and hot water, perform such balletic maneuvers as the Barracuda Back Pike Somersault Swimming 360, the Swordfish Straight Leg, the Heron Continuous Spin and the Dolphin Foot First Full Twist. Almost everyone said it was like watching an old Esther Williams movie, except the expert commentator on ABC, who was Esther Williams.

Kelly McCormick, daughter of a gold medal winner, earns a silver in the springboard diving.

DIVING

Kelly McCormick, the 24-year-old daughter of the most successful diver in Olympic history, was about to attempt her final dive, a back two-and-a-half somersault, and if her execution was perfect, or close, she would win the springboard event, one of the four gold medals her mother, Pat, won in 1952 and 1956.

Kelly needed 70 points from the judges. She made a good dive, a very good dive, but not a great dive. She earned 67.20 points, and the silver medal, and the gold went for the first time to a Canadian, a 20-year-old named Sylvie Bernier.

The best part was that all three of the medalists—Bernier, McCormick and Chris Seufert of the U.S.—seemed genuinely happy for one another. They were rivals, and they were friends. "I'm just so glad I made the Olympic team, competed in the Olympic Games and got an Olympic medal," said Seufert, who added that, at the age of 27, just to make certain that she was retiring, she might "get my suit bronzed so I can't ever get into it again."

Gold medalist Sylvie Bernier of
Canada off the springboard.

Action in the synchronized swimming duet.

BOXING

He jabbed, jabbed, jabbed, swift not punishing blows, but under international amateur scoring rules, each of Mark Breland's jabs was as potent as each of the left hooks his opponent, Romania's Rudel Obreja, occasionally landed on him. Obreja hit harder, but Breland hit more often, and when the judges gave the American welterweight a unanimous victory, Breland experienced a new reaction. He was booed. He couldn't console himself by saying, like Carl Lewis, that the fans booed because they wanted to see more of him. They wanted to see less. They wanted to see him use his right hand to score a knockout, not his left to score points. "I'll be sharper next time," Breland vowed.

Now, the preliminaries over, eight boxers remained in each of the 12 Olympic divisions, and in 11 of the divisions, one of the quarter-finalists was an American. U.S. boxers had won 22 of 23 bouts.

After a 60-year absence, tennis returned to the Olympics, as an exhibition sport, not an official one, and on the first day of competition, the American winners included a pair of teenagers, Kathy Horvath, who had won more than $100,000 in 1984 on the pro tour, and Andrea Jaeger, who had won more than a million dollars in her professional career, further proof that the amateur ideal, so important to Baron de Coubertin, was beginning to mean as little as it once did to the ancient Greeks.

Six American men's teams performed, and none damaged its reputation, not even the three losers. The handball team, which hadn't won a game, lost by only one goal to Spain; the field hockey team, which also hadn't won, lost by only one goal to undefeated Australia; and the volleyball team, already assured of a berth in the semifinals, lost a relatively meaningless match to Brazil, which needed to win to reach the semis.

On the other hand, the unbeaten baseball team beat Korea and advanced to the championship game, against Japan; the unbeaten water polo team, with Terry Schroeder, the inspiration for the Coliseum statue, scoring three goals, beat the Netherlands; and the unbeaten basketball team defeated a West German team that included Uwe Blab, Uwe Brauer and Uwe Sauce, inspiring Mark Heisler of the *Los Angeles Times* to commit the Games' most outrageous pun: "Like Uwes being led to the slaughter, the West Germans..."

The pun actually had a certain relevance in Los Angeles' sporting history. The cheerleaders for the Los Angeles Rams football team were called The Embraceable Ewes.

DAY 11
TUESDAY, AUGUST 7th

They were a unit, basketball's McGee twins, Paula and Pam, tall and strikingly attractive, and if sometimes people couldn't tell them apart, it really didn't matter. They were co-stars and co-captains in high school, both All-Americans on a two-time state championship team in Flint, Michigan. They were co-stars and co-captains in college, both All-Americans on a two-time NCAA championship team at the University of Southern California. Young, gifted and 6-foot-3, they once shared the cover of Jet magazine, and they also shared a dream, a dream of representing the United States in the Olympic Games.

Then in the spring of 1984, Paula and Pam McGee and their USC teammate Cheryl Miller tried out for the Olympic team. Miller made the team. Pam McGee made the team. Paula did not. When the squad was announced, when Pam realized her sister had been cut, she cried. And when she marched in the opening parade in her U.S. uniform, Pam cried again. "I'll never get over Paula not making it," Pam said. "I'm playing for both of us."

Hurt, feeling sorry for herself, Paula went home to Michigan, separated from her sister for the first time. She didn't want to be near the Olympics. But a week after the Games began, Paula decided to return to California, to watch the U.S. women's basketball team bid for the championship. "I felt it was time to grow up," Paula said, "and I wanted to support my sister. I wanted to see her take the gold."

Paula would be sitting in the stands at the championship game between the United States and South Korea. "I'll cheer like the rest of the Americans," Paula said. "I'll probably be waving a flag, and I'll probably cry because I'll be watching my sister and Cheryl, and I'll be happy—for them."

THE GOLD MEDALISTS

VOLLEYBALL

WOMEN'S CHAMPIONSHIP
  CHINA

WEIGHTLIFTING

110 KILOGRAMS
  NORBERTO OBERBURGER, ITALY

EQUESTRIAN

GRAND PRIX JUMPING
  USA

JUDO

78 KILOGRAMS
  FRANK WIENEKE, WEST GERMANY

BASKETBALL

WOMEN'S CHAMPIONSHIP
  USA

FIELD HOCKEY

Princess Anne arose at an unroyal hour to attend the 8:00 A.M. field hockey game between Pakistan and the undefeated British team that had suddenly become the darling of the nation, or at least of Fleet Street. Pakistan was a world power in field hockey, Great Britain was not even in the Olympics until the Soviet Union withdrew. But the two teams played to a scoreless tie, prompting the British goalie and hero, Ian Taylor, to say his team certainly deserved the attention it was getting. "We're the only amateur sport left," said Taylor.

The track and field athletes had the day off, to save and sharpen their bodies for the special confrontations that lay ahead, most notably the decathlon duel between Daley Thompson and Juergen Hingsen, the 3,000-meter dual between Mary Decker and Zola Budd, the high-jumping duel between the world-record holder, Zhu Jianhua of China, and the American-record holder, Dwight Stones, and the sprinting duel between Carl Lewis and the memory of Jesse Owens. Lewis hid away, spoke to no one. Stones chattered away, spoke to anyone. Budd was told by British Olympic officials to stop speaking exclusively to the *Mail,* the London newspaper that had financed her family's pilgrimage from South Africa to England. If any more of her thoughts popped up in the *Mail,* Budd was warned, she would be sacked, dropped from the team. Budd didn't say a public word. Mary Decker promised, "You can believe coming down the stretch Friday night, I'll be fighting."

And Daley Thompson, relaxed and confident, commissioned a friend to have a T-shirt made up for him, a shirt that would say in bold letters on the front, THANKS, AMERICA, FOR A GOOD GAMES AND A GREAT TIME, and on the back, mischievously, BUT WHAT ABOUT THE TV COVERAGE? Thompson said he would wear the shirt on his victory lap after he defeated Hingsen. The decathlon was to begin the following day, and Thompson said he had never in his life "felt so good, so prepared, physically and mentally, going into a competition."

BOXING

With six victories in the quarter-finals, the American boxing team ran its record to 28-1, which was almost too good to be believed. Some people didn't believe it. "All the Americans win," observed Kim Seung Wong, the president of the Korean Boxing Federation. "I think sometimes they lose and they still win."

Kim's credulity was severely taxed by the decision in a light-welterweight bout between Korea's Kim Dong Kil and Jerry Page of the U.S. When the American was judged the winner, the American crowd booed, and the South Koreans filed a protest and threatened to pull their boxers out of the Games. "I'm very worried that this can happen in America," said Kim the president, not Kim the boxer. "What do we do in Korea in 1988? Do we take all the gold medals?"

Another pro-American decision, for Virgil Hill over a Yugoslav named Damir Skaro, was also unpopular. Skaro cried, the crowd jeered and Hill admitted he wasn't positive he had won.

No one disputed Evander Holyfield's victory. The U.S. light-heavyweight landed a devastating left hook on a Kenyan named Syivaus Okello, and the fight ended in the first round.

Mark Breland, Paul Gonzales and Pernell Whitaker were the most publicized of the American boxers, but after three impressive victories in a row, Holyfield looked as if he might be the most talented.

Greg Louganis in the men's springboard competition.

For one day, Norberto Oberburger, a 24-year-old weightlifter from Merano, Italy, and Joe Fargis, a 36-year-old equestrian from Petersburg, Virginia, had something in common: Each played a part in Olympic history. Oberburger lifted 860 pounds in the heavyweight division to give Italy its first weightlifting gold medal in 60 years, and Fargis had two faultless rides aboard Touch of Class, an eleven-year-old mare, to lead the United States to its first gold medal ever in team show jumping.

BASEBALL

Relief pitcher Kazutomo Miyamoto loaded the bases in the 7th inning, but Japan got out of the jam and went on to defeat the U.S. in the baseball final, 6-3.

The American baseball team had everything going for it: A brilliant coach (Southern Cal's Rod Dedeaux, who had sent such players as Tom Seaver, Fred Lynn, Bill Lee and Ron Fairly to the major leagues), a brilliant squad (including thirteen men who had been selected in the first round of the major-league draft), a brilliant record (four straight Olympic victories by a combined score of 35 to 4) and more than a hundred years of rich tradition.

But in the championship game in the demonstration sport, Japan led the U.S. 3-1, in the bottom of the seventh, two out, the bases loaded with Americans. Reiichi Matsunaga, the Japanese coach, turned to his bullpen. He called on Yukio Yoshida, who had pitched nine full innings the previous night, to face Shane Mack, the number one draft choice of the San Diego Padres. A hometown hero from UCLA, Mack had already hit a home run for the only American run. Most of the 55,235 fans in Dodger Stadium— only a thousand fans fewer than the largest crowd in the park's history— wanted to see Shane come back and hit another.

Instead, the fans in Los Angeles found out how the fans in Mudville felt. Mighty Mack struck out, and Japan went on to a 6–3 victory and the gold medal.

Left fielder Shane Mack strikes out.

Gold medalists in the Los Angeles Games were already collecting bouquets topped by orange-and-purple birds of paradise, and now they were told they would be receiving another bonus, a gift from Levi Strauss, a pair of jeans with championship trim, five 22-karat gold-plated buttons and six 22-karat gold-plated rivets.

Waiting for a possible rebound, left to right, Lea Henry (5), Lee Hyung-Sook, Pam McGee, Cheryl Miller.

BASKETBALL

She darted. She floated. She soared. She shot. At the age of 20, with two years still to go at the University of Southern California, Cheryl Miller proved that she played the game of basketball more artfully and more passionately than any woman who had ever lived. Her presence—plus the Soviet absence—turned the 1984 Olympic women's basketball tournament into a one-team show. The United States won its closest game by 28 points, its average game by 33, its championship game, against South Korea, by 30. "I don't think anybody in the world could beat us now," Cheryl Miller said, but she had no way to prove her reasonable point.

Carol Menken-Schaudt (15) shooting against South Korea in the basketball final (left). Paula McGee, after getting her sister's gold medal (right).

The drama came after the championship game, not during it. "When the gold medals were presented, the flag raised and the "Star-Spangled Banner" played, Pam McGee bolted from the victory stand, forced her way through the crowd and reached the side of her sister Paula. Then Pam took the gold medal off her own neck and put it around the neck of her twin, and then, just as Pam had sobbed when Paula was cut from the team, Paula cried, the tears streaming down her cheeks, splashing onto the Olympic medal her sister had given her not for the moment, but for always.

Why? Why did Pam McGee give the medal she had dreamed of, the medal she had worked so hard for, to Paula McGee? Pam could have offered a dozen reasons, but she chose only one. "Because I love her," she said.

U.S. Coach Pat Head Summitt gets a victory lift from her players.

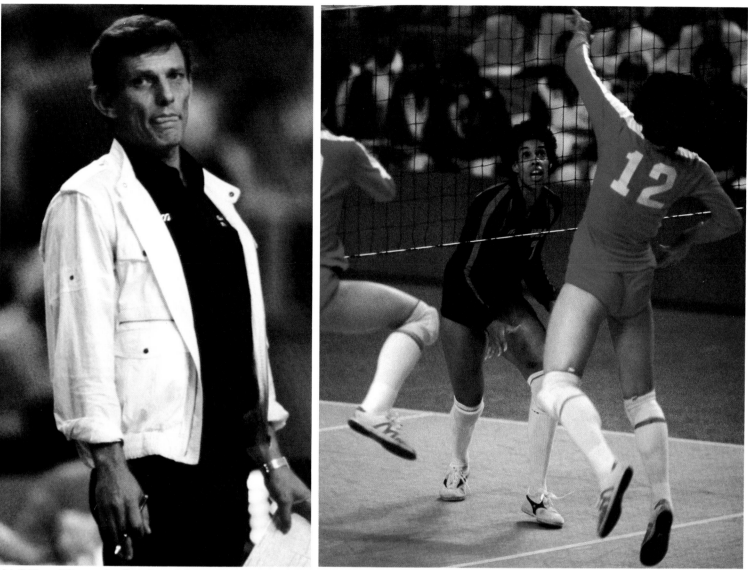

Arie Sellinger, U.S. women's volleyball coach (left). Flo Hyman of the U.S. facing China's Zhang Rongfang in the volleyball final (right).

VOLLEYBALL

As they had against Brazil, as they had in their first match against China, the United States women's volleyball team rallied. Trailing 14–8 in the opening game, one point from defeat, they battled back to tie the score, 14–14. Then it was China's serve, and Hou Yuzhu served deep, and Paula Weishoff thought the ball was going to go out. The ball fell in for an ace. China led, 15–14. Hou served again, and this time Weishoff took no chances. She returned the ball, across the net, and Lang Ping leaped high and slammed the ball down, and the Chinese won the opening game, 16–14, and the Americans' dream of a gold medal began to fade.

China breezed through the last two games, 15–3 and 15–9, and the United States' first medal ever in Olympic volleyball turned to silver. They had pursued the medal so long and so hard, and many of the American women cried. "The team has nothing to be sad about," said Arie Selinger.

Just as the players had responded to his harshest commands, they responded to his soft words. The sadness of defeat gave way to the joy of achievement. "We're the happiest women in the world," said Rita Crockett, "and it's a beautiful feeling, a feeling of love."

The love extended from player to player, and from all the players to their coach. "He's a special man," Debbie Green said. "It hurts us to read bad things about him. We wouldn't spend seven years with someone we hated."

"People think I'm a hard-driving coach," Selinger said. "I think I'm a humane coach." He paused. "I know what I want," he said, and then Arie Selinger smiled.

DAY 12

WEDNESDAY, AUGUST 8th

J im Thorpe did not invent the decathlon, but when the event was introduced in Stockholm in 1912, his winning display of skill and versatility was so impressive King Gustav V of Sweden told him, "Sir, you are the greatest athlete in the world."

The title endured—and so did the fame of the men who inherited it: Bob Mathias, the California teenager who won in London in 1948 and then in Helsinki in 1952 became the first to win the decathlon twice; Rafer Johnson, whose battle with C. K. Yang in Rome in 1960 added drama to the decathlon's glamour; and Bruce Jenner, whose world-record performance in Montreal in 1976 catapulted him from anonymity to a show-business career.

Now, finally, Daley Thompson and Juergen Hingsen were about to begin their two-day duel for the 1984 decathlon championship, a pair of handsome and engaging 26-year-olds, each of whom had broken the world record three times, each of whom was fiercely proud of mastering an event that demanded speed, strength, stamina, spring—and nerve.

"If people are willing to call me, or whoever wins, the world's greatest athlete," said Thompson, the 1980 Olympic champion, "then, fine, we'll accept it, that's for sure."

Hingsen held the world record, 8,798 points, but head to head he had never defeated Thompson. "Everybody thinks they might win, or hopes they might win, but there's always one guy who toes the line and knows he's going to win," Thompson said.

"Do you always know you're going to win?" Thompson, unbeaten since 1978, was asked.

Thompson winked. "So far, so good," he said.

In lane one, Juergen Hingsen starts the decathlon 100-meter dash. He finished third to Daley Thompson and Guido Kratschmer.

DECATHLON

In the 100-meter dash, the opening test of the decathlon, Daley Thompson finished first in 10.44 seconds, matching his fastest 100 ever in a decathlon, and Juergen Hingsen placed fourth in 10.91. Thompson took the lead, 948 points to 826.

ARCHERY

The paraplegic archer from New Zealand, Neroli Fairhall.

The duel was anticipated, but the crowd was not, 9,000 people turning out on the first of the four days of the archery competition to watch Darrell Pace, the 1976 Olympic champion, take the lead among the men over his fellow American, his longtime rival, Rick McKinney, the world champion. Many of the spectators who flocked to El Dorado Park in Long Beach were drawn by neither Pace nor McKinney but by Neroli Fairhall, the paraplegic New Zealand archer whose wheelchair had been so thoroughly searched before the Games began.

Fairhall, 39, lost the use of her legs in a motorcycle crash in 1969, but didn't lose her sense of humor. Asked if she were at a disadvantage because she had to shoot sitting down, she said, "I don't know. I've never tried it standing up." Pressed about the impact of her accident, Fairhall said, "I didn't have to buy shoes any more." She downplayed the importance of her paralysis and told reporters, "I live in a home. I drive a car. I do housework. I go shopping. Isn't that amazing?"

The reigning Australian women's champion, Fairhall did not have a good first day, placing 40th among 47 women, but the crowd still found her amazing.

DECATHLON

In the long jump, the second test of the decathlon, Juergen Hingsen leaped 25 feet 7 inches, a superb jump, and of his 25 rivals, only one could go farther. Daley Thompson went 26 feet 3½ inches, his best legal jump ever in a decathlon, and widened his lead to 1,970 points to 1,806. In the individual Olympic long jump, only four men—Carl Lewis and three others—had surpassed 26 feet 3½ inches.

SYNCHRONIZED SWIMMING

The second phase of the synchronized swimming competition—the *figures*, the unfrozen-water version of ice skating's compulsory figures—was held in the Olympic Swimming Stadium and was considered so boring the LAOOC elected not to put tickets up for sale. *That's* boring. Wearing drab black swimsuits, nothing like the sparkling suits they donned in front of crowds, performing without music, the favored pair—Tracie Ruiz and Candy Costie of the United States—moved into first place.

DECATHLON

In the shot put, the third test of the decathlon, Juergen Hingsen's best throw measured 52 feet ¾ inch, almost two feet short of his effort when he set the world record. Thompson achieved another personal best, 51 feet 7 inches, and lost only nine points of his lead, now 2,801 to 2,646. Thompson was 76 points ahead of his best decathlon performance, Hingsen 77 points behind his. Obviously in high spirits, Thompson chatted with his fellow decathletes, especially his two British teammates and his American training companion, John Crist. Understandably, Thompson and Hingsen did not speak. "It's funny," Thompson had said, before the competition began, "we look at each other often, but we never see each other looking at each other. I mean, he always looks when I'm not looking. But I know he's looking."

Thompson (above) and Hingsen (below) prepare to put the shot.

Tacking in a Soling class race.

The American boat leading in a Soling race.

YACHTING

The United States ruled the seas, or at least the waters of Long Beach Harbor, the site of the yachting competition. In the seven sailing classes, Americans won three gold medals and four silver, and the gold medalists included the only father-and-son combination on the 597-man U.S. Olympic team, Bill and Carl Buchan. They weren't boatmates, however; Bill Buchan teamed up with Steve Erickson to win the Star Class, and son Carl joined Jonathan McKee in the Flying Dutchman.

DECATHLON

In the high jump, the fourth test of the decathlon, Juergen Hingsen needed a special effort to get back in contention and produced one. He soared 6 feet 11½ inches, and when Daley Thompson, troubled by erratic jumps all year, managed only a respectable 6 feet 8 inches, the German gained 77 points. He now trailed 3,683 to 3,605, within striking distance of the rival for whom, he said, he felt a certain kinship. "Why should we hate each other?" Hingsen had said. "We need each other, that's for sure. We're like Bjorn Borg and John McEnroe."

"Did he say which one was McEnroe?" Thompson had rejoindered.

Robert Berland hoped to be the first American ever to win a gold medal in judo, and Mario Martinez hoped to be the first in 24 years to win a gold in weightlifting. Both came up short. Middleweight Berland, only 22, lost to Austria's Peter Seisenbacher and settled for the U.S.'s first silver medal. Martinez also settled for silver. The bus driver from San Francisco was outlifted by a fellow super-heavyweight, Dinko Lukin, a 305-pound millionaire tuna fisherman from Australia.

DIVING

Only an expert could figure out a diver's score: Take the votes of seven judges on a scale up to 10, discard the high score and the low and multiply the sum of the remaining five by .6 and then by the degree of difficulty of the dive.

But anybody could figure out who was the best diver in the springboard competition. Greg Louganis was so clearly the class of the field that 10's—he got four in the finals, and no one else got any—seemed too low for him. He leaped higher than any of his rivals, which gave him extra time to execute more demanding dives with greater grace, and then he sliced into the water so smartly the surface barely rippled.

"Diving should be like poetry, it should always be flowing," his first coach had told him, and Louganis unquestionably was the poet laureate of his sport. At 16, he had earned a silver medal in Montreal, but now, at 24, after fifteen years of diving and several of dance and theater classes, he was a consummate artist.

Born in California, of Samoan descent, adopted at the age of nine months, Louganis earned his first gold medal in the springboard and seemed certain to collect his second, later, in the platform competition.

On the victory stand after the springboard event, Tan Liangde (2nd), Greg Louganis (1st), Ronald Merriott (3rd).

Greg Louganis.

TRACK AND FIELD

Carl Lewis wins the 200-meter dash.

Carl Lewis, leading from start to finish, ran the 200-meter dash in 19.80 seconds, an Olympic record, the third-fastest 200 ever run, earned his third individual gold medal, keeping him even with Jesse Owens' 1936 pace, and by a two-meter margin led teammates Kirk Baptiste and Thomas Jefferson to a one-two-three finish, the fifth time the United States had swept the Olympic 200. This time, after he and his teammates kneeled briefly to say thanks for their sweep, Lewis was enthusiastically cheered.

And yet Lewis' achievement, as remarkable as it was, did not seem to create the sort of excitement many people, including Lewis and his advisers, had expected. Perhaps because he won each event so handily, never threatened with defeat, perhaps because he stood so aloof, perhaps because he was not making a sociopolitical point the way Owens had, Lewis seemed to be turning not into a bigger hero than he was before the Games, but, strangely, a lesser one.

On the other hand, Pietro Mennea of Italy, who came in seventh in the 200, was a hero to everyone over 30. Mennea had reached the finals of the same event for the fourth straight Olympics, a feat unprecedented for a runner. He had won a bronze medal in 1972, finished fourth in 1976 and won the gold in 1980.

DECATHLON

Daley Thompson on the victory lap after his win in the decathlon 400-meter run.

In the 400-meter run, the fifth test of the decathlon, Juergen Hingsen raced to the finish in 47.69 seconds, lifting himself to within 17 points of his world-record pace. But Daley Thompson turned in a 46.97 clocking, and with 4,633 points, moved 114 ahead of Hingsen, 84 ahead of his own previous best. No decathlete had ever before scored 4,600 points on the first day of the event, but Hingsen was not ready to concede. "Being 114 points back is no reason for me to let my wings drop," said Hingsen. "My second day is always my best."

Thompson had one problem. He had lost his usual mid-decathlon roommate, the British discus thrower Richard Slaney. "I know that no matter what happens," Thompson said before the Games, "in the middle of the night I can start talking to Richard and he'll always be awake because he knows I'm going to talk to him so there's no sense in going to sleep. And we just chat away for an hour or so, and then I go back to sleep, and he stays awake in case I wake up again. At the end of the two days, Richard looks terrible."

But now Richard was staying in a Beverly Hills hotel with his new roommate, his fiancée, Mary Decker.

BOXING

Boxing fans saw what they wanted to see: less of Mark Breland. He rushed out and hit Mexico's Genaro Leon with thirteen stiff jabs, then dropped him with a right. Leon got up, ran into another flurry of jabs, then a right, and went down for good. The crowd chanted, "U!S!A! U!S!A!" and Breland admitted, "I'd started to wonder myself where the real Mark Breland was."

No one debated Breland's victory, or four other U.S. quarter-final triumphs, three by knockout, one by unanimous decision, except Tonga's Tevita Taufoou, who thought his heavyweight bout with Henry Tillman shouldn't have been stopped. "He was nothing at all," Taufoou insisted.

Tillman and Frank Tate, who also scored a knockout, advanced to semifinal bouts against a pair of Canadians with impressive records and magnificent names, light-middleweight Shawn O'Sullivan and heavyweight Willie deWit. The latter knocked out a Ugandan with one left hand, then apologized, saying, "It wasn't my best punch."

TRACK AND FIELD

Nawal El Moutawakil, surprise winner of the women's 400-meter hurdles.

It was the best of times for Nawal El Moutawakil, it was the worst of times for Antonio McKay. El Moutawakil was an Iowa State sophomore from Morocco, and at 2:00 A.M. in her homeland, her countrymen, including King Hassan II, who had given her $10,000 toward training expenses, were able to watch the 5-foot-2½-inch Casablancan win the first Olympic 400-meter hurdles race for women, the first Olympic gold medal for Morocco. She took the customary victory lap, waving her national flag, and said she had never been happier.

"This is one of the saddest days of my life," said Antonio McKay. A Georgia Tech sophomore from Atlanta. McKay was the favorite to win the men's 400-meter run after the world champion, Bert Cameron of Jamaica, dropped out of the final. In his heat, Cameron had suffered a cramp in his left leg, slowed down till the pain eased, started running again and still qualified for the final, a performance that awed his rivals. But he had pushed his leg too hard and had to withdraw only minutes before the final.

McKay had been predicting victory for himself even before Cameron pulled out. But in the final, a 22-year-old U.S. Air Force lieutenant, Alonzo Babers, ran the fastest 400 of his life, the fourth-fastest ever, and in the stretch overtook Gabriel Tiacoh of the Ivory Coast and the Pacific Coast, a student at Washington State. Tiacoh came in second, the Ivory Coast's first Olympic medal, and McKay placed third. "I ran my best race and I was defeated," McKay said. "I lost to the best 400 runner in the world today."

The pole vault, too, produced an upset. The medals went to a quartet of 19-foot vaulters, but the gold went to the least-known of the four, France's Pierre Quinon, who under Olympic pressure came the closest to his potential, 18 feet 10¼ inches. Mike Tully of the U.S. took the silver medal, and an American and a Frenchman, Earl Bell and Thierry Vigneron, shared the bronze.

Finish of the men's 400-meter run: left to right, Sunder Nix (5th), Darren Clark (4th), Alonzo Babers (1st), Innocent Egbunike (7th).

After the only American medal sweep in track and field: left to right, Kirk Baptiste (2nd), Carl Lewis (1st), Thomas Jefferson (3rd) (top). A joyous vault by gold medal winner Pierre Quinon (left). Babers wins the 400-meter run (right).

VOLLEYBALL

The women had won America's first medal in volleyball, and now the men were in position to win the first gold. The U.S. eliminated Canada in three straight games and moved into the final for a rematch against Brazil, which defeated Italy. American coach Doug Beal had been downplaying his team's chances, calling reporters who praised the team too lavishly "stupid, petty and ill-informed."

TRACK AND FIELD

Arch-rivals who had never met, on the track or off, Mary Decker and Zola Budd qualified for the final of the 3,000-meter run, Decker with ease and Budd with effort. The American breezed home first in her heat, Budd no better than third in hers. Budd, who ran barefoot as usual, despite a new contract with Brooks sneakers, admitted she wasn't accustomed to racing in a pack—she ran away from opponents in South Africa and England—but said the texture of the track was fine: "It didn't bother my feet." Decker, well rewarded to wear her Nikes, said her Achilles tendon didn't flare up, but she didn't enjoy having her heels hit twice by women who were chasing her. "If they do that in the final," Decker said, "I'll kill 'em."

The confrontation between Decker and Budd had been so masterfully promoted few people noticed that Maricica Puica, a 33-year-old Romanian who won the heat in which Budd finished third, ran her 3,000 meters a full second faster than Decker.

BASKETBALL

Spain upset Yugoslavia in the semifinals of the men's basketball tournament, which put the Spaniards in a very awkward position: They would play the U.S. for the championship. "The game has to be played," Antonio Diaz-Miguel, the Spanish coach, said gloomily. The Americans, who had defeated Spain earlier by 33 points, defeated Canada by 19 in their semifinal. "Can the U.S. be stopped?" someone asked Jack Donahue, the coach of Canada. "Only by a terrorist attack," he said.

The Spanish coach saw one hope. "I will speak to Bobby Knight," he said, "and try to exchange players. If he says yes..." Diaz-Miguel said he would settle for Patrick Ewing and Wayman Tisdale, the most muscular of the Americans.

SOCCER

The two largest crowds ever to watch soccer games in the United States showed up for the semifinals, 97,451 in the Rose Bowl to watch France beat Yugoslavia, 4–2, and 83,642 in Stanford Stadium to watch Brazil beat Italy, 2–1. The fans got their money's worth: Both France and Brazil won in overtime and advanced to a final that would produce Brazil's first Olympic medal and France's second in 84 years.

Action in France's 4–2 soccer victory over Yugoslavia: Jean-Christoph Thouvenel (13) approaches the ball, covered by Mehmed Bazdarevic (10).

DAY 13
THURSDAY, AUGUST 9th

It was wonderful that the rebellious Romanians (sixteen gold medals so far, the second-highest total) and the emerging Chinese (fourteen) were doing so well in Los Angeles, but the truth was that the United States was dominating the Games of the XXIII Olympiad so thoroughly, and at times so boorishly—frenzied shouts of "U!S!A!" were starting to grate even on the nerves of proud Americans—it was almost embarrassing.

The U.S. had already won 54 gold medals, the most for any American team in 80 years, since the debacle of St. Louis, when only twelve nations showed up, and the U.S. won 70 of 100 gold medals, some in sports in which only Americans competed. There were no walkover sports in Los Angeles in 1984, but with the Soviet Union and the German Democratic Republic both boycotting, some (certainly not all) of the American victories were, like the first-place medals themselves, only 5.2 percent pure gold.

It wasn't the fault of the U.S. athletes—any more than it was their fault that many of them didn't get to earn the medals they deserved in 1980—but it was worth noting that the last time the world's three strongest athletic nations all competed, in Montreal in 1976, the Soviet Union won 49 gold medals and 125 overall, East Germany 40 and 90, and the United States 34 and 94, a very competitive three-way split. Logically, with the home-team advantage and the relaxed rules of amateurism, the United States would have done better in 1984, might even have outscored both East Germany and the USSR. At least it would have been a contest.

The main losers were, of course, the Soviet-bloc athletes who didn't get to compete. But the spectators, who didn't always get to see the best, and the champions, who didn't always get to beat the best, lost something, too.

THE GOLD MEDALISTS

TRACK AND FIELD

WOMEN'S 200 METERS
    VALERIE BRISCO-HOOKS, USA

WOMEN'S LONG JUMP
    ANISOARA STANCIU, ROMANIA

DECATHLON
    DALEY THOMPSON, BRITAIN

FENCING

MEN'S TEAM SABRE
    ITALY

JUDO

95 KILOGRAMS
    HYOUNG ZOO HA, SOUTH KOREA

SYNCHRONIZED SWIMMING

DUET
    CANDY COSTIE
    TRACIE RUIZ, USA

FREESTYLE WRESTLING

48 KILOGRAMS
    ROBERT WEAVER, USA

62 KILOGRAMS
    RANDY LEWIS, USA

90 KILOGRAMS
    ED BANACH, USA

TEAM HANDBALL

WOMEN'S CHAMPIONSHIP
    YUGOSLAVIA

Jon Svendsen readying a pass over Armando Fernandez of West Germany. The U.S. won, 8–7.

TENNIS

Americans were not dominating one sport they had been expected to dominate, the demonstration sport of tennis, and when the last U.S. woman, Kathy Horvath, was eliminated by Sabrina Goles in the quarter-finals, Horvath complained bitterly that the crowd favored her Yugoslav opponent over her, that the shouts were of "Goles!" and not of "U!S!A!" and that she felt "ashamed to be an American."

WATER POLO

The water polo game between the United States and West Germany came down to two shots in the final minute, one by Doug Burke of the U.S. with 26 seconds to play, one by Rainer Osselman of West Germany with three seconds to play. Burke scored, Osselman didn't and the American team, with an 8–7 victory, advanced undefeated to the championship game against Yugoslavia.

DECATHLON

Juergen Hingsen and Daley Thompson spoke before the first test on the second day of their decathlon competition. "Good morning, Mr. Thompson," Hingsen said. "Hello," Thompson replied. It didn't take them much longer to run the 110-meter hurdles, 14.29 seconds for the German, 14.34 for the Londoner, a six-point difference, cutting Thompson's lead to 108.

CANOEING

All 29 gold medals in canoeing and kayaking in the previous three Olympics had been won by Eastern Europeans, 25 of them by athletes from countries boycotting the Los Angeles Games. But in 1984 the U.S., which had never won a gold medal in the sport, sent eight boats into the finals, most notably Greg Barton in the 1,000-meter kayak singles. A 24-year-old mechanical engineer from the University of Michigan, Barton was born with clubfeet and had to have special braces built into his boat.

DECATHLON

In the discus, the seventh test of the decathlon, Juergen Hingsen's second throw measured 166 feet 9 inches, farther than he had ever thrown before, an effort worth 886 points. Daley Thompson felt the discus slipping out of his hand on his second throw, which sailed only 135 feet 4 inches, worth merely 710 points. His first throw had been even worse.

Hingsen did not improve on his third and final attempt, and if Thompson did not improve on his, his 108-point lead would turn into a 68-point deficit. Hingsen would be in a commanding position. "I was sure that I would be equal with his pole vault," Hingsen said, "and in the javelin we are also the same, and in the fifteen hundred, I would blow him away."

For the first time in two days, the pressure was squarely on Thompson. He positioned himself in the back of the circle, and froze. His mind spoke, and his body wouldn't listen. His muscles refused to respond. Finally, after seconds that felt like minutes to him, Thompson told his body it had no choice, it had to throw the discus. He felt every hair on his arms standing up. Then he spun and released, and the discus flew 152 feet 9 inches, a personal best. He earned 810 points. Instead of trailing by 68, he led by 32. Exulting, Thompson fired a right uppercut into the air, a knockout gesture.

FIELD HOCKEY

The U.S. women's field hockey team, needing a victory to clinch a medal, could do no better than tie West Germany, 1–1, the American goal scored by Beth Anders, her seventh, the most in the tournament. The Americans now were 2–2–1 and could win a medal only if the Netherlands defeated Australia the next day by two or more goals.

Mary Lou Retton was coming out of the Olympics one of its most popular and publicized stars, a champion and a cover girl, but she still didn't know if her other dream was going to come true, if she was going to get to meet the young actor, Matt Dillon, of whom she had said repeatedly, "I'm in love with him. He's sexy." So far her words were unrequited. Did Dillon know how she felt? "It's been in every newspaper and magazine around the country," Retton said. "If he doesn't know by now…"

Daley Thompson finished second to Juergen Hingsen in the decathlon 110-meter hurdles.

The two great competitors on the last day of the decathlon: Juergen Hingsen in the discus (2nd), pole vault (10th), 1,500-meter run (3rd);

DECATHLON

In the pole vault, the eighth test of the decathlon, Daley Thompson and Juergen Hingsen both started at the fairly modest height of 14 feet 9¼ inches. Thompson succeeded easily on his first vault, but Hingsen, suddenly struck by a stomachache producing dizziness and nausea, had trouble holding the pole and missed on his first two attempts. If he failed on his third, he would receive no score, and the decathlon, for all practical purposes, would be over. Under the most extreme pressure, Hingsen lifted himself, barely, over the bar. His pain subsided. "It happened to you in the discus," Hingsen said to Thompson, "and for me the same in the pole vault."

But the pole vault wasn't over. Hingsen, who had cleared 16 feet when he set the world record, failed now on all three tries at 15 feet 5 inches, a height Thompson cleared without difficulty. Thompson moved the bar up to 16 feet ¾ inch, a 1,028-point vault, which would increase his lead, if he made it, to 128 points, the brink of certain victory.

Thompson failed on his first two attempts. On his third he sprinted down the runway, planted his pole and sprang safely over. He jumped up, did a back flip to celebrate and broke out his best grin. Minutes later, Thompson achieved 16 feet 4¾ inches. His lead was 152 points. For the second time, he would be the Olympic champion.

SYNCHRONIZED SWIMMING

Tracie Ruiz and Candy Costie of the U.S. won the first gold medal in synchronized swimming, hailed by the crowd and assailed by the runners-up, Canada's Kelly Kryczka and Sharon Hambrook, who in their disappointment suggested that the judges were blind, ignorant and biased, among worse things.

Daley Thompson in the discus (6th), pole vault (2nd), javelin (6th).

DECATHLON

In the javelin, the ninth test of the decathlon, Daley Thompson's first and best throw traveled 214 feet, surpassing Juergen Hingsen's best by almost 16 feet. Thompson's lead, 209 points, barring physical collapse, was insurmountable. Thompson was 130 points ahead of his own previous best score and 104 ahead of Hingsen's pace the day Hingsen set the world record.

TRACK AND FIELD

The First Family of American track and field, the Lewis family, suffered its first Olympic setback in the women's long jump. Carol Lewis, among the favorites, failed to qualify in the final, no American earned a medal and the gold went to a beaming Anisoara Stanciu, a member of the First Family of Romanian track and field. She had recently married the Romanian 100-meter dash champion.

The men of the Hooks family, Alvin Sr. and Jr., once again celebrated Mother's Day, Valerie Brisco-Hooks winning the 200-meter dash and, just as she had at 400 meters, setting an American and Olympic record. No man or woman had ever before won both the Olympic 200 and 400, and with her spot secure on the favored American team in the 1,600-meter relay, 24-year-old Valerie Brisco-Hooks seemed likely to earn another place in history, to become only the second American woman to win three gold medals in track and field. Wilma Rudolph was the first, 24 years earlier.

Among the men, in the heats of the 1,500, traditionally a glamour event, Jose Absacal of Spain ran the fastest time, Americans Steve Scott and Jim Spivey qualified for the semifinals and so did Britain's three stars, Steve

The championship duo in synchronized swimming: Candy Costie and Tracie Ruiz (left). Valerie Brisco-Hooks (364) and Florence Griffith (381) accepting the cheers of the Coliseum crowd after they ran 1, 2 in the 200-meter dash (right).

Cram, Sebastian Coe and, surprisingly, Steve Ovett. Only one day out of the hospital, showing no effect of his earlier collapse, Ovett finished first in his heat.

Just before the finish of the heat, Ovett did slow up, and when he did, the man in third place, Pierre Deleze of Switzerland, an excellent runner, accidentally stepped on Ovett's foot. It didn't affect Ovett, but Deleze, only a few meters from qualifying, stumbled, fell to the track and watched the rest of the field go past him. Deleze didn't even bother to finish. "That's life," he said.

DECATHLON

Before the start of the 1,500-meter run, the final test of the decathlon, Juergen Hingsen conceded. "Congratulations," he said. "Thanks," Daley Thompson responded. A student of the decathlon, as well as its master, Thompson had, as always, been studying the charts. He knew that 9,000 points, his ultimate goal, was unreachable, and that 8,900 would require a faster 1,500 than he had ever run. He also knew that to break Hingsen's world record of 8,797 points—to become the first track and field athlete in the 1984 Olympics to set a world record—he merely had to run the 1,500 in 4:34.8, well within his reach. Eight years earlier, at the age of 18, he set his personal best of 4:20.3. He couldn't do that anymore. He could do 4:30.

But now, threatened neither by Hingsen nor by defeat, Thompson simply did not have the will to push his body to its limit. The lure of a world record wasn't sufficient incentive. He ran 4:35 flat. He missed the world record by two-tenths of a second, by one decathlon point.

Thompson still had the strength for a victory lap, carrying the Union Jack. He had the strength to accept congratulations from Princess Anne. He had the strength to climb the victory stand and whistle "God Save the Queen."

Was he surprised he beat Hingsen so easily?

He seemed more surprised by the question. "No," Thompson said. "I always do."

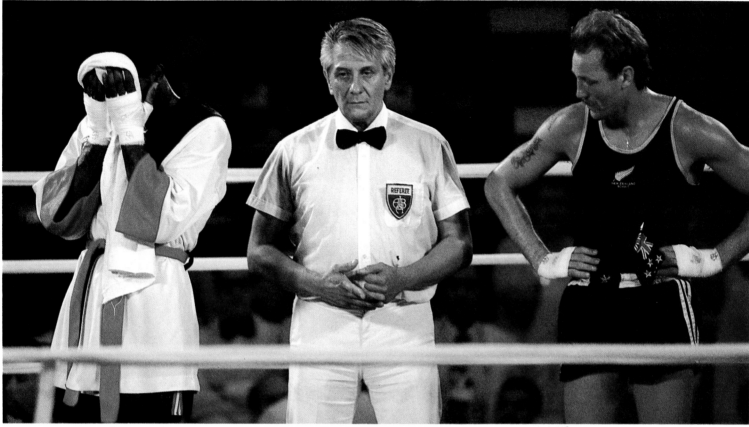

A distraught Evander Holyfield hears of his disqualification for hitting Kevin Barry on the break during their semifinal 178-pound bout. In the center is referee Gligorije Novicic.

BOXING

Sara Guido, who swam in both breast-stroke events and the medley relay for Mexico, had a communications problem. She was born and raised in Texas, and even though her father was Mexican, she spoke no Spanish. The coach of the Mexican Olympic team spoke no English. He also spoke no Spanish. He was German. When he wanted to communicate with Guido, his words were translated first from German to Spanish, then from Spanish to English. For instance, if he wanted to tell her to go for the gold, the German word "Gold" had to be translated to the Spanish word "oro" and then to the English word "gold," which could explain why Sara Guido didn't win any.

Of all the baffling decisions that marred the boxing competition, perhaps the most shocking went—finally—against an American, against Evander Holyfield, the light-heavyweight some boxing people considered the best fighter in the Olympics.

In the closing seconds of the second round of his semifinal bout against Kevin Barry, a New Zealander who had already received enough cautions and warnings to justify disqualification, Holyfield delivered a devastating combination, a right to the body and a left hook to the head, a fraction of a second after the referee, breaking the fighters, called, "Stop!" Barry hit the floor, knocked out, but when his head cleared he found that the referee, Gligorije Novicic of Yugoslavia, had disqualified Holyfield for hitting on the break.

The decision was not only stunning—so stunning Barry promptly lifted Holyfield's hand as the winner—it was suspect, suspect because the Yugoslav's decision gave the gold medal to a Yugoslav fighter, who had, one bout earlier, advanced to the final. Under amateur rules, Barry couldn't fight in the final, or anywhere else, for 28 days after being knocked out by a blow to the head. That meant a walkover for the Yugoslav, a silver medal for Barry and a bronze, even though he had been disqualified, for Holyfield, who behaved remarkably like a gentleman, not like the victim of a robbery. His coach, Pat Nappi, stormed away from the ring, away from the referee. "I was afraid if I didn't," Nappi said, "I'd hit the guy."

Five other Americans advanced to the finals, remarkably only one, Henry Tillman, on a debatable decision, over an Italian heavyweight, Angelo Musone. The judges voted Musone a 3–2 victory, but when the decision was reviewed—automatically, for all 3–2 decisions—the jury, by a 5–0 vote, reversed the outcome. Musone cried—and so did light-middleweight Christophe Tiozzo of France, whose 3–2 victory over Canada's Shawn O'Sullivan was similarly reversed. The reversals set up the anticipated finals between Tillman and Canada's Willie deWit, and between O'Sullivan and American Frank Tate. Cynics cried, too. They cried, "Fix."

WRESTLING

Bobby Weaver, carrying his infant son around the mat after his victory in the light-flyweight free-style wrestling class.

Five Americans scored decisive victories in freestyle wrestling, and as a reward, three got gold medals, and the other two got reprimands. The smallest of the bunch, but not the meekest was light-flyweight Bobby Weaver. Every pound of his 105½ pounds was fired up. He came out mad, took a fierce slap across the face from coach Dan Gable, just to get madder, then pinned his Japanese opponent in less than three minutes, earned a gold medal and celebrated with a world-class back flip. Still brimming with excess energy, Weaver raced around the arena carrying his eight-month-old son, Bobby Jr., who could probably lick any kid on the block.

Featherweight Randy Lewis and light-heavyweight Ed Banach also earned gold medals, each with a ferocious one-sided decision over a Japanese rival. But when the "Star-Spangled Banner" played, Lewis, a tiger a few minutes earlier, stood on the victory stand and cried.

The Schultz brothers from Palo Alto, Dave and Mark, made opponents cry. In preliminary matches, Dave pinned a Yugoslav, whose knee was ripped up in the process, and Mark pinned a Turk with a move so punishing he broke the Turk's left elbow. Turkish officials cried, "Brutality! Brutality!" Olympic officials agreed. Mark Schultz was not disqualified, but he was set down one match, and a wrestling judge, Mario Saletnig of Canada, was assigned, for the rest of the Olympics, just to keep an eye on the Schultzes. "They're trying to turn this into a sissy sport," said Dave.

Dave Schultz, on his way to pinning Saban Sejdi of Yugoslavia in the 163-pound class.

Gligorije Novicic, the Yugoslav referee whose decision to disqualify American boxer Evander Holyfield stirred up so much controversy, retired from his sport one day ahead of schedule. He was planning to quit anyway, after the Games, but his assignment to referee in the finals was canceled "as a precautionary measure," to keep him away from the fans. "Boxing was just a hobby for me," said Novicic, a physician specializing in nuclear medicine. "I've had enough."

Daley Thompson's victory lap. His T-shirt reads: "Thanks, America, for a good Games and a great time."

DECATHLON

At news conferences in separate but adjoining tents, Daley Thompson and Juergen Hingsen matched wits, the eleventh test of the decathlon. Asked, after several joking remarks about Princess Anne, "How can you say things like that about royalty?" Thompson replied: "It's easy when you're as close as we are." Asked if he thought he would ever defeat Thompson, Hingsen replied: "Someday I'll beat him, I'm sure. Of course I may be eighty by then."

One of the two was only kidding.

Michael Jordan performed the impossible routinely. When aroused, Patrick Ewing took over a basketball court. On a hot streak, Chris Mullin hit jump shots with his eyes closed. The United States men's basketball team boasted talent beyond belief—more quickness, strength and skill than any amateur squad ever—and yet the star of the ensemble was a 43-year-old man with a protruding paunch and a penetrating screech. Bobby Knight was not only coach of the U.S. team; he was commanding general, director, conductor and even choreographer. He turned his post-game press conferences into a pas de deux with Marie Holgado, the attractive young woman who translated his remarks into French and with whom he traded gifts and gibes. She gave him a set of constantly chattering teeth; he gave her flowers. She translated one of his favorite nouns, a short synonym for posterior, into the far more elegant derrière. By his own sometimes abrasive standards, Knight was a master of charm in Los Angeles.

But above all else, Knight was a teacher. He taught individuals to play as a team, wizards of offense to stress and enjoy defense. "This is like going to Harvard for a basketball player," said Johnny Dawkins, an alternate on the U.S. team.

Most of Knight's players savored the demanding experience ("I tell people I like playing for him," said Leon Wood, "and they look at me like I'm crazy"), some dreamed about it ("Nightmares, really," said Wayman Tisdale) and none was so brash as to contradict him openly. Yet each seemed to relish replying to a leading question: What kind of an animal does coach Knight remind you of? Answers ranged from fox ("He's so clever," said Jeff Turner) to shark ("He'll bite on you," said Sam Perkins), but Dawkins had the best response. "I think," he said, "I'd create a whole new species for coach Knight."

Action in a women's field hockey game between the U.S. (white) and Australia (yellow).

FIELD HOCKEY

The United States came precariously close to losing the wooden spoon, the trophy traditionally presented to the last-place team in men's field hockey, but by losing an overtime shoot-out to Malaysia, the Americans remained consistent, seven games, seven defeats. Gavin Featherstone, the British-born American coach, looked forward to better days in 1988. "Of course I'm committed to '88," he said. "It would be a bit daft now to say to someone, 'C'mon, buddy, the Englishman's done all the hard work, come in and grab the glory.'"

TENNIS

Kathy Horvath would have loved it. Spectators waved flags and shouted "U!S!A!" But even with the crowd on his side, top-seeded Jimmy Arias, the last American in the tennis demonstration, demonstrated little more than good sportsmanship in losing his semifinal match to Sweden's Stefan Edberg in swift straight sets. "He was more inspired than I was," said Arias, who gave up defending his U.S. Clay Courts championship to appear in the Olympics. "I played like a plumber."

FIELD HOCKEY

The United States came perilously close to losing the bronze medal in women's field hockey, but after the Dutch did their share, a 2–0 victory that dropped Australia into a tie for third place, the American women came down out of the stands and, in a special shoot-out to break the tie, beat the Aussies. The crowd cheered the bronze medal by chanting, "U!S!A! Holland! U!S!A! Holland!"

The American men's team (blue) tied Malaysia (yellow) 3–3, but lost in a penalty shoot-out.

DIVING

From their perches atop a 33-foot-high block of cement, the platform divers performed a perfect reversal of form. In other words, the second-best diver in the People's Republic of China and the second-best diver in the United States became the two best divers in the world in the women's platform final. Zhou Jihong, a 97-pound 19-year-old, won the gold medal, and Michele Mitchell, a 22-year-old former gymnast, won the silver, surprising their more celebrated teammates, the 19-year-old world champion, Wendy Wyland, who earned the bronze, and the Chinese champion, Chen Xiaoxia, who on her 22nd birthday placed fourth and got no medal as a present.

Michele Mitchell, diving for a silver medal in the women's 10-meter platform.

Gold medalist in the women's 10-meter platform dive, Zhou Jihong of China.

TRACK AND FIELD

The world champion took the lead at the start, the barefoot South African fell in behind her and the dream race became reality, the former prodigy and the present, 26-year-old Mary Decker and 18-year-old Zola Budd, battling for the Olympic 3,000-meter championship. Decker set a swift pace for 800 meters, then eased up, slowed to the point where Budd, at 1,600 meters, decided she had to attack, had to step up the pace to give herself a chance against Decker's kick, against Maricica Puica's kick.

Budd accelerated, moved in front. She ran in the center of lane one, which was wide enough to contain three runners, Decker on the inside, in second place, Wendy Sly on the outside, in third, Decker in the red uniform of the United States, Sly and Budd in the white of Great Britain. Puica, wearing the yellow and blue of Romania, held fourth.

As they came off a turn, with a little more than 1,200 meters to go, Budd edged toward the inside, narrowing the opening in front of Decker. The American, only a step off the lead, could have reached out and touched Budd's shoulder, pushed her gently, let the front runner know how perilously close they were. Instead, Decker cut down her stride, held back. As Budd's bare left foot flew up behind her, it brushed the outside of Decker's right thigh. Tilted slightly off stride, Budd edged farther toward her left, and now Decker's right foot struck Budd's left, and as the 92-pound South African struggled to maintain her balance, Decker lost hers.

Early in the women's 3,000-meter run: left to right, Wendy Sly, Zola Budd, Maricica Puica (partly hidden), Mary Decker, Lynn Williams.

Decker fell. She fell hard, her gluteus, the muscle that stabilizes the hip, painfully strained. She fell to the grass on the inside of the track, looked up to see the pack moving away from her, then rolled over in obvious anguish, mental and physical, her Olympic hopes shattered. Budd looked back briefly, her dismay visible, too, and as the crowd began to boo, blaming the young South African for cutting down the American heroine, tears slid down Budd's face. The confrontation in the Coliseum had ended in a collision. The dream race had turned into a nightmare.

Puica, who had deftly avoided the falling Decker's feet, bolted to the front. The 34-year-old Romanian knew how to run in a pack—by getting away from the pack, getting away from the dangers of inexperience. Budd, her ankle mildly spiked and bleeding, began to lose ground, and while Richard Slaney rushed to the side of his sobbing fiancée, Maricica Puica pulled away and, by a comfortable margin, defeated Wendy Sly for the gold medal. Budd wound up seventh, then trotted into the tunnel leading away from the track, the tunnel into which Slaney had carried Decker, still in agony. Budd approached Decker, sought to speak to her for the first time. "Don't bother," Decker said, brushing her rival away.

Budd retreated, hurt and bewildered, and Decker, hurt and frustrated, advanced toward the interview tent, to place the blame squarely on Budd, to accuse the teenager of cutting her off illegally. At first Decker's view had considerable support from, among others, a race official, who promptly disqualified Budd, and Marty Liquori, the ABC broadcaster who said flatly Budd was in the wrong. But as the tapes of the race were studied and restudied, perceptions changed. Budd was reinstated. Liquori apologized,

The race continues as Decker receives assistance.

Jim Ryun knew how Mary Decker felt. Ryun was elbowed by a rival in a preliminary heat of the 1,500-meter run in Munich in 1972 and tumbled to the track, his dream of a gold medal destroyed. He was the world-record holder in the mile, a silver medalist at 1,500 meters in Mexico City in 1968. Coincidentally, he was in a hotel room in Southern California watching the 3,000-meter run on television when Mary Decker fell. "Get up, Mary, get up," Ryun yelled, then turned to his wife and said, "It's happened again."

Just after the collision Decker writhes in the infield as Sly and Puica take the lead (top). Puica leads Sly on the final turn (bottom).

said his initial reaction was incorrect. The collision didn't seem to be anyone's fault, although Decker, because she had experience behind her and Budd in front of her, appeared to be in a better position to avoid the accident.

It really didn't matter whose fault it was. Both had suffered, not for the first time, and both bodies, both psyches were scarred. Ironically, Mary Decker and Zola Budd were now linked even more closely than before.

In their controversial 178-pound semifinal, Kevin Barry and Evander Holyfield.

BOXING

In its formal protest, the United States Amateur Boxing Federation argued that (a) Kevin Barry, the light-heavyweight from New Zealand, should have been disqualified earlier, (b) Barry had his arm wrapped so tightly around Evander Holyfield's headgear that Holyfield couldn't hear the referee call "Stop," and (c) eight times earlier in the bout, four times apiece, the two fighters had without penalty ignored "Stop" calls.

In its formal response, the five-man protest committee of the International Amateur Boxing Association ruled, "The decision of the referee stands."

That left merely ten Americans going into the finals of the weight divisions. No other country had more than two.

BASKETBALL

Bobby Knight was not entirely pleased with the way his men played in the championship basketball game. They permitted Spain to score first, and if that wasn't bad enough, they permitted Spain to score again, every once in a while. The Spanish, in fact, scored 19 points to the first 42 for the U.S. The final score was 96–65—three points closer than the average American game—and Michael Jordan, who had showed up at the Forum without his proper uniform, then had faked half the Spanish players out of theirs, wound up with 20 points. His players carried Knight off the court with the net draped around his neck, but he escaped before they could pull the cords tight. During his post-game act, he told reporters and Marie Holgado that the Soviet Union wouldn't have had a chance in the tournament. "We'll beat their *derrière* anywhere they want to play," Knight promised.

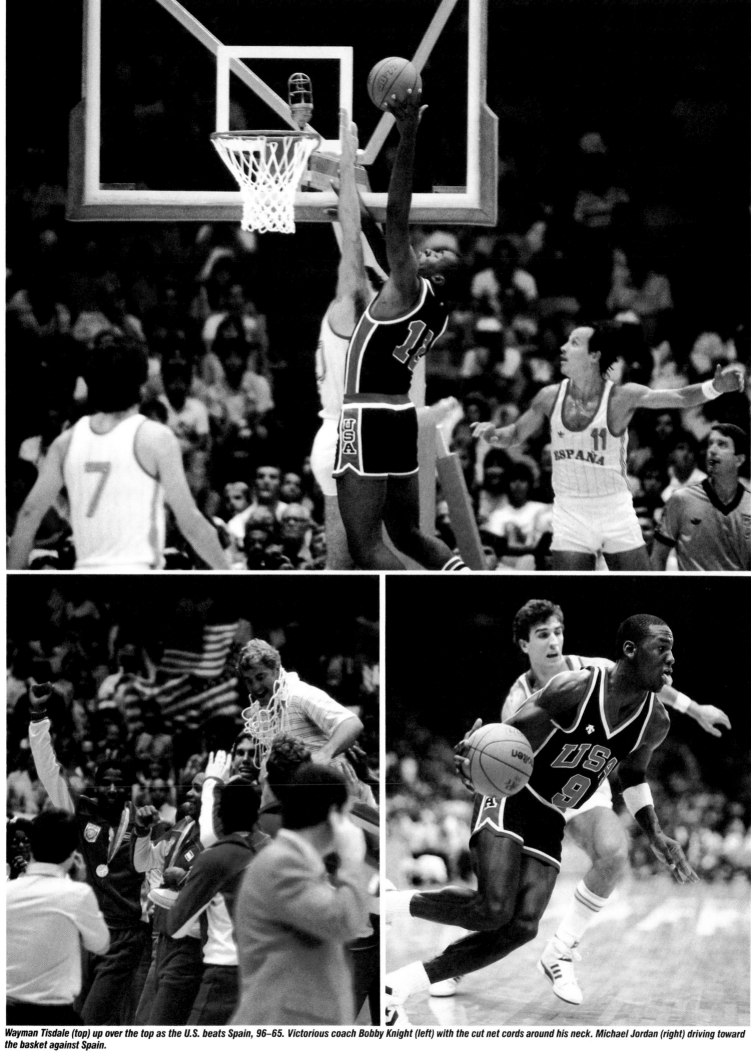

Wayman Tisdale (top) up over the top as the U.S. beats Spain, 96–65. Victorious coach Bobby Knight (left) with the cut net cords around his neck. Michael Jordan (right) driving toward the basket against Spain.

TRACK AND FIELD

Benita Fitzgerald-Brown, like Valerie Brisco-Hooks a fleet-footed American with a hyphenated name and a pass catcher for a husband, won the women's high hurdles, an event in which the U.S. had not taken a medal for more than half a century.

Joni Huntley, who was married to a biology professor but chose to use her maiden name, earned the bronze medal in the women's high jump, the first medal for the U.S. in that event since 1956, the year in which Huntley was born.

Despite Huntley's unexpected medal and Fitzgerald-Brown's unexpected and exciting victory—she had to watch the replay on the scoreboard before she knew her fast finish had paid off—it was not a good day for the U.S. in track and field.

Mac Wilkins and John Powell, who were supposed to finish one-two in the discus, instead finished two-three, behind Rolf Danneberg of West Germany, and Henry Marsh, who was supposed to win the 3,000-meter steeplechase, was weakened by a virus infection and distracted by an interloper (who invaded the track with a banner hailing "Our Earth at Peace, One Human Family"). Marsh finished fourth behind Julius Korir, who was the first Washington State University undergraduate to win the steeplechase and the third Kenyan. At the finish, half an hour after Mary Decker fell, Marsh collapsed on the track and was carried off on a stretcher.

Bronze medalist Joni Huntley (top) over the high jump bar. Henry Marsh's collapse (bottom) after the 3,000-meter steeplechase.

Benita Fitzgerald-Brown leading Michele Chardonet in the 100-meter hurdles (top). Julius Korir, the eventual winner, is ahead of Henry Marsh (919) and Julius Kanuki (579) in the 3,000-meter steeplechase (bottom).

Ulrike Meyfarth, gold medalist in the women's high jump. She won the same event in 1972.

Huntley, incidentally, was working on a master's degree in gerontology, which seemed appropriate, because the two women who beat her offered wonderful studies in aging. West Germany's 6-foot-2 Ulrike Meyfarth, the gold medalist, had aged 12 years since, as a precocious 16-year-old, she finished first in the high jump in Munich, and Sara Simeoni, the silver medalist, was 31, ancient for a jumper. La Simeoni, as her Italian countrymen called her, had won the silver medal in 1976 in Montreal, the gold in 1980 in Moscow. She had never dreamed she would win three Olympic medals. She had dreamed, however, of becoming a classical ballerina. At the age of 12 she wanted to be one of the little Ethiopians in *Aida,* but was turned down because she was too tall.

The day after Nawal El Moutawakil won Morocco's first Olympic gold medal, King Hassan II came up with the perfect way to commemorate her feat. The King decreed that, during the next month, all female babies born in Morocco should be named Nawal.

The veteran Mac Wilkins tossing the discus for a silver medal.

Dave Schultz (red), wrestling in the 163-pound class.

WRESTLING

Super-heavyweight Bruce Baumgartner, a college honor student whose wife called him a Teddy bear, and welterweight Dave Schultz, who had also been called an animal, became the fourth and fifth Americans to win gold medals in freestyle wrestling. Each won by a decisive decision in the final, and neither maimed nor crippled his opponent. "I'm sorry I'm perceived as an element that's dangerous," Schultz said. "I've never tried to hurt anybody. I'm interested in scoring points, pinning and winning."

WATER POLO

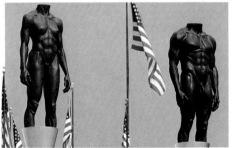

Before the United States played Yugoslavia for the water polo championship, Terry Schroeder, the model for athletic perfection, said he would rather be remembered for a gold medal than for a bronze statue. But when the American team that had spent so many pre-dawn hours training for the Olympics couldn't hold a 5–2 lead, Terry and the pool rats had to settle for a silver medal. The game ended in a 5–5 tie, but Yugoslavia won the title because it had outscored its Olympic opponents by 14 goals, while the U.S. margin was only nine. After almost eight years together, most of the U.S. water polo players were retiring, but the poster they had posed for, a beefcake classic, would endure.

TEAM HANDBALL

Two rare and wonderful things happened in the men's team handball game between the United States and Japan. A goalie, Bill Kessler of the United States, unguarded by the opposition, blocked a shot, moved down court and, from 30 feet out, fired and scored, the only goal scored by a goalie in the whole tournament. The U.S. went on to beat Japan, 24–16, an equally rare and wonderful thing, the only game the Americans won in the whole tournament.

SOCCER

Playing a game many Americans still did not fully comprehend, to determine nothing more important than third place, a pair of teams more than 6,000 miles from their homes drew 100,374 fans to the Rose Bowl. The record crowd saw Yugoslavia beat Italy for the bronze medal in soccer, 2–1. ABC, which had been criticized for ignoring soccer, did not show any of the game, even though the grass had been painted a darker shade of green to look better on the air.

THE GOLD MEDALISTS

TRACK AND FIELD

WOMEN'S 1,500 METERS
GABRIELLA DORIO, ITALY

WOMEN'S DISCUS
RIA STALMAN, NETHERLANDS

WOMEN'S 400-METER RELAY
USA

WOMEN'S 1,600-METER RELAY
USA

MEN'S 1,500 METERS
SEBASTIAN COE, BRITAIN

MEN'S 5,000 METERS
SAID AOUITA, MOROCCO

MEN'S 50-KILOMETER RACE WALK
RAUL GONZALEZ, MEXICO

MEN'S HIGH JUMP
DIETMAR MOEGENBURG, WEST GERMANY

MEN'S SHOT PUT
ALESSANDRO ANDREI, ITALY

MEN'S 400-METER RELAY
USA

MEN'S 1,600-METER RELAY
USA

CANOEING

MEN'S 1,000-METER KAYAK SINGLES
ALAN THOMPSON, NEW ZEALAND

MEN'S 1,000-METER KAYAK PAIRS
HUGH FISHER
ALWYN MORRIS, CANADA

MEN'S 1,000-METER KAYAK FOURS
NEW ZEALAND

WOMEN'S 500-METER KAYAK FOURS
ROMANIA

MEN'S 500-METER CANOE SINGLES
ULRICH EICKE, WEST GERMANY

MEN'S 1,000-METER CANOE PAIRS
IVAN PATZAICHIN
TOMA SIMIONOV, ROMANIA

FIELD HOCKEY

MEN'S CHAMPIONSHIP
PAKISTAN

SOCCER

CHAMPIONSHIP
FRANCE

RHYTHMIC GYMNASTICS

LORI FUNG, CANADA

ARCHERY

MEN'S CHAMPIONSHIP
DARRELL PACE, USA

WOMEN'S CHAMPIONSHIP
HYANG SOON SEO, SOUTH KOREA

FREESTYLE WRESTLING

57 KILOGRAMS
HIDEAKI TOMIYAMA, JAPAN

68 KILOGRAMS
IN TAK YOO, SOUTH KOREA

82 KILOGRAMS
MARK SCHULTZ, USA

100 KILOGRAMS
LOU BANACH, USA

JUDO

OPEN
YASUHIRO YAMASHITA, JAPAN

(continued on next page)

They did not quite have the flair of the Three Musketeers—the idea of "One for All and All for One" would have appalled them—or the universal appeal of the Three Stooges, yet the three slender young men were unmistakably a trio. They were all English, all in their twenties, and all Libras, and they were, individually and as a group, the world's dominant middle-distance runners in the five years leading up to the Los Angeles Olympics. Their names, which somehow seemed to overlap—Sebastian Coe, Steve Cram and Steve Ovett—were invariably linked, but their bodies rarely were. Never had the three of them run in the same race anywhere in Great Britain.

They had in fact run in the same race only once, in Moscow in 1980, in the Olympic 1,500-meter final. Cram, only 19 at the time, was thrilled to be in the same field with his distinguished countrymen. He finished eighth, while Ovett, the favorite, and Coe, the world-record holder, dueled for the championship. Surprisingly, Coe triumphed, and Ovett, who had won 45 straight races at 1,500 meters and a mile, slipped to third.

In 1981, Coe set the world record for the mile, and in 1983, Ovett the world record for 1,500 meters, but in between Cram outshone them both. Neither Ovett nor Coe won a major title in 1982 or 1983; Cram won the European and the Commonwealth 1,500-meter championships in 1982, the World Championship in 1983. Ovett placed fourth in the Worlds; Coe was sidelined by a glandular infection.

Now all three had come back from ailments to reach the final of the Olympic 1,500 meters. They had three strikingly different personalities —Ovett very private, Coe very proper and Cram very pleasant—and they had one goal.

(continued from previous page)

BOXING

48 KILOGRAMS
PAUL GONZALES, USA
51 KILOGRAMS
STEVE MCCRORY, USA
54 KILOGRAMS
MAURIZIO STECCA, ITALY
57 KILOGRAMS
MELDRICK TAYLOR, USA
60 KILOGRAMS
PERNELL WHITAKER, USA
63.5 KILOGRAMS
JERRY PAGE, USA
67 KILOGRAMS
MARK BRELAND, USA
71 KILOGRAMS
FRANK TATE, USA
75 KILOGRAMS
JOON SUP SHIN, SOUTH KOREA
81 KILOGRAMS
ANTON JOSIPOVIC, YUGOSLAVIA
91 KILOGRAMS
HENRY TILLMAN, USA
OVER 91 KILOGRAMS
TYRELL BIGGS, USA

FENCING

MEN'S TEAM ÉPEÉ
WEST GERMANY

Men's team-handball final, Yugoslavia (blue) against West Germany (white) (top). Sunder Nix in the blocks for the start of the 1,600-meter relay (bottom).

TENNIS

A pair of European teenagers named Steffi and Stefan won the titles in the demonstration sport of tennis: Steffi Graf, a 15-year-old West German, and Stefan Edberg, an 18-year-old Swede, both touring professionals. Sabrina Goles of Yugoslavia and Francisco Maciel of Mexico were the runners-up.

CANOEING

Ian Ferguson of New Zealand was the king of the kayakers, with three gold medals, in the 500-meter singles, the 500-meter pairs and the 1,000-meter fours, but he said he wouldn't mind if his two young sons did not succeed to his throne. "I'd like to see them get into a sport with a little more money in it," said Ferguson, who supported his training by installing video games in Auckland pubs.

Of the eight American entries in the canoeing and kayaking finals, only Greg Barton, in the 1,000-meter kayak singles, emerged with a medal, a bronze. No American had ever before earned a medal in the event, and certainly no American from a town, Homer, Michigan, in which the pig population outnumbered the human, 5,000 to 1,600. Barton's family supported his training by raising pigs.

West Germany went for the gold in men's team handball and in men's field hockey, and in both cases came up one goal short and settled for the silver. In team handball, Yugoslavia outscored the West Germans, 18–17, and in field hockey, Pakistan prevailed in overtime, 2–1, both victors regaining championships they had last won in 1968.

In the game for the bronze medal in field hockey, the upstart British team, led by its brilliant goalie Ian Taylor, scored a 3–2 victory over top-seeded Australia, led by Richard Charlesworth, a chronic overachiever who, in addition to being captain of the field hockey team in his third Olympics, was a physician, a Member of Parliament and a world-class cricket player.

TRACK AND FIELD

In a sense, Carl Lewis saved the best for last, his finest performance for his fourth gold medal, but once again its luster was slightly diminished because his brilliance was not seriously contested. When he started the anchor leg of the 400-meter relay, Lewis led by ten feet, and when he hit the tape 8.94 seconds later, sharing with his three American teammates the only track-and-field world record of the 1984 Games (37.83 seconds), Lewis led by more than 20 feet. The only opponent he did not run away from in Los Angeles was Jesse Owens. That duel ended, just as Lewis had hoped it would, in a tie.

David Moorcroft (385) of Britain leads Said Aouita of Morocco early in the 5,000-meter run.

The winning women's 1,600-meter relay foursome from the U.S.: left to right, Lillie Leatherwood, Valerie Brisco-Hooks, Chandra Cheeseborough, Sherri Howard.

"I'm sure Jesse would be very happy," said Owens' widow, Ruth, who watched Lewis run the relay on television.

"Jesse Owens is still the same to me—a legend," said Lewis, who had met the legend once. "Without the inspiration he gave me, I wouldn't be here today."

Yet even in his finest hour Lewis clearly could not please everyone. The first two questions of his first and last Olympic post-race news conference were directed not at him, but at his teammates—Sam Graddy, Calvin Smith and Ron Brown—asking them what they thought of him. After two questions, Graddy, who had run the lead-off leg, got up and walked out. "I'm tired of being made to feel less than Carl," said Graddy, who only a few minutes earlier had helped carry Lewis on a victory lap.

Lewis, of course, was asked for the several hundredth time about his commercial potential, and for almost the several hundredth time he felt compelled to pretend he didn't care. "If I make fifty cents or fifty thousand dollars," Lewis said, "it doesn't matter. I have four gold medals, and no one can take that away."

The United States, too, had four gold medals on this final day of track and field competition, victories in all four relays, the men's and women's 400 and the men's and women's 1,600, the latter notable mostly because Valerie Brisco-Hooks, running the third leg, earned her third gold medal. She matched Wilma Rudolph's achievement just as Lewis had matched Owens'. "She's such an outstanding lady," Brisco-Hooks said of Rudolph. "People honor me by comparing me to her." Brisco-Hooks had surpassed Rudolph in one respect. She now owned or shared three American and Olympic records.

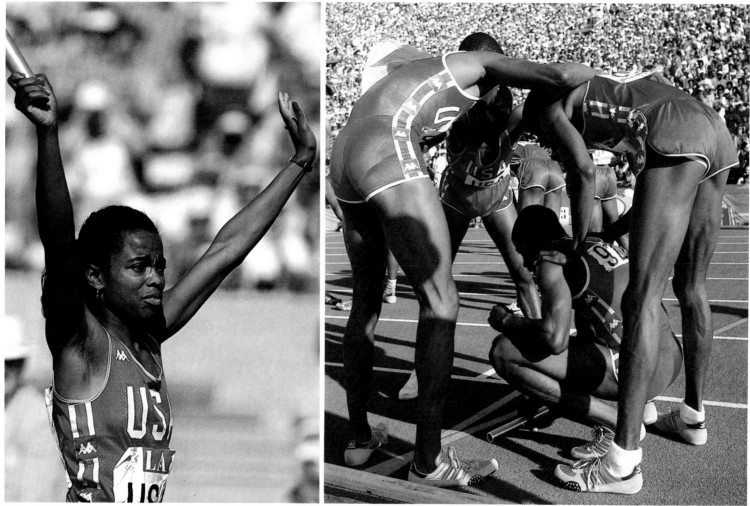

Evelyn Ashford, anchorwoman of the American women's 400-meter relay team (left). After their gold-medal victory, the American men's 1,600-meter quartet (right).

Twenty-four hours after the collision, the debate continued, most British journalists positive that Mary Decker was at fault, most Americans willing to concede that Zola Budd was not. Of the two principals, only Decker surfaced publicly and tried to assess her post-race feelings. "Imagine the worst," she said. "Imagine the worst." Did she feel sorry for Budd, too? "That's hard to say," Decker replied. "I still think it was her fault, but I don't think she did it deliberately." Budd spent the day seeing sights and saying nothing, except to her benefactors at the *London Daily Mail*. "I am upset that Mary fell and that the crowd seemed to think it was my fault," Budd told her Boswells. "I don't know what happened, but I think she ran into the back of me." In South Africa, ironically, a headline in the *Johannesburg Star* said, "Zola Trips Decker," and the *Rand Daily Mail* reported, "Zola clearly cut across the front of the American."

ARCHERY

Darrell Pace of the United States broke the Olympic archery record he had set in 1976, earned his second gold medal, then said he was looking forward to 1988, 1992 and 1996, which wasn't very encouraging to the runner-up, Rick McKinney.

Hyang Soon Seo of South Korea won the women's title, with Neroli Fairhall, the New Zealander in the wheelchair, placing 35th.

WRESTLING

Mark Schultz and Lou Banach, dutifully following the examples of their older brothers, won gold medals in freestyle wrestling, giving the U.S. a total of seven, its finest Olympic performance. When the competition ended, the crowd chanted the name of the American coach, Dan Gable of the University of Iowa, and the 220-pound Banach, who wrestled for Gable at Iowa, lifted his coach and carried him around the Anaheim Convention Center.

Coach Dan Gable on the shoulders of U.S. gold-medal wrestler Lou Banach.

Two weeks earlier, an official of Wrestling USA, the sport's governing body, had privately demanded that Gable, a former Olympic champion, resign. Gable was under pressure because, in a legal dispute to determine the American featherweight representative, he had vigorously supported Randy Lewis against the original selection, Lee Roy Smith. Lewis, coached by Gable at Iowa, won the court battle—and the gold medal. And Gable stayed on.

Mark Schultz, more than a year younger than brother Dave, and Lou Banach, precisely five minutes younger than twin Ed, scored overwhelming victories in the finals, Banach pinning a Syrian opponent in one second more than a minute, and Schultz blitzing a Japanese wrestler, 13–0, in one second less than two minutes.

Mark said he didn't realize that an extra judge had been watching him and his brother. "I guess it's because I broke the Turk's arm," he said. "My brother didn't help when he broke some guy's knee off."

Lou Banach, a reader and writer of poetry, did not speak so harshly. "The gold medal stands for persistence," he said, "and the mental part is probably the toughest." Coincidentally, the Banach twins, like Kitty and Peter Carruthers and Scotty Hamilton in Sarajevo and like Greg Louganis in Los Angeles, were adopted as children, adopted medalists.

Lou Banach working on Joseph Atiyeh of Syria in the final of the 220-pound freestyle wrestling class.

Alice Brown of the U.S., running the opening leg of the 400-meter relay.

TRACK AND FIELD

Steve Scott wanted to be the first American to win the Olympic 1,500 in 76 years, and after running the first 1,200 meters at a swift pace, he held a modest lead. His pace was too swift, his lead too modest. He had hoped to burn out the kickers, but instead he had burnt out himself. As Scott began fading toward tenth place, first Jose Abascal of Spain, then Sebastian Coe and Steve Cram of Great Britain stormed past him.

On the final turn, Coe and Cram overtook Abascal. As they faced the final straightaway, Coe, the defending champion, was in first place.

Coe wasn't supposed to be in contention. He wasn't even supposed to be in the race. A year earlier, he lay in a hospital bed. Several weeks earlier, he lost to Peter Elliott in the British championships, and when he was picked for the Olympic 1,500, over Elliott, some of his teammates resented the choice. Coe, who trained alone, coached by his father, was not immensely popular with his fellow athletes. His words, always articulate, always seemed rather calculated, too.

But now, in Los Angeles, Coe's legs were doing the talking, and they spoke eloquently of speed and stamina and courage. Twice Cram tried to kick past Coe, and twice Coe rejected the younger man's challenge. Coe pulled away, won by seven yards and set an Olympic record, 3:32.53.

If his victory in Moscow had brought him immense relief, his reputation preserved, his victory in Los Angeles brought Coe immense joy, his reputation revived. "To make a comeback within a year is something," Coe said. "But to do it in an Olympic year, with all the jitters that go with it, I am elated."

Gabriella Dorio of Italy wins the women's 1,500-meter run, ahead of Doina Melinte (obscured) and Maricica Puica (316)

Steve Ovett, tortured again by bronchial spasms, did not finish the race; once more, he left the Coliseum in an ambulance. Steve Cram came in second, without regrets. "I was beaten by a better athlete on this day," Cram said. "I'm happy for him. I didn't think Seb had it in his legs, but he did. I didn't think I had it in my legs, either, and I didn't."

Coe and Cram had preserved a remarkable tradition. In every Olympic Games except one in more than three-quarters of a century, an Englishman had placed among the top six in the 1,500-meter run.

Except for 1980, the boycott year, an American had always placed among the medalists in the high jump, but in 1984, that 88-year streak came to an end. Dwight Stones, who had kept the streak alive with his bronze-medal finishes in 1972 and 1976, jumped 7 feet 7 inches, four inches higher than he had ever gone in the Olympics, but this time, at the age of 30, he did not earn a medal. He came in fourth and blew kisses to the crowd. But Stones' failure to medal was only a minor shock; the major shock in the high jump was that Zhu Jianhua of China, the world-record holder at 7 feet 10 inches, could go no higher than Stones and won the bronze medal only on the basis of fewer misses. Dietmar Moegenburg of West Germany won the gold at 7 feet 8½ inches.

Italy launched an unexpected pair of champions, the Andrei-Dorio combination, Alessandro Andrei the first Italian to win the Olympic shot put, Gabriella Dorio the first Italian woman to win an Olympic running event, the 1,500 meters. Ria Stalman, from the Netherlands and Arizona State University, won the women's discus and got the inside story for her newspaper column; Said Aouita of Morocco won the men's 5,000 meters and got a congratulatory phone call from King Hassan II; and Raul Gonzalez of Mexico won the 50-kilometer walk and, as he entered the Coliseum looking remarkably fresh after his 31-mile stroll, got thunderous applause. Gonzalez and Stalman were both Olympic champions in their thirties.

It was a good day for Italy, as Alessandro Andrei won the shot put.

The medalists in the men's high jump: top, left, Patrick Sjoberg (silver); top, right, Zhu Jianhua (bronze); bottom, Dietmar Moegenburg (gold).

U.S. defeats Brazil in volleyball final. Center, Karch Kiraly (15).

VOLLEYBALL

Pat Powers, an All-American at the University of Southern California, knew that Brazil was beaten even before the match began. "I looked into their eyes," Powers said, "and I knew we had them. I had no doubts about it."

Seventy-nine minutes later—89 years after the game was invented in the United States, four days after the women's team won America's first Olympic medal ever in the sport—the American men struck gold in volleyball. They scored three straight one-sided victories, 15–6, 15–6 and 15–7, over the Brazilian team that had defeated them in an earlier, less meaningful match.

Powers, who spent several pre-game hours in a self-induced trance, awoke in time to succeed on 22 of 37 attempted spikes. "Balls hit 120 miles an hour looked like balloons to me," he said.

After the match, Tom Selleck, the actor and volleyball fanatic, entered the interview room to share his thoughts about the U.S. team. He said that even if all the boycotting nations had come to Los Angeles, the Americans would have won the gold medal. He said that the Americans, preparing for the Olympics, had beaten all the best Eastern European teams. He had conducted a very thorough private investigation.

SOCCER

The largest crowd to pay to see an Olympic event in Los Angeles, 101,799 people, stood up in the Rose Bowl to listen to the "Marseillaise," the stirring anthem that celebrated France's 2–0 victory over Brazil for the gold medal in soccer. The crowd broke the one-day-old record for soccer in the United States and produced one of the few monumental traffic jams to accompany the 1984 Games. The French victory left Joaquim Cruz the only Brazilian with a gold medal.

RHYTHMIC GYMNASTICS

Rhythmic gymnastics reared its Olympic head, a graceful game that, surprisingly, inspired verbal violence. When one reporter called rhythmic gymnastics "a kind of prettied-up aerobics," Millie Zimring, the mother of the top American, fired off a letter to the editor, calling the report "insensitive and insulting." The reporter's next story noted that Lori Fung of Canada won the individual all-around gold while "the world's best rhythmic gymnasts (were) twirling their ribbons at home." He also mentioned that Mrs. Zimring's daughter, Valerie, was "way back in the pack."

BOXING

Only Virgil Hill, among the ten American finalists, did not win a gold medal in boxing, but his silver helped lift the American medal total for the day, in all sports, to seventeen gold, six silver and three bronze, a haul both awesome and embarrassing. The U.S. now had 80 gold medals in the Games, matching the Olympic record set by the host country in Moscow in 1980, and there was still one day, and four finals, to go.

Paul Gonzales won without throwing a punch; his scheduled opponent bowed out with a broken thumb. Pernell Whitaker and Mark Breland won handsomely, punching brilliantly, living up to their reputations. Meldrick Taylor and Jerry Page earned unanimous but hard-fought decisions. Heavyweight Henry Tillman upset Willie deWit of Canada, super-heavyweight Tyrell Biggs won a decision that was booed and Frank Tate won a decision that was booed even more heartily. Tate took two standing eight-counts and a unanimous decision over Canada's Shawn O'Sullivan.

In post-fight interviews, Tillman dwelt on his past, the eighteen months he spent in prison for armed robbery, the heroin addiction he had overcome, and Breland dwelt on his future. "I'll fight professionally for three years," Breland said. "No longer. I have other things to fall back on, my education and my career in the movies. I don't like to get marked up too much in the face, but for a couple of million dollars, I'll let them mark me."

Breland, his amateur record 110–1, might be the one heading for show business, but Tillman had the best line of any boxer. Asked a few days earlier how far he lived from the Sports Arena, Tillman replied, "Three or four miles, depending on the traffic." He laughed, too, when he realized what he had said.

One of the most competitive boxing finals: Frank Tate (left) of the U.S. defeats Shawn O'Sullivan (right) of Canada in the 156-pound class.

He was generally considered the greatest judo player in history, but as Yasuhiro Yamashita of Japan approached the final in the open division, his winning streak, spanning five years and approaching 200 matches, was in jeopardy. In a preliminary match, he had torn a calf muscle in his right leg.

But in the final, his opponent—and admirer—Mohamed Rashwan of Egypt, did not attack Yamashita's leg. "That would be against my principles," said Rashwan. "I don't want to win that way."

The 27-year-old Yamashita won his way, by ippon, the judo equivalent of a knockout, in a match that lasted barely a minute. Afterward, the 280-pound Yamashita looked over at his parents and, like so many less formidable medalists, he cried.

Mark Breland (right) of the U.S. outpointing An Young Su (left) of South Korea in the 147-pound final.

DAY 16
SUNDAY, AUGUST 12th

More than any other track and field event in the Olympics, the marathon belonged to the world. Runners from ten nations and five continents had captured the race, and runners from 22 countries had earned medals. The last American to win the marathon, Frank Shorter, was born in West Germany; the last Frenchman, Alain Mimoun, in Algeria; the only Japanese, Kitei Son, in Korea (as Kee Chung Sohn); and the only South African, Kenneth McArthur, in Ireland. Since no one representing West Germany, Algeria, Korea or Ireland had ever won the race, fifteen nations could claim, legitimately, to have spawned or nurtured an Olympic marathon champion. One of the countries that could not was Australia, which had never even produced a medalist, a condition that was expected to be rectified on the final day of the Games in Los Angeles.

Rob de Castella of Australia, who had not been defeated in a marathon in four years, was favored to win the gold medal. Experts predicted he would be pressed by Toshihiko Seko, who wanted to be the first marathon champion born in Japan, and Alberto Salazar, the owner of the world's best time, representing the United States, who hoped to be the first born in Cuba.

But the most predictable aspect of the race was that the predicted winner rarely won. Perhaps the classic surprise was Waldemar Cierpinski of East Germany, whose unexpected victory in 1976 was an inspiration to the East German soccer team that was about to play Poland for the Olympic championship. "If this living example of mediocrity can lift himself up and win the marathon," said Juergen Croy, the German goalie, "and we don't beat Poland, we are never going to hear the end of it." East Germany beat Poland. Four years later, still an underdog, Cierpinski became only the second man to win the Olympic marathon for a second time.

THE GOLD MEDALISTS

TRACK AND FIELD

MEN'S MARATHON
  CARLOS LOPES, PORTUGAL

EQUESTRIAN

GRAND PRIX JUMPING
  JOE FARGIS, USA

DIVING

MEN'S PLATFORM
  GREG LOUGANIS, USA

SYNCHRONIZED SWIMMING

SOLO
  TRACIE RUIZ, USA

DIVING

Tucking it in off the platform, Greg Louganis.

In the platform diving final, Greg Louganis faced an opponent he had never defeated, the only opponent that had even a slight chance against him. He faced the 700-point barrier, a level he had never reached and no other diver had approached.

Louganis' bid to reach 700 came down to his final dive. He chose the one the rule book called No. 307C, a 3.4 degree of difficulty, the highest of any platform dive. But 307C was not only difficult; it was dangerous. It was known as the "Dive of Death," which was not mere hyperbole. In 1983 a gifted Soviet diver named Sergei Shlibashvili, attempting to execute 307C, struck his head against the platform, fractured his skull and, a week later, died of a massive cerebral hemorrhage.

Now Louganis stood on the tall platform in Los Angeles, facing 307C—and 700. "I was scared," he said later. He wasn't afraid of injury; he was afraid of a mistake, a small error that would destroy his bid for 700. He needed exceptionally high scores. If all the judges gave him 8's, which any other diver in the world would have considered exceptionally high for 307C, he would not quite achieve 700. "I stood there," Louganis said, "and told myself that no matter what I do here, my mother will still love me. That thought gives you a lot of strength." Louganis also thought of a song, "Believe in Yourself" from *The Wiz.* The music played in his head.

And then Louganis performed 307C, a reverse three-and-a-half somersault tuck, executed to the brink of perfection, high off the board, tight tuck, three and a half graceful flips to an entry, after a 33-foot drop, so precise he barely disturbed the surface. One judge said the dive was perfect. Another said it was worth a 9.5. All the others awarded Louganis 9's. He had cracked the 700 barrier; his final total was 710.91.

"It's like going over thirty feet in the long jump," said Ron O'Brien, one of the coaches of the U.S. diving team.

"It's like batting .450 for a whole season in baseball," said the other coach, Dick Kimball, whose son, Bruce, came in second, more than 60 points behind Louganis.

Louganis had a world record and his second gold medal, the record-breaking 81st of the Games for the United States. He had become the first male diver in 56 years to win both the springboard and platform golds.

"We won't see another like him in our lifetime," said O'Brien.

One of Greg Louganis' winning dives in the platform event.

Louganis soars to his second gold medal.

EQUESTRIAN

The individual show jumping competition ended in a jump-off between a pair of American teammates and friends, Joe Fargis and Conrad Homfeld, who for six years had been sharing a horse farm in Petersburg, Virginia. On the jump-off for the gold, Fargis turned in a flawless ride, Homfeld did not, and Fargis gave credit for his victory to his close relationship with his mount, A Touch of Class. "I've been overdosing her with carrots," Fargis said.

Joe Fargis astride Touch of Class in the show jumping competition.

Tracie Ruiz in the synchronized-swimming solo event.

Performing in front of her all-time favorite actress, Esther Williams, who was the star of her all-time favorite film, *Million-Dollar Mermaid,* Tracie Ruiz won the 83rd gold medal for the United States, in solo synchronized swimming, an event that sounded like a contradiction in terms. Solo synchronized swimming was added to the lineup of Olympic events only after the Eastern European nations decided to boycott. The victory for Ruiz reinforced a joke that had been circulating for days:

Question: Who won more gold medals for the United States than any man in history?

Answer: Chernenko.

West Germany had the second-highest number of medals, 59 overall, to 174 for the U.S., and both China, with 15 gold medals, and Canada, with 44 overall, made impressively strong showings.

Romania captured the second-highest number of gold medals, 20, which inspired one Romanian journalist to attempt an assessment—in English—of his country's athletes. "Romanians good boys," he explained. "Strong like bull. Smart like refrigerator."

The start of the men's marathon in Santa Monica.

TRACK AND FIELD

Six days after he came in second in the 10,000-meter run, Finland's Martti Vainio, who had long been suspected of blood doping, a technique not yet susceptible to testing, became the fifth Olympian in Los Angeles, and the second medalist, to be disqualified for using anabolic steroids. Vainio and the only other track and field athlete to be disqualified—Anna Verouli, a Greek javelin thrower—both claimed they were innocent. A California doctor, an advocate of anabolic steriods, Dr. Robert Kerr, claimed that he had prescribed forbidden drugs to twelve Olympic medalists who had escaped detection. Dr. Kerr named none. "I think he is seeking publicity," said Prince Alexandre de Merode, the chairman of the IOC Medical Commission.

Among the favorites in the marathon, Alberto Salazar was the first to fall back. By 20 miles, he was already more than a minute behind the leaders. Then Rob de Castella made his move, but not the move the experts anticipated. He reached for a drink of water, and while he drank, the leaders ran away from him. The Japanese star, Toshihiko Seko, also sipped, and slipped, far back, his bid finished. As the diminished pack of leaders passed the 20-mile mark, the figurative halfway point in the 26-mile test, one of them, John Treacy of Ireland, who had never run a marathon before, asked himself a question. "Where's the barrier?" he said.

His rivals for the lead were not experienced enough to supply an answer. After 21 miles, the race was among only three men—Treacy, Charlie Spedding of Great Britain and Carlos Lopes of Portugal—three men from countries which had never won an Olympic marathon. Spedding was 32 and had never been beaten in a marathon; he had run in only two. Lopes was 37 and had never won a marathon; he had completed only one.

But Lopes at least was an internationally known runner, the silver medalist in the 10,000 meters in Montreal in 1976, a mere 10–1 shot in the race, not 100–1 like Treacy and Spedding, the Irishman and the Englishman running side by side in Los Angeles on a day when Irish and English were firing at each other in Belfast.

In the final three miles, Lopes pulled away from his challengers, and by the time he trotted into the Coliseum, to be cheered in the twilight, he was more than half a minute in front, on his way to a winning time of 2:09:21, the fastest in Olympic history. Lopes, incidentally, had once been a goatherd; the first Olympic marathon champion, Spiridon Louis of Greece, had been a shepherd.

Treacy, 27, came in second, ahead of Spedding, and the medal for Ireland was its first of the Games, lifting the number of countries to earn at least one medal to 47, only one short of the Olympic high achieved in Munich in 1972. Lawrence Byrne, the coach of the Irish track and field team, said he was certain there would be suitable celebrations back home. "I'm sure a few people will raise their glasses tonight," he said. "Of course it doesn't take much for them to raise their glasses."

Carlos Lopes wins the marathon in the Coliseum. It was Portugal's first gold medal of the Games.

Sign at the closing ceremony.

Seventy-eight marathoners ran in to the closing ceremony on tired feet. Three equestrian medalists rode in on horseback. A man from outer space arrived in a spaceship and a blaze of laser beams. Cary Grant came in a bus. Mary Lou Retton showed up on the shoulders of a swimmer. Edwin Moses arrived in a fez and a Moroccan jacket. "I just feel like a citizen of the universe," Moses said.

One hundred thousand spectators brought the attendance for the 1984 Olympics close to six million, and the sixteen-day spectacle ended, without incident, in a kaleidoscope of actors and athletes, flags and fireworks and flashlights. It was Hollywood on parade, everyone marching to the beat of speeches advocating peace and prosperity and good will, everyone swaying to the music of "All Night Long," a special twelve-minute version of his hit sung by Lionel Richie, and "Auld Lang Syne."

Break dancers by the dozens put on the last display of athleticism, and the world's greatest athlete, Daley Thompson, as usual, had the final word, on a fresh T-shirt: "Thanks, L.A., See You in Seoul!"

The Games of the XXIII Olympiad conclude with a dazzling fireworks display.

USA

THE 1984 OLYMPIC GAMES

SUMMARY OF RESULTS AND STATISTICS

OFFICERS AND ADMINISTRATIVE LEADERS* UNITED STATES OLYMPIC COMMITTEE '81–'84

*All current officers, past presidents, and IOC members for the United States are also members of the Executive Board.

   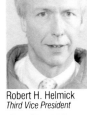

William E. Simon	John B. Kelly, Jr.	Dr. Evie G. Dennis	Robert H. Helmick	Stephen B. Sobel
President	First Vice President	Second Vice President	Third Vice President	Secretary

Lawrence A. Hough
Treasurer

Col. F. Don Miller
USA (ret.)
Executive Director

Baaron Pittenger
Assistant
Executive Director

Lt. Gen. W. H. Buse, Jr.
USMC (ret.)
Assistant to President

William E. Simon, President
John B. Kelly, Jr., First Vice President
Dr. Evie G. Dennis, Second Vice President
Robert H. Helmick, Third Vice President
Stephen B. Sobel, Secretary
Lawrence A. Hough, Treasurer
Clifford H. Buck, Past President
Robert J. Kane, Past President
Philip O. Krumm, Past President
Douglas F. Roby, IOC Member
Julian K. Roosevelt, IOC Member
Richard G. Kline, Counselor
George Gowen, Assistant Counselor
William Hybl, Assistant Counselor
James Morris, Assistant Counselor
Patrick H. Sullivan, Counselor Emeritus
Col. F. Don Miller, USA (ret.) Executive Director
Baaron Pittenger, Assistant Executive Director
Lt. Gen. W. H. Buse, Jr., USMC (ret.) Assistant to President

MEMBERS OF THE USOC EXECUTIVE BOARD

*Members with voice, but no vote.
**Members of the Executive Board during the quadrennium, but not members August 1, 1984.
***Deceased.
[1]AAC is the acronym for the Athletes' Advisory Council. The USOC Executive Board, by constitutional provision, must have at least 20 percent membership from active members who may be elected by the total membership of the Athletes' Advisory Council.

George Allen,* President's Council on Fitness and Sports
Lloyd Arnold,** YMCA, Cranbury, NJ
Loring Baker, Boxing, Atlanta, GA
David Brown, Public Sector, Springfield, NJ
Peter Buehning, Team Handball, Short Hills, NJ
Col. Howard Buxton, Biathlon, Winooski, VT
Timothy Caldwell, AAC[1], Putney, VT
Tony Carlino,** Bobsled, Lake Placid, NY
Jimmy Carnes, Track and Field, Gainesville, FL
Harlon B. Carter, Shooting, Washington, DC
Lt. Gen. A. P. Clark, Boy Scouts, Monument, CO
Matthew Cusack, CYO, Yonkers, NY
Ten Eyck Danko, AAC[1], New York, NY
Fred Danner,** Table Tennis, Huntington, NY
Anita DeFrantz, AAC, Vice Chair[1], Los Angeles, CA
Russell Dermond, Canoeing, Westwood, NJ
Dr. Brice Durbin, NFSHSA, Kansas City, MO
Gene Edwards, Soccer, Milwaukee, WI
John Ferrell, YMCA, Chicago, IL
Dr. Barbara Forker, AAHPERD, Ames, IA
Charles Foster, Figure Skating, Duxbury, MA
Herman Frazier, AAC[1], Tempe, AZ
Frank Fullerton, Judo, El Paso, TX
Ann Gerli,** Figure Skating, New York, NY
Charles Gibson, Skiing, Fairfield, CT
Robert F. Giegengack, Track and Field, Bethany, CT
Thomas Gompf, Aquatics, Miami, FL
John K. Greer, Field Hockey (M), Cos Cob, CT
Allan Hachigian, AAC[1], Lake Placid, NY
Richard Harkins, AAU, Kansas City, MO
Francis Heffron, Group D, Short Hills, NJ
Dr. Harold W. Henning, Aquatics, Naperville, IL
Capt. J. Henson,** USN, AAU, Falls Church, VA
William Hickey,** Bobsled, Keene, NY
Richard Hollander,** Track and Field, Richmond, VA
Werner Holzer, Wrestling, Des Plaines, IL
George Howie, Speed Skating, Oconomowoc, WI
Oscar T. Lobst, Jr.,** Figure Skating, Churchville, PA
Emily Johnson,** Fencing, San Francisco, CA
Laurel Kessel, AAC[1], Albuquerque, NM
Chris Knepp, AAC, Chair[1], Houston, TX
Edgar Knepper,** Gymnastics, Wilmington, DE
Kathy Kretschmer-Huss, AAC, Secretary[1] Tucson, AZ
John B. Layton,** Shooting, Washington, DC
Stephen Lieberman, Archery, Reading, PA
Peter Lippett, Rowing, San Francisco, CA
William H. Lynn, Yachting, Atlanta, GA
David Maggard, NCAA, Berkeley, CA
Stanley Malless, Tennis, Indianapolis, IN
Lt. Gen. W. Maloney, USMC—Armed Forces
Michel Mamlouk, Fencing, Washington, DC
Henry Marsh, AAC[1], Bountiful, UT
Jimmy McClure, Table Tennis, Indianapolis, IN
Richard McDevitt, Equestrian Sports, Philadelphia, PA
Adm. W. McDonald,** USN—Armed Forces, Norfolk, VA
Al McGuire,* President's Council on Fitness and Sports

William Middendorf, Public Sector, McLean, VA
Howard C. Miller, Public Sector, Boston, MA
Brig. Gen. R. Montague, Jr., Disabled in Sports, Washington, DC
James Moriarty,** Luge, Lake Placid, NY
Dr. Leotus L. Morrison,** AIAW, Harrisonburg, VA
Edwin H. Mosler, Jr.,*** Group D, New York, NY
Fred Newhouse, AAC¹, Houston, TX
Sheila Ochowicz, AAC¹, Peewaukee, WI
Wilbur H. Peck, Softball, Indianapolis, IN
Don E. Porter, McLean, VA, Oklahoma City, OK
Cynthia Potter, AAC¹, Tucson, AZ
Rudy Sablo, Weightlifting, New York, NY
Joseph Scalzo,** Wrestling, Toledo, OH
Peter Schnugg, AAC¹, Menlo Park, CA
Ernest Seubert, Cycling, Little Falls, NJ
Donna Shavlik, Public Sector, Washington, DC
Robert Sheppard, Public Sector, Carmel, CA
Alfred E. Smith,* Dept. of State, Washington, DC
Dr. Robert Smith, Baseball, Greenville, IL
Jack Starling, AAC¹, Midland, MI
Daniel Steinman, Modern Pentathlon, Hatboro, PA
Dr. Edward Steitz, Basketball, Springfield, MA
Andras Toro, AAC¹, El Cerrito, CA
W. Thayer Tutt, Ice Hockey, Colorado Springs, CO
Dr. LeRoy T. Walker, NAIA, Durham, NC
Marie Walker, Roller Skating, Groton, CT
Bruce Wilhelm, AAC¹, San Francisco, CA
Bud Wilkinson, Gymnastics, St. Louis, MO
Harold O. Zinman, Jewish Welfare Board, Marblehead, MA

USOC ADMINISTRATION/LOS ANGELES GAMES

William E. Simon, President
John B. Kelly, Jr., First Vice President, Chief of Mission and Chairman, Games Preparation Committee
Dr. Evie G. Dennis, Second Vice President and Chairman, Team Services Committee
Robert H. Helmick, Third Vice President and Asst. Chief of Mission
Stephen B. Sobel, Secretary
Lawrence A. Hough, Treasurer

Col. F. Don Miller, Secretary General
Lt. Gen. W. Henry Buse, Jr., Asst. to President
Robert J. Kane, Attaché
Richard Kline, Counselor
Irving Dardik, Chairman, Sports Medicine Council
Beatrice Toner, Chairman, Apparel and Supplies
William Tutt, Chairman, Housing
Hermann G. Rusch, Chairman, Food
George E. Killian, Chairman, Transportation

USOC SUPPORT STAFF

Baaron B. Pittenger, Asst. Executive Director
John Buck, Asst. Director of Fund Raising
Morton W. Butzen, Motorola
Lajuan Conner, Secretary to Col. Miller
Major Arthur Copeland, USAF, Armed Forces Rep.
Major J. Brian Egan, USMC, Armed Forces Rep.
Rochelle Evans, Headquarters Staff
Ernest Hinck, Business Manager
Sweela Hortick, United Air Lines
Arthur Kuman, Director of Corporate Participation
Jerry Lace, Director of Operations
Mike Moran, Director of Communications
Leroy Neiman, Official Artist
C. Robert Paul, Jr., Sp. Asst. to Executive Director

Linda Quayle, Asst. to Official Artist
James Warsinske, Ticket Distribution
M.L. Whiting, Director of Ticket Distribution
Paul Wiggin, LAOOC Liaison

ASSISTANTS IN OPERATIONS DEPARTMENT

Sheryl Abbot
Frank Aires
Marilyn Crawford
Thomas McLean
Sheila Walker

ATHLETES' REPRESENTATIVES

Karl Anderson
Laurel Brassey-Kessel
Katherine Kretschmer-Huss
Dorothy Morkis

Royden Hobson, Official Photographer

PRESS LIAISON STAFF

Bob Condron, Asst. Director
Gayle Bodin, Asst. Director
Hal Bateman, U.S. Air Force Academy
Rick Brewer, University of North Carolina
James Brock, Cotton Bowl Association
Bob Cornell, Colgate University
Jeff Dimond, U.S. Swimming, Inc.
Claude Felton, University of Georgia
Bill Hancock, Big Eight Conference
Dru Hancock, University of Missouri
Herb Hartnett, University of Pennsylvania
Debby Jennings, University of Tennessee
John Keith, University of New Mexico
Leslie King, USA Amateur Boxing Federation
Rich Lewis, Providence, RI
Jim Marchiony, Washington, DC
Jim McGrath, Butler University
Richard Rotkov, New York, NY
Nick Vista, Michigan State University

MEDICAL SERVICES

MEDICAL DOCTORS

Robert Leach, Head Team Physician, Boston, MA
Roy Bergman, Escanaba, MI
Eileen Haworth, Santa Monica, CA
Emily Lutz, Circleville, OH
Ben Mayne, Saginaw, MI
Capt. William McDaniel, USN, Annapolis, MD
Doug Shaw, Santa Barbara, CA
Debra Waters, Lackland AFB, TX

TRAINERS

Bob Beeten, Head Trainer, Colorado Springs, CO
Christine Bonci, University of Pennsylvania
Tom Bynum, Greensboro, NC
Gary Gardiner, Sea Cliff, NY
Tim Garl, Indiana University
Nancy Harris, Colorado Springs, CO
Terry Hazucha, Worthington, OH
Marguerite Higgins, Auburn University
Debbie Jackson, Eastern Kentucky University
Robert Moore, San Diego State University
Jack Moser, Albany, NY
Gayle Olson, North Easton, MA
George Roberts, Titusville, PA
Stanley Scott, Stanford University
Jennifer Stone, Colorado Springs, CO
Dean Weber, University of Arizona
Linda Zoller, Dartmouth College

ABBREVIATIONS USED FOR NATIONS LISTED IN STATISTICAL SUMMARIES

ALG Algeria	JPN Japan
ARG Argentina	KEN Kenya
AUS Australia	KOR South Korea
AUT Austria	LIE Liechtenstein
BAH Bahamas	MAL Malaysia
BAR Barbados	MAR Morocco
BEL Belgium	MEX Mexico
BER Bermuda	NGR Nigeria
BRA Brazil	NOR Norway
BUL Bulgaria	NZL New Zealand
CAN Canada	PAK Pakistan
CHI Chile	PAN Panama
CHN China	PER Peru
CIV Ivory Coast	POL Poland
CMR Cameroon	POR Portugal
COL Colombia	PUR Puerto Rico
CRC Costa Rica	QAT Qatar
DEN Denmark	ROM Romania
DJI Djibouti	SAU Saudi Arabia
DOM Dominican Republic	SEN Senegal
EGY Egypt	SMR San Marino
ESP Spain	SUD Sudan
FIN Finland	SUI Switzerland
FRA France	SWE Sweden
FRG West Germany	SYR Syria
GBR Great Britain	TAN Tanzania
GDR East Germany	TCH Czechoslovakia
GRE Greece	THA Thailand
HOL The Netherlands	TPE Chinese Taipei
HUN Hungary	TRI Trinidad and Tobago
INA Indonesia	TUR Turkey
IND India	UGA Uganda
IRL Ireland	URS Soviet Union
IRQ Iraq	USA United States
ISL Iceland	VEN Venezuela
ISR Israel	YUG Yugoslavia
ITA Italy	ZAM Zambia
JAM Jamaica	ZIM Zimbabwe

RESULTS ABBREVIATIONS

DISQ Disqualified
DNC Did Not Compete
DNF Did Not Finish
DNP Did Not Participate
DNQ Did Not Qualify
EOR Equals Olympic Record
EWR Equals World Record
NOR New Olympic Record
NWR New World Record

THE XIV OLYMPIC WINTER GAMES
Sarajevo, Yugoslavia

DATE BEGUN: 2/8/84
DATE ENDED: 2/19/84

This section has been written and compiled by
C. Robert Paul, Jr., Special Assistant to the USOC
Executive Director.

ALL-TIME MEDAL WINNINGS FOR THE OLYMPIC WINTER GAMES 1924-1984

(Ranked According to Total Medals Won)

Country	Gold	Silver	Bronze	Total
1. Norway	54	56	51	161
2. Soviet Union	67	48	41	156
3. USA	40	45	29	114
4. Finland	28	42	32	102
5. German Dem. Rep.	34	29	30	93
6. Austria	24	32	28	84
7. Sweden	29	23	28	80
8. Switzerland	18	20	20	58
9. Canada	13	8	16	37
10. France	12	9	13	34

THE MEDAL STANDINGS

1984 WINTER OLYMPICS

	Gold	Silver	Bronze	Total
Soviet Union	6	10	9	25
German Dem. Rep.	9	9	6	24
Finland	4	3	6	13
Norway	3	2	4	9
USA	4	4	0	8
Sweden	4	2	2	8
Czechoslovakia	0	2	4	6
Switzerland	2	2	1	5
German Fed. Rep.	2	1	1	4
Canada	2	1	1	4
France	0	1	2	3
Italy	2	0	0	2
Liechtenstein	0	0	2	2
Great Britain	1	0	0	1
Japan	0	1	0	1
Yugoslavia	0	1	0	1
Austria	0	0	1	1

BIATHLON

The United States has yet to earn a medal in the biathlon. Although there is a small, dedicated cadre of athletes participating in this testing sport, the results were no more promising in 1984 than they have been in the past. In the 10-kilometer race, a young Dartmouth graduate, Willie Carow, placed 20th. In the longer 20-kilometer race, the veteran biathlete Lyle Nelson was 26th among the 61 finishers.

The delicate balance required to put together a competitive biathlon relay quartet was not present when the United States finished 11th out of 17, almost six minutes behind the winner.

Peter Angerer, German Federal Republic, rated fourth among the biathletes, ignored the frightful weather conditions on Mount Igman and overcame Czechoslovakia's Jan Matousch on the final leg to capture the 20-kilometer test. Matousch fell apart and finished tenth because of the penalty for five missed shots at the target.

The fastest skier in the pack was bronze medalist Erik Kvalfoss, Norway, with a raw time of 1:09:02.4 (he was penalized five minutes for missed shots), opposed to the elapsed time of 1:09:52.7 for gold medalist Peter Angerer.

The 10-kilometer sprint was conducted three days after the longer race. Kvalfoss, with the fastest time on the snow for the longer race, used his speed to win the gold medal, although Angerer probably skied at a faster pace. The elapsed time was 30:53.8 for Kvalfoss and 31:02.4 for Angerer. But Angerer skied three penalty loops to two for Kvalfoss, providing Kvalfoss with the margin of victory.

One nostalgic note. It was probably the end of the road for Frank Ullrich, German Democratic Republic, winner of a gold and a silver in the individual events four years earlier. The 26-year-old biathlete finished fifth in the 20-kilometer event and was a disappointing 17th in the shorter race. He had been a top biathlete since 1977.

At Lake Placid the Soviet biathletes won two golds, a silver, and a bronze. At Sarajevo the Soviets came through to capture only a gold medal in the relay (nosing out Norway and the German Federal Republic).

The competitive life of a biathlete would appear to be short, based on a comparison of the results of 1980 and of 1984. Angerer, winner of a gold and two silvers at Sarajevo, placed eighth in the shorter race at Lake Placid. Yvon Mougel, bellwether of the French biathletes, was sixth in the 20-kilometer race at Lake Placid. At Sarajevo he upheld his reputation and was fourth in the 20 kilometer and sixth in the shorter race.

TEAM PERSONNEL

Willie Carow, 25, Putney, VT
Glenn Eberle, 20, McCall, ID
Martin Hagen, 29, Wilson, WY
Lyle Nelson, 35, Olympic Valley, CA
Donald Nielsen, 32, Boulder, CO
Joshua Thompson, 21, Ashford, WA

Marie Alkire, Mesa, AZ, shooting coach
Ken Alligood, Anchorage, AK, ski coach
Lt. Col. William Spencer, USAR, Essex Junction, VT, manager

BIATHLON

20-KILOMETER INDIVIDUAL (February 11, 1984)

1. **Peter Angerer, FRG**	1:11:52.7
2. **Frank-Peter Roetsch, GDR**	1:13:21.4
3. **Erik Kvalfoss, NOR**	1:14:02.4
4. Yvon Mougel, FRA	1:14:53.1
5. Frank Ullrich, GDR	1:14:53.7
6. Rolf Storsveen, NOR	1:15:23.9
7. Fritz Fischer, FRG	1:15:49.7
8. Leif Andersson, SWE	1:16:19.3
26. Lyle Nelson, USA	1:21:05.4
33. Glenn Eberle, USA	1:22:15.0
53. Martin Hagen, USA	1:30:19.8

10-KILOMETER INDIVIDUAL (February 14, 1984)

1. **Erik Kvalfoss, NOR**	30:53.8
2. **Peter Angerer, FRG**	31:02.4
3. **Matthias Jacob, GDR**	31:10.5
4. Kjell Soebak, NOR	31:19.7
5. Algimantas Shalna, URS	31:20.8
6. Yvon Mougel, FRA	31:32.9
7. Frank-Peter Roetsch, GDR	31:49.8
8. Toivo Makikyro, FIN	31:52.4
20. Willie Carow, USA	33:05.8
40. Josh Thompson, USA	35:10.5

4 x 7.5-KILOMETER RELAY (February 17, 1984)

1. **URS (Dimitri Vasiliev, Yuri Kashkarin,** **Algimantas Shalna, Sergei Bulygin)**	1:38:51.7
2. **NOR (Odd Lirhus, Erik Kvalfoss,** **Rolf Storsveen, Kjell Soebak)**	1:39:03.9
3. **FRG (Ernst Reiter, Walter Richler,** **Peter Angerer, Fritz Fischer)**	1:39:05.1
4. GDR	1:40:04.7
5. ITA	1:42:32.81
6. TCH	1:42:40.5
7. FIN	1:43:16.0
8. AUT	1:43:28.1
11. USA (Willie Carow, Don Nielsen, Lyle Nelson, Josh Thompson)	1:44:31.9

TEAM PERSONNEL

W. Carow   G. Eberle   M. Hagen

L. Nelson   D. Nielsen   J. Thompson

M. Alkire   K. Alligood   Lt. Col. W. Spencer

BOBSLED

The sweep of the German Democratic Republic bob-sledders, who won the gold and silver in both the two-man and four-man events, may be of secondary importance when the history of the sport is rewritten.

"Technology" was the buzz word among the bobsled-ding aficionados attending the Olympic Winter Games. By way of introduction, the U.S. bobsledders had been promised an innovative sled developed in the States through American sports technology. This goal was never achieved.

The USSR and the GDR showed up at Sarajevo with magnificent bobsleds considered light-years ahead of everyone else's. For years the sport had been depen-dent on and dominated by sleds manufactured by an Italian company, with minor changes in design when suggested by the purchasers.

So fast were the Soviet and the GDR bobsledders that there was talk the International Bobsled Federation would adopt regulations for a standard design for global competitions. It was another case of discussions aimed at achieving mediocrity and maintaining the status quo in this sport that has been a part of the Winter Olym-pics since the inaugural Games in Chamonix, France, in 1924.

Just how much a Swiss bobsled bought for the Ameri-cans meant to the U.S. I four-man team is exemplified by its fifth-place finish. Off the first two runs the team was unfamiliar with the new sled, posting the eleventh- and eighth-fastest times. On the final two runs the sled had the fifth- and fourth-fastest runs respectively to achieve a fifth-place finish.

Again, the four-man event was a race of milliseconds. The winning margin for the GDR I sled over that coun-try's No. II team was .56 seconds. The U.S. I sled was 3.11 seconds in the rear after the four runs.

The U.S. bobsled federation has four years to design modern sleds in order to become competitive with the GDR, the USSR, and Switzerland.

After recruiting potential bobsledders from other sports like track and field, the GDR entered bobsled competi-tion in Innsbruck, 1976, for the first time, winning both the two and four-man events. At Lake Placid the GDR

and Switzerland had the best balanced bobsled combi-nations. With the rise of the Soviet Union, experts pre-dicted the Big Two would become the Big Three.

So in the 1984 two-man event, the order of finish was GDR II, GDR I, USSR II, USSR I, Swiss II, Swiss I. The superiority of the GDR II two-man team of Wolfgang Hoppe and Dietmar Schauerhammer was obvious after analyzing the statistics. This pair had the fastest times for three of the four runs and was the second fastest behind the USSR I sled on the second trip down the course. So the German Democratic Republic bobsled-ders have captured five of the six gold medals available during the last three Olympic Winter Games.

Conversely, the finishes for the United States in 1984 were 5th and 16th in the four-man, 15th and 17th in the two-man. At Lake Placid the U.S. wound up 12th and 13th in the four-man and 5th and 6th in the two-man. At Innsbruck in 1976 U.S. forces recorded 15th- and 19th-place finishes in the four-man, and 14th- and 19th-place finishes in the two-man. There remains room for improvement and consistency, and a need for develop-ing a broader base in the bobsledding cadre at its per-manent headquarters in Lake Placid. Money may be one need, but an expansive program and the infusion of new technology are musts.

TEAM PERSONNEL

Thomas Barnes, 24, U.S. I four-man, Dover, DE
Joseph Briski, 28, U.S. I four-man, LaMesa, CA
John Wayne DeAtley, 25, U.S. II two-man, Virginia Beach, VA
Frederick Fritsch, 30, U.S. II two-man, Virginia Beach, VA
Robert Hickey, 31, reserve driver, Keene, NY
Hal A. Hoye, 26, U.S. I four-man, Malone, NY
Jeffrey W. Jost, 30, U.S. I four-man, Burke, NY
Brent Rushlaw, 32, U.S. I two-man and U.S. II four-man, Saranac Lake, NY
James Tyler, 23, U.S. II two-man and U.S. II four-man, Denver, CO

Michael Beauvais, West Point, NY, assistant head coach
Lester Fenner, Peru, NY, head coach
Allan Hashigian, Plattsburgh, NY, head manager and president of national federation

BOBSLED

TWO-MAN (February 11, 1984)

1. **GDR II (Wolfgang Hoppe,**	3:25.56
Dietmar Schauerhammer)	
2. **GDR I (Bernhard Lehmann,**	3:26.04
Bogdan Musiol)	
3. **URS II (Zintis Ekmanis,**	3:26.16
Vladimir Aleksandrov)	
4. URS I	3:26.42
5. SUI II	3:26:76
6. SUI I	3:28.23
7. ITA I	3:29.09
8. FRG I	3:29.18
15. USA I (Brent Rushlaw, Jim Tyler)	3:30.75
17. USA II (Fred Fritsch, Wayne DeAtley)	3:32.20

FOUR-MAN (February 18, 1984)

1. **GDR I (Wolfgang Hoppe, Roland Wetzig,**	3:20.2
Dietmar Schauerhammer,	
Andreas Kirchner)	
2. **GDR II (Bernhard Lehmann,**	3:20.78
Bogdan Musiol, Ingo Voge,	
Eberhard Weise)	
3. **SUI I (Silvio Giobellina, Hans Stettler,**	3:21.39
Urs Salzmann, Rico Freiermuth)	
4. SUI II	3:22.90
5. USA I (Jeff Jost, Joe Briski,	3:23.33
Tom Barnes, Hal Hoye)	
6. URS I	3:23.51
16. USA II (Brent Rushlaw, Ed Card,	3:25.50
Jim Tyler, Frank Hansen)	

TEAM PERSONNEL

T. Barnes   J. Briski   J. DeAtley

R. Hickey   H. Hoye   J. Jost

B. Rushlaw   J. Tyler   L. Fenner

A. Hashigian

ICE HOCKEY

Before the XIV Olympic Winter Games commenced, it was necessary for the Executive Committee of the International Olympic Committee to settle disputes over the use of professional ice hockey players. The United States was among the nations protesting the inclusion of professional players on the Canadian squad list.

The Executive Committee, after hearing the protests and carrying on deliberations, came up with a decision that left many questions unanswered. Flying in direct opposition to Rule 26, governing the eligibility of ath-letes for the Olympic Games, the committee ruled ineli-gible *only* those players who had signed contracts with, and played in games of, the National Hockey League in North America.

Thus, players who had participated in the defunct World Hockey Association or were playing in any one of several leagues in Europe where they were being paid handsomely for their services were allowed to be Olympians.

How much the decision worked against the Canadian team was not immediately apparent. The Canadians took the ice against the USA and within the first half minute Canada had scored the first of four goals to win the opening contest, 4–2. The U.S. ice hockey express was derailed and really never regained its poise until a play-off game to determine seventh place.

The majority of the U.S. press incorrectly played up the fact that this was the poorest finish ever for the USA hockey team. However, in 1964, 1968, and 1976 the United States finished fifth out of eight teams. Perhaps it is significant that those three teams that represented the U.S. in the past, plus the 1984 U.S. team, all finished at the top of the second division of play.

The level of play in the Olympic Games is extremely high. Certainly the 1980 Olympic finalists—USSR, Czechoslovakia, Sweden, and Canada—could play with any team in the world, including those in the NHL.

After round-robin play in the two divisions, the four teams advancing to the final four were the USSR and Sweden from one group, Czechoslovakia and Canada from the other.

The USSR made a strong comeback after being jolted to third place at Lake Placid. After defeating arch-rival Czechoslovakia for the title, 2–0, the Soviets raised their overall Olympic record since 1956 to 48 victories, four defeats, and two ties—the United States having inflicted defeats on the Soviets in 1960 and 1980 on their way to Olympic championships.

In the preliminary pool play, the United States won once (over Austria), lost twice (to Czechoslovakia and Canada), and played two ties (against Norway and Finland). Coach Lou Vairo summed up the play of the U.S. in the Olympics: "It has not been our year, but we have not played in 65 [exhibition] games the way we are [playing] now. The only thing that I can attribute it to is sheer, absolute frustration."

In Game No. 1, the key to the Canadian 4–2 triumph was the defense that Canadian coach Dave King rigged up to shadow Pat LaFontaine, center on the USA "Diaper Line." The USA could never really get into the flow of the game. Carey Wilson, who had played the last three seasons in Finland, scored three goals and assisted on the other for Canada. David A. Jensen, an 18-year-old high school student, scored both goals for the USA.

In Game No. 2, Czechoslovakia scored a 4–1 triumph to establish itself as one of the two best teams in the division. At the end of the first period the score was 1–1, the USA having scored in the 15th minute of the game on a goal by Mark Krumpel. Igor Liba scored twice for the winners and Darius Rusnak added a goal and three assists.

Game No. 3 was a frustrating 3–3 tie with Norway. Pat LaFontaine put the USA ahead in the first period, 2–1, and Ed Olczyk, the third high school student on the "Diaper Line," tied the game at 3–3 midway in the third period on a power-play goal.

Game No. 4 presented a 7–3 rout of Austria. Pat LaFontaine scored three times and his two linemates, David A. Jensen and Ed Olczyk, contributed two goals and four assists, respectively.

Game No. 5 could have, and perhaps should have, been a victory over a good Finnish team. In the final period, Bob Brooke gave the USA a short-lived 3–2 advantage with his unassisted goal. Then Anssi

Melametsa fired a screened 40-footer past U.S. goalie Marc Behrend with 21 seconds to play to cause a 3–3 deadlock.

The playoff for 7th place resulted in a convincing 7–4 triumph for the USA over outmanned Poland. The second period was a game for the spectators—five goals were scored within three minutes, the last one by captain Phil Verchota.

The so-called winning goal, giving the United States a commanding 5–3 advantage, was scored by David A. Jensen on a pass from LaFontaine. LaFontaine had snapped an early 2–2 deadlock by scoring unassisted after 15 seconds of the second period.

TEAM PERSONNEL

Marc Behrend, 23, Madison, WI (goalie)
Scott Bjugstad, 22, New Brighton, MA (forward)
Bob Brooke, 23, Acton, MA (forward, defense)
Chris Chelios, 22, San Diego, CA (defense)
Mark Fusco, 22, Burlington, MA (defense)
Scott Fusco, 21, Burlington, MA (forward)
Steven J. Griffith, 22, St. Paul, MN (forward)
Paul F. Guay, 20, North Smithfield, RI (forward)
John Harrington, 26, Colorado Springs, CO (forward)
Thomas W. Hirsch, 21, Minneapolis, MN (defense)
Al Iafrete, 17, Livonia, MI (defense)
David A. Jensen, 18, Needham, MA (forward)
David H. Jensen, 22, Crystal, MN (defense)
Mark Krumpel, 22, Wakefield, MA (forward)
Patrick M. LaFontaine, 18, Pontiac, MI (center)
Robert T. Mason, 22, International Falls, MN (goalie)
Corey E. Millen, 19, Cloquet, MN (forward)
Edward W. Olczyk, 17, Palos Heights, IL (forward)
Gary Sampson, 24, International Falls, MN (forward)
Tim Thomas, 20, Virginia, MN (defense)
Capt. Phil Verchota, 27, Duluth, MN (defense)

Lawrence Johnson, Edina, MN, team manager
Tim Taylor, Yale University, assistant coach
Lou Vairo, Colorado Springs, CO, head coach
Douglas Woog, South St. Paul, MN, assistant coach

ICE HOCKEY

TEAM CHAMPIONSHIP (February 7–19, 1984)

Team	Win	Lose	Tie
1. **Soviet Union (URS)**	7	0	0
2. **Czechoslovakia (TCH)**	6	1	0
3. **Sweden (SWE)**	5	2	0
4. Canada (CAN)	4	3	0
5. West Germany (FRG)	4	1	1
6. Finland (FIN)	2	2	2
7. United States (USA)	2	2	2
8. Poland (POL)	1	5	0
Italy (ITA)	1	0	4
Yugoslavia (YUG)	1	4	0
Austria (AUT)	1	4	0
Norway (NOR)	0	4	1

Medal Round Standings

	W	L	T	PTS
1. URS	3	0	0	6
2. TCH	2	1	0	4
3. SWE	1	2	0	2
4. CAN	0	3	0	0

Medal Round Scores

2/15 URS 10 – SWE 1	TCH 4 – CAN 0
2/17 TCH 2 – SWE 0	URS 4 – CAN 0
2/19 SWE 2 – CAN 0	URS 2 – TCH 0

Pool "A" Standings

	W	L	T	GF	GA	PTS
1. URS	5	0	0	42	5	10
2. SWE	3	1	1	34	15	7
3. FRG	3	1	1	27	17	7
4. POL	1	4	0	16	37	2
5. ITA	1	4	0	15	31	2
6. YUG	1	4	0	8	37	2

Pool "B" Standings

	W	L	T	GF	GA	PTS
1. TCH	5	0	0	38	7	10
2. CAN	4	1	0	24	10	8
3. FIN	2	2	1	27	19	5
4. USA	1	2	2	16	17	4
5. AUT	1	4	0	13	37	2
6. NOR	0	4	1	15	43	1

TEAM PERSONNEL

M. Behrend   S. Bjugstad   B. Brooke

C. Chelios   M. Fusco   S. Fusco

S. Griffith   P. Guay   J. Harrington

T. Hirsch   A. Iafrete   D. A. Jensen

D. H. Jensen   M. Krumpel   P. LaFontaine

R. Mason   C. Millen   E. Olczyk

G. Sampson   Capt. P. Verchota   L. Johnson

T. Taylor   L. Vairo

LUGE

Luge can be safely classified as the most exciting sport on the program for the Olympic Winter Games. The light sleds travel down the course at speeds reaching almost 70 miles an hour. But this is more than a sport of speed. The skill factor is how you play the course, avoiding riding high on the curves of the frozen luge run that causes the luger to travel a greater distance. Steering is done by the feet; the head at times extends beyond the limits of the sled.

This is truly another sport of milliseconds. In the four runs in the singles competition, the women's gold medal was decided by a .303 second; in the men's, the difference in the elapsed time between first and second place was .704 second.

There are only two runs in the men's doubles, and the difference in elapsed time between the gold and silver medalists was a mere .04 second.

The lugers were generous with praise for the course constructed in Sarajevo, feeling it was equal to any other in the world.

Unsurprisingly, eight of the nine medals were won by either the USSR or the GDR. A clean sweep was prevented when the FRG duo of Hans Stanggassinger and Franz Wembacher won the gold in the doubles. The West German pair trailed the Soviet duo of Yevgeni Byelousov and Aleksandr Belyakov by a scant .067 second after the first run.

However, on the second run Stanggassinger and Wembacher were a .107 second faster. The East German bronze medalists were only a .267 second slower than the winners in the elapsed time for the two runs.

The United States had its highest finish ever in doubles. Ron Rossi and Doug Bateman at ninth were a mere 1.031 seconds behind the winning elapsed time.

The only repeat 1984 medal winner in the three races was Paul Hildgartner, Italy. He was the gold medalist this time and a silver medalist at Lake Placid. He had lost by less than a half second of elapsed time for the four runs in 1980. This time his margin of victory was about .7 second. Hildgartner trailed after the first two runs, but then he registered the two fastest runs of the competition in the final two runs, 45.871 and 45.934 seconds respectively.

Frank Masley, a veteran of the 1980 Olympic Games in Lake Placid (placing 28th in the doubles race), finished a respectable 14th in the singles. He was the flag-bearer for the USA in the Opening Ceremony.

At the end of two runs the USA's Bonny Warner was eighth in the women's singles. On the third run Warner went for broke, fell off her sled, regained the sled, and managed to finish. However, the almost two seconds she lost caused her to drop in the standings to 15th.

There was no questioning the ability, talent, and technique of the women's winner, Steffi Martin, GDR. In the parlance of the horse race set, Steffi made every post a winning one. She had the fastest runs on each of the four dashes down the course. Yet her margin of victory in elapsed time was a mere .3 second ahead of her most persistent challenger, teammate Bettina Schmidt.

The German Democratic Republic swept the medals in the women's singles event at Sarajevo and placed third in the men's doubles. The Soviet lugers were impressive with a pair of silvers and one bronze. They blamed their relatively poor showing on their lack of experience on the Sarajevo track. They had preferred to train at Innsbruck.

TEAM PERSONNEL

Douglas Bateman, 30, Doubles, Somerville, NJ
Raymond Bateman, 28, Doubles, Neshanic Station, NJ
Antoinette (Tony) Damigella, 17, Singles, Lake Placid, NY
Ty Danco*, 29, Brooklyn, NY
Capt. David Gilman, 29, Singles, Berkeley, CA
Frank Masley, 23, Singles, Doubles, Newark, DE
Timothy Nardiello, 23, Singles, Lake Placid, NY
Ron Rossi, 27, Doubles, Yonkers, NY
Theresa Riedl, 19, Singles, Lake Placid, NY
Bonny Warner, 21, Singles, Mt. Baldy, CA

Robert Hughes, Pearl River, NY, manager
Sven Romstad, Athens, GA, coach

*Injured in training and did not compete.

LUGE

MEN'S SINGLES (February 9–12, 1984)

1. **Paul Hildgartner, ITA**	3:04.258
2. **Sergei Danilin, URS**	3:04.962
3. **Valeri Dudin, URS**	3:05.012
4. Michael Walter, GDR	3:05.031
5. Torsten Guerlitzer, GDR	3:05.129
6. Ernst Haspinger, ITA	3:05.327
7. Yuri Kharchenko, URS	3:05.548
8. Markus Prock, AUT	3:05.839
14. Frank Masley, USA	3:07.750
17. David Gilman, USA	3:09.857
21. Tim Nardiello, USA	3:11.320

WOMEN'S SINGLES (February 9–12, 1984)

1. **Steffi Martin, GDR**	2:46.570
2. **Bettina Schmidt, GDR**	2:46.873
3. **Ute Weiss, GDR**	2:47.248
4. Ingrida Amantova, URS	2:48.480
5. Vera Zozulya, URS	2:48.641
6. Marie Luise Rainer, ITA	2:49.138
7. Annefried Goellner, ATU	2:49.373
8. Andrea Hatle, FRG	2:49.491

15. Bonny Warner, USA	2:51.910
19. Theresa Riedl, USA	2:55.265
20. Tony Damigella, USA	2:56.981

MEN'S DOUBLES (February 15, 1984)

1. **FRG (Hans Stanggassinger, Franz Wembacher)**	1:23.620
2. **URS (Yevgeni Byelousov, Aleksandr Belyakov)**	1:23.660
3. **GDR (Joerg Hoffmann, Jochen Pietzsch)**	1:23.887
4. AUT	1:23.902
5. AUT	1:24.133
6. ITA	1:24.353
7. URS	1:24.366
8. FRG	1:24.634
9. USA (Ron Rossi, Doug Bateman)	1:24.651
13. USA (Frank Masley, Ray Bateman)	1:26.331

TEAM PERSONNEL

D. Bateman   R. Bateman   A. Damigella

F. Masley   T. Nardiello   T. Riedl

S. Romstad   R. Rossi   B. Warner

FIGURE SKATING

Again the figure skating competitions drew near-capacity crowds for every performance. It was a year for the "chalk players" in that all the favorites, save Rosalynn Sumners, won. There were few surprises in the awarding of the medals.

The skaters seemed to be placed where they belonged, except for the U.S. ice dancers Judy Blumberg and Michael Seibert, but the televiewers expressed dismay with the judging. It is difficult to assess the reason for these concerns, since judging figure skating requires years of experience. Those selected by the International Skating Union for the Olympic Games are the most experienced and top-rated arbiters.

The United States was number one among the nations, placing in the three disciplines and four events. Scott Hamilton won the gold medal in men's singles prior to going on to capture his fourth straight world title.

Rosalynn Sumners, reigning world champion and favorite for the gold medal, was outskated by Katarina Witt, 18, who gave the German Democratic Republic its second straight title in the ladies' singles. Californian Tiffany Chin, four feet eight inches and a mere 88 pounds, placed fourth, and 1982 world champion Elaine Zayak pulled up to sixth with a superb free skating routine.

In the pairs skating competition Kitty and Peter Carruthers closed out their Olympic career by landing the silver medal as Jill Watson and Burt Lancon finished sixth.

In ice dancing the assignment to fourth place for Blumberg and Seibert was not satisfying. The scoring by one judge was questionable, since she penalized Judy and Michael for their interpretation of Rimsky-Korsakov's "Scheherazade." The judge claimed that the work of classical music failed to reflect four different "tempos" as required under the difficult-to-interpret rules of competition.

Of all the Olympic figure skating champions, the ice dancing team of Jayne Torvill and Christopher Dean of Nottingham, England, earned the loudest hurrahs of the Games from an enthusiastic and appreciative audience. The current world champions swept all three phases of the program: compulsory dances, original set pattern, and the free dancing.

In the pairs skating Elena Valova and Oleg Vasiliev assured the Soviet Union of its sixth straight gold medal. In the Olympics Elena and Oleg were placed first in both the short program and the free skating.

Kitty and Peter Carruthers tied for second in the short program and then captured the silver medal by outskating the second Soviet pair of Larisa Selezneva and Oleg Makarov. Americans Jill Watson and Burt Lancon wound up sixth by virtue of a splendid free skating program.

In the men's singles, Scott Hamilton was not at the top of his game in the free skating program. He built up a tremendous lead with his almost flawless performance in the three compulsory figures. Although the public does not appreciate the importance of this aspect of skating, it is this first phase of the competition that greatly influences the final placings. Considered the finest amateur free skater, Hamilton actually was placed second behind Canada's Brian Orser in both the short program and the free skating.

The final title to be decided was in the women's singles; Rosalynn Sumners, reigning world champion, and the 1982 world champion, Elaine Zayak, were tabbed as possible gold medalists. It was not to be.

Katarina Witt, European champion at 18, wowed the judges with her all-around ability, although she was only third in the compulsory figures, behind Sumners, who was first. The big break came in the short program. Katarina out-skated the field of 23 as Sumners slumped to fifth. The surprise in the short program was the thrilling skating of Tiffany Chin.

Going into the free skating, Witt had established herself as the favorite to succeed Anett Poetzsch, GDR, who outskated Linda Fratianne, USA, at Lake Placid four years earlier.

In the order of lineup, Katarina skated 22nd, and Rosalynn 23rd and last in the free skating. The pressure of being the final two skaters on the ice would prey on less stout-hearted athletes. Rosalynn may not have watched the marks for Witt, but the unrestrained cheering of the near-capacity audience of enthusiasts must have made her apprehensive.

Although Chin was a disappointing 12th in the compulsory figures, she was second in the short program plus the free skating scoring, and placed fourth. Any solace

for the United States came in the free skating portion of the program where Sumners was second, Tiffany Chin third, and Elaine Zayak fourth.

___

TEAM PERSONNEL

SINGLES SKATING

Brian Boitano, 20; coach: Linda Leaver, Sunnyvale, CA
Tiffany Chin, 16; coach; John Nicks, Toluca Lake, CA
Mark Cockerell, 21; coach: Betty Berens, Burbank, CA
Scott Hamilton, 25; coach: Donald Laws, Denver, CO
Rosalynn Sumners, 19; coach: Lorraine Borman, Edmonds, WA
Elaine Zayak, 18; coach: Peter Burrows, Paramus, NJ

PAIRS SKATING

Caitlin (Kitty) Carruthers, 24; coach: Ron Ludington, Wilmington, DE
Peter Carruthers, 24; coach: Ron Ludington, Wilmington, DE
William Fauver, 29; coach: Ron Ludington, Claymont, DE
Burt Lancon, 23; coach: John Nicks, Costa Mesa, CA
Lea Ann Miller, 23; coach: Ron Ludington, Wilmington, DE
Jill Watson, 20; coach: John Nicks, Costa Mesa, CA

ICE DANCING

Judy Anne Blumberg, 26; coach: Bobby Thompson, Summit, NJ
Carol Fox, 27; coach: Ron Ludington, Wilmington, DE
Richard J. Dalley, 26; coach: Ron Ludington, Wilmington, DE
Scott Gregory, 24; coach: Ron Ludington, Wilmington, DE
Michael Seibert, 24; coach: Bobby Thompson, Washington, D.C.
Elisa Spitz, 20; coach: Ron Ludington, Short Hills, NJ

Janet Griffiths, Minneapolis, MI, head manager
John B. Nelson, Tulsa, OK, assistant manager

___

FIGURE SKATING

PAIRS (February 10 and 12, 1984)

		SP	FS
1.	**Elena Valova and Oleg Vasiliev, URS**	1	1
2.	**Kitty Carruthers and Peter Carruthers, USA**	2	2
3.	**Larisa Selezneva and Oleg Makarov, URS**	2	3
4.	Sabine Baess and Tassilo Thierbach, GDR	4	4
5.	Birgit Lorenz and Knut Schubert, GDR	5	5
6.	Jill Watson and Burt Lancon, USA	8	6
7.	Barbara Underhill and Paul Martini, CAN	6	7
8.	Katerina Matousek and Lloyd Eisler, CAN	9	8
10.	Lea Ann Miller and William Fauver, USA	10	10

ICE DANCING (February 14, 1984)

		CD	OSP	FD
1.	**Jayne Torvill and Christopher Dean, GBR**	1	1	1
2.	**Natalia Bestemianova and Andrei Bukin, URS**	2	2	2
3.	**Marina Klimova and Sergei Ponomarenko, URS**	4	4	3
4.	Judy Blumberg and Michael Seibert, USA	3	3	4.
5.	Carol Fox and Richard Dalley, USA	6	5	5
6.	Karen Barber and Nicky Slater, GBR	5	6	6
7.	Olga Volozhinskaya and Aleksandr Svinin, URS	8	7	7
8.	Tracy Wilson and Robert McCall, CAN	7	8	8
10.	Elisa Spitz and Scott Gregory, USA	10	10	10

MEN'S (February 16, 1984)

		CF	SP	FS
1.	**Scott Hamilton, USA**	1	2	2
2.	**Brian Orser, CAN**	7	1	1
3.	**Josef Sabovcik, TCH**	4	5	3
4.	Rudi Cerne, FRG	3	6	4
5.	Brian Boitano, USA	8	3	5
6.	Jean Christophe Simond, FRA	2	4	8
7.	Aleksandr Fadeyev, URS	5	8	7
8.	Vladimir Kotin, URS	11	9	6
13.	Mark Cockerell, USA	18	17	10

WOMEN'S (February 18, 1984)

		CF	SP	FS
1.	**Katarina Witt, GDR**	3	1	1
2.	**Rosalynn Sumners, USA**	1	5	2
3.	**Kira Ivanova, URS**	5	3	5
4.	Tiffany Chin, USA	12	2	3
5.	Anna Kondrashova, URS	7	4	6
6.	Elaine Zayak, USA	13	6	4
7.	Manuela Ruben, FRG	6	11	7
8.	Elena Vodorezova, URS	2	8	11

SP = Short Program, FS = Free Skating,
CD = Compulsory Dances,
OSP = Original Set, Pattern, FD = Free Dancing

___

SPEED SKATING

Gone was Eric Heiden, winner of five gold medals in world record time at Lake Placid four years earlier. Returning were two women's defending champions: Karin Enke, German Democratic Republic, 500 meters, and Natalia Petruseva, USSR, 1,000 meters. Neither retained their laurels, although Miss Enke, a reprogrammed figure skater, won the 1,000 and 1,500 meters and finished runner-up in the 500 and 3,000 meters.

Andrea Schoene, German Federal Republic, assumed the top rung in the 3,000 meters and placed second in the 1,000 and 1,500 meters. Schoene, 23, was skating in her third Olympic Winter Games.

The record busting at Lake Placid, where Heiden set five world records and the women established four Olympic marks, receded at Sarajevo. No Olympic or world marks were created for the men, but Olympic records in all four women's races were set. Enke established a world record in the 1,500 meters and an Olympic record in the 1,000 meters. Miss Schoene won the 3,000 meters in Olympic record time and Christa Rothenburger, German Democratic Republic, set an Olympic record in the 500 meters.

The German Democratic Republic swept the four gold and silver medals in the women's competition. The USSR won three bronze medals with two being credited to Petruseva.

In the men's competition the USSR accounted for 6 of the 15 medals available, including a pair of gold medals. Canada's Gaetan Boucher, also in his third Olympic Winter Games, won a pair of titles and placed third in the 500 meters. Another championship was garnered by Sweden's Tomas Gustafson in the 5,000 meters. Gustafson was runner-up to Igor Malkov, USSR, in the final event, the 10,000 meters.

Malkov was the youngest of the gold medal winners, having attained his 19th birthday immediately prior to the Games.

Gaetan Boucher yielded the 500-meter title to Sergei Fokichev, USSR, a virtual unknown outside of the USSR. Boucher was third. But he skated brilliantly to win both the 1,000 and 1,500-meter titles.

The speed skaters are divided into groups. Each country is permitted to slot its skaters in one of three groups. Customarily the top skater for each country is slotted with the first group. Eric Heiden was placed there, and thus he enjoyed the luxury of skating against the second best skater in virtually every race.

The Canadians exerted gamesmanship by placing Boucher with the second group of skaters. This is a dangerous ploy because if the ice softens it is more difficult to skate fast times. But it worked for Boucher, who clearly was the class of the fields in the two events he captured.

The performances of the U.S. skaters, of course, couldn't equal those of Eric Heiden, Leah Poulos Mueller, and Beth Heiden at Lake Placid. In fact, the USA's 1984 Olympians earned no medals.

The bright spots were Dan Jansen and Nick Thometz placing fourth and fifth in the 500 meters, Thometz fourth in the 1,000, Dr. Mike Woods seventh in the 10,000, and Mary Docter sixth in the women's 3,000 meters.

In the men's 500 meters, Jansen and Thometz missed medals by narrow margins: .16 and .17 seconds respectively.

The men's 10,000 meters was a classic. Malkov is the only man who has ever skated under 14 minutes for the six-miles-plus distance. In the final standings he earned the gold medal by .05 second over Gustafson, winner of the 5,000 meters.

In the 5,000 meters, Gustafson had skated in the first pairing, while Malkov skated with the fourth pair. In the 10,000 meters, Gustafson skated with the second pair and Malkov with the fourth. In reviewing the splits, victory was Malkov's by virtue of a faster final 400-meter lap, 35.10 seconds to 35.27 for Gustafson. Malkov's first 400 meters was timed at 36.17 seconds.

TEAM PERSONNEL

Bonnie Blair, 19, Champaign, IL (500 m)
Dorothea Boyce, 20, Oak Lawn, IL (did not compete)
Jim Chapin, St. Louis, MO (did not compete)
Kathryn H. Class, 20, St. Paul, MN (500 m, 1,000 m)
Mary Docter, 23, Madison, WI (1,000 m, 1,500 m, 3,000 m)
Jan Goldman, 19, Glenview, IL (1,500 m, 3,000 m)
Erik Henriksen, 25, Champaign, IL (500 m, 1,000 m, 1,500 m)
Mark Huck, Lake Forest, IL (5,000 m)
Daniel Immerfall, 28, Madison, WI (did not compete)
Dan Jansen, 18, West Allis, WI (500 m, 1,000 m)
Mark Mitchell, 22, Minnetonka, MN (1,500 m, 5,000 m, 10,000 m)
Connie Paraskevin, 22, Detroit, MI (500 m)
Dave W. Silk, 18, Butte, MT (did not compete)
Lydia R. Stephans, 23, Northbrook, IL (1,000 m)
Nancy Swider, 27, Park Ridge, IL (1,500 m, 3,000 m)
Nick Thometz, 20, Minnetonka, MN (500 m, 1,000 m, 1,500 m)
Kent Thometz, 25, Minnetonka, MN (did not compete)
Dr. Michael Woods, 31, Wauwatosa, WI (5,000 m, 10,000 m)

Bill Cushman, St. Paul, MN, head coach
Dianne Holum, Elgin, IL, head coach
Michael Crowe, Whitehall, MT, assistant coach

SPEED SKATING

WOMEN'S 1,500 METERS (February 9, 1984)

1. **Karin Enke, GDR**		2:03.42 NWR
2. **Andrea Schoene, GDR**		2:05.29
3. **Natalia Petruseva, URS**		2:05.78
4. Gabi Schoenbrunn, GDR		2:07.69
5. Erwina Rys-Ferens, POL		2:08.08
6. Valentina Lalenkova, URS		2:08.17
7. Natalia Kurova, URS		2:08.41
8. Bjoerg Eva Jensen, NOR		2:09.53
14. Mary Docter, USA		2:12.14
17. Jan Goldman, USA		2:12.94
18. Nancy Swider, USA		2:13.74

MEN'S 500 METERS (February 10, 1984)

1. **Sergei Fokichev, URS**	38.19
2. **Yoshihiro Kitazawa, JPN**	38.30
3. **Gaetan Boucher, CAN**	38.39
4. Dan Jansen, USA	38.55
5. Nick Thometz, USA	38.56
6. Vladimir Kozlov, URS	38.57
7. Frode Roenning, NOR	38.58
8. Jens-Uwe Mey, GDR	38.65
20. Erik Henriksen, USA	39.45

WOMEN'S 500 METERS (February 10, 1984)

1. **Christa Rothenburger, GDR**	41.02 NOR
2. **Karin Enke, GDR**	41.28
3. **Natalia Chive, URS**	41.50
4. Irina Kuleshova, URS	41.70
5. Skadi Walter, GDR	42.16
6. Natalia Petruseva, URS	42.19
7. Monika Holzner, FRG	42.40
8. Bonnie Blair, USA	42.53
10. Kathryn Class, USA	42.97
13. Connie Paraskevin, USA	43.05

MEN'S 5,000 METERS (February 12, 1984)

1. **Tomas Gustafson, SWE**	7:12.28
2. **Igor Malkov, URS**	7:12.30
3. **Rene Schoefisch, GDR**	7:17.49
4. Andreas Ehrig, GDR	7:17.63
5. Oleg Bogiyev, URS	7:17.96
6. Pertti Niittyla, FIN	7:17.97
7. Bjorn Nyland, NOR	7:18.27
8. Werner Jaeger, AUT	7:18.61
12. Mike Woods, USA	7:24.81
21. Mark Mitchell, USA	7:34.32
35. Mark Huck, USA	7:46.91

WOMEN'S 1,000 METERS (February 13, 1984)

1. **Karin Enke, GDR**	1:21.61 NOR
2. **Andrea Schoene, GDR**	1:22.83
3. **Natalia Petruseva, URS**	1:23.21
4. Valentina Lalenkova, URS	1:23.68
5. Christa Rothenburger, GDR	1:23.98
6. Yvonne Van Gennip, HOL	1:25.36
7. Erwina Rys-Ferens, POL	1:25.81
8. Monika Holzner, FRG	1:25.87
13. Lydia Stephans, USA	1:26.73
17. Kathryn Class, USA	1:27.57
24. Mary Docter, USA	1:28.55

MEN'S 1,000 METERS (February 14, 1984)

1. **Gaetan Boucher, CAN**	1:15.80
2. **Sergei Khlebnikov, URS**	1:16.63
3. **Kai Arne Engelstad, NOR**	1:16.75
4. Nick Thometz, USA	1:16.85
5. Andre Hoffmann, GDR	1:17.33
6. Viktor Chacherin, URS	1:17.42
7. (tie) Hilbert van der Duim, HOL	1:17.46
7. (tie) Andreas Dietel, GDR	1:17.46
11. Erik Henriksen, USA	1:17.64
16. Dan Jansen, USA	1:18.73

WOMEN'S 3,000 METERS (February 15, 1984)

1. **Andrea Schoene, GDR**	4:24.79 NOR
2. **Karin Enke, GDR**	4:26.33
3. **Gabi Schoenbrunn, GDR**	4:33.13
4. Olga Pleshkova, URS	4:34.42
5. Yvonne Van Gennip, HOL	4:34.80
6. Mary Docter, USA	4:36.25
7. Bjoerg Eva Jensen, NOR	4:36.28
8. Valentina Lalenkova, URS	4:37.36
10. Nancy Swider, USA	4:40.10
12. Jan Goldman, USA	4:42.49

MEN'S 1,500 METERS (February 16, 1984)

1. **Gaetan Boucher, CAN**	1:58.36
2. **Sergei Khlebnikov, URS**	1:58.83
3. **Oleg Bogiyev, URS**	1:58.89
4. Hans Van Helden, FRA	1:59.39
5. Andreas Ehrig, GDR	1:59.41
6. Andreas Dietel, GDR	1:59.73
7. Hilbert van der Duim, HOL	1:59.77
8. Viktor Chacherin, URS	1:59.81
14. Nick Thometz, USA	2:00.77
21. Erik Henriksen, USA	2:02.20
33. Mark Mitchell, USA	2:04.26

MEN'S 10,000 METERS (February 18, 1984)

1. **Igor Malkov, URS**	14:39.90
2. **Tomas Gustafson, SWE**	14:39.95
3. **Rene Schoefisch, GDR**	14:46.91
4. Geir Karlstad, NOR	14:52.40
5. Michael Hadschieff, AUT	14:53.78

6. Dmitri Bochkarev, URS	14:55.65
7. Mike Woods, USA	14:57.30
8. Henry Nilsen, NOR	14:57.81
21. Mark Mitchell, USA	15:21.24

TEAM PERSONNEL

B. Blair   D. Boyce   J. Chapin

K. Class   M. Docter   J. Goldman

E. Henriksen   M. Huck   D. Immerfall

D. Jansen   M. Mitchell   C. Paraskevin

D. Silk   L. Stephans   N. Swider

N. Thometz   K. Thometz   Dr. M. Woods

B. Cushman   D. Holum   M. Crowe

ALPINE SKIING

If Nordic skiing is considered the heart and soul of the Olympic Winter Games, since World War II, Alpine skiing has had the glamour.

It is amazing that 60,000 fans will gather on a wind-swept mountain to catch a glimpse of unrecognizable skiers whizzing down the slopes at more than 60 miles an hour. In weather better suited for penguins, ski fans crowd together to talk about the latest exploits of the heroes and heroines of the Alpine set—perhaps the most exclusive and elite athletic group in sports.

Even with the tremendous expansion of recreational ski opportunities all over the world, the United States, until comparatively recent times, was never a real factor in Alpine skiing. In fact, prior to Sarajevo no American man had ever won a gold medal in any of the three Alpine events.

But since 1972 the managers of the U.S. Ski Association have worked hard to retain as national team members the top skiers. They understood that in Olympic World Cup, and World Championship competitions, the awards usually went to the experienced skiers.

In the last two years the United States has been rated among the top nations on the World Cup circuit. And on the basis of medals won, the U.S. was the leading nation at Sarajevo.

Debbie Armstrong, a member of the national team for only two years as a downhill specialist, won the first gold medal of the 1984 Games for the USA in the giant slalom, followed closely by teammate Christin Cooper.

Downhill victor Bill Johnson surprised everyone except himself as he made good his every pre-race boast and found the new snow and his skis just letter-perfect.

And the Alpine competition was closed out on the final day by America's most famous and most successful Alpine artists, Phil and Steve Mahre, who skied to a magnificent one-two finish in the men's slalom.

In the toughest of all nerve-wracking competitions, the three women's champions are all very young: Debbie Armstrong, 20, won the giant slalom; Michela Figini, 17, took the downhill event; and Paoletta Magoni, 19, captured the gold medal in the slalom in a major upset of the Alpine events.

Magoni's triumph was the first for Italy since Piero Gros won the men's giant slalom eight years earlier. Also, she was the first Italian woman to win a gold in skiing.

Phil Mahre, one of four 1980 medalists skiing for honors at Sarajevo, improved his second-place finish at Lake Placid by winning the 1984 slalom; Andreas Wenzel, of the skiing Liechtenstein Wenzels, finished third in the giant slalom both in 1980 and again at Sarajevo. Canada's downhill specialist Steve Podborski, third in 1980, could do no better than eighth at Sarajevo.

One word of mention for Perrine Pelen, 23, France. She had been third in the giant slalom at Lake Placid. She was at the top of her game at Sarajevo and was the only skier to win two medals—a silver in the slalom, and the bronze in the giant slalom behind the two Americans.

Franz Klammer, Austria, has been a leading figure in skiing for a decade. He had won the downhill in 1976, much to the delight of his Austrian fans. But, in what was probably his swan song, he was relegated to tenth place at Sarajevo.

As in speed skating, the sport of Alpine skiing is also a game of milliseconds. In four of the six events, no more than 1.18 seconds separated the leaders. The closest competition was in the men's downhill; Bill Johnson finished only one second ahead of Steve Podborski, who was eighth. In the women's downhill, the difference between Figini and Lea Soelkner, eighth, was 1.03 seconds. Phil Mahre finished 1.07 seconds ahead of Italian Oswald Toetsch, fifth, in the slalom; and Max Julen was timed 1.18 seconds faster than Boris Strel, Yugoslavia, fifth in the giant slalom's two runs.

The women's slalom and giant slalom, with two runs determining the final placing, still had the leaders bunched. There was 1.28 seconds' difference between Magoni and Daniela Zini, Italy, ninth. The spread in the first ten places in the giant slalom (Debbie Armstrong, first, and Anne-Flore Rey, France, tenth) was only 1.57 seconds.

For many, the most glamorous event in Alpine skiing is the men's slalom. The USA did superbly in that event thanks to the efforts of the Mahre twins. Phil and Steve Mahre hadn't clicked on the World Cup circuit and had even left the team to finish preparations for the Olympics on their own, in the U.S. After the first run of the slalom race, Phil trailed brother Steve by .70 second. However, on the next run, Phil had the second fastest time (bettered only by Italy's Toetsch) while Steve slumped to eighth. Phil captured the gold medal and, despite his bad second run, Steve won the silver medal.

Debbie Armstrong and Bill Johnson, both U.S. Alpine winners, displayed opposing personalities during the Games. Armstrong is the All-American girl, almost oblivious of her accomplishments. She gave much credit to her roommate, Cynthia Nelson, America's long-time best and most beloved Alpine skier, who prepared Debbie mentally for the giant slalom and downhill races.

Armstrong gave herself pep talks at the starting gate of the giant slalom. Teammate Christin Cooper, the silver medalist (edged out by a mere .4 second), told the press after the race, "She [Debbie] was so excited before the second run I heard her say, 'Okay, Deb, have a good time, have a good time, have the run of your life.' Then she turned to me and said, 'Have the run of your life, Coop, have a good time.'"

Bill Johnson was the darling of the media prior to the eventual downhill race. All along he proclaimed that he would win.

After turning in the second fastest time in the final training run, Johnson told the assembled reporters, "My chances are good. If I can get through the turns a little better than I have lately, I think my chances are better than most."

After the first postponement, Johnson gave the reporters another quotable tidbit by saying, "I've got skis that are fantastic on new snow. The others don't have skis like mine and I'm not going to let them out of my sight."

After the third postponement, Johnson again made news for the scribes by declaring, "Doug Lewis [a teammate] is going to finish in the top fifteen and I'm going to win, no doubt about it." Later he admitted that the big thing for him was winning races and beating Europeans.

Johnson finally had to put it on the line on February 16, although the original date had been February 9. Charlie Meyers of the Denver Post summed up Johnson's achievement best when he wrote, the following day: "In a fairyland setting of bright sunshine dancing on ghost trees, Johnson made an American dream come true.

"Bill is part Babe Ruth, part Muhammad Ali, part Broadway Joe [Namath], part Evel Knievel, and all determination."

"Johnson did precisely what he told the Denver Post 12 days earlier he'd do. It was the Babe pointing to the center-field stands (in the 1932 World Series), Joe Namath guaranteeing the Super Bowl, Ali measuring up Liston."

TEAM PERSONNEL

Debra Armstrong, 20, Downhill and Giant Slalom, Seattle, WA

Michael Brown, 21, Downhill, Vail, CO

John Buxman, 23, Slalom and Giant Slalom, Vail, CO

Christin Cooper, 24, Slalom and Giant Slalom, Sun Valley, ID

Holly Flanders, 26, Downhill, Deerfield, NH

William D. Johnson, 23, Downhill, Van Nuys, CA

Douglas Lewis, Downhill, Salisbury, VT

Philip F. Mahre, 26, Slalom and Giant Slalom, Yakima, WA

Steven I. Mahre, 26, Slalom and Giant Slalom, Yakima, WA

Maria Maricich, 22, Downhill, Hailey, ID

Tamara McKinney, 21, Slalom and Giant Slalom, Lexington, KY

Cynthia Nelson, 28, Giant Slalom, Vail, CO & Reno, NV

Gale (Tiger) Shaw, 22, Slalom and Giant Slalom, Stowe, VT

ALPINE SKIING

WOMEN'S GIANT SLALOM (February 13, 1984)

1. **Debbie Armstrong, USA**	2:20.98
2. **Christin Cooper, USA**	2:21.38
3. **Perrine Pelen, FRA**	2:21.40
4. Tamara McKinney, USA	2:21.83
5. Marina Kiehl, FRG	2:22.03
6. Blanca Fernandez-Ochoa, ESP	2:22.14
7. Erika Hess, SUI	2:22.51
8. Olga Charvatova, TCH	2:22.57
18. Cindy Nelson, USA	2:24.88

MEN'S GIANT SLALOM (February 14, 1984)

1. **Max Julen, SUI**	2:41.18
2. **Jure Franko, YUG**	2:41.41
3. **Andreas Wenzel, LIE**	2:41.75
4. Franz Gruber, AUT	2:42.08
5. Boris Strel, YUG	2:42.36
6. Hubert Strolz, AUT	2:42.71
7. Alex Giorgi, ITA	2:43.00
8. Phil Mahre, USA	2:43.25
17: Steve Mahre, USA	2:46.03
Tiger Shaw, USA	DNF first run

DNF = Did Not Finish

MEN'S DOWNHILL (February 16, 1984)

1. **Bill Johnson, USA**	1:45.59
2. **Peter Mueller, SUI**	1:45.86
3. **Anton Steiner, AUT**	1:45.95
4. Pirmin Zurbriggen, SUI	1:46.05
5. (tie) Urs Raeber, SUI	1:46.32
5. (tie) Helmut Hoeflehner, AUT	1:46.32
7. Sepp Wildgruber, FRG	1:46.53
8. Steve Podborski, CAN	1:46.59
24. Doug Lewis, USA	1:48.49

WOMEN'S DOWNHILL (February 16, 1984)

1. **Michela Figini, SUI**	1:13.36
2. **Maria Walliser, SUI**	1:13.41
3. **Olga Charvatova, TCH**	1:13.53
4. Ariane Ehrat, SUI	1:13.95
5. Jana Gantnerova, TCH	1:14.14
6. (tie) Marina Kiehl, FRG	1:14.30
6. (tie) Gerry Sorensen, CAN	1:14.30
8. Lea Soelkner, AUT	1:14.39
16. Holly Flanders, USA	1:15.11
19. Maria Maricich, USA	1:15.55
21. Debbie Armstrong, USA	1:15.57

WOMEN'S SLALOM (February 17, 1984)

1. **Paoletta Magoni, ITA**	1:36.47
2. **Perrine Pelen, FRA**	1:37.38
3. **Ursula Konzett, LIE**	1:37.50
4. Roswitha Steiner, AUT	1:37.50
5. Erika Hess, SUI	1:37.91
6. Malgorzata Tlalka, POL	1:37.95
7. Maria Rosa Quario, ITA	1:37.99
8. Anni Kronbichler, AUT	1:38.05
Tamara McKinney, USA	DNF first run
Christin Cooper, USA	DNF first run

DNF = Did Not Finish

MEN'S SLALOM (February 19, 1984)

1. **Phil Mahre, USA**	1:39.41
2. **Steve Mahre, USA**	1:39.62
3. **Didier Bouvet, FRA**	1:40.20
4. Jonas Nilsson, SWE	1:40.25
5. Oswald Toetsch, ITA	1:40.48
6. Petar Popangelov, BUL	1:40.68
7. Bojan Krizaj, YUG	1:41.51
8. Lars Halvarsson, SWE	1:41.70
Tiger Shaw, USA	DNF second run

DNF = Did Not Finish

TEAM PERSONNEL

D. Armstrong   C. Cooper   H. Flanders

W. Johnson   D. Lewis   P. Mahre

S. Mahre   M. Maricich   T. McKinney

C. Nelson   G. Shaw

NORDIC SKIING

The Nordic ski events are the heart of the Olympic Winter Games. The program for the Olympic Winter Games was built around the Nordic events: cross-country races, ski jumping, and the Nordic combined event (cross-country skiing and ski jumping).

The United States has won only two medals in the Nordic events. In the first Olympic Winter Games, at Chamonix in 1924, the U.S. placed third in the ski jumping. This accomplishment was not appreciated at the time, however, and it took fifty years to discover a scoring error and thus elevate the American Anders Haugen from fourth to third place.

The United States did not participate in a victory ceremony again until 1976 at Innsbruck when Bill Koch won the silver medal in the 30-kilometer race. Although the U.S. media expressed great surprise at Koch's prowess, those close to the U.S. Ski Association had plotted at least one medal for Koch.

The United States has stepped up its Nordic program with an infusion of funds to help underwrite year-round training for its cadre of specialists. In the men's cross-country events the most notable achievement was for all 12 USA starters in the three races to finish. Likewise, all 12 starters in the three women's races finished.

Norway, Sweden, and Finland dominated the Nordic Ski events for the first ten Winter Games. But the Soviet Union's women and men skiers took over after 1972. Sarajevo, then, was a return to the early days. The three Scandinavian countries captured nine of the eleven gold medals.

In the women's competition Marja-Liisa Haemaelaeinen, 28, the defending World Cup champion, made a clean sweep of the three individual events. This was her third Winter Olympics appearance, but only the first time the tall blond Finn had been in the winner's circle.

The three gold medals earned by Haemaelaeinen led Finland's dash for the number one ranking in the Nordic events. In all, Finland accounted for four gold, three silver, and six bronze medals. Prior to this year's Winter Olympics the medal haul for the small Scandinavian country was 24–39–26, of which 17 gold medals had been earned in the Nordic ski events.

Gunde Anders Svan, who had turned 22 only a month earlier, was the Swedish star. He won the 15-kilometer event, finished second in the 50-kilometer race, third in the 30-kilometer race, and anchored the Swedish 4×10-kilometer relay team to victory with a come-from-behind win over the Soviet ace Nikolai Zimyatov.

The only winner of a cross-country race at Lake Placid to repeat at Sarajevo was Sweden's veteran Thomas Wassberg, winner of the shortest race in 1980 and the longest race in 1984. Wassberg overcame teammate Svan in the final five kilometers to win the men's 50-kilometer race.

It could be said that the Sarajevo Olympics would be the final Olympic Games for two of the finest cross-country skiers in history. Raissa Smetanina, USSR, collected two more silver medals to go along with five medals she had won previously, giving her a total of seven.

Among the men, Juha Mieto of Finland stands out. He is six feet seven inches tall and weighs approximately 235 pounds. At Lake Placid, after he lost the 15-kilometer race to Wassberg by .01 second, the skiing lords rewrote the rule on timing, decreeing that in the future the placing would be based on timing to the nearest tenth of a second. (In Nordic skiing the skiers take off at intervals, so they are not actually skiing head-to-head as in track races.)

The best attended of the Nordic disciplines has always been the ski jumping, and Finland's jumpers did not disappoint. Although the winner off the 70-meter hill was Jens Weissflog, German Democratic Republic, the real hero among the jumpers was Finland's Matti Nykaenen.

This is an event of some mystery, since distance is combined with style points to determine final placings. This year, much to the delight of the real ski jump fans, the victories went to the longest jumpers.

There were more than 60,000 spectators watching the jumpers soar off the 90-meter hill. Nykaenen put together leaps of 380 and 364 feet to avenge his second-place finish to Weissflog a week earlier. But in the matter of points, where Nykaenen had lost the 70-meter jump by a mere 1.2, he won off the big hill by 17.5. This victory was the result of his wide edge in style points and his long-distance jumping, 30 feet and 13 feet farther than Weissflog, respectively. Nykaenen was timed at 62 miles an hour coming down the take-off slide.

Jeff Hastings of the USA earned a place on the team by his expert jumping in the final selection trials. He did well in the pre-Olympic meets yet was anything but impressive in the Olympic training jumps. However, on the day of the 90-meter competition, Hastings was at his best. His fourth-place finish was the highest achieved by an American since Anders Haugen's corrected third-place finish in 1924. Hastings jumped within a couple of feet of third-place winner Pavel Ploc, Czechoslovakia, and his style points were comparable. Overall, he was a scant 1.7 points behind the bronze medalist.

In a set of Games comparatively free of controversy, there was much speculation about the stopping of the ski-jumping portion of the Nordic Combined event. Rightly or wrongly, the USA was almost certainly deprived of a medal because of the decision of the judges.

On the fateful first day, Pat Ahern was leading the competition and fellow American Kerry Lynch was in the top ten. Then the second round of jumping started; there were four jumpers to go in a field of 28 when the judges threw out the results.

In the "re-start" the eventual winner—Tom Sandberg, Norway—hit on both jumps to get back into contention after two miserable attempts were cancelled.

However, Ahern and Lynch never did as well and placed 16th and 22nd respectively. Thus, it was difficult to pick up points during the 15-kilometer cross-country run although Lynch was the third fastest over the course, trailing Jouko Karjalainen, Finland, the silver medalist, and eventual winner Sandberg.

It should be noted that under the rules of the International Ski Federation, the jury of appeal must vote on continuing the competition when skiers go past

a predetermined critical ("K") point. The skiers had outjumped "K," and the jury voted "No more jumping from that point."

Lynch reported that Sandberg had told him, "I am the luckiest man in the world because I had two poor jumps and I got to take both of them over."

TEAM PERSONNEL

Patrick L. Ahern, 23, Nordic combined, Breckenridge, CO
Landis Arnold, 23, ski jumping, Winter Park, CO
Todd Boonstra, 21, cross-country, Eagan, MN
Kevin Brochman, cross-country
Timothy Caldwell, 30, cross-country, Putney, VT
Audun Endestad, 31, cross-country, Fairbanks, AK
James Galanes, 27, cross-country, Anchorage, AK
Lynn Spencer Galanes, 29, cross-country, Anchorage, AK
Jeffrey Hastings, 24, ski jumping, Norwich, VT
Michael Holland, 22, ski jumping, Norwich, VT
Bill Koch, 28, cross-country, Eugene, OR
Susan Long, 23, cross-country, Somers, CT
Kerry Lynch, 26, Nordic combined, Granby, CO
Dennis McGrane, 21, ski jumping, Littleton, CO
Judy Rabinowitz, 25, cross-country, Fairbanks, AL
Michael Randall, 21, Nordic combined, Cloquet, MN
Patricia Ross, 24, cross-country, Cornwall, VT
Dan Simoneau, 25, cross-country, Livermore Falls, ME
Reed Zuehlke, 23, ski jumping, Eau Claire, WI

James Page, Park City, UT, Nordic director
Michael Gallagher, Pittsfield, VT, men's cross-country coach
Robert Patterson, Sun Valley, ID, women's cross-country coach
Gregory Windsperger, Shoreview, MN, jumping coach
Joseph Lamb, Lake Placid, NY, Nordic combined coach

NORDIC SKIING

WOMEN'S 10-KILOMETER CROSS-COUNTRY
(February 9, 1984)

1. **Marja-Liisa Haemaelaeinen, FIN**	31:44.2
2. **Raissa Smetanina, URS**	32:02.9
3. **Brit Pettersen, NOR**	32:12.7
4. Berit Aunli, NOR	32:17.7
5. Anne Jahren, NOR	32:26.2
6. Marie Risby, SWE	32:34.6
7. Marit Myrmael, NOR	32:35.3
8. Julia Stepanova, URS	32:45.7
26. Judy Rabinowitz, USA	34:35.1
32. Susan Long, USA	34:58.9
3?. Patty Ross, USA	35:41.3
40. Lynn Galanes, USA	35:47.4

MEN'S 30-KILOMETER CROSS-COUNTRY
(February 10, 1984)

1. **Nikolai Zimyatov, URS**	1:28:56.3
2. **Aleksandr Zavialov, URS**	1:29:23.3
3. **Gunde Svan, SWE**	1:29:35.7
4. Vladimir Sakhnov, URS	1:30:30.4
5. Aki Karvonen, FIN	1:30:59.7
6. Lars Erik Eriksen, NOR	1:31:24.8
7. Harri Kirvesniemi, FIN	1:31:37.4

8. Juha Mieto, FIN	1:31:48.3
21. (tie) Bill Koch, USA	1:33:44.4
29. Dan Simoneau, USA	1:35:50.7
36. Jim Galanes, USA	1:37:21.2
47. Kevin Brochman, USA	1:39:24.6

NORDIC COMBINED (February 11–12, 1983)

		70m	15km	TOTAL
1.	**Tom Sandberg, NOR**	1	2	422.595
2.	**Jouko Karjalainen, FIN**	15	1	416.900
3.	**Jukka Ylipulli, FIN**	5	5	410.825
4.	Rauno Miettinen, FIN	6	9	402.970
5.	Thomas Mueller, FRG	3	12	401.995
6.	Aleksandr Prosvirnin, URS	13	6	400.185
7.	Uwe Dotzauer, GDR	12	7	397.780
8.	Hermann Weinbuch, FRG	10	10	397.390
13.	Kerry Lynch, USA	22	3	388.165
17.	Pat Ahern, USA	16	17	384.620
28.	Mike Randall, USA	27	25	320.950

WOMEN'S 5-KILOMETER CROSS-COUNTRY
(February 12, 1984)

1. **Marja-Liisa Haemaelaeinen, FIN**	17:04.0
2. **Berit Aunli, NOR**	17:14.1
3. **Kveta Jeriova, TCH**	17:18.3
4. Marie Risby, SWE	17:26.3
5. Inger Nybraaten, NOR	17:28.2
6. Brit Pettersen, NOR	17:33.6
7. Anne Jahren, NOR	17:38.3
8. Ute Noack, GDR	17:46.0
27. Lynn Galanes, USA	18:30.8
30. Judy Rabinowitz, USA	18:41.5
38. Susan Long, USA	19:28.5
40. Patty Ross, USA	19:30.9

MEN'S 15-KILOMETER CROSS-COUNTRY
(February 13, 1984)

1. **Gunde Svan, SWE**	41:25.6
2. **Aki Karvonen, FIN**	41:34.9
3. **Harri Kirvesniemi, FIN**	41:45.6
4. Juha Mieto, FIN	42:05.8
5. Vladimir Nikitin, URS	42:31.6*
6. Nikolai Zimyatov, URS	42:34.5
7. Uwe Bellmann, GDR	42:35.8
8. Tor-Haakon Holte, NOR	42:37.4
18. Dan Simoneau, USA	43:03.4
27. Bill Koch, USA	43:53.7
39. Tim Caldwell, USA	45:21.2

*Ove Aunli, NOR, disqualified from tie for 5th

WOMEN'S 4 × 5-KILOMETER CROSS-COUNTRY
RELAY (February 15, 1984)

1. **NOR (Inger Nybraaten, Anne Jahren, Bill Pettersen, Berit Aunli)**	1:06:49.7
2. **TCH (Dagmar Shvubova, Blanka Paulu, Gabriela Svobodova, Kveta Jeriova)**	1:07:34.7

3. FIN (Pirkko Maeaettae, 1:07:36.7
   Eija Hyytiaeinen, Marjo Matikainen,
   Marja-Liisa Haemaelaeinen)

7. USA (Susan Long, Judy Rabinowitz, 1:10:03.4
   Lynn Galanes, Patty Ross)

MEN'S 4 × 10-KILOMETER CROSS-COUNTRY RELAY (February 16, 1984)

1. SWE (Thomas Wassberg, Benny 1:55:06.3
   Kohlberg, Jan Ottoson, Gunde Svan)

2. URS (Aleksandr Batiuk, Aleksandr 1:55:16.5
   Zavialov, Vladimir Nikitin, Nikolai Zimyatov)

3. FIN (Kari Ristanen, Juha Mieto, 1:56:31.4
   Harri Kirvesniemi, Aki Karvonen)

8. USA (Dan Simoneau, Tim Caldwell, 1:59:52.3
   Jim Galanes, Bill Koch)

MEN'S 50-KILOMETER CROSS-COUNTRY (February 19, 1984)

1. Thomas Wassberg, SWE	2:15:55.8
2. Gunde Svan, SWE	2:16:00.7
3. Aki Karvonen, FIN	2:17:04.7
4. Harri Kirvesniemi, FIN	2:18:34.1
5. Jan Lindvall, NOR	2:19:27.1
6. Andreas Gruenenfelder, SUI	2:19:46.2
7. Aleksandr Zavialov, URS	2:20:27.6
8. Vladimir Sakhnov, URS	2:20:53.7
17. Bill Koch, USA	2:24:02.3
18. Audun Endestad, USA	2:24:14:4
26. Dan Simoneau, USA	2:25:43.1
31. Jim Galanes, USA	2:28:00.7

WOMEN'S 20-KILOMETER CROSS-COUNTRY (February 18, 1984)

1. Marja-Liisa Haemaelaeinen, FIN	1:01:45.0
2. Raisa Smetanina, URS	1:02:26.7
3. Anne Jahren, NOR	1:03:13.6
4. Blanka Paulu, TCH	1:03:16.9
5. Marie Risby, SWE	1:03:31.8
6. Brit Pettersen, NOR	1:03:49.0
7. Lyubov Liadova, URS	1:03:53.3
8. Evi Kratzer, SUI	1:03:56.4
27. Judy Rabinowitz, USA	1:07:11.4
28. Susan Long, USA	1:07:25.9
33. Lynn Galanes, USA	1:08:25.0

70-METER JUMP (February 12, 1984)

1. Jens Weissflog, GDR	215.2
2. Matti Nykaenen, FIN	214.0
3. Jari Puikkonen, FIN	212.8
4. Stefan Stannarius, GDR	211.1
5. Rolf Aage Berg, NOR	208.5
6. Andreas Felder, AUT	205.6
7. Piotr Fijas, POL	204.5
8. Vegard Opaas, NOR	203.8
9. Jeff Hastings, USA	203.5
28. Landis Arnold, USA	182.0

33. Dennis McGrane, USA	178.4
41. Mike Holland, USA	164.3

90-METER JUMP (February 18, 1984)

1. Matti Nykaenen, FIN	231.2
2. Jens Weissflog, GDR	213.7
3. Pavel Ploc, TCH	202.9
4. Jeff Hastings, USA	201.2
5. Jari Puikkonen, FIN	196.6
6. Armin Kogler, AUT	195.6
7. Andreas Bauer, FRG	194.6
8. Vladimir Podzimek, TCH	194.5
29. Reed Zuehlke, USA	168.5
37. Mike Holland, USA	154.8
53. Dennis McGrane, USA	79.9

TEAM PERSONNEL

M. Gallagher R. Patterson G. Windsperger

J. Lamb

P. Ahern L. Arnold T. Boonstra

T. Caldwell A. Endestad J. Galanes

L. Galanes J. Hastings M. Holland

B. Koch S. Long K. Lynch

D. McGrane J. Rabinowitz M. Randall

P. Ross D. Simoneau J. Page

THE GAMES OF THE XXIII OLYMPIAD
Los Angeles, California, USA

DATE BEGUN: 7/28/84
DATE ENDED: 8/12/84

ALL-TIME MEDAL WINNINGS FOR THE SUMMER OLYMPIC GAMES, 1896–1984

(Ranked According to Total Medals Won)

(Unofficial)

Country	Gold	Silver	Bronze	Total
1. United States	717	540	459	1716
2. Soviet Union	340	288	240	868
3. Great Britain	167	213	200	580
4. France	149	166	168	483
5. Sweden	128	139	161	428
6. Italy	142	117	120	379
7. German Dem. Rep.	123	118	111	352
8. Hungary	113	107	131	351
9. Finland	97	75	108	280
10. Japan	83	72	75	230

THE MEDAL STANDINGS

1984 SUMMER OLYMPICS

(unofficial tally):

	Gold	Silver	Bronze	Total
United States	83	61	30	174
West Germany	17	19	23	59
Romania	20	16	17	53
Canada	10	18	16	44
Great Britain	5	10	22	37
China	15	8	9	32
Italy	14	6	12	32
Japan	10	8	14	32
France	5	7	15	27
Australia	4	8	12	24
South Korea	6	6	7	19
Sweden	2	11	6	19
Yugoslavia	7	4	7	18
Netherlands	5	2	6	13
Finland	4	3	6	13
New Zealand	8	1	2	11
Brazil	1	5	2	8
Switzerland	0	4	4	8
Mexico	2	3	1	6
Denmark	0	3	3	6
Spain	1	2	2	5
Belgium	1	1	2	4
Austria	1	1	1	3
Portugal	1	0	2	3
Jamaica	0	1	2	3
Norway	0	1	2	3
Turkey	0	0	3	3
Venezuela	0	0	3	3
Morocco	2	0	0	2
Kenya	1	0	1	2
Greece	0	1	1	2
Nigeria	0	1	1	2
Puerto Rico	0	1	1	2
Algeria	0	0	2	2
Pakistan	1	0	0	1
Colombia	0	1	0	1
Egypt	0	1	0	1
Ireland	0	1	0	1
Ivory Coast	0	1	0	1
Peru	0	1	0	1
Syria	0	1	0	1
Thailand	0	1	0	1
Cameroon	0	0	1	1
Chinese Taipei	0	0	1	1
Dominican Republic	0	0	1	1
Iceland	0	0	1	1
Zambia	0	0	1	1

The Games of the XXIII Olympiad may go down in history as the most memorable of the 19 renewals that have been held in the modern era since inauguration of the quadrennial sports extravaganza in 1896. There is much evidence to support this observation.

Probably for the first time, the Games were conducted without a single day of rain to mar the festive atmosphere.

The Organizing Committee in Los Angeles reported a surplus of income over expenses of $150 million, by any measuring stick the most financially successful Games.

The general public bought 93 percent of all available tickets.

No athletes missed a competition because of clogged roadways blocking their path to the Games.

A record number of Perfect Tens were awarded in gymnastics.

Greg Louganis scored higher in the diving events than any previous competitor in any springboard or platform diving competition.

Cheryl Miller, USA, proved herself the most versatile women's basketball player in the world.

There were tremendous performances by the athletes from the People's Republic of China and South Korea.

There were also a number of notable firsts at the Games:
- The women's marathon.
- The United States finished first in 15 different sports.
- The entertainment capital of the world choreographed the Opening and Closing Ceremony.
- Medalists of the United States were taken on a cross-country tour to accept the cheers and adulation of millions of Americans, thanks to the civic-minded Southland Corporation.
- A USOC President, William E. Simon, participated in the Olympic Torch Run leading up to the Opening Ceremony.
- A United States President proclaimed the opening of the Olympic Games.
- Professionals were openly permitted (e.g., soccer and tennis).
- The International Olympic Committee didn't berate countries for showering life-time monthly stipends on their returning medalists (e.g., the People's Republic of China and South Korea).
- Complete national anthems of the gold medalists' countries were played at victory ceremonies, in place of the usual abbreviated versions.
- Headgear was authorized for the boxing tournament.
- A full-time U.S. deputy sheriff won a gold medal—Steve Fraser, Greco-Roman wrestling.
- Women equaled men in splitting the first ten places in the demanding 3-day event in equestrian sports.
- A paraplegic participated in an event—New Zealand's archer Neroli Fairhall.
- One nation won all four relay races in track and field—the United States.
- The family name Kim outdistanced the Smiths among the nearly 7,200 athletes entered. By actual count there were 54 Kims and only 34 Smiths.
- No world records were set in the women's swimming races.
- Foreign swimmers led U.S. men swimmers in setting world records, six to four.
- Spectators played an integral part in the Opening Ceremony, with everyone participating in the salute to the 140 nations participating by forming flags in a massive card stunt. (The undersigned was proud to have been part of the flag of Britain.)
- A bearer who was the first to carry the torch at the beginning of the Torch Run and also was involved in bringing it into the Stadium for the Opening Ceremony—Gina Hemphill, granddaughter of Jesse Owens, four-time gold medalist at the 1936 Olympic Games in Berlin.

The United States had its finest record in the ten team sports—placing first in men's and women's basketball and men's volleyball; second in women's volleyball and water polo; and third in women's field hockey.

J. Michael Plumb, a member of the 3-day team in the equestrian sports, became a seven-time Olympian.

Two U.S. gold medalists from 1976 repeated their previous triumphs at Montreal—Edwin Moses in the 400-meter hurdles and archer Darrell Pace.

The first three finishers in the men's marathon had a combined experience of only six marathon races. Silver medalist John Treacy of Ireland had never previously run the distance.

U.S. yachtsmen finished first or second in all seven sailing classes, an unparalleled Olympic performance.

One 1972 Munich champion returned to regain her title —Ulrike Meyfarth, German Federal Republic, in the high jump, in which she had set a world record at the age of sixteen.

At every Olympic Games there are many priceless quotations, usually comments from athletes or officials:

Ambrose (Rowdy) Gaines, in full flush of victory, remarked, "Was it worth all the hell? I'd swim another eight years and go through another boycott for the feeling I have now."

After *Rick Carey,* world recordholder, won the 200-meter backstroke, he philosophized, "I expected a little more out of myself. I've been that fast in workouts, so I should have been a lot better in the Olympics. To be two seconds off my best time, I don't find satisfying."

After the U.S. men's gymnastics team had upset the world champion People's Republic of China, coach *Abie Grossfeld,* bursting with pride, commented, "This is certainly comparable to the hockey upset [in the 1980 Olympic Winter Games]. There was no way the world thought we were ready for this."

Before the Olympic boxing tournament opened, flyweight *Steve McCrory,* younger brother of a world professional champion, mused, "If Frank Tate and I both win gold medals, we'll be like Michael Jackson back in Detroit. We'll be as big as Thomas Hearns and bigger than Mayor Young." (P.S. They both won gold.)

Mark Schubert, assistant swimming coach for the U.S. team, soberly analyzed the world situation in his sport when he remarked, "We can't kid ourselves by thinking that we are best in the world and, because of all these medals, we are superior. There is another country [the German Democratic Republic] that has great athletes and is very competitive with us. But I don't think they're any better than we are."

Pope John Paul II, in a message to the Archbishop of Los Angeles on the eve of the Games, wrote, "This great event has significance not only for the world of sport as the expression of friendly athletic competition and the striving for human excellence, but also for the future of the human community, which through sport gives external expression to the desire of all for universal cooperation and understanding…and I hope that at this worldwide encounter they will be worthy models of peaceful harmony and human fellowship."

Film producer *David Wolper* on his Opening Ceremony: "Of course, all Olympic Opening Ceremonies have goosebumps already built in with the march of the athletes and the raising of the Olympic flags….But I wanted to add to that, creating something unexpected that would kick off the Los Angeles Games in a festive spirit—a 20-goosebump experience."

Sebastian Coe, Great Britain, winner of the 1,500 meters and second in the 800 meters in track and field: "The air is cleaner here than in most European cities."

IOC President *Juan Antonio Samaranch* beaming at his closing press conference as he remarked, "The most important thing to happen at these Games? The participation of the people of California and the people of the United States of America. Never in my life have I seen such great participation in an Olympics.

"I did nothing to eliminate the smog. But the smog was eliminated by the grace of good weather and the caring of the people and the industries of Southern California who cooperated with us so well."

And then, commenting on amateurism and eligibility of athletes, the IOC world leader continued, "In every Games the rules are more open and for many years now we have not had to disqualify anyone for professional reasons in sport. We realize we are in the 1980's and have to move. We have to live with the times."

Frank Deford, writing in *Sports Illustrated,* said it best, perhaps: "Professionalism has just sort of oozed into acceptance and amateurism has ended with a whimper, not a bang."

President Ronald Reagan, wearing an official team red blazer, at a final breakfast for the team waxed enthusiastically, if not eloquently, saying, "You did us proud. You're heroes, every one of you is living proof of what happens when America sets its sights high and says, 'Let's create a little excellence.'

"I say to you, the great melting-pot team of 1984, the members of America's team at the Games of the XXIII Olympiad, 'Thanks for the memories, thanks for being what you are—genuine heroes.'"

MULTIPLE MEDAL WINNERS (Three or More)

SIX MEDALS

Li Ning, CHN (Gymnastics 3G, 2S, 1B)

FIVE MEDALS

Mary Lou Retton, USA (Gymnastics (1G, 2S, 2B)
Ecaterina Szabo, ROM (Gymnastics 4G, 1S)

FOUR MEDALS

Mitchell Gaylord, USA (Gymnastics 1G, 1S, 2B)
Michael Gross, FRG (Swimming 2G, 2S)
Nancy Hogshead, USA (Swimming 3G, 1S)
Carl Lewis, USA (Track and Field, 4G)

THREE MEDALS

Agneta Andersson, SWE (Kayak 2G, 1S)
Valerie Brisco-Hooks, USA (Track and Field 3G)
Rick Carey, USA (Swimming 3G)
Tracy Caulkins, USA (Swimming 3G)
Chandra Cheeseborough, USA (Track and Field 2G, 1S)
Ian Ferguson, NZL (Kayak 3G)
Rowdy Gaines, USA (Swimming 3G)
Mike Heath, USA (Swimming 2G, 1S)
Julie McNamara, USA (Gymnastics 1G, 1S, 1B)
Mary T. Meagher, USA (Swimming 3G)
Pablo Morales, USA (Swimming 1G, 2S)
Lars-Erik Moberg, SWE (Kayak 3S)
Simona Pauca, ROM (Gymnastics 2G, 1B)
Mark Stockwell, AUS (Swimming 2S, 1B)
Annemarie Verstappen, HOL (Swimming 1S, 2B)
Peter Vidmar, USA (Gymnastics 2G, 1S)

ARCHERY

Archery, since World War II, has been one sport in which the United States has been internationally pre-eminent. In Olympic tournaments in 1972 and 1976, archery—returning to the Olympics for the first time since 1920 for the men and 1908 for the women—found the United States winning both men's and women's gold medals.

The men have continued to dominate the international scene. However, Asians have moved to the head of the class in women's competition.

The two dominant American men were the 1976 Olympic champion, Darrell Pace, formerly of the United States Air Force, and Rick McKinney, an Arizona college student, the reigning world champion. Those who know their way around the archery range freely predicted that McKinney would win.

However, Pace has always come to the fore with his winning performance in the most important international competitions. He had worked equally hard for the Olympic Games as the much more publicized women in volleyball and gymnastics.

Pace made every post a winning one. He was stronger during his first round (144 arrows) when he scored 1,317; he added 1,299 during the second round of 144 arrows. His total score of 2,616 bettered his previous Olympic mark of 2,571, then a world record.

The United States was never in contention for women's honors. Katrina King, the 7th-place finisher, was the third qualifier for the team and had never finished higher than fourth in national championships.

Whereas Pace outscored teammate McKinney 2,616 to 2,564, in the women's division Hyang Soon Seo, Korea, only 17 years old, won in the last two quivers from the 50- and 30-meter distances. Her margin of victory over Li Lingjuan, China, was a mere nine points.

The reigning world champion, Korea's Jin Ho Kim, became the bronze medalist, only 13 points off the pace.

TEAM PERSONNEL

Benita Edds, 26, Terre Haute, IN
Katrina King, 25, Grand Rapids, MI
Rick McKinney, 30, Glendale, AZ
Glenn Meyers, 23, Fremont, MI
Darrell Pace, 27, Hamilton, OH
Ruth Rowe, 41, McLean, VA

Ann Weber Hoyt, Bridgeton, MO, manager
John Williams, Fullerton, CA, coach

ARCHERY

MEN'S

1. **Darrell Pace, USA**	2,616
2. **Rick McKinney, USA**	2,564
3. **Hiroshi Yamamoto, JPN**	2,563
4. Takayoshi Matsushita, JPN	2,552
5. Tomi Poikolainen, FIN	2,538
6. Goran Bjerendal, SWE	2,522
7. Marnix Vervinck, BEL	2,519
8. Koo Ja-Chung, KOR	2,500
12. Glenn Meyers, USA	2,488

TEAM PERSONNEL

B. Edds   K. King   R. McKinney

G. Meyers   D. Pace   R. Rowe

A. Hoyt   J. Williams

ATHLETICS (Track and Field) Men's

There never had been a more enthusiastic and cheering gathering of fans at a track meet. The spectators got in the festive spirit early and rooted for the U.S. athletes with unrestrained shouts of encouragement, and were generous in their praise as well for foreign stars doing well on the track.

Disappointment: Only one world record in the track and field events—the U.S. sprint relay team anchored by Carl Lewis.

Most Versatile Athlete: Daley Thompson of Britain won his second straight decathlon title and extended his personal log with West German Juergen Hingsen (current world recordholder) to 5 out of 5. Thompson hasn't lost a decathlon.

Best All-Around Athlete: Carl Lewis. He won four races over the 100-meter route, four more in the 200 meters, his one qualifying jump was best among the long jumpers, he won the gold medal on his first jump in the final, and he anchored the sprint relay team to three victories on the way to the gold medal.

Unnoticed, Unrewarded, but Bemedaled: John Powell won the bronze medal in the discus throw. He was third in Montreal, and was running third in Munich until he was edged out for the bronze on Sweden's Ricky Bruch's final throw.

Superior Performance: Dietmar Moegenburg, West Germany (a onetime world recordholder), cleared all three attempts in the qualifying round and then achieved every height in the regular high jump competition until he clinched the gold medal.

Biggest Form Reversal: Ireland's John Treacy finished an undistinguished 10th in the 10,000 meters on August 6. Six days later he placed second in the marathon, the first time he had run this distance.

"The" Defending Champion: Among those who won at Moscow The Peerless Brit, Sebastian Coe, retained his laurels in Los Angeles, winning the 1,500 meters and placing second in the 800 meters. This was a carbon copy of his successes four years earlier.

How Good is "Good"? Ask those who watched the classic running machine from Brazil, Joaquim Cruz, 800-meter winner. The sometime University of Oregon student seemingly has unlimited potential and can be as good as the spirit moves him.

Who's He? Many in the Coliseum asked "Who's he?" when Lt. Alonzo Babers won the 400 meters. For one, Lt. Babers, son of a career officer in the U.S. Air Force, is the only person who's beaten the Jamaica wunderkind, Bert Cameron, twice. Cameron withdrew from the final 400 meters with a hamstring injury.

Comparisons May Be Odious: One world record at Los Angeles compared to 16 set at Munich in 1972; 20 Olympic records fashioned at Los Angeles compared to the all-time high of 38 set at Munich.

Olé, Mexicanos: Raul Gonzalez, peerless Mexican race walker, completed a historic double by winning the 50-kilometer race walk and placing second in the shorter 20-kilometer walk to his teammate, Ernesto Canto.

Gold Count: The USA men accounted for nine golds, short of the 12 earned at Mexico in 1968. The overall U.S. medal production of 24 doesn't really reflect the lack of medals earned in any flat race over 800 meters.

Interesting statistic: The last-place finisher in the men's marathon was timed in 2 hours 51 minutes 18 seconds, exactly one second faster than the 44th and last-place finisher for the women.

TEAM PERSONNEL, MEN'S

Ray Armstead, 24, Kirksville, MO (4 x 400m relay)
Duncan Atwood, 28, Santa Barbara, CA (javelin)
Alonzo Babers, USAF, 22, Montgomery, AL (400m, 4 x 400m relay)
Willie Banks, 28, Los Angeles, CA (triple jump)
Kirk Baptiste, 22, Houston, TX (200m)
Earl Bell, 28, Jonesboro, AR (pole vault)
Tim Bright, 24, Klamath Falls, OR (decathlon)
Ron Brown, 23, Chandler, AZ (100m, 4 x 100m relay)
Edward Burke, 44, Los Gatos, CA (hammer throw)
Art Burns, 30, San Jose, CA (discus)
Anthony Campbell, 24, Carson, CA (110m hurdles)
Michael Carter, 23, Dallas, TX (shot-put)
Don Clary, 27, Eugene, OR (5,000m)
Mike Conley, 21, Fayetteville, AK (triple jump)
John Crist, 29, Irvine, CA (decathlon)
Paul Cummings, 30, Orem, UT (10,000m)
Brian Diemer, 22, Grand Rapids, MI (3,000m steeplechase)
Marco Evoniuk, 26, Colorado Springs, CO (20km & 50km race walk)
Greg Foster, 26, Los Angeles, CA (110m hurdles)
Harvey Glance, 27, Auburn, AL (reserve)
Milton Goode, 24, Oakland, CA (high jump)
Sam Graddy, 20, Atlanta, GA (100m, 4 x 100m relay)
Johnny Gray, 24, Los Angeles, CA (800m)

Bill Green, 24, Lakewood, CA (hammer throw)
John Gregorek, 24, McLean, VA (3,000m steeplechase)
Danny Harris, 18, Ames, IA (400m hurdles)
Tranel Hawkins, 21, San Angelo, TX (400m hurdles)
James Heiring, 28, Colorado Springs, CO (20km race walk)
Thomas Jefferson, 22, Kent, OH (200m)
Earl Jones, 20, Ypsilanti, MI (800m)
Al Joyner, 24, Los Angeles, CA (triple jump)
Emmit King, 25, Bessemer, AL (reserve)
Roger Kingdom, 21, Pittsburgh, PA (110m hurdles)
Steve Lacy, 28, Madison, WI (5,000m)
David Laut, 27, Goleta, CA (shot-put)
Carl Lewis, 23, Houston, TX (100m, 200m, 4 x 100m relay, long jump)
Jud Logan, 25, Canton, OH (hammer throw)
Doug Lytle, 22, Manhattan, KS (pole vault)
Sydney Maree, 27, Rosemont, PA (1,500m)
Henry Marsh, 30, Bountiful, UT (3,000m steeplechase)
John Marshall, 20, Villanova, PA (800m)
Walter McCoy, 25, Tallahassee, FL (reserve)
Antonio McKay, 20, Atlanta, GA (400m, 4 x 400m relay)
Mike McRae, 29, Fremont, CA (long jump)
Edwin Moses, 28, Laguna Hills, CA (400m hurdles)
Larry Myricks, 28, Ontario, CA (long jump)
Sunder Nix, 22, Chicago, IL (400m, 4 x 400m relay)
Doug Nordquist, 25, Brea, CA (high jump)
Daniel O'Connor, 32, Westminster, CA (20km race walk)
Vincent O'Sullivan, 27, Sherman Oaks, CA (50km race walk)
Doug Padilla, 27, Provo, UT (5,000m)
Tom Petranoff, 26, Northridge, CA (javelin)
Peter Pfitzinger, 26, West Newton, MA (marathon)
Pat Porter, 25, Alamosa, CA (10,000m)
John Powell, 37, Cupertino, CA (discus)
Steven Roller, 30, San Bruno, CA (javelin)
Alberto Salazar, 26, Eugene, OR (marathon)
Carl Schueler, 28, Colorado Springs, CO (50km race walk)
Steve Scott. 28, Leucadia, CA (1,500m)
Calvin Smith, 23, Tuscaloosa, AL (4 x 100m relay)
Willie Smith, 28, Birmingham, AL (reserve)
Jim Spivey, 24, Noblesville, IN (1,500m)
Dwight Stones, 30, Irvine, CA (high jump)
Mike Tully, 27, Encino, CA (pole vault)
John Tuttle, 25, Auburn, AL (marathon)
Craig Virgin, 29, Lebanon, IL (10,000m)
Mac Wilkins, 33, San Jose, CA (discus)
August Wolf, 22, White Plains, NY (shot-put)
Jim Wooding, 30, Coatesville, PA (decathlon)

Albert Buehler, Durham, NC, assistant manager
William Dellinger, Eugene, OR, assistant coach
Larry Ellis, Skillman, NJ, head coach
Roy Griak, St. Louis Park, MN, manager
Fred Newhouse, Houston, TX, assistant manager
Mel Rosen, Auburn, AL, assistant coach
Kenyon Shannon, Snohomish, WA, assistant coach
Steve Simmons, San Jose, CA, assistant manager
Tom Tellez, Houston, TX, assistant coach

TRACK AND FIELD, MEN'S

100 METERS

1. **Carl Lewis, USA**	9.99
2. **Sam Graddy, USA**	10.19
3. **Ben Johnson, CAN**	10.22
4. Ron Brown, USA	10.26

5. Michael McFarlane, GBR — 10.27
6. Ray Stewart, JAM — 10.29
7. Donovan Reid, GBR — 10.33
8. Tony Sharpe, CAN — 10.35

200 METERS
1. **Carl Lewis, USA** — 19.80 NOR
2. **Kirk Baptiste, USA** — 19.96
3. **Thomas Jefferson, USA** — 20.26
4. Joao Batista Silva, BRA — 20.30
5. Ralf Luebke, FRG — 20.51
6. Jean-Jacques Boussemart, FRA — 20.55
7. Pietro Mennea, ITA — 20.55
8. Adeoye Mafe, GBR — 20.85

400 METERS
1. **Alonzo Babers, USA** — 44.27
2. **Gabriel Tiacoh, CIV** — 44.54
3. **Antonio McKay, USA** — 44.71
4. Darren Clark, AUS — 44.75
5. Sunder Nix, USA — 44.75
6. Sunday Uti, NGR — 44.93
7. Innocente Egbunike, NGR — 45.35
   Bertland Cameron, JAM — DNS

DNS = Did not start, injured

800 METERS
1. **Joaquim Cruz, BRA** — 1:43.00 NOR
2. **Sebastian Coe, GBR** — 1:43.64
3. **Earl Jones, USA** — 1:43.83
4. Billy Konchellah, KEN — 1:44.03
5. Donato Sabia, ITA — 1:44.53
6. Edwin Koech, KEN — 1:44.86
7. Johnny Gray, USA — 1:47.89
8. Steven Ovett, GBR — 1:52.28

1,500 METERS
1. **Sebastian Coe, GBR** — 3:32.53 NOR
2. **Steve Cram, GBR** — 3:33.40
3. **Jose Abascal, ESP** — 3:34.30
4. Joseph Chesire, KEN — 3:34.52
5. Jim Spivey, USA — 3:36.07
6. Peter Wirz, SUI — 3:36.97
7. Andres Vera, ESP — 3:37.02
8. Khalifa Omar, SUD — 3:37.11
10. Steve Scott, USA — 3:39.86
   Sydney Maree, USA — DNS

DNS = Did not start, injured

5,000 METERS
1. **Said Aouita, MAR** — 13:05.59 NOR
2. **Markus Ryffel, SUI** — 13:07.54
3. **Antonio Leitao, POR** — 13:09.20
4. Tim Hutchings, GBR — 13:11.50
5. Paul Kipkoech, KEN — 13:14.40
6. Charles Cheruiyot, KEN — 13:18.41
7. Doug Padilla, USA — 13:23.56
8. John Walker, NZL — 13:24.46
   Steve Lacy, USA — DNQ
   Don Clary, USA — DNQ

DNQ = Did not qualify, eliminated in semi-final round

10,000 METERS
1. **Alberto Cova, ITA** — 27:47.54
2. **Michael McLeod, GBR** — 28:06.22
3. **Mike Musyoki, KEN** — 28:06.46
4. Salvatore Antibo, ITA — 28:06.50
5. Christoph Herle, FRG — 28:08.21
6. Sosthenes Bitok, KEN — 28:09.01
7. Yutaka Kanai, JPN — 28:27.06
8. Steve Jones, GBR — 28:28.08
16. Pat Porter, USA — 28:34.59
   Craig Virgin, USA — DNQ
   Paul Cummings, USA — DNQ

NOTE: Marri Vainio, FIN, finished 2nd but was disqualified for a positive drug test.

MARATHON (26 MILES, 385 YARDS)
1. **Carlos Lopes, POR** — 2:09:21
2. **John Treacy, IRL** — 2:09:56
3. **Charles Spedding, GBR** — 2:09:58
4. Takeshi So, JPN — 2:10:55
5. Rob De Castella, AUS — 2:11:09
6. Juma Ikangaa, TAN — 2:11:10
7. Joseph Nzau, KEN — 2:11:28
8. Djama Robleh, DJI — 2:11:39
11. Peter Pfitzinger, USA — 2:13:53
15. Alberto Salazar, USA — 2:14:19
   John Tuttle, USA — DNF

110-METER HURDLES
1. **Roger Kingdom, USA** — 13.20 NOR
2. **Greg Foster, USA** — 13.23
3. **Arto Bryggare, FIN** — 13.40
4. Mark McKoy, CAN — 13.45
5. Anthony Campbell, USA — 13.55
6. Stephane Caristan, FRA — 13.71
7. Carlos Sala, ESP — 13.80
8. Jeff Glass, CAN — 14.15

400-METER HURDLES
1. **Edwin Moses, USA** — 47.75
2. **Danny Harris, USA** — 48.13
3. **Harald Schmid, FRG** — 48.19
4. Sven Nylander, SWE — 48.97
5. Amadou Dia Ba, SEN — 49.28
6. Tranel Hawkins, USA — 49.42
7. Michel Zimmerman, BEL — 50.69
8. Henry Amike, NGR — 53.78

3,000-METER STEEPLECHASE
1. **Julius Korir, KEN** — 8:11.80
2. **Joseph Mahmoud, FRA** — 8:13.31
3. **Brian Diemer, USA** — 8:14.06
4. Henry Marsh, USA — 8:14.25
5. Colin Reitz, GBR — 8:15.48
6. Domingo Ramon, ESP — 8:17.27
7. Julius Kariuki, KEN — 8:17.47
8. Pascal Debacker, FRA — 8:21.51
   John Gregorek, USA — DNQ

20-KILOMETER RACE WALK
1. **Ernesto Canto, MEX** — 1:23:13
2. **Raul Gonzalez, MEX** — 1:23:20
3. **Maurizio Damilano, ITA** — 1:23:26
4. Guillaume LeBlance, CAN — 1:24:29
5. Carlo Mattioli, ITA — 1:25:07
6. Jose Marin, ESP — 1:25:32
7. Marco Evoniuk, USA — 1:25:42
8. Erling Andersen, NOR — 1:25:54
23. Jim Heiring, USA — 1:30:20
33. Daniel O'Connor, USA — 1:35:12

50-KILOMETER RACE WALK
1. **Raul Gonzalez, MEX** — 3:47:26
2. **Bo Gustafsson, SWE** — 3:53:19
3. **Sandro Belluci, ITA** — 3:53:45
4. Reima Salonen, FIN — 3:58:30
5. Raffaello Ducceschi, ITA — 3:59:26
6. Carl Schueler, USA — 3:59:46
7. Jorge Llopart, ESP — 4:03:09
8. Jose Pinto, POR — 4:04:42
14. Vincent O'Sullivan, USA — 4:22:51
   Marco Evoniuk, USA — DNF

4 x 100-METER RELAY
1. **USA (Sam Graddy, Ron Brown, Calvin Smith, Carl Lewis)** — 37.83 NOR/NWR
2. **JAM (Albert Lawrence, Gregory Meghoo, Donald Quarrie, Ray Stewart)** — 38.62
3. **CAN (Ben Johnson, Tony Sharpe, Desai Williams, Sterling Hinds)** — 38.70
4. ITA — 38.87
5. FRG — 38.99
6. FRA — 39.10
7. GBR — 39.13
8. BRA — 39.40

4 x 400-METER RELAY
1. **USA (Sunder Nix, Ray Armstead, Alonzo Babers, Antonio McKay)** — 2:57.91
2. **GBR (Kriss Akabusi, Garry Cook, Todd Bennett, Philip Brown)** — 2:59.13
3. **NGR (Sunday Uti, Moses Ugbusien, Rotimi Peters, Innocente Egbunike)** — 2:59.32
4. AUS — 2:59.70
5. ITA — 3:01.44
6. BAR — 3:01.60
7. UGA — 3:02.09
8. CAN — 3:02.82

DECATHLON
1. **Daley Thompson, GBR** — 8,797 NOR
2. **Juergen Hingsen, FRG** — 8,673
3. **Siegfried Wentz, FRG** — 8,412
4. Guido Kratschmer, FRG — 8,326
5. William Motti, FRA — 8,266
6. John Crist, USA — 8,130
7. Jim Wooding, USA — 8,091
8. Dave Steen, CAN — 8,047
12. Tim Bright, USA — 7,862

SHOT PUT

1. **Alessandro Andrei, ITA**	21.26m (69–9)
2. **Michael Carter, USA**	21.09m (69–2½)
3. **Dave Laut, USA**	20.97m (68–9¾)
4. August Wolf, USA	20.93m (68–8)
5. Werner Guenthoer, SUI	20.28m (66–6½)
6. Marco Montelatici, ITA	19.98m (65–6¾)
7. Soeren Tallhem, SWE	19.81m (65–0)
8. Erik De Bruin, HOL	19.65m (64–5¾)

DISCUS

1. **Rolf Danneberg, FRG**	66.60m (218–6)
2. **Mac Wilkins, USA**	66.30m (217–6)
3. **John Powell, USA**	65.46m (214–9)
4. Knut Hjeltnes, NOR	65.28m (214–2)
5. Art Burns, USA	64.98m (213–2)
6. Alwin Wagner, FRG	64.72m (212–4)
7. Luciano Zerbini, ITA	63.50m (208–4)
8. Stefan Fernholm, SWE	63.22m (207–5)

JAVELIN

1. **Art Haerkoenen, FIN**	86.76m (284–8)
2. **David Ottley, GBR**	85.74m (281–3)
3. **Kenth Eldebrink, SWE**	83.72m (274–8)
4. Wolfram Gambke, FRG	82.46m (270–6)
5. Masami Yoshida, JPN	81.98m (268–11)
6. Einar Vihjalnsson, ISL	81.58m (267–8)
7. Roald Bradstock, GBR	81.22m (266–6)
8. Laslo Babits, CAN	80.68m (264–8)
10. Tom Petranoff, USA	78.40m (257–3)
11. Duncan Atwood, USA	78.10m (256–3)
Steven Roller, USA	DNQ

HAMMER

1. **Juha Tiainen, FIN**	78.08m (256–2)
2. **Karl-Hans Riehm, FRG**	77.98m (255–10)
3. **Klaus Ploghaus, FRG**	76.68m (251–7)
4. Giampaolo Urlando, ITA	75.96m (249–2)
5. Orlando Bianchini, ITA	75.94m (249–2)
6. Bill Green, USA	75.60m (248–0)
7. Harri Huhtala, FIN	75.28m (247–0)
8. Walter Ciofani, FRA	73.46m (241–0)
Jud Logan, USA	DNQ
Edward Burke, USA	DNQ

LONG JUMP

1. **Carl Lewis, USA**	8.54m (28–0¼)
2. **Gary Honey, AUS**	8.24m (27–0½)
3. **Giovanni Evangelisti, ITA**	8.24m (27–0½)
4. Larry Myricks, USA	8.16m (26–9¼)
5. Liu Yuhang, CHN	7.99m (26–2¾)
6. Joey Wells, BAH	7.97m (26–1¾)
7. Juinchi Usui, JPN	7.87m (25–10)
8. Kim Jong-Il, KOR	7.81m (25–7½)
11. Mike McRae, USA	7.63m (25–0½)

TRIPLE JUMP

1. **Al Joyner, USA**	17.26m (56–7½)
2. **Mike Conley, USA**	17.18m (56–4½)
3. **Keith Connor, GBR**	16.87m (55–4¼)

4. Zou Zhenxian, CHN	16.83m (55–2¾)
5. Peter Bouschen, FRG	16.77m (55–0¼)
6. Willie Banks, USA	16.75m (54–11½)
7. Ajayi Agbebaku, NGR	16.67m (54–8¼)
8. Eric McCalla, GBR	16.66m (54–8)

HIGH JUMP

1. **Dietmar Moegenburg, FRG**	2.35m (7–8½)
2. **Patrik Sjoeberg, SWE**	2.33m (7–7¾)
3. **Zhu Jianhua, CHN**	2.31m (7–7)
4. Dwight Stones, USA	2.31m (7–7)
5. Doug Nordquist, USA	2.29m (7–6)
6. Milt Ottey, CAN	2.29m (7–6¼)
7. Liu Yunpeng, CHN	2.29m (7–6)
8. Cai Shu, CHN	2.27m (7–5¼)
Milton Goode, USA	DNF

POLE VAULT

1. **Pierre Quinon, FRA**	5.75m (18–10¼)
2. **Mike Tully, USA**	5.65m (18–6½)
3. **(tie) Earl Bell, USA**	5.60m (18–4½)
3. **(tie) Thierry Vigneron, FRA**	5.60m (18–4½)
5. Kimmo Pallonen, FIN	5.45m (17–10½)
6. Doug Lytle, USA	5.40m (17–8½)
7. Felix Boehni, SUI	5.30m (17–4½)
8. Mauro Barella, ITA	5.30m (17–4½)

TEAM PERSONNEL, MEN'S

R. Armstead D. Atwood A. Babers

W. Banks K. Baptiste E. Bell

T. Bright R. Brown  E. Burke

A. Burns A. Campbell  M. Carter

D. Clary  M. Conley  J. Crist

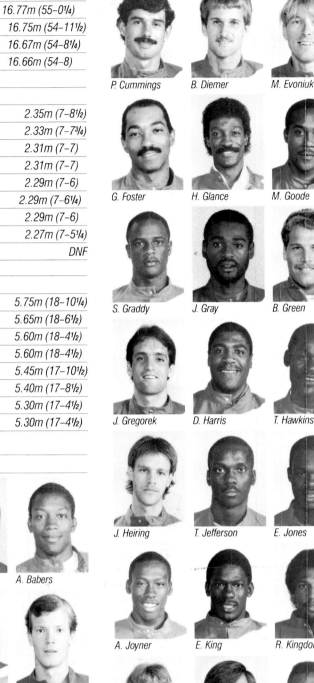

P. Cummings B. Diemer  M. Evoniuk

G. Foster H. Glance M. Goode

S. Graddy J. Gray B. Green

J. Gregorek D. Harris T. Hawkins

J. Heiring T. Jefferson E. Jones

A. Joyner E. King R. Kingdom

S. Lacy D. Laut  C. Lewis

J. Logan  D. Lytle S. Maree

H. Marsh J. Marshall W. McCoy

M. McRae

E. Moses

L. Myricks

L. Ellis

R. Griak

F. Newhouse

S. Nix

D. Nordquist

D. O'Connor

M. Rosen

K. Shannon

S. Simmons

V. O'Sullivan

D. Padilla

T. Petranoff

T. Tellez

P. Pfitzinger

J. Powell

S. Roller

A. Salazar

C. Schueler

S. Scott

C. Smith

W. Smith

J. Spivey

D. Stones

M. Tully

J. Tuttle

M. Wilkins

A. Wolf

C. Virgin

J. Wooding

A. Buehler

W. Dellinger

ATHLETICS (Track and Field) Women's

The women's events were just that—for women, not young girls. The two youngest winners were long jumper Anisoara Stanciu, Romania, and 400-meter hurdler Nawal El Moutawakil, Morocco (a student at Iowa State), both 22.

The oldest champion was discus thrower Ria Stalman, Holland (a onetime student at Arizona State). She was 32. Tessa Sanderson, Great Britain, javelin, and high jumper Ulrike Meyfarth, West Germany, were 28. There were four 27-year-olds—Evelyn Ashford and Joan Benoit, USA; Doina Melinte, Romania; and Gabriella Dorio, Italy.

Speaking of Meyfarth, when she won the high jump at Munich she was the youngest Olympic high jump champion ever—16 years, 123 days.

The great performance of the U.S. 4x400-meter relay team is further accentuated when analysis shows that three of the four members covered their one lap under 50 seconds. No other runner in the relay beat 50 seconds.

The Day That Wasn't to Be: Al Joyner won the triple jump the same day his sister, Jackie, was competing in the final day of the heptathlon. It looked like a brother/sister double gold production. Jackie led the world through the first six events, in spite of a painful thigh injury. Her world came apart in the final event, the 800 meters. The Australian, Glynis Nunn, finished far enough ahead to erase Joyner's lead and earn the gold medal by a mere five points. Joyner was second.

The Closest of All Finishes: In the shot-put, on the first day of track and field in the Coliseum, Claudia Losch, West Germany, won the gold medal over Romania's Mihaela Loghin by one centimeter, one-quarter of an inch (67–2¼ to 67–2).

Statistical Note: Joan Benoit took the lead at the 3-kilometer mark in the marathon and never relinquished it. After the race she told the media, "I promised myself months ago that I'd run my race, nobody else's. That's exactly what I did."

Psychological Note: Benoit's top rivals mistakenly were psyched to believe that she would unravel sometime during the race. Benoit had arthroscopic surgery on one of her knees a scant seventeen days before the May Olympic trials. The "knee syndrome" was on everyone's mind—except hers.

A Small Woman Finishes First: Moutawakil at 5 feet 3 inches, 108 pounds, was the shortest of the women in the 400-meter hurdles. Yet this timber-topper from Morocco made every hurdle first on her way to victory.

Joni Huntley, 28, USA, placed third in the high jump with the greatest day of her ten-year career. She announced her retirement following the victory ceremony. Incidentally, the high jump was for the mature athlete: Huntley, 28; Meyfarth, 28, and Italy's 1980 Olympic winner, Sara Simeoni, 31, won the medals at the Coliseum.

Valerie Brisco-Hooks became the first ever to double in the 200 meters and the 400 meters. She became the second U.S. runner to win three gold medals. The other, Wilma Rudolph, 1960, was dubbed in Europe La Gazelle Noire. We hereby dub Mrs. Hooks La Gazelle Noire II.

TEAM PERSONNEL, WOMEN'S

Jodi Anderson, 26, Inglewood, CA (heptathlon)
Evelyn Ashford, 27, Venice, CA (100m, 4 x 100m relay)
Sharrieffa Barksdale, 23, Knoxville, TN (400m hurdles)
Roberta Belle, 24, West Los Angeles, CA (reserve)
Joan Benoit, 27, Freeport, ME (marathon)
Jeanette Bolden, 24, Los Angeles, CA (100m, 4 x 100m relay)
Cindy Bremser, 31, Madison, WI (3,000m)
Valerie Brisco-Hooks, 24, Los Angeles, CA (200m, 400m, 4 x 400m relay)
Alice Brown, 23, Los Angeles, CA (100m, 4 x 100m relay)
Judi Brown, 23, Eugene, OR (400m hurdles)
Julie Brown, 29, Eugene, OR (marathon)
Carol Cady, 22, Stanford, CA (shot put)
Robin Campbell, 25, Palo Alto, CA (800m)
Chandra Cheeseborough, 25, Gainesville, FL (400m, 4 x 100m relay, 4 x 400m relay)
Brenda Cliette, 21, Macon, GA (reserve)
Mary Decker, 26, Eugene, OR (3,000m)
Leslie Deniz, 22, Tempe, AZ (discus)
Laura DeSnoo, 21, San Diego, CA (discus)
Diane Dixon, 20, Brooklyn, NY (reserve)
Benita Fitzgerald-Brown, 23, Knoxville, TN (100m hurdles)
Kim Gallagher, 20, Santa Monica, CA (800m)
Randy Givens, 22, Tallahassee, FL (200m)
Cindy Greiner, 27, Eugene, OR (heptathlon)
Lorna Griffin, 28, Huntington Beach, CA (discus)
Florence Griffith, 24, Los Angeles, CA (200m)
Joan Hansen, 26, Phoenix, AZ (3,000m)
Denean Howard, 19, Granada Hills, CA (4 x 400m relay-heat)
Sherrie Howard, 22, Granada Hills, CA (4 x 400m relay)
Joni Huntley, 28, Seal Beach, CA (high jump)
Julie Isphording, 22, Cincinnati, OH (marathon)
Jackie Joyner, 22, Los Angeles, CA (heptathlon, long jump)
Missy Kane, 29, Knoxville, TN (1,500m)
Lillie Leatherwood, 22, Ralph, AL (400m, 4 x 400m relay)
Carol Lewis, 21, Willingboro, NJ (long jump)

Pamela Page, 26, Evanston, IL (100m hurdles)
Ramona Pagel, 22, Santee, CA (shot put)
Diana Richburg, 21, Troy, NY (1,500m)
Louise Ritter, 26, Denton, TX (high jump)
Karin Smith, 29, San Luis Obispo, CA (javelin)
Pamela Spencer, 26, Northridge, CA (high jump)
Cathy Sulinski, 26, South San Francisco, CA (javelin)
Lynda Sutfin, 21, Seal Beach, CA (javelin)
Angela Thacker, 20, Lincoln, NE (long jump)
Kim Turner, 23, El Paso, TX (100m hurdles)
Wenda Vareen, Trenton, NJ (reserve)
Jackie Washington, Houston, TX (reserve)
Diane Williams, 22, Montery Park, CA (reserve)
Angela Wright, 22, Tallahassee, FL (400m hurdles)
Ruth Wysocki, 27, El Toro, CA (800m, 1,500m)

John Griffin, Frederick, MD, assistant coach
Doris Heritage, Seattle, WA, assistant coach
Brooks Johnson, Stanford, CA, head coach
Patricia Rico, Croton-on-the-Hudson, NY, manager
Robert Seaman, Cerritos, CA, assistant manager

TRACK AND FIELD, WOMEN'S

100 METERS

1. **Evelyn Ashford, USA**	10.97 NOR
2. **Alice Brown, USA**	11.13
3. **Merlene Ottey-Page, JAM**	11.16
4. Jeanette Bolden, USA	11.25
5. Grace Jackson, JAM	11.39
6. Angela Bailey, CAN	11.40
7. Heather Oakes, GBR	11.43
8. Angella Taylor, CAN	11.62

200 METERS

1. **Valerie Brisco-Hooks, USA**	21.81 NOR
2. **Florence Griffith, USA**	22.04
3. **Merlene Ottey-Page, JAM**	22.09
4. Kathryn Cook, GBR	22.10
5. Grace Jackson, JAM	22.20
6. Randy Givens, USA	22.36
7. Rose Aimee Bacoul, FRA	22.78
8. Liliane Gaschet, FRA	22.86

400 METERS

1. **Valerie Brisco-Hooks, USA**	48.83 NOR
2. **Chandra Cheeseborough, USA**	49.05
3. **Kathryn Cook, GBR**	49.42
4. Marita Payne, CAN	49.91
5. Lillie Leatherwood, USA	50.25
6. Ute Thimm, FRG	50.37
7. Charmaine Crooks, CAN	50.45
8. Ruth Waithera, KEN	51.56

800 METERS

1. **Doina Melinte, ROM**	1:57.60
2. **Kim Gallagher, USA**	1:58.63
3. **Fita Lovin, ROM**	1:58.83
4. Gabriella Dorio, ITA	1:59.05
5. Lorraine Baker, GBR	2:00.03
6. Ruth Wysocki, USA	2:00.34
7. Margrit Klinger, FRG	2:00.65
8. Caroline O'Shea, IRL	2:00.77
Robin Campbell, USA	DNQ

DNQ = Did not qualify, eliminated in the semi-final round

1,500 METERS

1. **Gabriella Dorio, ITA**	4:03.25
2. **Doina Melinte, ROM**	4:03.76
3. **Maricica Puica, ROM**	4:04.15
4. Roswitha Gerdes, FRG	4:04.41
5. Christine Benning, GBR	4:04.70
6. Christina Boxer, GBR	4:05.53
7. Brit McRoberts, CAN	4:05.98
8. Ruth Wyoscki, USA	4:08.92
Missy Kane, USA	DNQ
Diana Richburg, USA	DNQ

DNQ = Did not qualify, eliminated in the semi-final round

3,000 METERS

1. **Maricica Puica, ROM**	8:35.96 NOR
2. **Wendy Sly, GBR**	8:39.47
3. **Lynn Williams, CAN**	8:42.14
4. Cindy Bremser, USA	8:42.78
5. Cornelia Buerki, SUI	8:45.20
6. Aurora Cunha, POR	8:46.37
7. Zola Budd, GBR	8:48.80
8. Joan Hansen, USA	8:51.53
Mary Decker, USA	DNF

MARATHON (26 MILES, 383 YARDS)

1. **Joan Benoit, USA**	2:24:52 EOR
2. **Grete Waitz, NOR**	2:26:18
3. **Rosa Mota, POR**	2:26:57
4. Ingrid Kristiansen, NOR	2:27:34
5. Lorraine Moller, NZL	2:28:34
6. Priscilla Welch, GBR	2:28:54
7. Lisa Martin, AUS	2:29:03
8. Sylvia Ruegger, CAN	2:29:09
36. Julie Brown, USA	2:47:33
Julie Isphording, USA	DNF

HEPTATHLON

1. **Glynis Nunn, AUS**	6,390 NOR
2. **Jackie Joyner, USA**	6,385
3. **Sabine Everts, FRG**	6,363
4. Cindy Greiner, USA	6,281
5. Judy Simpson, GBR	6,280
6. Sabine Braun, FRG	6,236
7. Tineke Hidding, HOL	6,147
8. Kim Hagger, GBR	6,127
Jodi Anderson, USA	DNF

100 METER HURDLES

1. **Benita Fitzgerald-Brown, USA**	12.84
2. **Shirley Strong, GBR**	12.88
3. **Kim Turner, USA**	13.06
4. Michele Chardonnet, FRA	13.06
5. Glynis Nunn, AUS	13.20
6. Marie Noelle Savigny, FRA	13.28
7. Ulrike Denk, FRG	13.32
8. Pamela Page, USA	13.40

400-METER HURDLES

1. **Nawal El Moutawakil, MOR**	54.61 NOR
2. **Judi Brown, USA**	55.20
3. **Cristina Cojocaru, ROM**	55.41
4. P.T. Usha, IND	55.42
5. Ann Louise Skoglund, SWE	55.43
6. Debbie Flintoff, AUS	56.21
7. Tuija Helander, FIN	56.55
8. Sandra Farmer, JAM	57.15
Sharrieffa Barksdale, USA	DNQ
Angela Scott, USA	DNQ

4 x 100-METER RELAY

1. **USA (Alice Brown, Jeannette Bolden, Chandra Cheeseborough, Evelyn Ashford)**	41.65
2. **CAN (Angela Bailey, Marita Payne, Angella Taylor, France Gareau)**	42.77
3. **GBR (Simone Jacobs, Kathryn Cook, Beverley Callender, Heather Oakes)**	43.11
4. FRA	43.15
5. FRG	43.57
6. BAH	44.18
7. TRI	44.23
8. JAM	53.54

4 x 400-METER RELAY

1. **USA (Lillie Leatherwood, Sherrie Howard, Valerie Brisco-Hooks, Chandra Cheeseborough)**	3:18.29 NOR
2. **CAN (Charmaine Crooks, Jillian Richardson, Molly Killingbeck, Marita Payne)**	3:21.21
3. **FRG (Heike Schulta-Mattler, Ute Thimm, Heide Gaugel, Gaby Bussman)**	3:22.98
4. GBR	3:25.51
5. JAM	3:27.51
6. ITA	3:30.82
7. IND	3:32.49
8. PUR	DNS

LONG JUMP

1. **Anisoara Stanciu, ROM**	6.96m (22-10)
2. **Vali Ionescu, ROM**	6.81m (22-4¼)
3. **Susan Hearnshaw, GBR**	6.80m (22-3¾)
4. Angela Thacker, USA	6.78m (22-3)
5. Jackie Joyner, USA	6.77m (22-2½)
6. Robyn Lorraway, AUS	6.67m (21-10¾)
7. Glynis Nunn, AUS	6.53m (21-5¼)
8. Shonel Ferguson, BAH	6.44m (21-1½)
9. Carol Lewis, USA	6.43m (21-1¼)

HIGH JUMP

1. **Ulrike Meyfarth, FRG**	NOR 2.02m (6-7½)
2. **Sara Simeoni, ITA**	2.00m (6-6¾)
3. **Joni Huntley, USA**	1.97m (6-5½)
4. Maryse Ewanje-Epee, FRA	1.94m (6-4¼)
5. Debbie Brill, CAN	1.94m (6-4¼)
6. Vanessa Browne, AUS	1.94m (6-4¼)
7. Zheng Dazhen, CHN	1.91m (6-3¼)
8. Louise Ritter, USA	1.91m (6-3¼)
11. Pamela Spencer, USA	1.85m (6-0¾)

SHOT PUT

1. **Claudia Losch, FRG**	20.48m (67–2¼)	
2. **Mihaela Loghin, ROM**	20.47m (67–2)	
3. **Gael Martin, AUS**	19.19m (62–11½)	
4. Judith Oakes, GBR	18.14m (59–6¼)	
5. Li Meisu, CHN	17.96m (58–11¼)	
6. Venissa Head, GBR	17.90m (58–8¾)	
7. Carol Cady, USA	17.23m (56–6½)	
8. Florenta Craciunescu, ROM	17.23m (56–6½)	
11. Ramona Pagel, USA	16.06m (52–8¼)	

JAVELIN

1. **Tessa Sanderson, GBR**	NOR 69.56m (228–2)	
2. **Tiina Lillak, FIN**	69.00m (226–4)	
3. **Fatima Whitbread, GBR**	67.14m (220–3)	
4. Tuula Laaksalo, FIN	66.40m (217–10)	
5. Trine Solberg, NOR	64.52m (211–8)	
6. Ingrid Thyssen, FRG	63.26m (207–6)	
7. Beate Peters, FRG	62.34m (204–6)	
8. Karin Smith, USA	62.06m (203–7)	
10. Cathy Sulinski, USA	58.38m (191–6)	
Lynda Sutfin, USA	DNQ	

DISCUS

1. **Ria Stalman, HOL**	65.36m (214–5)	
2. **Leslie Deniz, USA**	64.86m (212–9)	
3. **Florenta Craciunescu, ROM**	63.64m (208–9)	
4. Ulla Lundholm, FIN	62.84m (206–2)	
5. Meg Ritchie, GBR	62.58m (205–4)	
6. Ingra Manecke, FRG	58.56m (192–1)	
7. Venissa Head, GBR	58.18m (190–10)	
8. Gael Martin, AUS	55.88m (183–4)	
10. Laura DeSnoo, USA	54.84m (179–11)	
12. Lorna Griffin, USA	50.16m (164-7)	

TEAM PERSONNEL, WOMEN'S

J. Anderson

E. Ashford

S. Barksdale

R. Belle

J. Benoit

J. Bolden

C. Bremser

V. Brisco-Hooks

A. Brown

Judi Brown

Julie Brown

C. Cady

D. Richburg

L. Ritter

K. Smith

R. Campbell

C. Cheeseborough

B. Cliette

P. Spencer

C. Sulinski

L. Sutfin

M. Decker

L. Deniz

L. DeSnoo

A. Thacker

K. Turner

W. Vareen

D. Dixon

B. Fitzgerald-Brown

K. Gallagher

J. Washington

D. Williams

A. Wright

R. Givens

C. Greiner

L. Griffin

R. Wysocki

J. Griffin

D. Heritage

F. Griffith

J. Hansen

D. Howard

B. Johnson

P. Rico

R. Seaman

S. Howard

J. Huntley

J. Isphording

J. Joyner

M. Kane

L. Leatherwood

C. Lewis

P. Page

R. Pagel

BASKETBALL

There is no way of assessing the true prowess of the two U.S. gold medalist basketball teams; but, until proved otherwise, it might be said candidly that these are two of the finest squads ever to win gold in the Olympic Games.

Other teams had higher scorers. But the real assessment of the two U.S. squads was the balance achieved with strong and deep squads of 12 each. In no game did either team trail at half-time.

Both coaches, Robert Knight and Patricia Head Summitt (herself a member of the U.S. silver medalist team in 1976), molded impressive teams that played defense immeasurably better than any rival and presented a gaggle of shooters possessed of more fire power than could be mustered by any of the opponents.

The men depended on college players exclusively. Coach Summitt employed several women graduates who had gained valuable additional experience playing in European leagues over the last several years.

Whereas the men's squad had 12 standouts, Cheryl Miller was the cynosure of all eyes in the women's tournament. It is doubtful if any single player has ever dominated an international tournament as did Miller, a sophomore at the University of Southern California and a two-time member of the U.S. National Team. In the championship game against Korea, Miller scored 16 points, copped 16 rebounds, and made five assists.

In the men's tournament the United States had dispatched Spain, 101–68 in the preliminary pool play. For the championship round Spain earned a rematch by a second-half semi-final rally to unseat the defending champion, Yugoslavia. But the final game was no contest after the U.S. scored 14 straight points after Spain had crept up to within nine.

TEAM PERSONNEL

MEN'S

Steve Alford, 19, New Castle, IN
Patrick Ewing, 21, Cambridge, MA
Vern Fleming, 23, Long Island City, NY
Michael Jordan, 21, Wilmington, NC
Joseph Kleine, 22, Slater, MO
Jon Koncak, 21, Kansas City, MO
Chris Mullin, 21, Brooklyn, NY
Sam Perkins, 23, Lathan, NY
Alvin Robertson, 22, Fayetteville, AR
Wayman Tisdale, 20, Tulsa, OK
Jeff Turner, 22, Brandon, FL
Leon Wood, 22, Santa Monica, CA

Robert Knight, Bloomington, IN, coach
Charles Newton, Nashville, TN, manager
George Raveling, Iowa City, IA, assistant coach

TEAM PERSONNEL

WOMEN'S

Cathy Boswell, 21, Shorewood, IL
Denise Curry, 24, Davis, CA
Anne Donovan, 22, Ridgewood, NJ
Teresa Edwards, 20, Cairo, GA
Lea Henry, 22, Damascus, GA
Janice Lawrence, 22, Lucedale, MS
Pamela McGee, 21, Flint, MI
Carol Menken-Schaudt, 26, Eugene, OR
Cheryl Miller, 21, Riverside, CA
Kim Mulkey, 22, Tickfaw, LA
Cindy Noble, 23, Clarksburg, OH
Lynette Woodard, 25, Wichita, KS

Betty Jo Graber, Weatherford, TX, manager
Patricia Head Summitt, Seymour, TN, coach
Kay Yow, Cary, NC, assistant coach

BASKETBALL, MEN'S

GOLD MEDAL GAME

USA 96, Spain 65

BRONZE MEDAL GAME

Yugoslavia 88, Canada 82

5TH PLACE GAME

Italy 111, Uruguay 102

7TH PLACE GAME

Australia 83, West Germany 78

9TH PLACE GAME

Brazil 86, China 76

11TH PLACE GAME

France 102, Egypt 78

SCORES OF USA GAMES

July 29	USA 97, China 49
July 31	USA 89, Canada 68
Aug. 1	USA 104, Uruguay 68
Aug. 2	USA 120, France 62
Aug. 4	USA 101, Spain 68
Aug. 6	USA 78, West Germany 67*
Aug. 8	USA 78, Canada 59*
Aug. 10	USA 96, Spain 65*

* Championship Round

LEADING SCORERS FOR USA

Jordan 137, Mullin 93, Ewing 88, Alford 82, Tisdale 69, Perkins 65, Robertson 62, Fleming 54, Wood 47

TEAM STATISTICS

Field Goals: 271 of 492—55%
Foul Goals: 125 of 173—72%
Rebounds: 326 (Tisdale 45, Ewing 41, Perkins 36)
Assists: 166 (Wood 55, Fleming 19, Alford 19)
Steals: 82 (Robertson 16, Mullin 14, Alford 11)

BASKETBALL, WOMEN'S

GOLD MEDAL GAME

USA 85, South Korea 55

BRONZE MEDAL GAME

China 63, Canada 57

SCORES OF USA GAMES

July 30	USA 83, Yugoslavia 55
July 31	USA 81, Australia 47
Aug. 2	USA 84, South Korea 47
Aug. 3	USA 91, China 55
Aug. 5	USA 92, Canada 61
Aug. 7	USA 85, South Korea 55

SCORERS FOR USA (6 GAMES)

Miller 37–25–99, Woodard 25–13–63, Lawrence 20–17–57, Noble 21–10–52, Curry 18–6–42, Donovan 19–7–45, McGee 15–7–37, Mulkey 13–6–32, Henry 11–3–25, Menken-Schaudt 11–3–25, Boswell 11–2–24, Edwards 6–3–15

TEAM STATISTICS

Field Goals: 207 of 395—52%
Foul Goals: 102 of 154—66%
Rebounds: 294 (Lawrence 37, Miller 42)
Assists: 126 (Miller 25, Henry 15)
Steals: 76 (Miller 19, Boswell 10)

TEAM PERSONNEL, MEN'S

S. Alford

P. Ewing

V. Fleming

M. Jordan

J. Kleine

J. Koncak

C. Mullin

S. Perkins

A. Robertson

W. Tisdale

J. Turner

L. Wood

R. Knight

C. Newton

G. Raveling

TEAM PERSONNEL, WOMEN'S

C. Boswell

D. Curry

A. Donovan

T. Edwards

L. Henry

J. Lawrence

P. McGee

C. Menken-Schaudt

C. Miller

K. Mulkey

C. Noble

L. Woodard

B. Graber

P. Summitt

K. Yow

BOXING

The U.S. boxers won a record nine championships, and added one silver and one bronze medal in the 12 weight classes. The U.S. boxers started fast and won 16 straight bouts before Robert Shannon, the only hold-over from the 1980 Olympic team, was stopped in the third round by Korea's Sung-Kil Moon in the bantam-weight class. Then in the quarter-final Sung was stopped in the first round by Pedro Nolasco, Dominican Republic. In turn, Nolasco in the semifinals was deci-sioned by Italy's Maurizio Stecca, who went on to win the gold medal.

Overall, the U.S. boxers compiled an enviable record: 53 victories; one loss by disqualification (Evander Holyfield in the light heavyweight match when he had a New Zealander out on his feet); one by decision (Virgil Hill in the final of the middleweight class at the hands of another Korean, Shin Joon-Sup); and Shannon's third-round knock-out.

The International Amateur Boxing Association awards the Val Barker Trophy to the best boxer in the tourna-ment. The award this year went to Paul Gonzales, USA, the light flyweight champion who only a year earlier had been deprived of a Pan American gold medal when a jury reversed a decision and awarded the title to his South American opponent. Gonzales was magnificent in Los Angeles (his hometown) and didn't have to fight for the gold medal. His opponent was unable to enter the ring because of a broken thumb.

Two significant policy changes were adopted by IABA since the last Olympic Games that had a marked impact on the conduct of the tournament.

Judges' decisions have long been the center of contro-versy in amateur boxing. Some years previous the IABA took a major step forward by adopting a policy of assigning five judges to each match, one from each continent, with the provision that no judge could be from the country of either boxer.

Then, in 1982, the IABA decided to inaugurate a "supe-rior panel" of five judges who would work every match. However, the judgment of these men would only be brought into play when the regular judges voted a split decision, 3–2.

Although Gonzales lost in the Pan American Games on a reversal by the superior panel, their work at Los Angeles was all-important in deciding 33 close bouts. Many consider the introduction of a superior panel as extremely beneficial to the sport.

The other major policy change was approval of the use of headguards for the boxers. While not minimizing chances for a knockout, it virtually eliminates the num-ber of men defeated by cut eyes as the result of butting, whether intentional or not.

A pair of Canada's national heroes—light-middleweight Shawn O'Sullivan and heavyweight Willie DeWit—benefited from the superior panel's judgment. Both advanced to the finals when decisions against them, 3–2, were reversed by the panel.

O'Sullivan and USA's Frank Tate and DeWit and Henry Tillman, also USA, had live slugfests for the gold medal. O'Sullivan doesn't mind taking two jabs to the face to try a haymaker right. Many spectators think he is doing well, but his opponent scores heavily with clean blows.

Likewise, DeWit loves to mix it up. What he lacks in technical boxing skills he strives to make up for with his relentless plodding forward.

The number one plodder in the tournament was Italy's super-heavyweight, Francisco Damiani. Damiani was an aggressive foe in his match with Tyrell Biggs, USA. But the judges scored the match 4–1 in favor of Biggs.

In the final matches there were five 5–0 decisions, three 4–1 decisions, one 3–2 decision, and two walk-overs. Pernell Whitaker, USA, won the lightweight title when the seconds for Puerto Rico's Luis Ortiz waved a white towel of surrender after 2:57 of the second round.

TEAM PERSONNEL

Tyrell Biggs, 23, Philadelphia, PA
Mark Breland, 21, Brooklyn, NY
Paul Gonzales, 20, Los Angeles, CA
Virgil Hill, 20, Williston and Grand Forks, ND
Evander Holyfield, 21, Atlanta, GA
Steve McCrory, 20, Detroit, MI
Jerry Page, 23, Columbus, OH
Robert Shannon, 21, Edmonds, WA
Frank Tate, 20, Detroit, MI
Meldrick Taylor, 17, Philadelphia, PA
Henry Tillman, 24, Los Angeles, CA
Pernell Whitaker, 20, Norfolk, VA

Pat Nappi, Syracuse, NY, coach
Roosevelt Sanders, Colorado Springs, CO, assistant coach
Edward Silverglade, Trenton, NJ, manager

BOXING

(In boxing the winner receives the gold medal, the defeated finalist is awarded the silver medal, and the defeated semi-finalists in each weight class receive bronze medals)

106 LBS./48 KG. LIGHT FLYWEIGHT
Final: **Paul Gonzales, USA** won by walkover over **Salvatore Todisco, ITA**
Semifinal: Gonzales, USA dec. **Jose Marcelino Bolivar, VEN;** Todisco, ITA dec. **Keith Mwila, ZAM**

112 LBS./51 KG. FLYWEIGHT
Final: **Steven McCrory, USA** dec. **Redzep Redzepovski, YUG, 4–1**
Semifinal: McCrory, USA dec. **Eyup Can, TUR;** Redzepovski, YUG dec. **Ibrahim Bilali, KEN**

119 LBS./54 KG. BANTAMWEIGHT
Final: **Maurizio Stecca, ITA** dec. **Hector Lopez, MEX, 4–1**
Semifinal: Stecca, ITA dec. **Pedro Nolasco, DOM;** Lopez, MEX dec. **Dale Walters, CAN** Robert Shannon, USA eliminated in 1/16th final by Sung-Kil Moon, KOR, when referee stopped the contest in the third round.

126 LBS./57 KG. FEATHERWEIGHT
Final: **Meldrick Taylor, USA** dec. **Peter Konyegwachie, NGR, 5–0**
Semifinal: Taylor, USA dec. **Omar Catari Peraza, VEN;** Konyegwachie, NGR dec. **Turgut Aykac, TUR**

132 LBS./60 KG. LIGHTWEIGHT
Final: **Pernell Whitaker, USA** won over **Luis Ortiz, PUR** in 2:57 of the second round. Ortiz "retired."
Semifinal: Whitaker, USA dec. **Chun Chil-Sung, KOR;** Ortiz, PUR dec. **Martin Ndongo Ebanga, CMR**

139 LBS./63 KG. LIGHT WELTERWEIGHT
Final: **Jerry Page, USA** dec. **Dhawee Umponmaha, THA** 5–0
Semifinal: Page, USA dec. **Mirk O. Puzovic, YUG;** Umponmaha, THA dec. **Mircea Fulger, ROM**

148.5 LBS./67 KG. WELTERWEIGHT
Final: **Mark Breland, USA** dec. **An Young-Su, KOR** 5–0
Semifinal: Breland USA dec. **Luciano Bruno, ITA;** Young-Su dec. **Joni Nyman, FIN**

157 LBS./71 KG. LIGHT MIDDLEWEIGHT
Final: **Frank Tate, USA** dec. **Shawn O'Sullivan, CAN** 5–0
Semifinal: Tate, USA won by walkover over **Manfred Zielonka, FRG;** O'Sullivan CAN dec. **Christophe Tiozzo, FRA**

165 LBS./75 KG. MIDDLEWEIGHT
Final: **Shin Joon-Sup, KOR** dec. **Virgil Hill, USA,** 3–2
Semifinal: Joon-Sup, KOR dec. **Aristides Gonzalez, PUR;** Hill, USA dec. **Mohamed Zaoui, ALG**

179 LBS./81 KG. LIGHT HEAVYWEIGHT
Final: **Anton Josipovic, YUG** won by walkover over **Kevin Barry, NZL**
Semifinal: Josipovic, YUG dec. **Mustapha Moussa, ALG;** Barry, NZL won by disq. over **Evander Holyfield, USA**

201 LBS./91 KG. HEAVYWEIGHT
Final: **Henry Tillman, USA** dec. **Willie deWit, CAN,** 5–0
Semifinal: Tillman, USA dec. **Angelo Musone, ITA;** deWit, CAN dec. **Arnold Vanderlijde, HOL**

OVER 201 LBS./OVER 91 KG. SUPER-HEAVYWEIGHT
Final: **Tyrell Biggs, USA** dec. **Francisco Damiani, ITA** 4–1
Semifinal: Biggs, USA dec. **Salihu Azis, YUG;** Damiani, ITA won over **Robert Wells, GBR,** referee stopped contest

TEAM PERSONNEL

T. Biggs   M. Breland   P. Gonzales

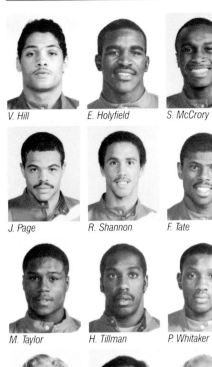

V. Hill	E. Holyfield	S. McCrory
J. Page	R. Shannon	F. Tate
M. Taylor	H. Tillman	P. Whitaker

P. Nappi	R. Sanders	E. Silverglade

CANOEING

The only 1980 champions to repeat were the Romanians Ivan Potzaichin and Toma Simionov in the 1,000-meter Canadian pairs (double-bladed paddles).

The two outstanding paddlers were New Zealand's Ian Ferguson with three gold medals in the kayak events and Sweden's Agneta Andersson, two gold medals and a silver in women's kayaking.

The USA's Greg Barton distinguished himself by winning the bronze medal in the kayak singles, 1,000-meter race. The previous highest placed U.S. kayaker was Ernest Riedel's fourth in 1936.

The United States showed a slight improvement over previous paddling performances. In addition to Barton, the team had a fourth in men's kayak doubles. In the Canadian canoe events, out of four races, the United States placed fifth, seventh, and ninth and was eliminated in the semi-finals of the 500-meter singles.

In the women's kayak races the United States notched a sixth place in the singles, fifth in the pairs, and a fourth in the fours, all over the 500-meter distance.

Sweden won two of the three women's kayak races, while Romania was the victor in the fours. Romania was a disappointment in the men's canoe and kayak events, New Zealand winning four out of five.

TEAM PERSONNEL

Greg Barton, 24, Homer, MI (Kayak)
Norman Bellingham, 19, Rockville, MD (K)
Sheila L. Conover, 21, Costa Mesa, CA (K)
Shirley Dery, 22, Fort Lauderdale, FL (K)
Capt. David R. Gilman, USA, 29, Berkeley, CA (K)
David Halpern, 28, Seattle, WA (K)
Olney (Terry) Kent, 21, Rochester, NY (K)
Leslie G. Klein (Kearney), 29, Lexington, KY (K)
Rodney S. McLain, 23, Gloversville, NY (Canoe)

Bruce P. Merritt, 26, Ridge, MD (C)
John Robert Plankenhorn, 29, Roselle, IL (C)
Daniel W. Schnurrenberger, 28, Mt. Airy, MD (K)
Chris A. Spelius, 32, Deerfield, IL (K)
Jim Ross Terrell, 19, Milford, OH (C)
Ann C. Turner, 27, St. Charles, IL (K)
Terry White, 28, Peru, VT (K)
J. Brett Young, 24, Hastings-on-Hudson, NY (C)

Clyde C. Britt, Ridgefield Park, NJ, coach
Robert M. Hahn, Long Beach, CA, manager
Powel Podgorski, Hartford, CT, assistant coach

CANOEING, WOMEN'S

500-METER KAYAK SINGLES

1. **Agneta Andersson, SWE**	1:58.72
2. **Barbara Schuttpelz, FRG**	1:59.73
3. **Annemiek Derckx, HOL**	2:00.11
4. Tecia Marinescu, ROM	2:00.12
5. Beatrice Basson, FRA	2:02.21
6. Sheila Conover, USA	2:02.38
7. Lucie Guay, CAN	2:02.49
8. Elizabeth Blencowe, AUS	2:02.63

500-METER KAYAK DOUBLES

1. **SWE (Agneta Andersson, Anna Olsson)**	1:45.25
2. **CAN (Alexandra Barre, Sue Holloway)**	1:47.13
3. **FRG (Josefa Idem, Barbara Schuttpelz)**	1:47.32
4. USA (Shirley Dery, Leslie Klein Kearney)	1:49.51
5. FRA	1:51.40
6. NOR	1:51.61
7. GBR	1:51.73

500-METER KAYAK FOURS

1. **ROM (Agafia Constantin, Nastasia Ionescu, Tecia Marinescu, Maria Stefan**	1:38.34
2. **SWE (Agneta Andersson, Anna Olsson, Eva Karlsson, Susanne Wiberg)**	1:38.37
3. **CAN (Alexandra Barre, Lucie Guay, Sue Holloway, Barb Olmsted)**	1:39.40
4. USA (Sheila Conover, Shirley Dery, Leslie Klein Kearney, Ann Turner)	1:40.49
5. FRG	1:42.68
6. NOR	1:42.97
7. GBR	1:46.30

CANOEING, MEN'S

500-METER KAYAK SINGLES

1. **Ian Ferguson, NZL**	1:47.84
2. **Lars-Erik Moberg, SWE**	1:48.18
3. **Bernard Bregeon, FRA**	1:48.41
4. Vasile Diba, ROM	1:48.77
5. David Upson, GBR	1:49.32
6. Daniele Scarpa, ITA	1:49.60
7. Guillermo Del Riego, ESP	1:49.71
8. Reiner Scholl, FRG	1:49.89
Terry White, USA	DNQ

500-METER KAYAK DOUBLES

1. **NZL (Ian Ferguson, Paul MacDonald)**	1:34.21
2. **SWE (Per-Inge Bengtsson, Lars-Erik Moberg)**	1:35.26

3. **CAN (Hugh Fisher, Alwyn Morris)**	1:35.41
4. ITA	1:35.50
5. ROM	1:35.60
6. FRA	1:36.20
7. FRG	1:36.51
8. GBR	1:36.73
USA (David Halpern, Terry Kent)	DNQ

1,000-METER KAYAK SINGLES

1. **Alan Thompson, NZL**	3:45.73
2. **Milan Janic, YUG**	3:46.88
3. **Greg Barton, USA**	3:47.38
4. Kalle Sundqvist, SWE	3:48.69
5. Peter Genders, AUS	3:49.11
6. Philippe Boccara, FRA	3:49.38
7. Vasile Diba, ROM	3:51.61
8. Stephen Jackson, GBR	3:52.25

1,000-METER KAYAK DOUBLES

1. **CAN (Hugh Fisher, Alwyn Morris)**	3:34.22
2. **FRA (Bernard Bregeon, Patrick Lefoulon)**	3:25.97
3. **AUS (Barry Kelly, Grant Kenny)**	3:26.80
4. USA (Terry Kent, Terry White)	3:27.01
5. FRG	3:27.28
6. ITA	3:27.46
7. ESP	3:27.53
8. SWE	3:29.39

1,000-METER KAYAK FOURS

1. **NZL (Grant Bramwell, Ian Ferguson, Paul MacDonald, Alan Thompson)**	3:02.28
2. **SWE (Per-Inge Bengtsson, Tommy Karls, Lars-Erik Moberg, Thomas Ohlsson)**	3:02.81
3. **FRA (Francois Barouh, Philippe Boccara, Pascal Boucherit, Didier Vavasseur)**	3:03.94
4. ROM	3:04.29
5. GBR	3:04.59
6. ESP	3:04.71
7. AUS	3:06.02
8. FRG	3:06.47
USA (Norman Bellingham, David Gilman, Dan Schnurrenberger, Chris Spelius)	DNQ

500-METER CANOE SINGLES (CANADIAN)

1. **Larry Cain, CAN**	1:57.01
2. **Henning Jakobsen, DEN**	1:58.45
3. **Costica Olaru, ROM**	1:59.86
4. Philippe Renaud, FRA	1:59.95
5. Timo Gronlund, FIN	2:01.00
6. Kiyoto Inoue, JPN	2:01.79
7. Harmut Faust, FRG	2:01.86
8. Robert Rozanski, NOR	2:01.12
John Plankenhorn, USA	DNQ

500-METER CANOE DOUBLES (CANADIAN PAIRS)

1. **YUG (Matja Ljubek, Mirko Nisovic)**	1:43.67
2. **ROM (Ivan Potzaichin, Toma Simionov)**	1:45.68
3. **ESP (Enrique Miguez, Narsciso Suarez)**	1:47.71

4. FRA	1:47.72
5. CAN	1:48.81
6. FRG	1:48.97
7. GBR	1:49.59
8. JPN	1:50.22
9. USA (J. Brett Young, Bruce Merritt)	1:50.55

1,000-METER CANOE SINGLES (CANADIAN)

1. **Ulrich Eicke, FRG**	4:06.32
2. **Larry Cain, CAN**	4:08.67
3. **Henning Jakobsen, DEN**	4:09.51
4. Timo Gronlund, FIN	4:15.58
5. Costica Olaru, ROM	4:16.39
6. Stephen Train, GBR	4:16.64
7. Bruce Merritt, USA	4:18.17
8. Kiyoto Inoue, JPN	4:18.72

1,000-METER CANOE DOUBLES (CANADIAN PAIRS)

1. **ROM (Ivan Potzaichin, Toma Simionov)**	3:40.60
2. **YUG (Matija Ljubek, Mirko Nisovic)**	3:41.56
3. **FRA (Didier Hoyer, Eric Renaud)**	3:48.01
4. FRG	3:52.69
5. USA (John Plankenhorn, Rodney McClain)	3:52.72
6. ESP	3:56.92
7. CAN	3:56.99
8. MEX	3:57.49

TEAM PERSONNEL

G. Barton   N. Bellingham   S. Conover

D. Gilman   D. Halpern   O. Kent

R. McLain   B. Merritt   J. Plankenhorn

D. Schnurren-   C. Spelius   J. Terrell
berger

A. Turner   T. White   J. Young

CYCLING

Perhaps no Olympic sport has prospered more than cycling as a result of the USOC adoption of the National Training Center concept.

Over a six-year period cycling has made excellent use of the training center at Colorado Springs as the prime base for both the track and road cyclists. Since 1983 the U.S. Cycling Federation has concentrated on the honing of cyclists' skills at a velodrome built in Colorado Springs under the sponsorship of the Southland Corporation.

Corporate sponsorship has made it possible for the cyclists to cover their personal living, training, and travel expenses. In addition, the USCF has made it possible to step up cyclists' opportunities for international competitions both at home and abroad.

Before the Olympics the United States had done well in international competition. The two top U.S. women road cyclists, Rebecca Twigg and Connie Carpenter-Phinney, were ranked Nos. 1 and 2, respectively, in the world.

The opening test was the women's individual road race, and the finish was close to a dead heat. But coming down the last 100 meters of the 49-mile test Carpenter-Phinney nosed out Twigg by a couple of inches.

The men's individual road race was a real shocker. Alexi Grewal, a free spirit among free spirits in a sport where they are the rule rather than the exception, sped over the 119-mile distance in just under five hours. His margin of victory over Canada's Steve Bauer was a few inches.

The success of the United States in the individual road races served as a catalyst for the track performers.

The United States had never earned a medal of any color in the track events until 1984. The old six-day bike racers, wherever they may be today, can shake their heads as they question anyone and everyone, "Can you imagine? In the Olympic match sprint it came down to a race between two Americans, Gorski and Vails." Gorski won in two straight heats.

The 4,000-meter individual pursuit is a difficult one for the uninitiated to understand at first glance. This is a match race where the two cyclists start on opposite sides of the track. Thus, two timing instruments are kept going, just in case the naked eye doesn't conclusively show the winner...or else the race is over if the one rider catches up and passes his opponent.

The two American entries, Steve Hegg and Leonard Harvey Nitz, showed their understanding of tactics connected with this race.

In the semifinals Hegg was a victor, Nitz a loser. In the finals Hegg completely dominated Rolf Golz of West Germany. The timing devices showed that Nitz won the bronze medal by a .05 second.

Aided by research under the USOC Sports Equipment and Technology Committee, chaired by Andras Toro, the U.S. track cyclists turned up with "funny bikes," the backwheel being solid to cut down on wind resistance and turbulence. Look for other major technical changes before the cyclists of the world gather at Seoul in 1988.

TEAM PERSONNEL

John C. Beckman, 25, Beaverton, OR
Jeff A. Bradley, 23, Davenport, IO
Jon Carmichael, 23, Miami, FL
Connie Carpenter-Phinney, 27, Boulder, CO
Brent R. Emery, 26, Allentown, PA
Mark B. Gorski, 24, La Jolla, CA
Alexi Grewal, 23, Aspen, CO
David M. Grylls, 26, San Diego, CA
Steve Edward Hegg, 20, Dana Point, CA
Ronald Kiefel, 24, Boulder, CO
Clarence (Roy) Knickman, 19, Colorado Springs, CO
Patrick McDonough, 23, Long Beach, CA
Leonard Harvey Nitz, 27, Sacramento, CA
Rory T. O'Reilly, 29, Costa Mesa, CA
Janelle Parks, 20, Big City, WY
Davis Phinney, 25, Boulder, CO
Thurlow Rogers, 24, Van Nuys, CA
Douglas Shapiro, 24, Boulder, CO
Kristina Thompson, 20, Reno, NV
Rebecca Twigg, 21, Colorado Springs, CO
Nelson B. Vails, 23, New York, NY
Danny Van Haute, 27, Chicago, IL
Andrew T. Weaver, 25, Coral Springs, FL
Mark Whitehead, 23, Whittier, CA

Edward Borysewicz, Phoenix, AZ, head coach
Edward R. Burke, Colorado Springs, CO, mechanic
Michael A. Fraysee, Teaneck, NJ, manager
Timothy Kelly, Boulder, CO, road coach
Carl Leusenkamp, Beaverton, OR, track coach

CYCLING, WOMEN'S

INDIVIDUAL ROAD RACE (79.2 kilometers, 49.5 miles)

1. **Connie Carpenter-Phinney, USA**	2:11:14
(36.210 kilometers per hour, 22.7 miles per hour)	
2. **Rebecca Twigg, USA**	Group
3. **Sandra Schumacher, FRG**	Group
4. Unni Larsen, NOR	Group
5. Maria Canins, ITA	Group
6. Jeannie Longo, FRA	2:12:35
7. Helle Soerensen, DEN	2:13:28
8. Ute Enzenauer, FRG	Group

CYCLING, MEN'S

INDIVIDUAL ROAD RACE (190.2 kilometers, 119 miles)

1. **Alexi Grewal, USA**	4:59:57
(38.056 kilometers per hour, 23.8 miles per hour)	
2. **Steve Bauer, CAN**	Group
3. **Dag Otto Lauritzen, NOR**	5:00:18
4. Morten Saether, NOR	Group
5. Davis Phinney, USA	5:01:16
6. Thurlow Rogers, USA	Group
7. Bojan Ropret, YUG	
8. Nestor Mora, COL	

100-KILOMETER ROAD TEAM TRIALS

1. **ITA (Marcello Bartalini, Marco Giovannetti, Eros Poli, Claudio Vandelli)**	1:58.24
2. **SUI (Alfred Acherman, Richard Trinkler, Laurent Vial, Benno Wiss)**	2:02.34
3. **USA (Ronald Kiefel, Roy Knickman, Davis Phinney, Andrew Weaver)**	2:02.46
4. HOL	2:02.57
5. SWE	2:04.46
6. FRA	2:05.07
7. DEN	2:05.31
8. GBR	2:05.51

MATCH SPRINT

1. **Mark Gorski, USA**	NOR	10.49/10.96
2. **Nelson Vails, USA**		
3. **Tsutomu Sakamoto, JPN**		11.06/11.03
4. Philippe Vernet, FRA		
5. Gerhard Scheller, FRG		
6. Marcelo Alexandre, ARG		
7. Kenrick Tucker, AUS		
8. Fredy Schmidtke, FRG		

1,000-METER TIME TRIALS

1. **Fredy Schmidtke, FRG**	1:06.10
2. **Curtis Harnett, CAN**	1:06.44
3. **Fabrice Colas, FRA**	1:06.65
4. Gene Samuel, TRI	1:06:69
5. Craig Adair, NZL	1:06.96
6. David Weller, JAM	1:07.24
7. Marcello O. Alexandre, ARG	1:07.29
8. Rory O'Reilly, USA	1:07.39

4,000-METER INDIVIDUAL PURSUIT

1. **Steve Hegg, USA**	4:39.35
2. **Rolf Golz, FRG**	4:43.82
3. **Leonard Harvey Nitz, USA**	4:44.03
4. Dean Woods, AUS	4:44.08
5. Joergen V. Pedersen, DEN	
6. Jelle Nijdam, HOL	
7. Robert Pascal, FRA	
8. Michael Grenada, AUS	

4,000-METER TEAM PURSUIT

1. **AUS (Michael Grenda, Kevin Nichols, Michael Turtur, Dean Woods)**	4:25.99
(54.137 kilometers per hour, 33.8 miles per hour)	
2. **USA (David Grylls, Steve Hegg, Patrick McDonough, Leonard Harvey Nitz)**	4:29.85
3. **FRG (Reinhard Alber, Rolf Golz, Roland Gunther, Michael Marx)**	4:25.60
4. ITA (Roberto Amadio, Massimo Brunelli, Maurizio Colombo, Silvio Martinello)	4:26.90
5. DEN	4:25.16
6. FRA	4:30.28
7. SUI	4:30.47
8. BEL	4:31.53

POINTS RACE

	Laps Down	Points Earned
1. **Roger Ilegems, BEL**	0	37
2. **Uwe Messerschmidt, FRG**	0	15
3. **Jose Manuel Youshimatz, MEX**	1	29
4. Joerg Mueller, SUI	1	23
5. Juan Esteban Curuchet, ARG	1	20
6. Glen Clarke, AUS	1	13
7. Brian Fowler, NZL	1	12
8. Derk Jan Van Egmond, HOL	2	56
Danny Van Haute, USA		DNQ
Mark Whitehead, USA		DNQ

TEAM PERSONNEL

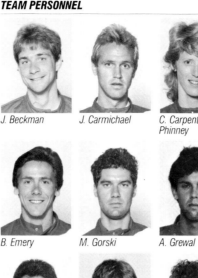

J. Beckman   J. Carmichael   C. Carpenter-Phinney

B. Emery   M. Gorski   A. Grewal

D. Grylls   S. Hegg   P. McDonough

L. Nitz   R. O'Reilly   J. Parks

D. Phinney   T. Rogers   D. Shapiro

K. Thompson   R. Twigg   M. Whitehead

E. Borysewicz   E. Burke   M. Fraysee

T. Kelly

DIVING

Following his third straight gold medal in the platform diving event at Montreal, 1976, the Italian Klaus Dibiasi predicted, "In 1980 Greg Louganis will own everything in diving."

But Louganis never had an opportunity to prove Dibiasi right in 1980. Still, the long wait didn't dampen his enthusiasm or his burning desire to perfect his techniques off the platform or the 3-meter springboard.

This year would have been difficult to find a single follower of diving to predict gold for anyone other than Louganis. And they were right, for Louganis won both diving events. Ron Merriott was third in the springboard event when China's Tan Liangde nipped him by the margin of a .99 point. Bruce Kimball was second to Louganis' record platform high of 710.91 points.

At the 1982 world championships Louganis had won both diving events. In the 1982 women's competition Megan Neyer and Wendy Wyland, both U.S. teenagers just starting on international careers, won the springboard and platform events. Neyer didn't make the Olympic team and Wyland finished third at Los Angeles behind China's Zhou Jihong and the virtually unknown Michele Mitchell, a late bloomer whose biographical notes were not even included in the USA Media Guide.

Canada's Sylvie Bernier was the steadiest of the springboard divers and won the title. Kelly McCormick placed second and Christina Seufert third.

It may be difficult for most spectators to follow the intermediate standings of the divers posted on electronic leader boards as they move through their programs. However, divers seemingly possess a sixth sense permitting them to keep in mind the sequence of dives they have signed up for as well as their relative standings.

Not so for Bernier. Two of her comments to the assembled media following her triumph are worthy of preservation in the official record of the USOC:

(1) "I've had the same selection of dives for six years. The program has worked well for me. I saw no need to change it [the program] for the Olympics. Now I may never change it."

(2) "It wasn't until a few minutes before my final dive when my coach told me I was doing a good job that I realized I had a chance for a medal. I refused to look at the scoreboard because I didn't want to put any extra pressure on myself. Instead, I plugged in my Walkman and listened to music from *Flashdance*. That relaxed me."

For the record: Bernier won the title on her eighth dive. Both she and Kelly McCormick had selected the same dive. Bernier was scored 60.48 points, McCormick only 51.24. Bernier's final margin of victory was a scant 2.24 points.

TEAM PERSONNEL

Bruce Kimball, 21, Ann Arbor, MI (Platform)
Greg Louganis, 24, Mission Viejo, CA (Platform, Springboard)
Kelly McCormick 24, Columbus, OH (Springboard)
Ron Merriott, 24, Ann Arbor, MI (Springboard)
Michele Mitchell, 19, Mission Viejo, CA (Platform)
Christina Seufert, 27, Ambler, PA (Springboard)
Wendy Wyland, 19, Mission Viejo, CA (Platform)

Thomas Gompf, Miami, FL, manager
Richard Kimball, Ann Arbor, MI, coach
Dr. Ronald O'Brien, Mission Viejo, CA, coach

DIVING, MEN'S

PLATFORM DIVING

1. **Greg Louganis, USA**	710.91
2. **Bruce Kimball, USA**	643.50

3. **Li Kongzheng, CHN**		638.28
4. Tong Hui, CHN		604.77
5. Albin Killat, FRG		551.97
6. Dieter Doerr, FRG		536.07
7. Christopher Snode, GBR		524.40
8. David Bedard, CAN		518.13

SPRINGBOARD DIVING

1. **Greg Louganis, USA**	754.41
2. **Tan Liangde, CHN**	662.31
3. **Ron Merriott, USA**	661.32
4. Li Hongping, CHN	646.35
5. Christopher Snode, GBR	609.51
6. Piero Italiani, ITA	578.94
7. Albin Killat, FRG	569.52
8. Stephen Foley, AUS	561.93

DIVING, WOMEN'S

SPRINGBOARD DIVING

1. **Sylvie Bernier, CAN**	530.70
2. **Kelly McCormick, USA**	527.46
3. **Christina Seufert, USA**	517.62
4. Li Yihua, CHN	506.52
5. Li Qiaoxian, CHN	487.68
6. Elsa Tenorio, MEX	463.56
7. Lesley Smith, ZIM	451.89
8. Debbie Fuller, CAN	450.99

PLATFORM DIVING

1. **Zhou Jihong, CHN**	435.51
2. **Michele Mitchell, USA**	431.19
3. **Wendy Wyland, USA**	422.07
4. Chen Xiaoxia, CHN	419.76
5. Valerie Beddoe, AUS	388.56
6. Debbie Fuller, CAN	371.49
7. Elsa Tenorio, MEX	360.45
8. Guadalupe Canseco, MEX	352.89

TEAM PERSONNEL

B. Kimball   G. Louganis   K. McCormick

R. Merriott   M. Mitchell   C. Seufert

W. Wyland   T. Gompf   R. Kimball

Dr. R. O'Brien

EQUESTRIAN

Touch of Class, a resurrected reject from flat racing ridden by Joe Fargis, earned two gold medals with perhaps the single finest performance of any jumper in Olympic history. In the team competition Touch of Class and Fargis had two perfect rounds to lead the United States to the gold medal. In the individual show jumping Touch of Class became the second U.S. horse to win the blue Ribbon. (Snowbound had won with Bill Steinkraus astride sixteen years earlier.)

In the individual show jumping, Touch of Class had two perfect rounds up to the last rail fence. She knocked it down and had to go against a teammate, Abdullah, for the gold. Touch of Class had a fourth perfect round out of the five in the jump-off.

After the U.S. victory in the team show jumping, West German Paul Schockemohle was quoted as saying, "The Americans made us look like fools today, they were so good. Today they would have won everywhere."

At Montreal in 1976 the U.S. three-day team showed Great Britain's Princess Anne and the rest of the riders and horses that there was no one better.

Since Montreal the Olympic candidates had been training at South Hamilton, Massachusetts. This event is perhaps the second toughest on the Olympic program, ranking only behind the modern pentathlon. What makes it difficult is the endurance ride the second day of competition.

ABC-TV did a stupendous job showing the entire endurance ride conducted on a golf course within a ranch outside San Diego. The beauty of this event had only been captured one time previously, by Leni Riefenstahl in *Olympiad*, the official film of the 1936 Games.

Perhaps the best U.S. combination for the gold medal was Bruce Davidson riding J.J. Babu. But J.J. Babu came a cropper at one difficult fence and lost enough time to eliminate him and his rider from contention.

The surprise was Karen Stives, little known before the Olympic Games. In fact, on the victory stand at the conclusion of the three-day, there were two surprises: the winner was Charisma, ridden by Mark Todd of New Zealand, followed by Ben Arthur, ridden by Stives. Priceless of Great Britain, ridden by Virginia Holgate, came in third.

In the three-day competition the team of Ben Arthur, Blue Stone, and Finvarra brought home the blue ribbon and gold medals for the United States. The riders were Stives, J. Michael Plumb, and Torrance Watkins Fleischmann, respectively.

For many years, the grueling three-day event was strictly for members of the military. However, today women have made their mark. Two of the three top riders were women; and so were five of the top ten.

One of the grand old men of equestrian sports, Dr. Reiner Klimke, German Federal Republic, rode Ahlerich to victory in the individual dressage competition.

TEAM PERSONNEL

Leslie M. Burr, 27, Westport, CT
Bruce D. Davidson, 34, Unionville, PA
Robert J. Dover, 28, Alexandria, VA
Joseph H. Fargis, 36, Petersburg, VA
Torrance Fleischmann, 35, The Plains, VA
Hilda C. Gurney, 40, Moorpark, CA
Conrad E. Homfeld, 32, Petersburg, VA
Anne Kursinski, 25, Pasadena, CA
Sandy Pflueger-Clarke, 30, Lafayette Hill, PA
J. Michael Plumb, 44, Dover, MA
Melanie Smith, 35, Litchfield, CT
Karen E. Stives, 33, Dover, MA
James C. Wofford, 39, Upperville, VA

Frank Chapot, Neshanic Station, NJ, jumping coach
Chrystine Jones, Gladstone, NJ, manager
Jack LeGoff, South Hamilton, MA, 3-day coach
A. Martin Simensen, Hamilton, MA, veterinarian
George Teodorescu, West Germany, dressage coach

EQUESTRIAN

THREE-DAY EVENT, INDIVIDUAL

1. **Mark Todd (horse: Charisma), NZL**	51.60
2. **Karen Stives (horse: Ben Arthur), USA**	54.20
3. **Virginia Holgate (horse: Priceless), GBR**	56.80
4. Torrance Fleischmann (Finvarra), USA	60.40
5. Paschal Morvillers (Gulliver B), FRA	63.00
6. Lucinda Green (Regal Realm), GBR	63.80
7. Marina Sciocchetti (Master Hunt), ITA	67.00
8. Mauro Checcoli (Spey Cast Boy), ITA	67.00
10. J. Michael Plumb (Blue Stone), USA	71.40
13. Bruce Davidson (J.J. Babu), USA	75.20

THREE-DAY EVENT, TEAM

1. **USA (Plumb, Davidson, Stives, Fleischmann)**	186.00
2. **GBR (Holgate, Green, Stark, Clapham)**	189.20
3. **FRG (Hogrefe, Overesch, Erhorn, Tesdorph)**	234.00
4. FRA	236.00
5. AUS	258.40
6. NZL	280.00
7. ITA	280.70
8. SWE	339.85

DRESSAGE, INDIVIDUAL

1. **Reiner Klimke (horse: Ahlerich), FRG**	1,504
2. **Anne Grethe Jensen (horse: Marzog), DEN**	1,442
3. **Otto J. Hofer (horse: Limandus), SUI**	1,364
4. Ingamay Bylund (Aleks), SWE	1,332
5. Herbert Krug (Muscadeur), FRG	1,323
6. (tie) Christopher Bartle (Wily Trout), GBR	1,279
6. (tie) Uwe Sauer (Montevideo), FRG	1,279
8. Annemarie Sanders-Keyzer (Amon), HOL	1,271

DRESSAGE, TEAM

1. **FRG (Klimke, Sauer, Krug)**	4,955
2. **SUI (Hofer, Stuckelberger, DeBary)**	4,673
3. **SWE (Bylund, Hakanson, Nahhorst)**	4,630
4. HOL	4,586
5. DEN	4,574
6. USA (Gurney, Pflueger-Clarke, Dover)	4,559
7. CAN	4,503
8. GBR	4,463

PRIX DE NATIONS SHOW JUMPING, INDIVIDUAL

1. **Joe Fargis (horse: Touch of Class), USA**	4.00 WG
2. **Conrad Homfeld (horse: Abdullah), USA**	4.00
3. **Heidi Robbiani (horse: Jessica V), SUI**	8.00 WB
4. Mario Deslauriers (Aramis), CAN	8.00
5. Bruno Candrian (Slygof), SUI	8.00
6. Luis Cervera Alvarez (Jexico de Park), ESP	8.50
7. (tie) Frederic Cottier (Flambeau C), FRA	12.00
7. (tie) Melanie Smith (Calypso), USA	12.00
7. (tie) Paul Schockemohle (Deister), FRG	12.00

WG = Won jump-off for gold medal
WB = Won jump-off for bronze medal

PRIX DE NATIONS SHOW JUMPING, TEAM

1. **USA (Fargis, Homfeld, Smith, Burr)**	12.00
2. **GBR (M. Whitaker, J. Whitaker, Smith, Grubb)**	36.75
3. **FRG (Schockemohle, Sloothaak, Luther, Ligges)**	39.25
4. CAN	40.00
5. SUI	41.00
6. FRA	49.75
7. ESP	52.00
8. ITA	75.25

TEAM PERSONNEL

L. Burr   B. Davidson   R. Dover

J. Fargis   T. Fleischmann   H. Gurney

C. Homfeld   A. Kursinski   S. Pflueger-Clarke

J. Plumb   M. Smith   K. Stives

J. Wofford   F. Chapot   C. Jones

J. LeGoff   A. Simensen   G. Teodorescu

FENCING

For the first time in twenty-four years the United States won an individual medal in Olympic fencing. It was not surprising that the medalist was Peter Westbrook, a three-time Olympian and an eight-time national sabre champion. He followed up the gold medal he had won in the 1983 Pan-American Games sabre competition.

The U.S. fencing cadre showed a modicum of improvement with its placings:

Debra Waples was 20th in the women's foil.

The women's foil team placed sixth, with Vincent Bradford winning three individual matches.

Newcomer Peter Lewison moved into the direct elimination and wound up 11th in the men's foil.

The men's foil team placed fifth by defeating Britain 9–6 in a fence-off.

Westbrook won the bronze in the individual sabre, Steve Mormando finished 12th, and Michael Lofton 17th.

In the sabre team competition the U.S. placed sixth, losing to China 9–7 in a bid for fifth.

The best finishes for the U.S. in the individual epee were Steve Trevor, 17th, and Bob Marx, 18th.

The USA was 10th out of 16 teams in the epee.

TEAM PERSONNEL

Jana Marie Angelaikis, 22, Peabody, MA (Foil)
Susan J. Badders, 32, Beaverton, OR (Foil)
Vincent H. Bradford, 29, San Antonio, TX (Foil)
Joel A. Glucksman, 35, New York, NY (Sabre)
Peter Lewison, 22, Brooklyn, NY (Foil)
Michael Lofton, 20, Hempstead, NY (Sabre)
Michael A. Marx, 26, Portland, OR (Foil)
Robert G. Marx, 27, Portland, OR (Epee)
Gregory Massialas, 28, San Jose, CA (Foil)
Michael J. McCahey, 29, Leonia, NJ (Foil)
Sharon M. Monplaisir, 23, Woodside, NY (Foil)
John A. Moreau, 33, San Antonio, TX (Epee)
Steve Mormando, 29, Lakewood, NJ (Sabre)
Philip Reilly, 32, New York, NY (Sabre)
Peter Schifrin, 26, San Francisco, CA (Epee)
C. Lee Shelley, 28, Hackensack, NJ (Epee)
Mark J. T. Smith, 28, Atlanta, GA (Foil)
Stephen Trevor, 20, Shaker Heights, OH (Epee)
Debra Lynn Waples, 31, Geneva, Switzerland (Foil)
Peter J. Westbrook, 32, New York, NY (Sabre)

Yves L. Auriol, Beaverton, OR, coach
Joseph Byrnes, Roselle Park, NJ, armorer
Casaba Elthes, New York, NY, coach
Henry Harutunian, Woodbridge, CT, coach
Anthony Keane, East New Brunswick, NJ, team captain

FENCING, MEN'S

FOIL, INDIVIDUAL

1. **Mauro Numa, ITA**
2. **Matthias Behr, FRG**
3. **Stefano Cerioni, ITA**
4. Frederick Pietruszka, FRA
5. Andrea Borella, ITA
6. Mathias Gey, FRG
7. Phillippe Omnes, FRA
8. Thierry Soumagne, BEL
11. Peter Lewison, USA
28. Gregory Massialas, USA
30. Michael McCahey, USA

SABRE, INDIVIDUAL

1. **Jean Francois Lamour, FRA**
2. **Marco Marin, ITA**
3. **Peter Westbrook, USA**
4. Herve Granger-Veyron, FRA
5. Pierre Guichot, FRA
6. Marin Mustata, ROM
7. Giovanni Scalzo, ITA
8. Ioan Pop, ROM
12. Steve Mormando, USA
17. Michael Lofton, USA

EPEE, INDIVIDUAL

1. **Philippe Boisse, FRA**
2. **Bjorne Vaggo, SWE**
3. **Philippe Riboud, FRA**
4. Stefano Bellone, ITA
5. Michel Poffet, SUI
6. Elmar Bormmann, FRG
7. Alexander Pusch, FRG
8. Volker Fischer, FRG
17. Stephen Trevor, USA
18. Robert Marx, USA
38. C. Lee Shelley, USA

FOIL TEAM

1. **ITA (Mauro Numa, Andrea Borella, Stefano Cerioni, Angelo Scuri; Andrea Cipressa, DNC)**
2. **FRG (Behr, Gey, Hein, Beck; Reichert, DNC)**
3. **FRA (Omnes, Groc, Pietruszka, Jolyot; Cerboni, DNC)**
4. AUT
5. USA (Michael Marx, Gregory Massialas, Peter Lewison, Mark Smith; Michael McCahey, DNC)
6. GBR
7. CHN
8. BEL

SABRE, TEAM

1. **ITA (Marco Marin, Gianfranco Della Barba, Giovanni Scalzo, Ferdinando Meglio; Angelo Arcidiacono, DNC)**
2. **FRA (Lamour, Guichot, Granger-Veyron, Delrieu; Ducheix, DNC)**
3. **ROM (Mustata, Pop, Chiculita, Marin, DNC)**

4. FRG

5. CHN

6. USA (Peter Westbrook, Steve Mormando,
        Philip Reilly, Joel Glucksman, Michael Lofton)

7. CAN

8. GBR

EPEE, TEAM

1. **FRG (Elmar Borrmann, Volker Fischer,
   Rafael Nickel, Alexander Pusch;
   Gerhard Heer, DNC)**

2. **FRA (Boisse, Lenglet, Riboud, Salesse;
   Henry, DNC)**

3. **ITA (Bellone, Cuomo, Manzi, Mazzoni;
   Ferro, DNC)**

4. CAN

5. SWE

6. CHN

7. KOR

8. GBR

10. USA (Robert Marx, John Moreau, Peter Schifrin,
        C. Lee Shelley, Stephen Trevor)

FENCING, WOMEN'S

FOIL, INDIVIDUAL

1. **Luan Jujie, CHN**

2. **Cornelia Hanisch, FRG**

3. **Dorina Vaccaroni, ITA**

4. Elisabeta Guzganu, ROM

5. Veronique Brouquier, FRA

6. Laurence Modaine, FRA

7. Sabine Bischoff, FRG

8. Brigitte Gaudin, FRA

20. Debra Waples, USA

23. Vincent Bradford, USA

28. Jana Angelaikis, USA

FOIL, TEAM

1. **FRG (Christiane Weber, Cornelia Hanisch,
   Sabine Bischoff, Zita Funkenhauser;
   Ute Wessel, DNC)**

2. **ROM (Dan, Weber, Oros, Zsak, Guzganu)**

3. **FRA (Modaine, Trinquet-Hachin, Gaudin,
   Broquier; Meygret, DNC)**

4. ITA

5. CHN

6. USA (Vincent Bradford, Sharon Monplaisir,
        Susan Badders, Debra Waples;
        Jana Angelaikis, DNC)

7. GBR

8. JPN

TEAM PERSONNEL

J. Angelaikis   S. Badders   V. Bradford

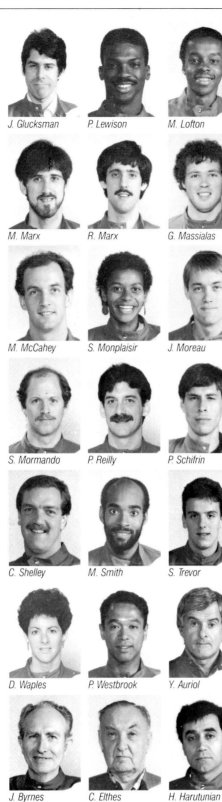

J. Glucksman   P. Lewison   M. Lofton

M. Marx   R. Marx   G. Massialas

M. McCahey   S. Monplaisir   J. Moreau

S. Mormando   P. Reilly   P. Schifrin

C. Shelley   M. Smith   S. Trevor

D. Waples   P. Westbrook   Y. Auriol

J. Byrnes   C. Elthes   H. Harutunian

A. Keane

FIELD HOCKEY

The United States may be the only country in the world where women play a more highly-developed game of field hockey than men. For ages the women in secondary schools and a few selected Eastern colleges and amateur clubs have competed strenuously. However, on the international women's scene the United States has not enjoyed as much success as one would suspect based on an analysis of the organization of the sport.

Men's field hockey simply hasn't caught on. The bronze medal won by the men at Los Angeles in 1932 was tainted. There were only three teams in the tournament. In fact, since 1956 when qualifying tournaments were introduced, the United States really hadn't come close to making to the Olympics. The two US teams automatically qualified for the 1984 Games as the host nation.

In preliminary play the men's team was 0–5. In a classification match to decide 12th place (out of 16) the USA played Malaysia to a 3–3 tie only to be relegated to 12th place on the basis of penalty strokes, 9–8 for Malaysia.

The women's field hockey team had been well organized. They played together for more than two years. They had based themselves in Philadelphia, perhaps the women's field hockey capital of the nation.

Experts had cited four of the six women's teams as definite medal contenders: USA, Australia, Holland, and West Germany. The six-team tournament was conducted as round-robin competition.

The United States opened with a 4–1 triumph over Canada and then played The Netherlands. This was really the gold medal game even though it was played early in the round-robin tournament. The Netherlands won, 2–1.

Later the United States lost to Australia and the best hope was for a bronze medal. As a result of Australia losing to The Netherlands 2–0 in the final game, a shootout was to be the deciding factor.

The U.S. team had watched the Australia-Netherlands game from the stands, understanding that a shootout immediately after the game would be called for if Australia was defeated.

The anxious Americans sent their goalie off to a practice field to warm up during the second half of the Australia-Netherlands game. The others warmed up in the final minutes of the game and were ready for the supreme effort. In the barrage that followed, the United States scored more goals than the Australians and were awarded the bronze.

TEAM PERSONNEL

MEN'S

Mohammed Barakat, 17, Moorpark, CA
Ken Barrett, 21, Simi Valley, CA
Rawle Cox, 23, Brooklyn, NY
Trevor Fernandes, 33, Seattle, WA
Robert Gregg, 30, Allentown, PA
Manzar Iqbal, 25, Livermore, CA
Michael Kraus, 26, Frankfurt, FR
Randy Lipscher, 23, Lawrenceville, NJ
David McMichael, 23, Flourtown, PA
Gary Newton, 26, Ventura, CA
Michael Newton, 32, Ventura, CA
Brian Spencer, 22, Canoga Park, CA
M. Morgan Stebbins, 24, Berkeley, CA
Robert Stiles, 24, Westlake Village, CA
Andrew Stone, 23, Marion, MA
Nigel Traverso, 25, Hollis, NY

William Bradbury, III, Flourtown, PA,
assistant manager
Gavin Featherstone, Camarillo, CA, coach
Lee Yoder, Ambler, PA, manager

TEAM PERSONNEL

WOMEN'S

Elizabeth R. Anders, 32, Norfolk, VA (midfielder)
Elizabeth A. Beglin, 27, Upper Saddle River, NJ (midfielder)
Regina Buggy, 24, Norristown, PA (midfielder)
Gwen W. Cheeseman, 32, Haddonfield, NJ (goalie)
Sheryl A. Johnson, 26, Cupertino, CA (forward)
Christine L. Mason, 28, Williamstown, MA (forward)
Kathleen A. McGahey, 24, Blackwood, NJ (forward)
Anita C. Miller, 33, Gladwyne, PA (back)
Leslie W. Milne, 27, Darien, CT (back)
Charlene Morett, 26, Aldan, PA (forward)
Diane Moyer, 26, Laureldale, PA (goalie)
Marcella Place, 25, Malibu, CA (back)
Karen Shelton, 26, Chapel Hill, CA (back)
Brenda L. Stauffer, 23, Elverson, PA (forward)
Julia A. Staver, DVM, 32, Sellersville, PA (midfield)
Judith A. Strong, 24, West Hatfield, MA (forward)

Marge D. Garinger, Harveys Lake, PA, manager
Vonnie Gros, West Chester, PA, coach
Margery Watson, Kimberton, PA, assistant coach

FIELD HOCKEY, MEN'S

GOLD MEDAL GAME

PAK 2, FRG 1

BRONZE MEDAL GAME

GBR 3, AUS 2

5th PLACE GAME

IND 5, HOL 2

7th PLACE: NZL
8th PLACE: ESP
9th PLACE: KEN
10th PLACE: CAN
11th PLACE: MAL
12th PLACE: USA

OLYMPIC CHAMPIONS

(PAK) Ishtiaq Ahmed, Mushtaq Ahmad, Naeem
    Akhtar, Nasir Ali, Tauqeer Dar, Khild Hameed,
    Manzoor Hussain, Kaleemullah Hanir Khan,
    Shahid Ali Kahn, Ayaz Mehmood, G. Moinud-
    din, A. Rashid, Hassan Sardar, Salleem
    Sherwani, Oasin Zia

SCORES OF U.S. GAMES IN PRELIMINARY ROUND

USA vs AUS, 1–3
    vs MAL, 1–4
    vs FRG, 0–4
    vs ESP, 1–3
    vs IND, 1–5

FIELD HOCKEY, WOMEN'S

ROUND-ROBIN TOURNAMENT	Won	Lost	Tied
1. **Netherlands,**	4	0	1
2. **West Germany,**	2	1	2
3. **United States,**	2	2	1
4. Australia,	2	2	1
5. Canada,	2	2	1
6. New Zealand,	0	5	0

SCORES OF GAMES

HOL vs NZL, 2–1, vs AUS, 2–0, vs FRG, 6–2,
    vs CAN, 2–2, vs USA, 2–1
FRG vs HOL, 2–6, vs NZL, 1–0, vs AUS, 2–2,
    vs CAN, 3–0, vs USA, 1–1
USA vs HOL, 1–2, vs NZL, 2–0, vs AUS, 1–3,
    vs FRG, 1–1, vs CAN, 4–1

Note: USA awarded third place on the basis of the number of penalty shots

OLYMPIC CHAMPIONS

(HOL) Bernadette De Beus, Alette Pos, Margriet
    Zegers, Laurien Willemse, Marjolein Eyesvogel,
    Josephin Boekhorst, Carina Benninga, Alexan-
    dre LePoole, Francisca Hillen, Marieke Van
    Doorn, Sophie Von Weiler, Aletta Van Manen,
    Irene Hendriks, Elisabeth Sevens,
    Martine Ohr, Annelos Nieuwenhuizen.
    Coach: Gijsbertus Van Heumen

TEAM PERSONNEL, MEN'S

M. Barakat   K. Barrett   R. Cox

T. Fernandes   R. Gregg   M. Iqbal

M. Kraus   R. Lipscher   G. Newton

M. Newton   B. Spencer   M. Stebbins

R. Stiles   A. Stone   N. Traverso

W. Bradbury   G. Featherstone   L. Yoder

TEAM PERSONNEL, WOMEN'S

E. Anders   E. Beglin   R. Buggy

G. Cheeseman   S. Johnson   C. Mason

K. McGahey   A. Miller   L. Milne

C. Morett   D. Moyer   M. Place

K. Shelton   B. Stauffer   J. Staver

J. Strong   M. Garinger   V. Gros

M. Watson

GYMNASTICS

The popularity of gymnastics dates back to the satellite telecasts of the Games from Mexico City in 1968. Up to that point there had been no world heroes or heroines in gymnastics. But at Mexico City Vera Caslavska of Czechoslovakia repeated her success at Tokyo in the women's events and Sawao Kato, Japan, led the Japanese to the team title. All the world watched and cheered.

Through television the sport has developed harsh critics of judges' decisions. Those judges assigned to inter-national competitions are certified as worthy by the International Gymnastics Federation. Also, they are required to show specific deductions for "false moves" by the gymnasts.

Many now regard the United States as the primary gymnastics power, both men's and women's. At Los Angeles the U.S. men unseated China, world champions, in the team competition; the U.S. women finished runners-up to Romania. In the women's all-around, Mary Lou Retton nosed out the pre-Olympic favorite, Ecaterina Szabo of Romania, by the scant margin of .05 point.

Retton won the gold medal in the all-around competition by the closest possible margin over Szabo. But in the apparatus finals, Szabo won three gold medals to a silver and two bronze for Retton.

Julie McNamara, one of the veterans of the USA team and a 1980 holdover, won a gold medal on the uneven parallel bars.

Among the men, Koji Gushiken of Japan nosed out the USA's Peter Vidmar by a .025 point for the all-around title. Li Ning of China, the favorite, placed third.

Then in the apparatus Li earned two gold and two silver medals. Vidmar on the pommel horse and three-time Olympian Bart Conner on the parallel bars were crowned champions. Thus, for the first time since 1932 the United States produced an individual gold medalist.

Coach Abie Grossfeld, a former Olympian and a long-time mentor at Southern Connecticut State College, expressed it well when he described the U.S. competitors as "the best gymnasts that I've ever been associated with athletically, mentally, spiritually—every way."

Previously, there were too many instances, especially in the last four Olympic Games, when the U.S. men's team was beset with problems caused by temperamental outbursts. Bart Conner best summed up the new attitude evident at Los Angeles. "I think everybody agreed before we came here," he said, "that all of our individual chances to win a medal are bound up in one thing—and that's the team."

Rhythmic Gymnastics was introduced to the Olympic program with the all-around competition involving hoops, streamers, beach balls, and Indian clubs. With the absence of the USSR and Bulgaria, Romania was considered the heavy favorite to produce the first Olympic champion.

But the winner turned out to be Canada's Lori Fung, 21, who had an opportunity to train with the Romanians following the world championships in which she did no better than 21st.

Fung echoed the words of diving champion Sylvie Bernier when she remarked, after the competition, "It was really a big surprise to me because I didn't know my placing as the meet went on."

TEAM PERSONNEL

MEN'S GYMNASTICS

Bart Conner, 26, Norman OK
Timothy Daggett, 24, West Springfield, MA
Mitch Gaylord, 23, Van Nuys, CA
James N. Hartung, 24, Omaha, NE
Scott Johnson, 23, Colorado Springs, CO
James A. Mikus, 22, Lincoln, NE, (alternate)
Peter Vidmar, 23, Los Angeles, CA

Abie Grossfeld, New Haven, CT, coach
Makoto Sakamoto, Los Angeles, CA, assistant coach

TEAM PERSONNEL

WOMEN'S GYMNASTICS

Pamela Jean Bileck, 15, Garden Grove, CA
Michelle Dusserre, 15, Garden Grove, CA
Kathy Ann Johnson, 24, Huntington Beach, CA
Julianne (Julie) McNamara, 18, San Romana, CA
Mary Lou Retton, 16, Fairmont, WV
Tracee Ann Talavera, 17, Walnut Creek, CA

Rosemary P. Kreutzer, Scottsdale, AZ, manager
Don Peters, Huntington Beach, CA, coach

TEAM PERSONNEL

RHYTHMIC GYMNASTICS

Michelle Rene Berube, 18, Rochester, MN
Valerie Lee Zimring, 19, Los Angeles, CA

Alla Svirsky, Van Nuys, CA, coach

GYMNASTICS, MEN'S

TEAM COMPETITION

	Compulsory	Optional	Total Points
1. **USA (Peter Vidmar, Bart Conner, Mitch Gaylord,**	295.30	296.10	591.40
Timothy Daggett, James Hartung, Scott Johnson)			
2. **CHN (Li Ning, Li Xiaoping, Li Yuejiu,**	294.25	296.55	590.80
Xu Zhigiang, Tong Fei, Lou Yun)			
3. **JPN (Koji Gushiken, Nobuyuki Kajitani,**	292.40	294.30	586.70
Noritoshi Hirata, Shinji Morisue,			
Koji Sotomura, Kyoji Yamawaki)			
4. FRG	290.30	291.80	582.10
5. SUI	289.95	290.00	579.95
6. FRA	287.65	290.60	578.25
7. CAN	288.85	288.30	577.15
8. KOR	287.15	287.80	574.95

ALL-ROUND

1. **Koji Gushiken, JPN**	118.700
2. **Peter Vidmar, USA**	118.675
3. **Li Ning, CHN**	118.575
4. Tong Fei, CHN	118.550
5. Mitch Gaylord, USA	118.525
6. Bart Conner, USA	118.350
7. Xu Zhiqiang, CHN	118.225
8. Nobuyuki Kajitani, JPN	117.375

FLOOR EXERCISES

1. **Li Ning, CHN**	19.925
2. **Lou Yun, CHN**	19.775
3. **(tie) Koji Sotomura, JPN**	19.700
3. **(tie) Philippe Vatuone, FRA**	19.700
5. Bart Conner, USA	19.675
6. Valentin Pintea, ROM	19.600
7. Peter Vidmar, USA	19.550
8. Koji Gushiken, JPN	19.450

SIDE (POMMEL) HORSE

1. **(tie) Li Ning, CHN**	19.950
1. **(tie) Peter Vidmar, USA**	19.950
3. **Tim Daggett, USA**	19.825
4. Tong Fei, CHN	19.750
5. Jean-Luc Cairon, FRA	19.700
6. Nobuyuki Kajitani, JPN	19.625
7. Benno Gross, FRG	19.525
8. Josef Zellweger, SUI	19.375

RINGS

1. **(tie) Koji Gushiken, JPN**	19.850
1. **(tie) Li Ning, CHN**	19.850
3. **Mitch Gaylord, USA**	19.825
4. (tie) Peter Vidmar, USA	19.750
4. (tie) Tong Fei, CHN	19.750
6. Kyoji Yamawaki, JPN	19.725
7. Emilian Nicula, ROM	19.500
8. Josef Zellweger, SUI	19.375

HORSE VAULT

1. **Lou Yun, CHN**	19.950
2. **(tie) Li Ning, CHN**	19.825
2. **(tie) Koji Gushiken, JPN**	19.825
3. **(tie) Mitch Gaylord, USA**	19.825
3. **(tie) Shinji Morisue, JPN**	19.825
6. James Hartung, USA	19.800
7. Warren Long, CAN	19.700
8. Daniel Wunderlin, SUI	19.625

PARALLEL BARS

1. **Bart Conner, USA**	19.950
2. **Nobuyuki Kajitani, JPN**	19.925
3. **Mitch Gaylord, USA**	19.850
4. Tong Fei, CHN	19.825
5. Koji Gushiken, JPN	19.800
6. Li Ning, CHN	19.775
7. (tie) Daniel Winkler, FRG	19.600
7. (tie) Juergen Geiger, FRG	19.600

HORIZONTAL BAR

1. **Shinji Morisue, JPN**	20.000
2. **Tong Fei, CHN**	19.975
3. **Koji Gushiken, JPN**	19.950
4. (tie) Lou Yun, CHN	19.850
4. (tie) Peter Vidmar, USA	19.850
4. (tie) Timothy Daggett, USA	19.850
7. Marco Piatti, SUI	19.800
8. Daniel Wunderlin, SUI	19.675

GYMNASTICS, WOMEN'S

TEAM COMPETITION

1. **ROM (Ecaterina Szabo,**	392.20
Laura Cutina, Cristina Grigoras,	
Simona Pauca, Mihaela Stanulet,	
Lavinia Agache)	
2. **USA (Mary Lou Retton,**	391.20
Julie McNamara, Tracee Talavera,	
Michelle Dusserre,	
Pamela Bileck, Kathy Johnson)	
3. **CHN (Qun Huang, Zhou Qiurui,**	388.60
Wu Jiani, Ma Yanhonjg, Zhou Ping,	
Chen Yongyan)	
4. FRG	379.15
5. CAN	378.90
6. JPN	376.75
7. GBR	373.85
8. SUI	373.50

ALL-AROUND

1. **Mary Lou Retton, USA**	79.175
2. **Ecaterina Szabo, ROM**	79.125
3. **Simona Pauca, ROM**	78.675
4. Julie McNamara, USA	78.400
5. Laura Cutina, ROM	78.300
6. Ma Yanhonjg, CHN	77.850
7. Zhou Ping, CHN	77.775
8. Chen Yongyan, CHN	77.725
10. Kathy Johnson, USA	77.450

HORSE VAULT

1. **Ecaterina Szabo, ROM**	19.875
2. **Mary Lou Retton, USA**	19.850
3. **Lavinia Agache, ROM**	19.750
4. Tracee Talavera, USA	19.700
5. Zhou Ping, CHN	19.500
6. (tie) Brigitta Lehmann, FRG	19.425
6. (tie) Kelly Brown, CAN	19.425
8. Chen Yongyan, CHN	19.300

UNEVEN PARALLEL BARS

1. **(tie) Ma Yanhonjg, CHN**	19.950
1. **(tie) Julie McNamara, USA**	19.950
3. **Mary Lou Retton, USA**	19.800
4. Mihaela Stanulet, ROM	19.650
5. Romi Kessler, SUI	19.425
6. Zhou Ping, CHN	19.350
7. Noriko Mochizuki, JPN	19.325
8. Lavinia Agache, ROM	19.150

BALANCE BEAM

1. **(tie) Ecaterina Szabo, ROM**	19.800
1. **(tie) Simona Pauca, ROM**	19.800
3. **Kathy Johnson, USA**	19.650
4. Mary Lou Retton, USA	19.550
5. Ma Yanhonjg, CHN	19.450
6. Romi Kessler, SUI	19.350
7. (tie) Anja Wilhelm, FRG	19.200
7. (tie) Chen Yongyan, CHN	19.200

FLOOR EXERCISES

1. **Ecaterina Szabo, ROM**	19.975
2. **Julie McNamara, USA**	19.950
3. **Mary Lou Retton, USA**	19.775
4. Zhou Qiurui, CHN	19.625
5. Romi Kessler, SUI	19.575
6. Ma Yanhonjg, CHN	19.450
7. Maiko Morio, JPN	19.373
8. Laura Cutina, ROM	19.150

RHYTHMIC GYMNASTICS

1. **Lori Fung, CAN**	57.950
2. **Doina Staiculescu, ROM**	57.900
3. **Regina Weber, FRG**	57.700
4. Alina Dragan, ROM	57.375
5. Milena Reljin, YUG	57.250
6. Marta Canton, ESP	56.950
7. Giulia Staccioli, ITA	56.775
8. Hiroko Yamasaki, JPN	56.675
11. Valerie Zimring, USA	56.250
14. Michele Berube, USA	55.800

TEAM PERSONNEL, MEN'S

B. Conner T. Daggett M. Gaylord

J. Hartung S. Johnson J. Mikus

P. Vidmar A. Grossfeld M. Sakamoto

TEAM PERSONNEL, WOMEN'S

P. Bilek M. Dusserre K. Johnson

J. McNamara M. Retton T. Talavera

R. Kreutzer D. Peters

TEAM PERSONNEL, RHYTHMIC GYMNASTICS

M. Berube V. Zimring A. Svirsky

JUDO

Judo may be the "most fluid" of all the combative sports on the program of the Olympics. The most recent addition to the Olympic program (dating back to 1964), judo records show that twelve different countries have won gold medals.

In 1980, seventeen different countries shared in the medals' awards in the eight different weight classes. As in boxing, two awards are made for third place.

The only country to show any dominance in the sport is the founding judo nation, Japan. The Japanese have won a minimum of three gold medals in every Olympic Games in which they played. Their judokas have accounted for a total of 13 (they did not compete in 1980), with an all-time high of 4 coming at Los Angeles.

By adding Ed Liddie's bronze in the 132-pound class, and a silver (the highest ever for a judoka from the U.S.) for Robert Berland in the 190-pound, the United States has won four medals.

Judo is conducted as a single elimination contest. Thus, the luck of the draw plays an important role in the success of the team. The growing popularity of the sport is attested to by a record entry of 222 judokas at Los Angeles.

Nostalgic Note: Angelo Parisi, France, winner of the heavyweight (over 209 pounds) title at Moscow, where he also garnered a silver in the "open" weight class category, placed second in the heavyweight class at Los Angeles. That silver medal was the fourth Parisi had earned in judo competition. His first medal was a bronze in the open category at Munich.

TEAM PERSONNEL

Craig Agina, 23, Fort Carson, CO
Brett Barron, 24, San Bruno, CA
Robert Berland, 22, Wilmette, IL
Edward (Eddie) Liddie, 25, Colorado Springs, CO
Dewey Mitchell, 27, New Port Richey, FL
Doug Nelson, 25, Englewood, NJ

Michael L. Swain, 23, Middletown, NY
Leo White, 26, Fort Carson, CO

Lt. Col. Paul K. Maruyama, Monument, CO, coach
Jim R. Wooley, El Toro, CA, manager

JUDO

EXTRA LIGHTWEIGHTS (60 KG./132 LBS.)
1. Shinji Hosokawa, JPN
2. Kim Jae-Yup, KOR
3. Eddie Liddle, USA
3. Neil Eckersley, GBR

HALF LIGHTWEIGHTS (65 KG./143 LBS.)
1. Yoshiyuki Matsuoka, JPN
2. Hwang Jung-Oh, KOR
3. Marc Alexandre, FRA
3. Josef Reiter, AUT
Craig Agina, USA, lost to Alfredo Chinchilla, NOR, in
first round of tournament.

LIGHTWEIGHTS (71 KG./156.2 LBS.)
1. Ahn Byeong-Keun, KOR
2. Ezio Gamba, ITA
3. Luis Onmura, BRA
3. Kerrith Brown, GBR
Michael Swain, USA, won two matches and then was
def. by Luis Onmura, BRA, in the third round

HALF MIDDLEWEIGHTS (78 KG./171.6 LBS.)
1. Frank Wieneke, FRG
2. Neil Adams, GBR
3. Michel Nowak, FRA
3. Mircea Fratica, ROM
Brett Barron, USA, was def. by Neil Adams, GBR, in
the first round. In the repêchage he lost to Robert
Henneveld, HOL

MIDDLEWEIGHTS (86 KG./190 LBS.)
1. Peter Seisenbacher, AUT
2. Robert Berland, USA
3. Seiki Nose, JPN
3. Walter Carmona, BRA

HALF HEAVYWEIGHT (95 KG./209 LBS.)
1. Ha Hyoung-Zoo, KOR
2. Douglas Vieira, BRA
3. Bjarni Fridriksson, ISL
3. Gunter Neureuther, FRG
Leo White, USA, won two matches and then was
eliminated by Bjarni Fridriksson, ISL

HEAVYWEIGHTS (OVER 95 KG./OVER 209 LBS.)
1. Hitoshi Saito, JPN
2. Angelo Parisi, FRA
3. Cho Yong-Chul, KOR
3. Mark Berger, CAN
Doug Nelson, USA, won two matches and then was
eliminated by Angelo Parisi, FRA

OPEN CATEGORY (NO WEIGHT LIMIT)
1. Yasuhiro Yamashita, JPN
2. Mohamed Rashwan, EGY

3. Mihai Cioc, ROM
3. Arthur Schnanel, FRG
Dewey Mitchell, USA, lost in first round to
Fred Blaney, CAN

TEAM PERSONNEL

C. Agina   B. Barron   R. Berland

E. Liddie   D. Mitchell   D. Nelson

M. Swain   L. White   P. Maruyama

J. Wooley

MODERN PENTATHLON

Over the years the official publication of the United
States Olympic Committee cites the gold medalist in
the modern pentathlon as the "Most Versatile Athlete in
the World."

This sport has never caught on with the American
media, nor does it have a large following. The activity in
the United States is housed at the Modern Pentathlon
Training Center, maintained by the Army at Fort Sam
Houston, Texas.

Perhaps the most celebrated participant in this sport
was General George S. Patton in 1912 at Stockholm.

Although the United States has never produced an
Olympic Champion, Bob Nieman in 1979 won the world
individual title.

Prior to the start of the competition, one of the
acknowledged authorities on the demands of the sport
(comprising show jumping, fencing, shooting, swimming, and cross-country running within a period of four
consecutive days) identified Italy's Daniele Masala as
the probable winner. Masala had missed the 1983 world
championships after winning the 1982 title, and had
eschewed all competitions to concentrate on training
for what has been described as the demanding and
most unpredictable of all Olympic sports.

At the end of the hectic competition Masala eked out
the gold medal by overtaking a fatigued Swede, Svante

Rasmuson, in the last 40 meters of the final event, the
cross-country run.

Italy also won the team event. The United States surprised by capturing the team silver, the first medal for
the U.S. in the team competition since 1964.

The top finisher for the United States was a former University of Pennsylvania swimmer/fencer, Mike Storm.
He placed fifth, but won the shooting discipline, scoring
198 out of a possible 200.

TEAM PERSONNEL

Dean William Glenesk, 26, Santa Maria, CA
R. Gregory Losey, 34, San Antonio, TX
Michael E. Storm, 24, Arlington, VA
Robert E. Stull, 23, Damascus, MD (alternate)

Col. John Paul Lingo, USA, San Antonio, TX, manager
Henry Weinbrecht, San Antonio, TX, coach

MODERN PENTATHLON

INDIVIDUAL COMPETITION

1. Daniele Masala, ITA	5,469
2. Svante Rasmuson, SWE	5,456
3. Carlo Massullo, ITA	5,406
4. Richard Phelps, GBR	5,391
5. Michael Storm, USA	5,325
6. Paul Four, FRA	5,287
7. Ivar Sisniega, MEX	5,282
8. Jorge Quesada, ESP	5,281
13. Gregory Losey, USA	5,158
18. Dean Glenesk, USA	5,085

WINNERS OF EACH INDIVIDUAL EVENT
Riding: Masala and Massullo, ITA; Phelps, GBR;
     Daizou Araki, JPN; Ihab Ellebedy, EGY;
     all 1,100 pts.
Fencing: Achim Bellmann, FRG; 1,066 pts.
Swimming: Christian Sandow, FRG; 1,324 pts.
Shooting: Storm, USA; 1,088 pts.
Cross-Country Run: Phelps, GBR; 1,295 pts.

TEAM COMPETITION

1. ITA (Daniele Masala, Carlo Massullo, Pierpaolo Cristofori)	16,060
2. USA (Michael Storm, Gregory Losey, Dean Glenesk)	15,568
3. FRA (Paul Four, Didier Boube, Joel Bouzou)	15,565
4. SUI	15,343
5. MEX	15,283
6. FRG	15,028
7. GBR	14,894
8. ESP	14,891

TEAM PERSONNEL

D. Glenesk   G. Losey   M. Storm

R. Stull   J. Lingo   H. Weinbrecht

ROWING

The United States flotilla did well on Lake Casitas as the rowing events were held on lake waters for the first time since 1960. The races, conducted in the early morning hours to avoid the winds that invariably sweep the lake in late morning, enjoyed prime conditions.

In 1980 Pertti Karppinen, Finland, won his second single sculls title and the German Democratic Republic took the seven other men's races. In the women's regatta that year the GDR won four gold medals, and Romania and the USSR one each. In fact, except for the three medals won by Romania, the other 15 were garnered by nations not competing this year in the women's events on Lake Casitas.

In the 1980 men's races, Karppinen won the only gold medal not earned by the GDR. Great Britain captured one silver and two bronze, and Yugoslavia one medal.

The United States won a single gold medal in the 1984 men's regatta as eight different nations shared in as many gold medals for the first time in the history of the Olympics. The United States also won three silver and one bronze, rowing in all but one final.

In the two most prestigious races (single sculls and eights with coxswain) the U.S. won the women's eight; and placed second in the men's eights; in the single sculls the U.S. had the silver medalist in the women's race and a fourth place in the men's.

Romania won the first six races in the women's finals. In the climactic race for eights, the favored U.S. boat trailed Romania at the 1,000-meter mark and then took up the beat to catch and pass the Romanians to win by about one-third of a boat length.

The closing race on the program for the men proved a heartbreaker for the U.S. sweep-swingers. The United States had cleaned up in a pre-Olympic trip to Europe. From that trip it appeared that its crews would have to outrow the likes of Australia, New Zealand, and Britain. And they did just that in the Olympic final.

But the surprising boat in the race was underrated Canada. Canada led at the 500 , 1,000 , and 1,500-meters, finally crossing the finish line less than one-half second ahead of the USA.

Canadian coxswain Brian McMahon had his crew rowing an even pace. Their splits for each 500 meters were 1:24.42, 1:26.70, 1:25.21, and 1:24.99. The USA, in fourth place after the first 500 meters, recorded splits of 1:25.59, 1:27.33, 1:25.56, and a fast 1:23.26.

Although rowing in the last two Olympic Games has suffered from the non-participation of great rowing nations, at Lake Casitas it still came up with competitive races through the heats, repêchages, semi-finals, and finals.

Finland's Pertti Karppinen became the first sculler to win three in a row Olympics since the Soviet's Vyacheslav Ivanov in 1956, 1960, and 1964.

TEAM PERSONNEL

MEN'S

Michael Bach, 24, West Hartford, CT (4's with cox)
John C. Bannan, Philadelphia, PA (Spare)
Bruce E. Beall, 32, Cambridge, MA (Quad)
John Biglow, 26, Bellevue, WA (Single)
Earl Borchelt, 30, Cambridge, MA (8's)
Charles Clapp III, 25, Seattle, WA (8's)
David R. Clark, 24, Columbia, MO (4's without)
Thomas W. Darling, 26, Swampscott, MA (8's)
David DeRuff, 23, Newport Beach, CA (Pairs without)
Paul Enquist, 28, Seattle, WA (Double sculls)
Robert Espeseth, Jr., 30, Champaign, IL (Pairs with)
Curtis Fleming, 29, Costa Mesa, CA (Quad)
Alan Forney, 24, Edmonds, WA (4's without)
David A. Grant, 46, Newport Beach, CA (Spare)
Douglas Herland, 32, Ann Arbor, MI (Pairs with)
Christoper Huntington, 23, New York, NY (Spare)
Bruce Ibbotson, 31, Tustin, CA (8's)
Edward Ives, 23, Seattle, WA (4's with)
Robert Jaugstetter, 36, Cambridge, MA (8's)
Ridgley Johnson, 26, Allston, MA (Quad)
Thomas Kiefer, 26, Salisbury, CT (4's with)
Bradley A. Lewis, 29, Corona Del Mar, CA
(Double sculls)
Walter Lubsen, Jr., 29, Arlington, VA (8's)
Stewart MacDonald, 34, Cambridge, MA (Spare)
Gregg Montesi, 25, Barrington, RI (Quad)
Christopher Penny, 22, Middletown, RI (8's)
Jonathan Smith, 23, Swampscott, MA (4's without)
Gregory Springer, 23, Canoga Park, CA (4's with)
Philip W. Stekl, 28, Hartford, CT (4's without)
Kevin Still, 23, North Hollywood, CA (Pairs with)
John Stillings, 29, Edmonds, WA (4's with)
John M. Strotbeck, 27, Philadelphia, PA
(Pairs without)
Andrew Sudduth, 22, Exeter, NH (8's)
John Terwilliger, 26, Watertown, MA (8's)
Michael Teti, 27, Upper Darby, PA (Spare)
Christopher Wood, 24, Cambridge, MA (Spare)

Kris Korzeniowski, Lawrenceville, NJ, sweeps coach
Harry Parker, Cambridge, MA, sculling coach
Dietrich Rose, Philadelphia, PA, small boats coach
Michael Vespoli, Guilford, CT, boatman
Julian Wolf, Los Angeles, CA, assistant manager
Peter Zandenbergen, Omaha, NE, manager

TEAM PERSONNEL

WOMEN'S

Victoria Baker, 29, San Luis Obispo, CA (Spare)
Hope Barnes, 25, Seattle, WA (Spare)
Betsy Beard, 22, Seattle, WA (8's)
Carol Bower, 28, New Haven, CT (8's)
Susan Broome, 26, Edmonds, WA (Spare)
Carol P. Brown, 31, Seattle, WA (Spare)
Sherri Cassuto, 37, Seattle, WA (Spare)
Christine Ernst, 30, New Haven, CT (Spare)
Jeanne Flanagan, 27, Somerville, MA (8's)
Charlotte Geer, 26, West Fairlee, VT (Single)
Julie Geer, 31, Morrisville, VT (Double)
Virginia Gilder, 26, Belmont, MA (Quad)
Carrie Graves, 31, Cambridge, MA (8's)
Janet Harville, 32, Seattle, WA (4's with)
Kathryn Keeler, 27, Northampton, MA (8's)
Barbara Kirch, 24, Penllyn, PA (Pairs without)
Joan Lind, 31, Long Beach, CA (Quad)
Anne Marden, 26, Concord, MA (Quad)
Valerie McLain-Ward, 28, Ewa Beach, HI (4's with)
Harriet Metcalf, 26, South Hadley, MA (8's)

Elizabeth Miles, 29, Fresno, CA (4's with)
Kristine Norelius, 27, Seattle, WA (8's)
Shyril O'Steen, 23, Seattle, WA (8's)
Abigail Peck, 27, Waltham, MA (4's with)
Kelly Rickon, 29, San Diego, CA (Quad)
Lisa Rohde, 21, Long Beach, CA (Quad)
Patricia Spratlen, 28, San Diego, CA (4's with)
Cathleen Thaxton, 27, Irvine, CA (Double)
Kristen Thorsness, 21, Anchorage, AK (8's)
Chari Towne, 24, Wild Rose, WI (Pairs without)

Robert G. Ernst, Edmonds, WA, coach
Lawrence Gluckman, Hightstown, NJ, coach
Peter E. Lippett, San Francisco, CA, manager
Thomas McKibbon, Newport Beach, CA, coach
John Van Blom, Long Beach, CA, coach
Vincent Ventura, White Plains, NY, coach

ROWING, MEN'S (2,000 Meters All Races)

SINGLE SCULLS

1. **Pertti Karppinen, FIN**		7:00.24
2. **Peter-Michael Kolbe, FRG**		7:02.19
3. **Robert Mills, CAN**		7:10.38
4. John Biglow, USA		7:12.00
5. Ricardo D. Ibarra, ARG		7:14.59
6. Kostantinos Kontomanolis, GRE		7:17.03

DOUBLE SCULLS

1. **USA (Bradley Lewis, Paul Enquist)**		6:36.87
2. **BEL (Pierre-Marie DeLoof, Dirk Crois)**		6:38.19
3. **YUG (Zoran Panic, Milorad Stanulov)**		6:39.59
4. FRG		6:40.41
5. ITA		6:44.29
6. CAN		6:46.68

PAIR OARS WITHOUT COXSWAIN

1. **ROM (Petru Iosub, Valer Toma)**	6:45.39
2. **ESP (Fernando Climent, Luis Lasurtgui)**	6:48.47
3. **NOR (Hans Magnus Grepperud,**	6:51.81
Sverre Loken)	
4. FRG	6:52.53
5. ITA	6:55.88
6. USA (David DeRuff, John Strotbeck)	6:58.46

PAIR OARS WITH COXSWAIN

1. **ITA (Carmine and Giuseppe Abbagnale,**	7:05.99
Giuseppe DiCapua)	
2. **ROM (Dimitrie Popescu,**	7:11.21
Vasile Tomoiaga, Dumitru Raducanu)	
3. **USA (Kevin Still, Robert Espeseth,**	7:12.81
Douglas Herland)	
4. BRA	7:17.07
5. CAN	7:18.98
6. FRG	7:25.16

QUADRUPLE SCULLS

1. **FRG (Albert Hedderich, Raimund**	5:57.55
Hormann, Dieter Wiedenmann,	
Michael Dursch)	
2. **AUS (Paul Reedy, Gary Gullock, Timothy**	5:57.98
McLaren, Anthony Lovrich)	
3. **CAN (Doug Hamilton, Mike Hughes,**	5:59.07
Phil Monckton, Bruce Ford)	

4. ITA	6:00.94
5. FRA	6:01.35
6. ESP	6:04.99
7. USA (Curtis Fleming, Gregg Montesi, Ridgley Johnson, Bruce Beall)	NT

FOUR OARS WITHOUT COXSWAIN

1. **NZL (Leslie O'Connell, Shane O'Brien, Conrad Robertson, Keith Trask)**	6:03.48
2. **USA (David Clark, Jonathan Smith, Philip Stekl, Alan Forney)**	6:06.10
3. **DEN (Michael Jessen, Lars Nielsen, Per Rasmussen, Erik Christiansen)**	6:07.72
4. FRG	6:09.27
5. SUI	6:09.50
6. SWE	6:11.71

FOUR OARS WITH COXSWAIN

1. **GBR (Martin Cross, Richard Budgett, Andrew Holmes, Steven Redgrave, Adrian Ellison)**	6:18.64
2. **USA (Thomas Kiefer, Gregory Springer, Michael Bach, Edward Ives, John Stillings)**	6:20.28
3. **NZL (Kevin Lawton, Donald Symon, Barrie Mabbot, Ross Tong, Brett Hollister)**	6:23.68
4. ITA	6:26.44
5. CAN	6:28.78
6. FRG	6:34.23

EIGHT OARS WITH COXSWAIN

1. **CAN (Pat Turner, Keven Neufield, Mark Evans, Grant Main, Paul Steele, Mike Evans, Dean Crawford, Blair Horm, Brian McMahon)**	5:41.32
2. **USA (Walter Lubsen, Andrew Sudduth, John Terwilliger, Christoper Penny, Thomas Darling, Earl Borchelt, Charles Clapp, Bruce Ibbotson, Bob Jaugstetter)**	5:41.74
3. **AUS (Muller, Hefer, Patten, Willoughby, Edmunds, Battersby, Popa, Evans, Thredgold)**	5:43.40
4. NZL	5:44.14
5. GBR	5:47.01
6. FRA	5:49.52
7. CHI	6:07.03

ROWING, WOMEN'S (1,000 Meters All Races)

SINGLE SCULLS

1. **Valeria Racila, ROM**	3:40.68
2. **Charlotte Geer, USA**	3:43.89
3. **Ann Haesebrouck, BEL**	3:45.72
4. Andrea Schreiner, CAN	3:45.97
5. Lise Marianne Justesen, DEN	3:47.79
6. Beryl Mitchell, GBR	3:51.20

DOUBLE SCULLS

1. **ROM (Marioara Popescu, Elizabeta Oleniuc)**	3:26.75
2. **HOL (Greet and Nicolette Hellemans)**	3:29.13
3. **CAN (Daniele and Silken Laumann)**	3:29.82
4. SWE	3:30.79
5. NOR	3:32.09
6. USA (Cathleen Thaxton, Julie Geer)	3:32.23

PAIR OARS WITHOUT COXSWAIN

1. **ROM (Rodica Arba, Elena Horvat)**	3:32.60
2. **CAN (Betty Craig, Tricia Smith)**	3:36.06
3. **FRG (Ellen Becker, Iris Volkner)**	3:40.50
4. HOL	3:44.01
5. USA (Barbara Kirch, Chari Towne)	3:44.35
6. GBR	3:48.53

QUADRUPLE SCULLS WITH COXSWAIN

1. **ROM (Titie Taran, Anisoara Sorohan, Ioana Badea, Sofia Corban, Ecaterina Oancia)**	3:14.11
2. **USA (Anne Marden, Lisa Rohde, Joan Lind, Virginia Gilder, Kelly Rickon)**	3:15.57
3. **DEN (Eriksen, Hanel, Koefoed, Rasmussen, Soeresen)**	3:16.02
4. FRG	3:16.81
5. FRA	3:17.87
6. ITA	3:21.48

FOUR OARS WITH COXSWAIN

1. **ROM (Florica Lavric, Maria Friciou, Chira Apostol, Olga Bularda, Viorica Ioja)**	3:19.30
2. **CAN (Brain, Schneider, Ambrust, Tregunno, Thompson)**	3:21.55
3. **AUS (Grey-Gardner, Brancourt, Chapman, Foster, Lee)**	3:23.29
4. USA (Abigail Peck, Patricia Spratlen, Janet Harville, Elizabeth Miles, Valerie McClain-Ward)	3:23.58
5. HOL	3:23.97
6. FRG	3:29.03

EIGHT OARS WITH COXSWAIN

1. **USA (Shyril O'Steen, Harriet Metcalf, Carol Bower, Carrie Graves, Jeanne Flanagan, Kristine Norelius, Kristen Thorsness, Kathryn Keeler, Betsy Beard)**	2:59.80
2. **ROM (Balan, Trasca, Plesca, Mihaly, Chelariu, Armasescu, Diaconescu, Sauca, Ioja)**	3:00.87
3. **HOL (Hellemans, N., Cornet, Van Ettekoven, Hellemans, G., Drogenbroek Van, Quist, Neelisssen, Vaandrager, Laurijsen)**	3:02.92
4. CAN	3:03.64
5. GBR	3:04.51
6. FRG	3:09.92

TEAM PERSONNEL, MEN'S

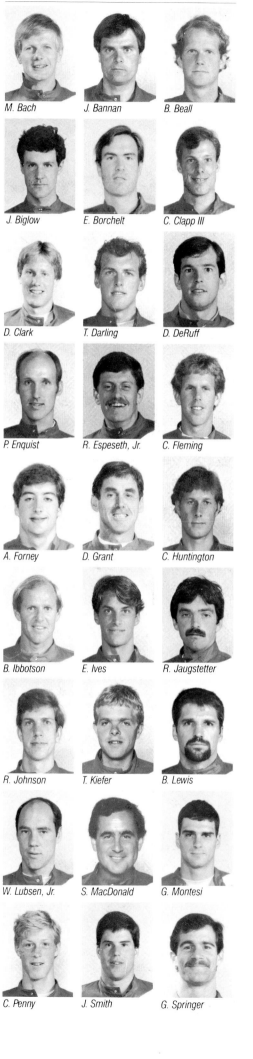

M. Bach   J. Bannan   B. Beall

J. Biglow   E. Borchelt   C. Clapp III

D. Clark   T. Darling   D. DeRuff

P. Enquist   R. Espeseth, Jr.   C. Fleming

A. Forney   D. Grant   C. Huntington

B. Ibbotson   E. Ives   R. Jaugstetter

R. Johnson   T. Kiefer   B. Lewis

W. Lubsen, Jr.   S. MacDonald   G. Montesi

C. Penny   J. Smith   G. Springer

P. Stekl   K. Still   J. Stillings

J. Strotbeck   A. Sudduth   J. Terwilliger

M. Teti   C. Wood   K. Korzeniowski

H. Parker   D. Rose   M. Vespoli

J. Wolf   P. Zanderbergen

TEAM PERSONNEL, WOMEN'S

V. Baker   H. Barnes   B. Beard

C. Bower   S. Broome   C. Brown

C. Cassuto   C. Ernst   J. Flanagan

C. Geer   J. Geer   V. Gilder

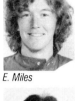
C. Graves   J. Harville   K. Keeler

B. Kirch   J. Lind   A. Marden

V. McLain-Ward   H. Metcalf   E. Miles

K. Norelius   S. O'Steen   A. Peck

K. Rickon   L. Rohde   P. Spratlen

C. Thaxton   K. Thorsness   C. Towne

R. Ernst   L. Gluckman   V. Ventura

SHOOTING

Shooting as a sport came of age at the 1984 Olympic Games. Heretofore the officials controlling the sport had decreed that women were eligible for the shooting events, but they had to compete with men for places on a nation's Olympic Team. In 1976, the United States produced one silver medalist, Margaret Murdock, the only female medalist in the history of shooting events.

For the 1984 Games, the international shooting body established three events for women only. The United States took advantage of these added events to show off the prowess of its modern-day Annie Oakleys who have been doing superbly well in national and international competitions.

Pat Spurgin won the gold medal in the women's air rifle and Ruby Fox placed second in the sport pistol with Wanda Jewell earning a bronze medal in the standard (small-bore) rifle. Thus, the United States took a medal in each of three female competitions.

Although by the established USOC scoring method the United States was rated no. 1 among the nations competing in shooting, success was not as great as had been anticipated. One men's gold medal was won by Edward Etzel, a graduate student at West Virginia University who doubles as amateur coach of the university shooting team. Etzel prevailed in the small-bore rifle, prone position (better known as the English match).

The other gold medal was deservedly won in skeet shooting by Matthew Dryke. It is difficult to believe that the Games closed down without Dan Carlisle, world champion, placing higher than third in his specialty, trap shooting. He was "eliminated" in a shoot-off after a three-way tie for first place.

It was significant that in the eleven-event program, Asian countries accounted for four gold and three bronze medals, their most successful Games yet in shooting.

The women produced the only double medal winner. Wu Xiaoxuan won the title in the standard (small-bore) rifle and took third place in the air rifle event.

Ragnar Skanaker, Sweden, shot an Olympic record of 567 in winning the free pistol title at Munich in 1972. In Los Angeles he placed second in the same event with a 565, one point behind the winner.

TEAM PERSONNEL

William F. Beard, 36, Indianapolis, IN (rifle 3 pos.)
Todd L. Bensley, 23, Lordsburg, NM (running game target)
Erich Buljung, 40, Fort Benning, GA (free pistol)
Daniel Carlisle, 28, Fort Benning, GA (trap)
Matthew A. Dryke, 25, Squim, WA (skeet)
Glen A. Dubis, 25, Fort Benning, GA (air rifle and rifle 3 pos.)
Donald L. Durbin, 47, Louisville, KY (English Match rifle)
Kim Dyer, 37, Waco, TX (sport pistol)
Edward Etzel, 31, Morgantown, WV (English Match rifle and rifle 3 pos.)
Ruby Fox, 38, Parker, AZ (sport pistol)
Wanda R. Jewell, 30, Redstone Arsenal, AL (rifle 3 pos.)
Allyn W. Johnson, 46, Fremont, CA (rapid-fire pistol)
Allan F. Knowles, 34, Ojai, CA (English Match rifle)
John T. McNally, 28 Fort Benning, GA (rapid-fire pistol)
Donald C. Nygord, 48, La Crescenta, CA (free pistol)
Gloria Parmentier, 26, Fort Benning, GA (rifle 3 pos.)
John A. Rost, 24, Pittsburgh, PA (air rifle)
Mary A. Schweitzer, 23, Lancaster, PA (air rifle)
Pat Spurgin, 19, Billings, MT (air rifle)
Randy W. Stewart, 32, Kirby, AK (running game target)
Michael E. Thompson, 28, Fredericksburg, VA (skeet)
Walter (Wally) Zobell, 34, Jackson, MT (trap)

Joseph Berry, Lorton, VA, manager
David S. Mattice, Nashville, TN, gunsmith
Jack Vincent, Amarillo, TX, assistant manager

SHOOTING, MEN'S

AIR RIFLE

1. **Philippe Heberle, FRA**	589 NOR	
2. **Andreas Kronthaler, AUT**	587	
3. **Barry Dagger, GBR**	587	
4. Nicolas Berthelot, FRA	585	
5. Peter Heinz, FRG	583	
6. John Rost, USA	583	
7. Harald Stenvaag, NOR	582	
8. Itzchak Yonassi, ISR	582	
15. Glenn Dubis, USA	579	

ENGLISH MATCH RIFLE (SMALL-BORE, PRONE)

1. **Edward Etzel, USA**	599 EOR
2. **Michel Bury, FRA**	596
3. **Michael Sullivan, GBR**	596
4. Alister Allan, GBR	594
5. Francesco Nanni, SMR	594
6. Hans Strand, SWE	594
7. John Duus, NOR	594
8. Ulrich Lind, FRG	593
13. Donald Durbin, USA	592

SMALL-BORE RIFLE, THREE POSITIONS

1. **Malcolm Cooper, GBR**	1,173 NOR/EWR
2. **David Nipkow, SUI**	1,163
3. **Alister Allan, GBR**	1,162
4. Kurt Hillenbrand, FRG	1,154
5. Bo Arne Lilja, DEN	1,153
6. Glen Dubis, USA	1,151
7. Jean Pierre Amat, FRA	1,150
8. Peter Heinz, FRG	1,150
15. Edward Etzel, USA	1,142

RUNNING GAME TARGET

1. **Li Yuwei, CHN**	587
2. **Helmut Bellingrodt, COL**	584
3. **Huang Shiping, CHN**	581
4. Uwe Schroder, FRG	581
5. David Lee, CAN	580
6. Kenneth Skoglund, NOR	576
7. Jorma Lievonen, FIN	576
8. Ezio Cini, ITA	576
9. Randy Stewart, USA	575
13. Todd Bensley, USA	572

CLAY TARGET TRAP SHOOTING

1. **Luciano Giovannetti, ITA**	192
2. **Francisco Boza, PER**	192
3. **Dan Carlisle, USA**	192
4. Timo Niemminen, FIN	191
5. Michel Carrega, FRA	190
6. Eli Ellis, AUS	190
7. Terry Rumbel, AUS	189
8. Johnny Pahlsson, SWE	189
22. Wally Zobell, USA	181

SKEET SHOOTING

1. **Matthew Dryke, USA**	198 NOR
2. **Ole Riber Rasmussen, DEN**	196
3. **Luca Scribani Rossi, ITA**	196
4. Johannes Pierik, HOL	194
5. Anders Berglind, SWE	194
6. Norbert Hofmann, FRG	194
7. Jorge Molina, COL	194
8. Ian Hale, AUS	193
38. Michael Thompson, USA	185

FREE PISTOL

1. **Xu Haifeng, CHN**	566
2. **Ragnar Skanaker, SWE**	565
3. **Wang Yifu, CHN**	564
4. Jurgen Hartmann, FRG	560
5. Vincenzo Tondo, ITA	560
6. Philippe Cola, FRA	559
7. Hector De Lima Carillo, VEN	558
8. Paavo Palokangas, FIN	558
9. Erich Buljung, USA	558
14. Donald Nygord, USA	554

RAPID-FIRE PISTOL

1. **Takeo Kamachi, JPN**	595
2. **Corneliu Ion, ROM**	593
3. **Rauno Bies, FIN**	591
4. Delival Nobre, BRA	591
5. Yang Choong-Yuli, KOR	590
6. Alfred Radke, FRG	590
7. Park Jong-Gil, KOR	590
8. Bernardo Tobar, COL	590
20. Allyn Johnson, USA	586
26. John McNally, USA	581

SHOOTING, WOMEN'S

AIR RIFLE

1. **Pat Spurgin, USA**	393 NOR
2. **Edith Gufler, ITA**	391
3. **Wu Xiaoxuan, CHN**	389
4. Sharon Bowes, CAN	388
5. Yvette Courault, FRA	386
6. Gisela Sailer, FRG	385
7. Siri Landsem, NOR	384
8. Sirpa Ylonen, FIN	383
18. Mary Schweitzer, USA	379

SMALL-BORE RIFLE, THREE POSITIONS

1. **Wu Xiaoxuan, CHN**	581 NOR
2. **Ulrike Holmer, FRG**	578
3. **Wanda Jewell, USA**	578
4. Gloria Parmentier, USA	576
5. Ann Grethe Jeppesen, NOR	574
6. Jin Dongxiang, CHN	571
7. Biserka Vrbek, YUG	569
8. Mirjana Jovovic, YUG	569

SPORT PISTOL

1. **Linda Thom, CAN**	585 NOR
2. **Ruby Fox, USA**	585 NOR
3. **Patricia Dench, AUS**	583
4. Liu Haiying, CHN	583
5. Kristina Fries, SWE	581
6. Wen Zhifang, CHN	578
7. Debora Srour, BRA	578
8. Maria Macovei, ROM	577
13. Kim Dyer, USA	574

TEAM PERSONNEL

W. Beard   T. Bensley   E. Buljung

D. Carlisle   M. Dryke   G. Dubis

D. Durbin   K. Dyer   E. Etzel

R. Fox   W. Jewell   A. Johnson

A. Knowles   J. McNally   D. Nygord

G. Parmentier   J. Rost   M. Schweitzer

P. Spurgin   R. Stewart   M. Thompson

W. Zobell   J. Berry   D. Mattice

J. Vincent

SOCCER

America adopted football (soccer) as its favorite team sport at the Olympic Games. Record crowds watched the games in the Rose Bowl, Stanford, Annapolis, and at Soldiers Field, Harvard University. The Rose Bowl with its capacity of more than 100,000 wasn't large enough to hold the many thousands clamoring for tickets to the semi-final and final games.

The United States didn't put together its Olympic squad until the last minute. For three years the officials of the international soccer football association had been negotiating from strength with the International Olympic Committee to open the Olympic games to professionals.

After a final compromise professional players were permitted to play; but most of the other Olympic soccer teams had been chosen by the time this decision was announced. The United States had been readying two separate squads—one composed of amateurs, and another including players from the professional North American Soccer League.

The U.S. Soccer Federation, charged with selecting the squad, sent its entry list to the USOC. All but four were players from the NASL.

The United States was placed in a preliminary pool with Italy, Egypt, and Costa Rica.

At Stanford, the U.S. opened its Olympic play with a resounding 3-0 triumph over Costa Rica before more than 78,000. Then the U.S. moved into the Rose Bowl for the important test with Italy. The Italians won 1-0, on a goal in the 54th minute (nine minutes into the second half) by Pietro Fanna.

To advance to the quarter-final round, the United States had to defeat Egypt. In case of a tie, Egypt would prevail because they had scored one more goal than the U.S.

It was a typically defensive game induced by the rules for advancing in the tournament. The U.S. scored first, and the Egyptians deadlocked the count at 1-1 after 27:30 of the first half. Although the Egyptians didn't actually sit on the ball for the final 62:30, they protected the ball from the U.S. team, and the resultant tie gave them a place in the quarter-finals.

France won the gold by defeating Brazil, 2-0, in the final.

TEAM PERSONNEL

Amr Aly, Brooklyn, NY
Hernan Borja, Bloomfield, NJ
David Brcic, Washingtown Township, NJ
Kevin Crow, San Diego, CA
Richard Davis, Manchester, MD

Angel Dibernardo, North Haledon, NJ
Jeff Durgan, Westwood, NJ
Michael Fox, La Verne, CA
Jeff Hooker, Walnut, CA
Erhardt Kapp, Sewickley Heights, PA
Steve Moyers, Washington Township, NJ
Hugo Perez, San Diego, CA
William Savage, Phoenix, AZ
Jamie Swanner, St. Louis, MO
Kazbek Tambi, Ridgewood, NJ
Gregg Thompson, Tampa, FL
Jean Willrich, San Diego, CA

Angus McAlpine, Duluth, GA, assistant coach
Charles Andrew Meeks, Clearwater, FL, manager
Alkis Panagoulias, Vienna, VA, coach

SOCCER

GOLD MEDAL GAME
FRA 2, BRA 0
BRONZE MEDAL GAME
YUG 2, ITA 1

SEMI-FINAL ROUND
FRA 4, YUG 2
BRA 2, ITA 1

QUARTER-FINAL ROUND
FRA 2, EGY 0
ITA 1, CHI 0
YUG 5, FRG 2
BRA 5, CAN 3

PRELIMINARY ROUND STANDINGS
Group A: FRA, CHI, NOR, QAT
Group B: YUG, CAN, CMR, IRQ
Group C: BRA, FRG, MAR, SAU
Group D: ITA, EGY, USA, CRC

SCORES OF USA GAMES
USA vs ITA 0-1, vs EGY 1-1, vs CRC 3-0

GROUP D STANDINGS

	Win	Lose	Tie	Goals For	Against	Pts
1. ITA	2	1	0	2	1	4
2. EGY	1	1	1	5	3	3
3. USA	1	1	1	4	2	3
4. CRC	1	2	0	2	7	2

THE CHAMPIONS
FRA: Albert Rust, William Ayache, Michel Bibard,
    Dominique Bijotat, Francois Brisson, Patrick
    Cubaynes, Patrice Carande, Philippe Jeannot,
    Guy Lacombe, Jean-Claude Lemoult,
    Jean-Philippe Rohr, Didier Senac, Jean-Christoph
    Thouvenel, Jose Toure, Daniel Xuereb,
    Jean-Louis Zanon, Michel Bensoussan.
    Coach: Henri Michel.

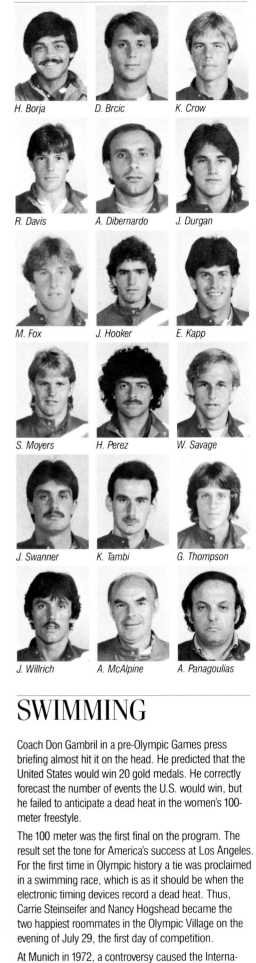

H. Borja   D. Brcic   K. Crow

R. Davis   A. Dibernardo   J. Durgan

M. Fox   J. Hooker   E. Kapp

S. Moyers   H. Perez   W. Savage

J. Swanner   K. Tambi   G. Thompson

J. Willrich   A. McAlpine   A. Panagoulias

SWIMMING

Coach Don Gambril in a pre-Olympic Games press briefing almost hit it on the head. He predicted that the United States would win 20 gold medals. He correctly forecast the number of events the U.S. would win, but he failed to anticipate a dead heat in the women's 100-meter freestyle.

The 100 meter was the first final on the program. The result set the tone for America's success at Los Angeles. For the first time in Olympic history a tie was proclaimed in a swimming race, which is as it should be when the electronic timing devices record a dead heat. Thus, Carrie Steinseifer and Nancy Hogshead became the two happiest roommates in the Olympic Village on the evening of July 29, the first day of competition.

At Munich in 1972, a controversy caused the International Amateur Swimming Federation (FINA) to change its own rules after America's Tim McKee lost a 400-meter individual medley race. Both McKee and Sweden's Gunnar Larsson had been electronically timed in

4:31.98. Somehow or other officials went behind the exposed digits and found that Larsson was actually a .002 second faster. The 1972 decision went to Larsson but FINA declared that, henceforth, timing would go no further than one-hundredths of a second.

On the U.S. team at Los Angeles were nine men and seven women from the 1980 Olympic squad who had been selected from the U.S. Swimming Champion-ships. Among those from the 1980 team were such familiar names as Gaines, Caulkins, Carey, Hogshead, Woodhead, Lundquist, and Meagher.

The last time the U.S. swam in the Olympics, at Mon-treal in 1976, the men prevailed, although the women won a single gold medal in a meet dominated by swim-mers from the German Democratic Republic.

There was no doubt about U.S. supremacy at Los Angeles.

The women went 1, 2 in six events (including three of the four freestyle events); the men swept three. Although the U.S. won the five relays, it took four com-bined herculean efforts in the 4 × 200-meter men's freestyle relay for the American quartet to overturn a determined team from the German Federal Republic, anchored by The Albatross, Michael Gross. Both relay teams shaved three seconds from the best previous record in the world.

The smashing of existing swimming records is expected at every Olympic Games. Here the women established six new Olympic marks (all but one by U.S. swimmers), but could not better any of the existing world records.

In the men's division, Olympic standards were eclipsed in 13 of the 15 events and the United States set four of the ten world records in the pool (three of them in the relays, the other by Steve Lundquist in the 100-meter breaststroke).

Although the depth of the U.S. team enabled it to win more medals than the competing nations, it should be noted that Michael Gross, of West Germany and Cana-da's adopted son Alex Baumann each swam to a pair of world records.

There is ample evidence that should the USSR and the GDR return to the Olympic Games four years hence the contest for winning medals will be highly competitive.

TEAM PERSONNEL

MEN'S

Matt Biondi, 18, Moraga, CA (4x100m free relay)
Rick Carey, 21, Mt. Kisco, NY (100m, 200m back-stroke, 4x100m medley relay)
Chris Cavanaugh, 22, Mountain View, CA (4x100 free relay)
George DiCarlo, 21, Denver, CO (400m, 1500m freestyle)
Jeff Float, 24, Sacramento, CA (200m freestyle, 4x200m free relay)
Geoff Gaberino, 22, Palm Harbor, FL (4x200m free relay-heat)
Anbrose (Rowdy) Gaines, 25, Winter Haven, FL (100m freestyle, 4x100m free relay, 4x100m medley relay)
Matt Gribble, 22, Miami, FL (100m 'fly)
Bruce Hayes, 21, Dallas, TX (4x200 free relay)
Mike Heath, 20, Dallas, TX (100m, 200m freestyle, 4x100m and 4x200m free relay, 4x100m medley relay-heat)
Tom Jager, 19, Collinsville, IL (4x100m free relay-heat, 4x100m medley relay-heat)

Patrick Kennedy, 20, Cockeysville, MD (200m 'fly)
Jeff Kostoff, 18, Upland, CA (400m I.M.)
David Larson, 25, Jessup, GA (4x200m free relay)
Robin Leamy, 23, Rancho Palos Verdes, CA (4x100m free relay-heat)
Steve Lundquist, 23, Jonesboro, GA (100m breast-stroke, 200m I.M., 4x100m medley relay)
John Moffet, 20, Costa Mesa, CA (100m breaststroke)
Pablo Morales, 19, Santa Clara, CA (100m and 200 'fly, 200m I.M., 4x100m medley relay)
John Mykkanen, 17, Placentia, CA (400m freestyle)
Michael O'Brien, 18, Mission Viejo, CA (1500m freestyle)
Richard Saeger, 20, Mission Viejo, CA (4x200m free relay-heat)
Richard Schroeder, 22, Santa Barbara, CA (200m breaststroke, 4x100m medley relay-heat)
Jesus Vassallo, 23, Mission Viejo, CA (200m backstroke, 400m I.M.)
David Wilson, 23, Cincinnati, OH (100m backstroke, 4x100m medley relay-heat)

TEAM PERSONNEL

WOMEN'S

Theresa Andrews, 21, Annapolis, MD (100m backstroke, 4x100m medley relay)
Tracy Caulkins, 21, Nashville, TN (100m breast-stroke, 200m and 400m I.M., 4x100m medley relay)
Tiffany Cohen, 18, Mission Viejo, CA (400m, 800m freestyle)
Susan Heon, 22, Clarks Summit, PA (400m I.M.)
Nancy Hogshead, 22, Jacksonville, FL (100m free-style, 200m 'fly, 200m I.M., 4x100m free relay, 4x100m medley relay)
Jenna Johnson, 16, La Habra, CA (100m 'fly, 4x100 free relay, 4x100m medley relay-heat)
Kimberly Linehan, 21, Sarasota, FL (400m freestyle)
Mary Meagher, 19, Louisville, KY (100m, 200m 'fly, 4x100m medley relay)
Betsy Mitchell, 18, Marietta, OH (100m backstroke, 4x100m medley relay-heat)
Susan Rapp, 19, Eden Prairie, MN (100m, 200m breaststroke, 4x100m medley relay-heat)
Kim Rhodenbaugh, 18, Cincinnati, OH (200m breaststroke)
Michelle Richardson, 15, Miami, FL (800m freestyle)
Carrie Steinseifer, 16, Saratoga, CA (100m freestyle, 4x100m free relay, 4x100m medley relay-heat)
Jill Sterkel, 23, Hacienda Heights, CA (4x100m free relay-heat)
Dara Torres, 17, Beverly Hills, CA (4x100m free relay)
Tori Trees, 19, Louisville, KY (200m backstroke)
Mary Wayte, 19, Mercer Island, WA (200m freestyle, 4x100m free relay-heat)
Amy White, 15, Irvine, CA (200m backstroke)
Cynthia Woodhead, 20, Riverside, CA (200m freestyle)

TEAM PERSONNEL

SWIMMING STAFF FOR MEN AND WOMEN

Ronald Ballatore, South Pasadena, CA, assistant coach
Raymond Bussard, Knoxville, TN, assistant coach
Donald Gambril, Tuscaloosa, AL, head coach
George Haines, San Jose, CA, assistant coach
James Ingram, Ft. Pierce, FL, manager
Frank Keefe, Lansdowne, PA, assistant coach

Beverly Montrella, Columbus, OH, assistant manager
Richard Quick, Austin, TX, assistant coach
Randy Reese, Gainesville, FL, assistant coach
Mark Schubert, Mission Viejo, CA, assistant coach
Carol Taylor, Ballwin, MO, assistant coach

SWIMMING, MEN'S

100-METER FREESTYLE

1. **Rowdy Gaines, USA**	49.80 NOR
2. **Mark Stockwell, AUS**	50.24
3. **Per Johansson, SWE**	50.31
4. Mike Heath, USA	50.41
5. Dano Halsall, SUI	50.50
6. (tie) Alberto Mestre Sosa, VEN	50.70
6. (tie) Stephan Caron, FRA	50.70
8. Dirk Korthals, FRG	50.93

200-METER FREESTYLE

1. **Michael Gross, FRG**	1:47.44 NOR/NWR
2. **Mike Heath, USA**	1:49.10
3. **Thomas Fahrner, FRG**	1:49.69
4. Jeff Float, USA	1:50.18
5. Alberto Mestre Sosa, VEN	1:50.23
6. Frank Drost, HOL	1:51.62
7. Marco Dell'Uomo, ITA	1:52.20
8. Peter Dale, AUS	1:53.84

400-METER FREESTYLE

1. **George DiCarlo, USA**	3:51.23
2. **John Mykkanen, USA**	3:51.49
3. **Justin Lemberg, AUS**	3:51.79
4. Stefan Pfeiffer, FRG	3:52.91
5. Franck Iacono, FRA	3:54.58
6. Darjan Petric, YUG	3:54.88
7. Marco Dell'Uomo, ITA	3:55.44
8. Ronald McKeon, AUS	3:55.48

Note: Thomas Fahrner, FRG 3:50.91 NOR in consolation final

1,500-METER FREESTYLE

1. **Michael O'Brien, USA**	15:05.20
2. **George DiCarlo, USA**	15:10.59
3. **Stefan Pfeiffer, FRG**	15:12.11
4. Rainer Henkel, FRG	15:20.03
5. Franck Iacono, FRA	15:26.96
6. Stefano Grandi, ITA	15:28.58
7. David Shemilt, CAN	15:31.28
8. Wayne Shillington, AUS	15:38.18

100-METER BACKSTROKE

1. **Rick Carey, USA**	55.79
2. **David Wilson, USA**	56.35
3. **Mike West, CAN**	56.49
4. Gary Hurring, NZL	56.90
5. Mark Kerry, AUS	57.18
6. Bengt Baron, SWE	57.34
7. Sandy Goss, CAN	57.46
8. Hans Kroes, HOL	58.07

200-METER BACKSTROKE

1. **Rick Carey, USA**	2:00.23
2. **Frederic Delcourt, FRA**	2:01.75
3. **Cameron Henning, CAN**	2:02.37
4. Ricardo Prado, BRA	2:03.05
5. Gary Hurring, NZL	2:03.10
6. Nicolai Klapkarek, FRG	2:03.95
7. Ricardo Aldabe, ESP	2:04.53
8. David Orbell, AUS	2:04.61
Jesus Vassallo, USA	DNQ

Note: Carey set an Olympic record in the heats, 1:58.99.

100-METER BREASTSTROKE

1. **Steve Lundquist, USA**	1:01.65 NOR/NWR
2. **Victor Davis, CAN**	1:01.99
3. **Peter Evans, AUS**	1:02.97
4. Adrian Moorhouse, GBR	1:03.25
5. John Moffet, USA	1:03.29
6. Brett Stocks, AUS	1:03.49
7. Gerald Morken, FRG	1:03.95
8. Raffaele Avagnano, ITA	1:04.11

200-METER BREASTSTROKE

1. **Victor Davis, CAN**	2:13.34 NOR/NWR
2. **Glenn Beringen, AUS**	2:15.79
3. **Etienne Dagon, SUI**	2:17.41
4. Richard Schroeder, USA	2:18.03
5. Ken Fitzpatrick, CAN	2:18.86
6. Pablo Restrepo, COL	2:18.96
7. Alexandre Yokochi, POR	2:20.69
8. Marco DelPrete, ITA	DISQ
John Moffet, USA	DNP

100-METER BUTTERFLY

1. **Michael Gross, FRG**	53.08 NOR/NWR
2. **Pablo Morales, USA**	52.23
3. **Glenn Buchanan, AUS**	53.85
4. Rafael Vidal Castro, VEN	54.27
5. Andrew Jameson, GBR	54.28
6. Anthony Mosse, NZL	54.93
7. Andreas Behrend, FRG	54.95
8. Bengt Baron, SWE	55.14

200-METER BUTTERFLY

1. **Jon Sieben, AUS**	1:57.04 NOR/NWR
2. **Michael Gross, FRG**	1:57.40
3. **Rafael Vidal Castro, VEN**	1:57.51
4. Pablo Morales, USA	1:57.75
5. Anthony Mosse, NZL	1:58.75
6. Tom Pointing, CAN	1:59.37
7. Peter Ward, CAN	2:00.39
8. Patrick Kennedy, USA	2:01.03

200-METER INDIVIDUAL MEDLEY

1. **Alex Baumann, CAN**	2:01.42 NOR/NWR
2. **Pablo Morales, USA**	2:03.05
3. **Neil Cochran, GBR**	2:04.38
4. Robin Brew, GBR	2:04.52
5. Steve Lundquist, USA	2:04.91
6. Andrew Phillips, JAM	2:05.60

7. Nicolai Klapkarek, FRG	2:05.88
8. Ralf Diegel, FRG	2:06.66

400-METER INDIVIDUAL MEDLEY

1. **Alex Baumann, CAN**	4:17.41 NOR/NWR
2. **Ricardo Prado, BRA**	4:18.45
3. **Robert Woodhouse, AUS**	4:20.50
4. Jesus Vassallo, USA	4:21.46
5. Maurizio Divano, ITA	4:22.76
6. Jeff Kostoff, USA	4:23.28
7. Stephen Poulter, GBR	4:25.80
8. Giovanni Franceschi, ITA	4:26.05

4 × 100-METER FREESTYLE RELAY

1. **USA (Cavanaugh, Heath, Biondi, Gaines)**	3:19.03 NOR/NWR
2. **AUS (Fasala, Brooks, Delany, Stockwell)**	3:19.68
3. **SWE (Leidstrom, Baron, Orn, Johansson)**	3:22.69
4. FRG	3:22.98
5. GBR	3:23.61
6. FRA	3:24.63
7. CAN	3:24.70
8. ITA	3:24.97

4 × 200-METER FREESTYLE RELAY

1. **USA (Heath, Larson, Float, Hayes)**	7:15.69 NOR/NWR
2. **FRG (Fahrner, Korthals, Schowtka, Gross)**	7:15.73
3. **GBR (Cochran, Easter, Howe, Asbury)**	7:24.78
4. AUS	7:25.63
5. CAN	7:26.51
6. SWE	7:26.53
7. HOL	7:26.72
8. FRA	7:30.16

4 × 100-METER MEDLEY RELAY

1. **USA (Carey, Lundquist, Morales, Gaines)**	3:39.30 NOR/NWR
2. **CAN (West, Davis, Pointing, Goss)**	3:43.23
3. **AUS (Kerry, Evans, Buchanan, Stockwell)**	3:43.25
4. FRG	3:44.26
5. SWE	3:47.13
6. GBR	3:47.39
7. SUI	3:47.93
8. JPN	DISQ

SWIMMING, WOMEN'S

100-METER FREESTYLE

1. **(tie) Carrie Steinseifer, USA**	55.92
1. **(tie) Nancy Hogshead, USA**	55.92
3. **Annemarie Verstappen, HOL**	56.08
4. Conny Van Bentum, HOL	56.43
5. Michele Pearson, AUS	56.83
6. June Croft, GBR	56.90
7. Susanne Schuster, FRG	57.11
8. Angela Russel, AUS	58.09

200-METER FREESTYLE

1. **Mary Wayte, USA**	1:59.23
2. **Cynthia Woodhead, USA**	1:59.50
3. **Annemarie Verstappen, HOL**	1:59.69
4. Michele Pearson, AUS	1:59.79
5. Conny Van Bentum, HOL	2:00.59
6. June Croft, GBR	2:00.64
7. Ina Beyermann, FRG	2:01.89
8. Anna McVann, AUS	2:02.87

400-METER FREESTYLE

1. **Tiffany Cohen, USA**	4:07.10 NOR
2. **Sarah Hardcastle, GBR**	4:10.27
3. **June Croft, GBR**	4:11.49
4. Kimberly Linehan, USA	4:12.26
5. Anna McVann, AUS	4:13.95
6. Jolande Van Der Meer, HOL	4:16.05
7. Birgit Kowalczik, FRG	4:16.33
8. Julie Daigneault, CAN	4:16.41

800-METER FREESTYLE

1. **Tiffany Cohen, USA**	8:24.95 NOR
2. **Michele Richardson, USA**	8:30.73
3. **Sarah Hardcastle, GBR**	8:32.60
4. Anna McVann, AUS	8:37.94
5. Carla Lasi, ITA	8:42.45
6. Jolande Van Der Meer, HOL	8:42.86
7. Monica Olmi, ITA	8:47.32
8. Karen Ward, CAN	8:48.12

100-METER BACKSTROKE

1. **Theresa Andrews, USA**	1:02.55
2. **Betsy Mitchell, USA**	1:02.63
3. **Jolanda De Rover, HOL**	1:02.91
4. Carmen Bunaciu, ROM	1:03.21
5. Aneta Patrascoiu, ROM	1:03.29
6. Svenja Schlicht, FRG	1:03.46
7. Beverley Rose, GBR	1:04.16
8. Carmel Clark, NZL	1:04.47

200-METER BACKSTROKE

1. **Jolanda De Rover, HOL**	2:12.38
2. **Amy White, USA**	2:13.04
3. **Aneta Patrascoiu, ROM**	2:13.29
4. Georgina Parkes, AUS	2:14.37
5. Tori Trees, USA	2:15.73
6. Svenja Schlicht, FRG	2:15.93
7. Carmen Bunaciu, ROM	2:16.15
8. Carmel Clark, NZL	2:17.89

100-METER BREASTSTROKE

1. **Petra Van Staveren, HOL**	1:09.88 NOR
2. **Anne Ottenbrite, CAN**	1:10.69
3. **Catherine Poirot, FRA**	1:10.70
4. Tracy Caulkins, USA	1:10.88
5. Eva-Marie Hakansson, SWE	1:11.14
6. Hiroko Nagasaki, JPN	1:11.33
7. Susan Rapp, USA	1:11.45
8. Jean Hill, GBR	1:11.82

200-METER BREASTSTROKE

1. **Anne Ottenbrite, CAN**	2:30.38
2. **Susan Rapp, USA**	2:31.15
3. **Ingrid Lempereur, BEL**	2:31.40
4. Hiroko Nagasaki, JPN	2:32.93
5. Sharon Kellett, AUS	2:33.60
6. Ute Hasse, FRG	2:33.82
7. Susannah Brownsdon, GBR	2:35.07
8. Kim Rhodenbaugh, USA	2:35.51

100-METER BUTTERFLY

1. **Mary T. Meagher, USA**	0:59.26
2. **Jenna Johnson, USA**	1:00.19
3. **Karin Seick, FRG**	1:01.36
4. Annemarie Verstappen, HOL	1:01.56
5. Michelle MacPherson, CAN	1:01.58
6. Janet Tibbits, AUS	1:01.78
7. Conny Van Bentum, HOL	1:01.94
8. Ina Beyermann, FRG	1:02.11

Note: Meagher set New Olympic Record of 0:59.05 in preliminary heat.

200-METER BUTTERFLY

1. **Mary T. Meagher, USA**	2:06.90 NOR
2. **Karen Phillips, AUS**	2:10.56
3. **Ina Beyermann, FRG**	2:11.91
4. Nancy Hogshead, USA	2:11.98
5. Samantha Purvis, GBR	2:12.33
6. Naoko Kume, JPN	2:12.57
7. Sonja Hausladen, AUT	2:15.38
8. Conny Van Bentum, HOL	2:17.39

200-METER INDIVIDUAL MEDLEY

1. **Tracy Caulkins, USA**	2:12.64 NOR
2. **Nancy Hogshead, USA**	2:15.17
3. **Michele Pearson, AUS**	2:15.92
4. Lisa Curry, AUS	2:16.75
5. Christiane Pielke, FRG	2:17.82
6. Manuela Dalla Valle, ITA	2:19.69
7. Petra Zindler, FRG	2:19.86
8. Katrine Bomstad, NOR	2:20.48

400-METER INDIVIDUAL MEDLEY

1. **Tracy Caulkins, USA**	4:39.24
2. **Suzanne Landells, AUS**	4:48.30
3. **Petra Zindler, FRG**	4:48.57
4. Susan Heon, USA	4:49.41
5. Nathalie Gingras, CAN	4:50.55
6. Donna McGinnis, CAN	4:50.65
7. Gaynor Stanley, GBR	4:52.83
8. Katrine Bomstad, NOR	4:53.28

4 × 100-METER FREESTYLE RELAY

1. **USA (Johnson, Steinseifer, Torres, Hogshead)**	3:43.43
2. **HOL (Verstappen, Voskes, Reijers, Van Bentum)**	3:44.40
3. **FRG (Zscherpe, Schuster, Pielke, Seick)**	3:45.56
4. AUS	3:47.79
5. CAN	3:49.50
6. GBR	3:50.12
7. SWE	3:51.24
8. FRA	3:52.15

4 × 100-METER MEDLEY RELAY

1. **USA (Andrews, Caulkins, Meagher, Hogshead)**	4:08.34
2. **FRG (Schlicht, Hasse, Beyermann, Seick)**	4:11.97
3. **CAN (Abdo, Ottenbrite, MacPherson, Rai)**	4:12.98
4. GBR	4:14.05
5. ITA	4:17.40
6. SUI	4:19.02
JPN	DISQ
SWE	DISQ

TEAM PERSONNEL, MEN'S

M. Biondi

R. Carey

C. Cavanaugh

G. DiCarlo

J. Float

G. Gaberino

A. Gaines

M. Gribble

B. Hayes

M. Heath

T. Jager

P. Kennedy

J. Kostoff

D. Larson

R. Leamy

S. Lundquist

J. Moffet

P. Morales

J. Mykkanen

M. O'Brien

R. Saeger

R. Schroeder

J. Vassallo

D. Wilson

TEAM PERSONNEL, WOMEN'S

T. Andrews

T. Caulkins

T. Cohen

S. Heon

N. Hogshead

J. Johnson

K. Linehan

B. Mitchell

S. Rapp

K. Rhodenbaugh

M. Richardson

C. Steinseifer

J. Sterkel

D. Torres

T. Trees

M. Wayte

A. White

C. Woodhead

SWIMMING STAFF FOR MEN AND WOMEN

R. Ballatore   R. Bussard   D. Gambril

G. Haines   J. Ingram   F. Keefe

R. Quick   R. Reese   M. Schubert

SYNCHRONIZED SWIMMING

Synchronized swimming has been an integral part of the world aquatic championships. It is now a regular discipline among the aquatic sports at the Pan-American Games.

The United States has pioneered the sport, perhaps the most technically judged discipline in the Olympic Games. But in the most recent world championships Canada had upset the U.S. entries.

Although only the duet competition had been on the original program for Los Angeles, the solo event was added just before the Games. This brought about the double head-to-head confrontation between the United States and Canada. Also, there were 15 other nations in the solo competition and 16 others in the duet.

Tracie Ruiz has dominated the sport in the United States for nine years. She and duet partner Candy Costie have been together throughout their careers.

Ruiz was scored 99.467 for her figures in the solo competition and was awarded 99.000 for her classic routine.

In the duet competition Ruiz-Costie were scored 99.000 for their routine and 96.584 for their figures.

Esther Williams, a great freestyle swimmer in the early 1940's, was denied an Olympic opportunity because of World War II. She turned to the movies and water ballet and now works to popularize synchronized swimming although she never appeared competitively in the discipline.

TEAM PERSONNEL

Candace (Candy) Costie, 21, Seattle, WA (duet)
Sarah Josephson, 20, Bristol, CT, (alternate)
Tracie Ruiz, 21, Bothell, WA, (solo, duet)

Charlotte Davis, Seattle, WA, coach
Gail Emery, Lafayette, CA, manager

SYNCHRONIZED SWIMMING

SOLO

1. **Tracie Ruiz, USA**	198.467
2. **Carolyn Waldo, CAN**	195.300
3. **Miwako Motoyoshi, JPN**	187.050
4. Marijke Engelen, HOL	182.632
5. Gudrun Hanisch, FRG	182.017
6. Caroline Holmyard, GBR	182.000
7. Muriel Hermine, FRA	180.534
8. Karin Singer, SUI	178.383

DUET

1. **USA (Tracie Ruiz, Candy Costie)**	195.584
2. **CAN (Sharon Hambrook, Kelly Kryszka)**	194.234
3. **JPN (Saeko Kimura, Miwako Motoyoshi)**	187.992
4. GBR	184.050
5. SUI	180.109
6. HOL	179.058
7. FRA	176.709
8. MEX	176.404

TEAM PERSONNEL

C. Costie   S. Josephson   T. Ruiz

C. Davis   G. Emery

TEAM HANDBALL

The United States has never distinguished itself in this typically American game, spawned in Europe, exploited in the socialist countries, and played on an extraordinarily limited basis in the United States.

On the basis of performances in international competitions and tournaments, hopes were not high for the success of the U.S. A women's national team had been formed and had played together for more than a year. The men's approach was not as strictly structured. However, no U.S. national teams preparing for the Olympic Games were given more opportunities to travel than these two teams.

Such travel must be considered important in the improved play of the two U.S. teams. There were no

medals, but at least the United States became competitive at the international level for the first time.

In the men's final the Yugoslavs defeated West Germany, 18–17. The Yugoslavian women beat China 31–25 after handing Korea its only loss, 29–23.

The U.S. women wound up in a tie for fourth with West Germany after defeating bronze medalist China 25–22 and Austria 25–21 while losing a pair of close games to Korea, silver medalist, 29–27, and West Germany, 18–17.

The U.S. men's team finished an all-time high in ninth place after defeating Japan 24–16 in the final classification round. Nine players contributed to the U.S. scoring, led by Jim Buehning, five, and Peter Lash and Steve Goss, four each.

In the preliminary round the U.S. ended up fifth after one tie (Korea, 22–22) and four defeats by margins of 3, 2, 3, and 1 goals, respectively. The closeness of the games indicates that the team handball leaders may be seeing the light at the end of the tunnel after twelve years of frustration.

TEAM PERSONNEL

MEN'S

James Buehning, 27, Short Hills, NJ
Robert Djokovich, 28, Tucson, AZ
Tim Dykstra, 22, Lagrange, IN
Tim Funk, 27, San Antonio, TX
Craig Gilbert, 27, Cranbury, NJ
Steven Goss, 23, Castro Valley, CA
William Kessler, 21, West Hempstead, NY
Stephen Kirk, 25, Short Hills, NJ
Peter Lash, Jr., 25, West Point, NY
Michael Lenard, 29, Los Angeles, CA
Joseph McVein, 27, Lebanon, OR
Gregory Morava, 25, Des Plaines, IL
Rod Oshita, 25, Palos Verdes Estates, CA
Thomas Schneeberger, 28, Ann Arbor, MI
Joe Story, 32, Colonial Heights, VA

Jorge Alvaro Alcaide, Barcelona, Spain, assistant coach
Javier Garcia Cuesta, Kendall Park, NJ, coach
Tor Holtan, Larchmont, NY, manager

TEAM PERSONNEL

WOMEN'S

Pamela Boyd, 28, Toms River, NJ
Reita Clanton, 29, Opelika, AL
Theresa Contos, 24, Syracuse, NY
Sandra de la Riva, 22, Chatsworth, CA
Mary Dwight, 32, Raytown, MO
Carmen Forest, 29, Houston, TX
Dorothy Franco, 26, Milford, CT
Melinda Hale, 29, Oil City, PA
Kimberly Howard, 24, Estherville, IO
Leora Jones, 24, Mount Olive, NC
Carol Lindsey, 29, Washburn, WI
Cynthia Stinger, 26, Lawrenceville, NJ
Penelope Stone, 21, Johnsonville, SC
Janice Trombly, 27, Chazy, NY
Sherry Winn, 22, Fort Worth, TX

Klement Capilar, Lake Placid, NY, coach
Ilya Milman, Brooklyn, NY, assistant coach
Camille Nichols, Mt. Holly, NJ, manager

TEAM HANDBALL, MEN'S

GOLD MEDAL GAME

YUG 18, FRG 17

BRONZE MEDAL GAME

ROM 23, *DEN 19*

FIFTH PLACE GAME

SWE 26, ISL 24

SEVENTH PLACE GAME

SUI 18, ESP 17

NINTH PLACE GAME

USA 24, JPN 16

11TH PLACE GAME

KOR 25, ALG 21

THE CHAMPIONS

YUG: Zlatan Arnautovic, Momir Rnic, Veselin Vukovic, Milan Kalina, Jovan Elezovic, Zdravko Zovko, Pavo Jurina, Veselin Vujovic, Slobodan Kuzmanovski, Mirko Basic, Zdravko Radjenovic, Mile Isakovic. Coach: Branislav Pokrajac.

PRELIMINARY ROUND STANDINGS

	Win	Lose	Tie	For	Against	Pts
				Goals		
1. FRG	5	0	0	114	95	10
2. DEN	4	1	0	115	99	8
3. SWE	3	2	0	119	110	6
4. ESP	2	3	0	105	106	4
5. USA	0	4	1	91	100	1
6. KOR	0	4	1	123	157	1
1. YUG	4	0	1	123	76	9
2. ROM	4	1	0	120	91	8
3. ISL	3	1	1	102	96	7
4. SUI	2	3	0	83	102	4
5. JPN	1	4	0	84	117	2
6. ALG	0	5	0	75	105	0

SCORES OF USA GAMES—PRELIMINARY ROUND

USA vs DEN 16–19, vs FRG 19–21, vs SWE 18–21, vs ESP 16–17, vs KOR 22–22

TEAM HANDBALL, WOMEN'S

FINAL STANDINGS

	Win	Lose	Tie	For	Against	Pts
				Points		
1. **YUG**	5	0	0	143	102	10
2. **KOR**	3	1	1	125	119	7
3. **CHN**	2	2	1	112	115	5
4. (tie) USA	2	3	0	114	123	4
4. (tie) FRG	2	3	0	91	100	4
6. AUT	0	5	0	91	117	0

THE CHAMPIONS

YUG: Jasna Ptujec, Mirjana Ognjenovic, Ljubinka Jankovic, Svetlana Anastasovski, Svetlana Dasic-Kitic, Alenka Cuderman, Svetlana Mugosa, Mirjana Djurica, Biserka Visnjic, Salvica Djukic, Jasna Kolar-Merden, Lilijana Mugosa. Coach: Josip Samarzija.

SCORES OF GAMES

YUG vs CHN 31–25, vs KOR 29–23, vs FRG 20–19, vs AUT 30–15, vs USA 33–20

USA vs YUG 20–33, vs CHN 25–22, vs KOR 27–29, vs FRG 17–18, vs AUT 25–21

TEAM PERSONNEL, MEN'S

J. Buehning   R. Djokovich   T. Dykstra

T. Funk   C. Gilbert   S. Goss

W. Kessler   S. Kirk   P. Lash, Jr.

M. Lenard   J. McVein   G. Morava

R. Oshita   T. Schneeberger   J. Story

J. Alvaro Alcaide   J. Garcia Cuesta   T. Holtan

TEAM PERSONNEL, WOMEN'S

P. Boyd   R. Clanton   T. Contos

S. de la Riva   M. Dwight   C. Forest

D. Franco   M. Hale   K. Howard

L. Jones   C. Lindsey   C. Stinger

P. Stone   J. Trombly   S. Winn

K. Capilar   I. Milman   C. Nichols

VOLLEYBALL

The United States made greater strides in 1984 in volleyball than in any other team sport on the program for the Olympic Games. Although the women had qualified for the Moscow Olympics, they never had the opportunity to prove their prowess.

The team preparation for 1984 was long and thorough, aimed at having both squads reach their peak at Los Angeles. For six years, the much publicized women's team had done extraordinarily well in international matches at home and abroad.

Shortly before the Olympic Games, the men's squad took a final swing around the Eastern Bloc countries, beating the Soviet national team in one match. Such news didn't make headlines, but it certainly brought smiles of satisfaction to U.S. volleyball leaders.

Teams are seeded in the Olympic Games from the world championships. U.S. women in recent years have been seeded high; such was not the case for the men, who invariably were placed in preliminary pools with stronger teams in which only two advanced.

On the basis of its ninth place world championship finish (out of 16), the U.S. was placed in a preliminary pool that included top-seeded Brazil, Argentina, Korea, and Tunisia. Actually the USA, Brazil, and Korea finished with identical 3–1 records. Brazil was accorded the top rung because it had defeated the USA, 3–0.

In the play-off to advance to the final, the United States won over Canada, and Brazil over Italy.

Not to downplay the Brazilian effort in the final, but the U.S. got the jump in the first game by winning 15–6. The Americans simply took the fight out of the Brazilians. The rest was easy.

The U.S. women advanced out of the preliminary pool with a perfect 3–0 record. In the semi-final round the U.S. got revenge on Peru for a loss on its home court in the most recent world championship. Thus was set up the climactic game bringing together the USA and China, acknowledged to be the two best teams in the world.

But the United States was never in the contest and dropped three straight games. It was the end of the dreams for titles. Still, the silver medal was not to be sneered at, nor were the players.

TEAM PERSONNEL, MEN'S

GOLD MEDALIST TEAM

Aldis Berzins, 27, San Diego, CA
Craig Buck, 25, San Diego, CA
Richard Duwelius, 29, San Diego, CA
Douglas Dvorak, 26, San Diego, CA
Charles (Karch) Kiraly, 23, Culver City, CA
Christian Marlowe, 32, Santa Monica, CA
Patrick Powers, 26, Coronado, CA
Steven Salmons, 26, San Diego, CA
David Saunders, 23, San Diego, CA
Paul Sunderland, 32, La Mesa, CA
Stephen Timmons, 25, Newport Beach, CA
Marc Waldie, 28, Coronado, CA

Douglas Beal, San Diego, CA, coach
Charles Crabb, San Diego, CA, manager
William Neville, Bozeman, MT, assistant coach

TEAM PERSONNEL, WOMEN'S

Jeanne Beauprey, 23, Mission Viejo, CA
Carolyn Becker, 25, Laguna Hills, CA
Linda Chisholm, 25, Van Nuys, CA
Rita Crockett, 26, San Antonio, TX
Laurie Flachmeier, 27, Detroit, MI
Debbie Green, 26, Westminister, CA
Flora Hyman, 30, El Toro, CA
Rose Mary Magers, 24, Big Springs, TX
Kim Ruddins, 20, Inglewood, CA
Julie Vollertsen, 25, Palmyra, NE
Paula Jo Weishoff, 22, Torrance, CA
Susan Woodstra, 27, Colton, CA

Ruth Becker, Santa Ana Heights, CA, manager
John Corbelli, San Clemente, CA, assistant coach
Arie Selinger, El Toro, CA, coach

VOLLEYBALL, MEN'S

GOLD MEDAL GAME

USA def. BRA 15–6, 15–6, 15–7

BRONZE MEDAL GAME

ITA def. CAN 15–11, 15–12, 15–8

FIFTH PLACE GAME

KOR def. ARG 15–13, 9–15, 15–9, 15–7

SEVENTH PLACE GAME

JPN def. CHN 16–14, 15–9, 15–6

SEMIFINAL ROUND

USA def. CAN 15–6, 15–10, 15–7

BRA def. ITA 12–15, 15–2, 15–3, 15–5

USA SCORES PRELIMINARY ROUND

USA vs BRA 0–3, vs ARG 3–1, vs KOR 3–0,
    vs TUN 3–0

THE CHAMPIONS

USA: Dvorak, Saunders, Salmons, Sunderland,
    Duwelius, Timmons, Buck, Waldie, Marlowe,
    Berzins, Powers, Kiraly. Coach: Douglas Beal.

VOLLEYBALL, WOMEN'S

GOLD MEDAL GAME

CHN def. USA 16–14, 15–3, 15–9

BRONZE MEDAL GAME

JPN def. PER 13–15, 15–4, 15–7, 15–10

FIFTH PLACE GAME

KOR def. FRG 15–10, 15–10, 15–2

SEVENTH PLACE GAME

BRA def. CAN 15–9, 15–3, 15–8

SEMIFINAL ROUND

USA def. PER 16–14, 15–9, 15–10

CHN def. JPN 15–10, 15–7, 15–4

FRG def. CAN 15–5, 15–7, 15–1

KOR def. BRA 13–15, 15–13, 15–9, 15–10

USA SCORES PRELIMINARY ROUND

USA def. FRG 17–15, 15–8, 15–10

USA def. BRA 12–15, 10–15, 15–5, 15–5, 15–12

USA def. CHN 15–13, 7–15, 16–14, 15–12

THE CHAMPIONS

CHN: Lang Ping, Liang Yan, Zhu Ling, Hou Yuzhu,
    Zhou Xiaolan, Yang Xilan, Su Huijuan, Jiang
    Ying, Li Yanjun, Yang Xiaojun, Zheng Meizhu,
    Zhang Rongfang. Coach: Yuan Weimin.

TEAM PERSONNEL, MEN'S

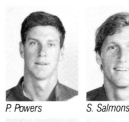
A. Berzins

C. Buck

R. Duwelius

D. Dvorak

C. Kiraly

C. Marlowe

P. Powers

S. Salmons

D. Saunders

P. Sunderland

S. Timmons

M. Waldie

C. Crabb

D. Beal

W. Neville

TEAM PERSONNEL, WOMEN'S

J. Beauprey

C. Becker

L. Chisholm

R. Crockett

L. Flachmeier

D. Green

F. Hyman

R. Magers

K. Ruddins

J. Vollertsen

P. Weishoff

S. Woodstra

R. Becker

J. Corbelli

A. Selinger

WATER POLO

The Olympic water polo tournament at beautiful Pepperdine University, Malibu, was to be the climax of a four-year U.S. crusade for excellence. Everything was working right for the national water polo team chosen for the 1980 Olympic Games until they had no place to go.

Coaches Monty NItzkowski and Ken Lindgren deserve praise for reinstilling confidence into the veterans of the 1980 team. Seven members of that squad earned places on the all-California 1984 team. In international play the United States had met with mixed success. Yet the potential was there for the team to do well in the Olympic Games.

The absence of the USSR and Hungary definitely reduced the overall quality of the field. Yugoslavia, silver medalist at Moscow, was installed as the favorite. In the preliminary round the U.S., West Germany, and Yugoslavia all won three victories, the U.S. outscoring its opponents 32–17.

A pair of one-goal defeats to the U.S., 8–7, and Yugoslavia, 10–9, eliminated the West German squad from gold medal contention.

Both the United States and Yugoslavia were undefeated going into the championship game. The Yugoslavs had won the silver medal at Moscow and the gold at Mexico City in 1968. The United States had been yearning for a medal of any color since the 1972 team won the bronze. Back in 1924 Johnny Weissmuller parlayed his talents in swimming and water polo and the Americans had finished third.

Under international rules for breaking ties, if the final game ends in a deadlock the issue is decided by statistical tables, not in the pool. Yugoslavia had outscored its opponents by 14, while the U.S. enjoyed only a nine-goal edge. That was it in a nutshell.

At the end of three of the four seven-minute periods the USA led 5–3. There was an all-out Yugoslav offense in the final period. Deni Lusic cut the margin to one goal when he scored with 4:01 minutes to play. The goal that tied the game 5–5 was made by Milivoj Bebic with 3:03 remaining.

That was to be the final score. The United States had earned a place among the elite of the world water polo powers.

TEAM PERSONNEL

Douglas Burke, 27, Modesto, CA
Jody Campbell, 24, Stanford, CA
Peter Campbell, 24, Irvine, CA
Christopher Dorst, 28, Atherton, CA
Gary Figueroa, 27, Salinas, CA
Andrew McDonald, 28, Orinda, CA
Kevin Robertson, 25, Santa Ana Heights, CA
Terry Schroeder, 25, Santa Barbara, CA
Timothy Shaw, 26, Long Beach, CA
John Siman, 33, Cypress, CA
Jon Svendsen, 30, Pleasant Hill, CA
Joseph Vargas, 28, Hacienda Heights, CA
Craig Wilson, 27, Cypress, CA

Kenneth Lindgren, Huntington Beach, CA, assistant coach
Kenneth (Monty) Nitzkowski, Huntington Beach, CA, coach
Terry Sayring, Manhattan Beach, CA, manager

WATER POLO

CHAMPIONSHIP ROUND

	Win	Lose	Tie	Goals For	Goals Against	Pts
1. **YUG**	4	0	1	47	33	9
2. **USA**	4	0	1	43	34	9
3. **FRG**	2	2	1	49	34	5
4. ESP	1	2	2	42	46	4
5. AUS	1	3	1	37	48	3
6. HOL	0	5	0	25	48	0

CHAMPIONSHIP ROUND SCORES

	YUG	USA	FRG	ESP	AUS	HOL
YUG	–	5–5	10–9	14–8	9–6	9–5
USA	5–5	–	8–7	10–8	12–7	8–7
FRG	9–10	7–8	–	8–8	10–6	15–2
ESP	8–14	8–10	8–8	–	10–10	8–4
AUS	6–9	7–12	6–10	10–10	–	8–7
HOL	5–9	7–8	2–15	4–8	7–8	–

CONSOLATION PLACINGS

7. ITA 8. GRE 9. CHN 10. CAN 11. JPN 12. BRA

LEADING SCORERS

Manuel Estiarte, ESP 34; Mario Fiorillo, ITA 19; Frank Otto, FRG 18; Charles Turner, AUS 17

THE CHAMPIONS

YUG: Milorad Krivokapic, Deni Lusic, Zoran Petrovic, Bozo Vuletic, Veselin Djuho, Zoran Roje, Milivoj Bebic, Perica Bukic, Goran Sukno, Tomislav Paskvalin, Igor Milanovic, Dragan Andric, Andrija Popovic. Coach: Ratko Rudik.

TEAM PERSONNEL

D. Burke   J. Campbell   P. Campbell

C. Dorst   G. Figueroa   A. McDonald

K. Robertson   T. Shaw   J. Siman

J. Svendsen   J. Vargas   C. Wilson

K. Lindgren   K. Nitzkowski   T. Sayring

WEIGHTLIFTING

If you don't participate in a competition, you cannot win. Even so, weightlifting was the sport most damaged by the nonparticipation of the Eastern Bloc countries. In the 1983 world championships the USSR had captured six gold medals, Bulgaria won three, and the tenth was earned by the German Democratic Republic.

The USSR had won five Olympic titles in both 1976 and 1980. Bulgaria accounted for three gold medals in 1976 and added two more in 1980.

If Yurik Vardanyan, USSR, 181.5-pound light-heavyweight class, was the star of the 1980 Olympics with his world record lift of 882 pounds (greater than the total lifts for the next two higher weight classes), Niku Vlad, Romania, was the most impressive of the 1984 lifters with his Olympic record total of 863.5 pounds. Vlad's total was higher than the winning scores in the next two higher weight classes. Vlad competed in the middle heavyweight (198 pounds); at age twenty, he was one of the youngest lifters at Los Angeles.

For the first time since Montreal, the United States won a medal. At Los Angeles the super heavyweight, Mario Martinez, a three-time national champion, pushed his Australian opponent Dinko Lukim to the limit before yielding, 907.5 to 902 pounds.

Earlier Guy Carlton, the lone carry-over from the 1980 team, had snared the bronze medal in the 242-pound second-heavyweight class.

Carlton wound up third after spurning an almost sure shot at the silver. He went for broke—attempting a higher lift than he had ever attempted in a bold move for the first U.S. gold in twenty-four years.

When Carlton missed, the gold medal went to Italy's Norberto Oberburger, for the first weightlifting medal awarded Italy in sixty years.

The U.S. lifters did establish two American records in the competition—Martinez with a total lift of 902 pounds and Albert Hood's snatch of 247 pounds.

The weightlifters had had the poorest record among all athletes since drug testing was introduced in 1968 at Mexico City. At Los Angeles only two lifters failed the drug tests (and subsequently were barred for life from international competition by the International Weightlifting Federation). They were Lebanon's Mahmoud Tarha and the Algerian Ahmed Tarbi.

The best human interest story is wound around West Germany's Rolf Milser, gold medalist in the 220-pound first-heavyweight class. A veteran of the 1972 and 1976 Olympic Games and a 1978 world champion, Milser did not participate at Moscow. He had retired from competition and entered business, but went back into training as the Los Angeles Games approached.

After clinching the gold medal Misler told a reporter, "It was not a matter of absolute strength, but rather one of nerves. I could have done more in the clean and jerk, but I took 437 pounds to get the gold medal. Even though the last lift was the heaviest, I was so psyched up by the audience that it was, in fact, the easiest."

TEAM PERSONNEL

Donald Abrahamson, 26, *Cupertino, CA*
Thomas Calandro, 26
Guy Carlton, 30, *Colorado Springs, CO*
Ken Clark, 28, *Pacifica, CA*
Derrick Crass, 24, *Colorado Springs, CO*
Michael Davis, 24, *Colorado Springs, CO*
Richard Eaton, 22, *Colorado Springs, CO*
Albert Hood, 20, *Los Angeles, CA*
Arn Paul Krinsky, 23, *Vienna, VA*
Mario Martinez, 27, *San Francisco, CA*
Lou Murcado, 26, *Colorado Springs, CO*
Rich Shanko, 24, *Colorado Springs, CO*

Marty Cypher, *Maywood, PA, manager*
Harvey Newton, *Colorado Springs, CO, coach*
Richard Smith, *York, PA, assistant coach*

WEIGHTLIFTING

FLYWEIGHT (UP TO 52 KG./115 LBS.)

	Kilograms			Pounds
	Snatch	C&J	Total	Total
1. **Zeng Guoqiang, CHN**	105	130	235	517 *
2. **Zhou Peishun, CHN**	107.5	127.5	235	517
3. **Kazushito Manabe, JPN**	102.5	130	232.5	511.5
4. Hidemi Miyashita, JPN	107.5	122.5	230	506
5. Maman Suryaman, INA	102.5	125.0	227.5	500.5
6. Hyo Mun Bang, KOR	100	125	225	495
7. Jose Diaz Lopez, PAN	95	125	220	484
8. Levent Erdogan, TUR	95	120	215	473

BANTAMWEIGHT (UP TO 56 KG./123 LBS.)

	Kilograms			Pounds
	Snatch	C&J	Total	Total
1. **Wu Shude, CHN**	120	147.5	267.5	588.5
2. **Lai Runming, CHN**	125 NOR/NWR	140	265	583
3. **Masahiro Kotaka, JPN**	112.5	140	252.5	555.5
4. Takashi Ichiba, JPN	110	140	250	550
5. Kim Chil Bong, KOR	105	140	245	539
6. Dioniso Munoz, ESP	110	132.5	242.5	533.5 *
7. Arvo Ojalehto, FIN	105	137.5	242.5	533.5
8. Albert Hood, USA	112.5	130	242.5	533.5

FEATHERWEIGHT (UP TO 60 KG./132 LBS.)

	Kilograms			Pounds
	Snatch	C&J	Total	Total
1. **Chen Weiquiang, CHN**	125	157.5	282.5	621.5
2. **Gelu Radu, ROM**	125	155	280	616
3. **Tsai Wen-Yee, TPE**	125	147.5	272.5	599.5
4. Kaoru Wabiko, JPN	120	150	270	594
5. Yosuke Muraki, JPN	120	147.5	267.5	588.5 *
6. Lee Myeong Su, KOR	117.5	150	267.5	588.5
7. Sori-Enda Nassution, INA	115	152.5	267.5	588.5
8. Uolevi Kahelin, FIN	112.5	155	267.5	588.5

LIGHTWEIGHT (UP TO 67.5 KG./148.5 LBS.)

	Kilograms			Pounds
	Snatch	C&J	Total	Total
1. **Yao Jingyuan, CHN**	142.5	177.5	320	704
2. **Andrei Socaci, ROM**	142.5	170	312.5	687.5 *
3. **Jouni Gronman, FIN**	140	172.5	312.5	687.5
4. Dean Willey, GBR	140	170	310	682
5. Choji Taira, JPN	132.5	162.5	305	671
6. Yasushige Sasaki, JPN	140	162.5	302.5	665.5 *
7. Basil Stellios, AUS	137.5	165	302.5	665.5
8. Ma Jianping, CHN	130	167.5	297.5	654.5
13. Donald Abrahamson, USA	122.5	155	277.5	610.5

MIDDLEWEIGHT (UP TO 75 KG./165 LBS.)

	Kilograms			Pounds
	Snatch	C&J	Total	Total
1. **Karl-Heinz Radschinsky, FRG**	150	190	340	748
2. **Jacques Demers, CAN**	147.5	187.5	335	737
3. **Dragomir Cioroslan, ROM**	147.5	185	332.5	731.5
4. David Morgan, GBR	145	185	330	726
5. Shunzhu Li, JPN	147.5	175	322.5	709.5
6. Mohammed Y Mohammed, IRQ	140	180	320	704
7. Tony Pignone, AUS	147.5	170	317.5	698.5
8. Park Chun Jong, KOR	137.5	175	312.5	687.5

LIGHT HEAVYWEIGHT (UP TO 82.5 KG./181.5 LBS.

	Kilograms			Pounds
	Snatch	C&J	Total	Total
1. **Petre Becheru, ROM**	155	200	355	781
2. **Robert Kabbas, AUS**	150	192.5	342.5	753.5
3. **Ryoji Isaoka, JPN**	150	190	340	748
4. Newton Burrowes, GBR	147.5	180	327.5	715
5. Ebraheem Elbakth, EGY	145	177.5	322.5	709.5
6. Lee Kang Seog, KOR	140	182.5	322.5	709.5 *
7. Yvan Darsigny, CAN	142.5	180	322.5	709.5
8. Allister Nalder, NZL	142.5	175	317.5	698.5
9. Arn Krinsky, USA	140	175	315	693

*Final placing decided on basis of lower bodyweight

MIDDLE HEAVYWEIGHT (UP TO 90 KG./198 LBS.)

	Kilograms			Pounds
	Snatch	C&J	Total	Total
1. **Niku Vlad, ROM**	172.5	220	NOR 392.5	NOR 863.5
2. **Petre Dumitru, ROM**	165	195	360	792
3. **David Mercer, GBR**	157.5	195	352.5	775.5
4. Peter Immesberger, FRG	155	195	350	770*
5. Hwang Woo Won, KOR	152.5	197.5	350	770
6. Nikos Iliadis, GRE	155	195	350	770
7. Henri Junch Hoeg, DEN	152.5	195	347.5	764.5
8. Jose Garces, MEX	150	192.5	342.5	753.5
21. Thomas Calandro, USA	142.5	172.5	315	693
Derrick Crass, USA	withdrew, injury			

FIRST HEAVYWEIGHT (UP TO 100 KG./220 LBS.)

	Kilograms			Pounds
	Snatch	C&J	Total	Total
1. **Rolf Milser, FRG**	167.5	NOR/NWR 217.5	385	847
2. **Vasile Gropa, ROM**	165	NOR/NWR 217.5	382.5	841.5
3. **Pekka Niemi, FIN**	160	207.5	367.5	808.5
4. Kevin Roy, CAN	160	197.5	357.5	786.5
5. Ken Clark, USA	155	197.5	352.5	775.5
6. Franz Langthaler, AUT	162.5	187.5	350	770*
7. Rich Shanko, USA	155	195	350	770
8. Jean-Marie Kretz, FRA	150	192.5	342.5	753.5

SECOND HEAVYWEIGHT (UP TO 110 KG./242 LBS.)

	Kilograms			Pounds
	Snatch	C&J	Total	Total
1. **Norberto Oberburger, ITA**	175	215	390	858
2. **Stefan Tasnadi, ROM**	167.5	212.5	380	836
3. **Guy Carlton, USA**	167.5	210	377.5	830.5
4. Frank Seipelt, FRG	160	207.5	367.5	808.5
5. Albert Squires, CAN	165	200	365	803
6. Goran Pettersson, SWE	165	195	360	792
7. Richard Eaton, USA	152.5	200	352.5	775.5
8. Ioannis Gerontas, GRE	152.5	197.5	350	770

SUPER HEAVYWEIGHT (OVER 110 KG./242 LBS.)

	Kilograms			Pounds
	Snatch	C&J	Total	Total
1. **Dinko Lukim, AUS**	172.5	NOR 240	412.5	907.5
2. **Mario Martinez, USA**	185	225	410	902
3. **Manfred Nerlinger, FRG**	177.5	220	397.5	874.5
4. Stefan Laggner, AUT	170	215	385	847
5. Ioannis Tsintsaris, GRE	162.5	185	347.5	764.5
6. Bartholomew Oluma, NGR	150	187.5	337.5	742.5
7. Mosad Mosbah, EGY	150	180	330	726

*Final placing decided on basis of lower bodyweight

TEAM PERSONNEL, MEN'S

D. Abrahamson   T. Calandro   G. Carlton

K. Clark   D. Crass   M. Davis

R. Eaton   A. Hood   A. Krinsky

M. Martinez   L. Murcado   R. Shanko

M. Cypher   H. Newton   R. Smith

WRESTLING

The Olympic wrestling trials did not exactly presage the success that the United States was to enjoy at the Games. There was an unusual amount of bickering among the grapplers on the selection methods, the officiating, and a general malaise that often amounted to internecine warfare.

Freestyle coach Dan Gable, 1972 Olympic wrestling champion and currently coach at the University of Iowa, was crestfallen when the Eastern Bloc countries withdrew. He had prepared well. He had conducted a year-long training camp on campus for a number of top candidates. The United States in pre-Olympic meets over the last three years had shown flashes of rare talent and depth in the freestyle division.

The honor of being the first American Greco-Roman wrestler to bring home the gold went to a deputy sheriff from Michigan, Steve Fraser, in the 198-pound class.

But the sentimental favorite was gold medalist Jeff Blatnick in the super-heavyweight class. Blatnick had defeated the 1981 world champion, Refik Memisevic of Yugoslavia, in the first round. In the final he nipped Thomas Johansson of Sweden, 2–0. However, when the Swede tested positive for steroids, he was barred and lost his medal.

Blatnick had overcome a bout with Hodgkin's disease. Diagnosed in 1982, he was wrestling again a year later.

Blatnick had won a place on the 1980 Olympic team and dedicated his efforts to his older brother who had been killed in a motorcycle crash.

In the ten freestyle classes, the United States captured seven gold and two silver medals. It was almost a family atmosphere. The Banach twins, Ed and Lou, and the Schultz brothers, Dave and Mark, accounted for four gold medals. The Schultzes were the "heavies" of the competition. Even in wrestling there were charges that they were too rough. In fact, the international federation assigned a special "official" to watch them closely.

Mark Schultz concentrated on gymnastics until his junior year in high school. Born in Palo Alto, he attended the University of Oklahoma and won three NCAA titles. In his final match, Mark won by a grand superiority, 13–0, over Japan's Hideyuki Nagashima, scoring his points in just 1:59 minutes.

Equally impressive was Randy Lewis in the 137-pound-class gold medal match. Lewis scored 24 points to 11 for his Japanese opponent, Kosei Akaishi, earning the decision by grand superiority in 4:42 minutes.

In the Greco-Roman class, the United States won 10 victories by a decision, 3 by a fall, 3 by grand superiority, 1 by injury, 1 by criterion, 3 by passivity with the opponent being disqualified, and 1 by forfeit. All three falls were achieved by Jim Martinez in the 150-pound class. The wrestlers lost 12 times.

On the freestyle team, there were two carry-overs from 1980—Bobby Weaver and Randy Lewis. Both won gold medals. There were three carry-overs on the Greco-Roman team: Jeff Blatnick won the gold medal in the super-heavyweight class; Dan Chandler and Mark Fuller were early-round losers.

TEAM PERSONNEL

FREESTYLE

Ed Banach, 24, Port Jervis, NY (198 lbs.)
Lou Banach, 24, West Point, NY (220 lbs.)
Bruce Baumgartner, 23, Haledon, NJ (super heavyweight)
Barry Davis, 22, Cedar Rapids, IA (126 lbs.)
Joe Gonzales, 26, Montebello, CA (115 lbs.)
Randy Lewis, 25, Rapid City, SD (137 lbs.)
Andrew Rein, 26, Stoughton, WI (150 lbs.)
David Schultz, 25, Palo Alto, CA (163 lbs.)
Mark Schultz, 23, Palto Alto, CA (181 lbs.)
Robert Weaver, 25, Rochester, NY (106 lbs.)

Stanley Dzedzic, Lincoln, NE, assistant coach
Dan Gable, Iowa City, IA, coach

TEAM PERSONNEL

GRECO-ROMAN

Jeff C. Blatnick, 27, Schenectady, NY (super heavyweight)
Christopher L. Catalfo, 24, Montvale, NJ (163 lbs.)
Daniel C. Chandler, 32, Minneapolis, MN (181 lbs.)
Frank S. Famiano, 23, Schenectady, NY (126 lbs.)
Steven H. Fraser, 26, Ann Arbor, MI (198 lbs.)
Mark A. Fuller, 23, Pleasant Hill, CA (106 lbs.)
Gregory P. Gibson, USMC, 30, Stafford, VA (220 lbs.)
Bert A. Govig, 23, Scottsdale, AZ (115 lbs.)
Abdurrahim Kuzu, 28, Lincoln, NE (137 lbs.)
James M. Martinez, 25, Brooklyn Park, MN (150 lbs.)

Ronald L. Finley, Eugene, OR, coach
Pavel Kasten, Portland, OR, assistant coach

WRESTLING, FREESTYLE

PAPERWEIGHT (48 kg./106 lbs.)
1. **Robert Weaver, USA, pinned**
2. **Takashi Irie, JPN, 2:58**
3. **Sohn Kab-Do, KOR,** dec.
4. Gao Wenhke, CHN, 3–7
5. Reiner Heugabel, FRG, won by passivity over
6. Kent Andersson, SWE, 5:21

FLYWEIGHT (52 kg./115 lbs.)
1. **Saban Trstena, YUG, won by injury over**
2. **Kim Jong-Kyu, KOR**
3. **Yuji Takada, JPN,** pinned
4. Roy Takahashi, CAN, 4:34
5. Aslan Seyhanli, TUR, dec.
6. Mahavir Singh, IND, 14–5
7. Fritz Niebler, FRG
8. Llang Dejin, CHN
Note: Joe Gonzales, USA, eliminated in third round

BANTAMWEIGHT (57 kg./126 lbs.)
1. **Hideaki Tomiyama, JPN, dec.**
2. **Barry Davis, USA, 8–3**
3. **Kim Eui-Kon, KOR,** dec.
4. Orlando Caceras, PUR, 7–4
5. Rohtas Songh, IND, dec.
6. Zoran Sorov, YUG, 3–2
7. Guanbunima, CHN
8. Ivrahim Akgun, TUR

FEATHERWEIGHT (62 kg./137 lbs.)
1. **Randy Lewis, USA, by superiority over**
2. **Kosei Akaishi, JPN, 24–11**
3. **Lee Jung-Keun, KOR,** dec.
4. Cris Brown, AUS, 11–6
5. Martin Herbster, FRG, dec.
6. Antonio LaBrua, ITA, 11–4

LIGHTWEIGHT (68 kg./150 lbs.)
1. **Yoo In-Tak, KOR,** dec.
2. **Andrew Rein, USA, 5–5**
3. **Jukka Rauhala, FIN,** won by injury over
4. Masakazu Kamimura, JPN, 3:02
5. Zsigmond Kelevitz, AUS, dec.
6. Fevzi Seker, TUR, 11–3
7. Erwin Knosp, FRG
8. Rene Neyer, Sui

WELTERWEIGHT (74 kg./163 lbs.)
1. **David Schultz, USA, dec.**
2. **Martin Knosp, FRG, 4–1**
3. **Saban Sejdi, YUG,** dec.
4. Rajender Singh, IND, 5–1
5. Naomi Higuchi, JAP, dec.
6. Han Myung-Woo, KOR, 7–3
7. Marc Mongeon, CAN
8. Pekka Rauhala, FIN

MIDDLEWEIGHT (82 kg./181 lbs.)
1. **Mark Schultz, USA, pinned**
2. **Hideyuki Nagashima, JPN, 1:59**

3. **Chris Rinke, CAN,** dec.
4. Reiner Trik, FRG, 5–2
5. Kim Tae-Wood, KOR, dec.
6. Kenneth Reinsfield, NZL, 10–3
7. Iraklis Deskoulidis, GRE
8. Luciano Ortelli, ITA

LIGHT HEAVYWEIGHT (90 kg./198 lbs.)
1. **Ed Banach, USA, won superiority dec. over**
2. **Akira Ohta, JPN, 15–3**
3. **Neil Loban, GBR,** dec.
4. Clark Davis, CAN, 5–1
5. MaCauley Appan, NGR, won by injury over
6. Ismail Temiz, TUR

HEAVYWEIGHT (100 kg./220 lbs.)
1. **Lou Banach, USA, pinned**
2. **Joseph Atiyeh, SYR, 1:01**
3. **Vasile Puscasu, ROM,** dec.
4. Hayri Sezgin, TUR, 4–3
5. Tamon Honda, JPN, won by injury over
6. George Pikilidis, GRE
7. Kartar Singh Dhillon, IND
8. Wayne Brightwell, CAN

SUPER HEAVYWEIGHT (Over 100 kg./Over 220 lbs.)
1. **Bruce Baumgartner, USA, dec.**
2. **Bob Molle, CAN, 10–2**
3. **Ayhan Taskin, TUR,** pinned
4. Hassan El Hadad, EGY, 1:44
5. Mamadou Sakho, SEN, won by injury over
6. Vasile Andrei, ROM
7. Koichi Ishimori, JPN
8. Panayotis Pikilidis, GRE

WRESTLING, GRECO-ROMAN

PAPERWEIGHT (48 kg./106 lbs.)
1. **Vicenzo Maenza, ITA, won by superiority over**
2. **Markus Scherer, FRG, 12–0**
3. **Ikuzo Saito, JPN,** dec.
4. Salih Bora, TUR, 7–5
5. Kent Andersson, SWE, dec.
6. Jun Dae-Je, LOR, 10–3
   Mark Fuller, USA, did not participate

FLYWEIGHT (52 kg./115 lbs.)
1. **Atsuji Miyahara, JPN, dec.**
2. **Daniel Aceves, MEX, 9–4**
3. **Bang Dae-Du, KOR,** won by superiority over
4. Hu Richa, CHN, 13–1
5. Jon Ronnington, NOR, won by superiority over
6. Taisto Halonen, FIN, 14–0
7. Erol Kemah, TUR
8. Mihai Cismasu, ROM

BANTAMWEIGHT (57 kg./126 lbs.)
1. **Pasquale Passarelli, FRG, dec.**
2. **Masaki Eto, JPN, 8–5**
3. **Haralambos Holidis, GRE,** dec.
4. Nicolae Zamfir, ROM, 2–1
5. Frank Famiano, USA, won by injury over

6. Benni Ljunbeck, SWE

7. Mehmets Erhat Karadag, TUR

8. Park Byung-Ho, KOR

FEATHERWEIGHT (62 kg./137 lbs.)

1. **Kim Weon-Kee, KOR, won by criteria over**

2. **Kentolle Johansson, SWE**

3. **Hugo Dietsche, SUI,** dec.

4. Abdurrahim Kuzu, USA, 8–4

5. Doug Yeats, CAN, won by superiority over

6. Salem Bekhit, EGY, 15–3

LIGHTWEIGHT (68 kg./150 lbs.)

1. **Vlado Lisjak, YUG, pinned**

2. **Tapio Sipila, FIN, 0:57**

3. **James Martinez, USA,** pinned

4. Stefan Negrisan, ROM, 0:25

5. Deitmar Streitler, AUT, dec.

6. Mohamed Mutei Alnakdali, SYR, 8–4

7. Shaban Ibrahim, EGY

8. Sumer Kocak, TUR

WELTERWEIGHT (74 kg./163 lbs.)

1. **Jouko Salomaki, FIN, dec.**

2. **Roger Tallroth, SWE, 5–4**

3. **Stefan Rusu, ROM,** dec.

4. Kim Young-Nam, KOR, 6–1

5. Karolj Kasap, YUG, dec.

6. Martial Mischler, FRA, 6–3

7. Christopher Catalfo, USA

8. Mohamed Hamad, EGY

MIDDLEWEIGHT (82 kg./181 lbs.)

1. **Ion Draica, ROM, dec.**

2. **Dimitrios Thanopoulos, GRE, 4–3**

3. **Soren Claeson, SWE,** dec.

4. Momir Petkovic, YUG, 5–2

5. Jarmo Overmark, FIN, dec.

6. Mohamed El Ashram, EGY, 5–3

7. Louis Santerre, CAN

8. Kim Sang-Kyu, KOR

   Daniel Chandler, USA, did not participate

LIGHT HEAVYWEIGHT (90 kg./198 lbs.)

1. **Steven Fraser, USA, dec.**

2. **Ilie Maftei, ROM, 1–1**

3. **Frank Andersson, SWE,** dec.

4. Uwe Sachs, FRG, 5–0

5. Jean-Francois Court, FRA, dec.

6. George Pozidis, GRE, 4–2

HEAVYWEIGHT (100 kg./220 lbs.)

1. **Vasile Andrei, ROM, won by superiority over**

2. **Greg Gibson, USA**

3. **Josef Tertelji, YUG,** dec.

4. George Pikilidis, GRE, 3–0

5. Fritz Gerdsmeier, FRG, dec.

6. Franz Pitschmann, AUT, 7–5

7. Yoshihiro Fujita, JPN

7. Karl-Johan Gustavsson, SWE

SUPER HEAVYWEIGHT (Over 100 kg./Over 220 lbs.)

1. **Jeff Blatnick, USA,** dec. over Thomas Johansson, SWE, 2–0, who was later disq. for failing drug test

2. **Refik Memisevic, YUG,** won by passivity over

3. **Victor Dolipschi, ROM**

4. Panayouis Pikilidis, GRE, dec.

5. Hassan El Hadad, EGY, 7–3

6. (tie) Masaya Ando, JPN

6. (tie) Antonio Lapenna, ITA

TEAM PERSONNEL, FREESTYLE

E. Banach   L. Banach   B. Baumgartner

B. Davis   J. Gonzales   R. Lewis

A. Rein   D. Schultz   M. Schultz

R. Weaver   S. Dzedzic   D. Gable

TEAM PERSONNEL, GRECO-ROMAN

J. Blatnick   C. Catalfo   D. Chandler

F. Famiano   S. Fraser   M. Fuller

G. Gibson   B. Govig   A. Kuzu

R. Finley   P. Kasten

YACHTING

The United States had a better record in the seven yachting regattas than any previous nation. It was the first time that a country placed in all seven classes—three winners, four runners-up.

It was not that the U.S. owned a home-water advantage. For the last three years the sailing nations of the world had been testing the waters and the winds in the Pacific Ocean off Long Beach. As recently as the fall of 1983 a full-dress rehearsal regatta was held.

In the pre-Olympics period there was a six-week controversy over the U.S. entrant in the Finn Class. A complicated set of incidents led to the final decision in a federal court. Finally, John Bertrand was tapped. A 1980 Olympian, sailmaker Bertrand was the 1978 Finn world champion and twice won the Laser world championship. Bertrand gave it all he had off Long Beach and gained a silver medal. A disqualification in the first race hurt his chances for gold.

The windsurfing/windglider class attracted more attention from the general public than all of the other classes combined. Here was a recreational sailing event for the masses included in the Olympics. Scott Steele of Annapolis won another silver medal for the United States.

For the first time the United States was represented by a father and son in separate boats. (In 1952 Hilary Smart, son, and Paul Smart, father, sailed to victory in the Star Class.) Now in 1984 there were two Buchans from the Seattle area. William E. Buchan, the father, was the skipper of the Star Class entry. William Carl Buchan, the son, crewed for Jonathan McKee in the Flying Dutchman Class. Buchan, the elder, won three of the six races to earn a gold medal. Buchan and McKee scored a narrow victory over a persistent Canadian boat.

The third gold medal for the United States was won by Robbie Haines, helmsman, in the Soling Class. The U.S. entry had clinched the gold after the first six races and didn't have to take to the water for the final race of the regatta.

TEAM PERSONNEL

Stephen Benjamin, 28, Oyster Bay, NY (470 Class, helmsman)

John Bertrand, 28, San Francisco, CA (Finn)

William Carl Buchan, 27, Kirkland, WA (Flying Dutchman)

William E. Buchan, 49, Bellevue, WA (Star Class, helmsman)

Roderick Davis, 28, Seal Beach, CA (Soling Class)

Stephen Erickson, 23, Edmonds, WA (Star Class)

Jay Glaser, 21, Newport Beach, CA (Tornado)

Robert (Robbie) Haines, 30, Coronado, CA (Soling Class, helmsman)

Jonathan McKee, 24, Seattle, WA (Flying Dutchman, helmsman)

Randy Smyth, 30, Huntington Beach, CA (Tornado, helmsman)

Scott Steele, 26, Annapolis, MD (Windglider, helmsman)
Christopher Steinfeld, 24, Oyster Bay, NY (470 Class)
Ed Trevelyan, 28, La Jolla, CA (Soling Class)

Carl Eichenlaub, San Diego, CA, boatman
Robert Hopkins, Manchester, MA, manager
Robert Mairs, Edgewater, MD, manager
Samuel V. Merrick, Washington, DC, head manager

YACHTING

Note: The best six finishes for medalists are listed after each name and nation. Total points are based on IYRU scoring table whereby the skipper with the lowest point score wins.

WINDGLIDER CLASS

1. **Stephan Van Den Berg, HOL**		27.70
(4-2-1-4-2-3)		
2. **Scott Steele, USA** (7-1-2-1-9-9)		46.00
3. **Bruce Kendall, NZL** (2-3-13-2-3-5)		46.40
4. Gildas Guillerot, FRA		52.40
5. Klaus Maran, ITA		54.40
6. Greg Hyde, AUS		55.70
7. Dirk Meyer, FRG		67.20
8. Bjoern Eybl, AUT		80.00

FINN CLASS

1. **Russell Coutts, NZL** (1-7-2-2-3-5)	34.70
2. **John Bertrand, USA** (5-1-1-2-5-8)	37.00
3. **Terry Neilson, CAN** (2-2-5-5-1-6)	37.70
4. Joaquin Blanco, ESP	60.70
5. Wolfgang Gerz, FRG	66.10
6. Chris Pratt, AUS	68.00
7. Michael McIntyre, GBR	70.70
8. Jorge Zarif Neto, BRA	78.70

TORNADO CLASS

1. **NZL (Rex Sellers, Christopher Timms)**	14.70
(3-2-1-2-1-2)	
2. **USA (Randy Smyth, Jay Glaser)**	37.00
(1-7-1-4-1-10)	
3. **AUS (Chris Cairns, John Anderson)**	50.40
(4-16-3-2-6-1)	
4. DEN	51.10
5. BER	53.50
6. GBR	53.70
7. BRA	74.70
8. FRA	81.00

STAR CLASS

1. **USA (William E. Buchan,**	29.70
Stephen Erickson) (1-9-2-6-1-1)	
2. **FRG (Joachim Griese,**	41.40
Michael Marcour) (4-4-6-1-4-3)	
3. **ITA (Giorgio Gorla,**	43.50
Alfio Peraboni) (3-6-3-3-2-6)	
4. SWE	43.70
5. AUT	53.40
6. GRE	67.00
7. ESP	74.00
8. HOL	76.00

FLYING DUTCHMAN CLASS

1. **USA (Jonathan McKee,**	19.70
William Carl Buchan) (2-1-2-3-1-4)	
2. **CAN (Terry McLaughlin,**	22.70
Evert Bastet) (3-2-1-1-8-1)	
3. **GBR (Jonathan Richards,**	48.70
Peter Allam) (3-5-4-4-8-2)	
4. DEN	52.40
5. FRG	56.70
6. BRA	61.70
7. ITA	78.70
8. ISR	79.40

470 CLASS

1. **ESP (Luis Doreste, Roberto Molina)**	33.70
(3-1-5-2-1-9)	
2. **USA (Stephen Benjamin,**	43.00
Christopher Steinfeld) (10-2-1-4-7-2)	
3. **FRA (Thierry Peponnet,**	49.40
Luc Pillot) (2-9-8-3-1-6)	
4. FRG	50.10
5. ITA	57.00
6. FIN	67.40
7. GBR	70.00
8. ISR	70.00

SOLING CLASS

1. **USA (Robert Haines, Edward Trevelyan,**	33.70
Roderick Davis) (1-9-3-5-1-2)	
2. **BRA (Torben Grael, Daniel Adler,**	43.40
Ronaldo Senfft) (3-7-2-10-1-3)	
3. **CAN (Hans Fogh, John Kerr,**	49.70
Steve Calder) (4-6-1-5-5-5)	
4. GBR	54.70
5. NOR	57.70
6. GRE	59.20
7. AUS	62.40
8. FRG	71.00

TEAM PERSONNEL

S. Steele

C. Steinfeld

E. Trevelyan

S. Merrick

R. Hopkins

R. Mairs

C. Eichenlaub

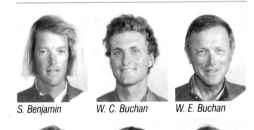
S. Benjamin   W. C. Buchan   W. E. Buchan

R. Davis   S. Erickson   J. Glaser

R. Haines   J. McKee   R. Smyth

ABOUT THE AUTHOR

Dick Schaap has been city editor of the New York Herald-Tribune, senior editor of Newsweek and editor of Sport Magazine. At present he is the Emmy Award–winning correspondent for ABC News, for whom he covered the 1984 Olympic Games, and sports editor of Parade Magazine. He has written 24 books on subjects ranging from Robert F. Kennedy to Joe Namath; one, Instant Replay, with Jerry Kramer of the Green Bay Packers, is the best-selling sports book of all time. He is also author of The Illustrated History of the Olympics. Schaap lives in New York with his wife and their daughter.